D1582474

Power and Faction in
Louis XIV's France

For John
Ten Years

Power and Faction in Louis XIV's France

ROGER METTAM

Basil Blackwell

British Library Cataloguing in Publication Data

Mettam, Roger
    Power and faction in Louis XIV's France.
    1. France—History—Louis XIV,
    1643–1715
    I. Title
    944'.033   DC125
    ISBN 0–631–15667–4

Library of Congress Cataloging in Publication Data

Mettam, Roger.
    Power and faction in Louis XIV's France.
    Bibliography: p.
    Includes index.
    1. France—Politics and government—1643–1715.
    2. Louis XIV, King of France, 1638–1715. 3. Monarchy—
France—History—17th century. I. Title.
DC126.M43 1987 944'.033 87–11442
ISBN 0–631–15667–4

Typeset in 10½ on 12pt Baskerville
by Cambrian Typesetters, Frimley, Surrey
Printed in Great Britain by
T.J. Press Ltd, Padstow

Contents

vi   *Contents*

Acknowledgements

In all fields of French history, whether social, economic, political, administrative, ecclesiastical, intellectual, military or naval, and in every period from the Wars of Religion to the present day, there will be found at least one book, and often many more, which begins by recording the debt of its author to the late Alfred Cobban. It was he who, in the early 1960s, encouraged me to examine the power of the high aristocracy under Louis XIV, at a time when the current historical orthodoxy still proclaimed that the king had reduced his nobility to impotence. If, after some twenty years of further investigation and reflection, it has been possible to incorporate some of that early research into this present book, that must be a tribute to the careful scrutiny, rigorous criticism and wise advice for which all his former students remember him with gratitude and affection.

Among other senior scholars who have encouraged my researches, offered penetrating comments, acted as referees and generally shown me much kindness, I must first mention John Bromley who, sadly, is also no longer here to be thanked in person. Nor can I ever repay Ragnhild Hatton for her continuing help over many years and in so many ways. It was she who invited me to join her in running the European History seminar at the Institute of Historical Research, from whose members I have derived so many ideas that it seems churlish, but is regretfully inevitable, for me to thank them collectively. Nevertheless I must add that my greatest debt to the seminar is for an introduction to Graham Gibbs, whose friendship, wisdom and support have been so important to me for many years. I am also most grateful to Douglas Johnson, who assumed the role of my principal referee on the death of Alfred Cobban, and who has willingly testified to my worth on numerous occasions since then.

It is largely due to the efforts on my behalf by these five historians that I am in a position to acknowledge, with my warmest thanks, the financial generosity of many institutions and trusts which have made grants towards this research: the Master and Fellows of Peterhouse, the Government of the French Republic, the CNRS, the British Academy, the Twenty-Seven Foundation, the Sir Ernest Cassell Foundation, the Leverhulme Trust for a six-month European Studies Fellowship, and the Central Research Fund of the University of London.

So many younger scholars have provided information and influenced my thinking that I hope they will not be offended if I do not name them all. My prime debt is to John Murphy, who has given me many insights into courtly society and has always been willing to argue about my interpretations of historical events. Robert Oresko, with his prodigious knowledge of European families and patronage networks, has often enabled me to see additional implications of my own research and has directed me towards many new channels of enquiry. Mark Greengrass has forced me to justify or to change the structure and content of this book, and its final form is undoubtedly better because of his telling observations. It is always comforting to discover that other historians, working from different premises or towards other goals, are nevertheless formulating ideas which are compatible with or give strength to one's own. I have therefore benefited greatly from the penetrating questions posed by David Parker on early modern France and by David Starkey on Tudor England. I do not agree with all their detailed conclusions, nor they with mine, but they have illuminated many dark areas of history, large and small. Most importantly from my point of view, every name that I have cited in these paragraphs has been that of a friend as well as an historian.

Finally it would be difficult to find a more congenial publisher than Philip Carpenter at Blackwell. His patience and good humour during the planning and writing of a book far outweigh his tyranny once the finished product is in sight. He has been responsible for publishing some fine historical works in recent years, and it is therefore with understandable apprehension that I invite the reader to consider whether this volume is worthy of inclusion among them.

Introduction:
Power and Faction

This book is concerned with the mechanisms of power in seventeenth-century France. It seeks to examine both the exercise of royal authority and the importance of social groups and institutions whose rights, jurisdictions and influence coexisted and sometimes conflicted with those of the crown. It will explain how the central government functioned, how it perceived its role in the kingdom, how it was regarded by the people of France and how far it was able to implement its policies. The crown was the senior, but not the sole, source of authority in the realm. A host of individuals and corporate bodies – ecclesiastical, aristocratic, military, bureaucratic, provincial, munici-pal and economic – possessed considerable privileges and powers. All played a part in the administration of the country, with the result that there was often tension either between the king and some of his influential subjects or among rival elites in the provinces and at court. It will therefore be essential to uncover the ambitions and priorities of these notables, and the methods by which they sought to advance themselves.

The title of this study introduces a vital element in any under-standing of power structures in Bourbon France – the notion of 'faction'. That word is used here without its modern overtones of factiousness, intrigue and the pursuit of selfish aims by unscrupulous means, although such undesirable characteristics might be present on occasion. Here it is intended as a description of a social group, whose members have banded together in order to further their own best interests, and whose methods, while undoubtedly opportunist, might be perfectly legitimate and legal. It was a commonplace of French society in this period that individual ambition was best advanced by associating with others who had similar or complementary goals. A single faction might include men and women who were related by blood or through carefully arranged marriages, and others who were

[handwritten marginal note: vying with power 8 kg]

bound by the tie between client and patron. The membership was not constant, as some elements might decide to join another and seemingly more successful group, but often there was an enduring core of members who had pursued their common advantage over many years. Thus, although institutions might be at odds because they saw themselves as rival corporations with conflicting jurisdictions, and social strata might challenge those above and below them as they sought to defend or even to improve their position in the hierarchy of rank and prestige, the combined family and patronage networks would be engaged in struggles which crossed these hierarchical and corporate boundaries because each faction had members from a variety of backgrounds, who were participating in different areas of the French power structure. Therefore, while it is not uncommon to discover confrontations which stemmed from corporate motives – court against court, gild against municipality, town against town – it is equally easy to find disputes among the members of a single corporation which were part of a wider conflict as two or more rival factions sought pre-eminence across the whole range of local institutions.

It is not the intention here to provide a detailed history of later seventeenth-century France in all its aspects, but to concentrate on those topics where a new interpretation may be suggested or where additional evidence has recently come to light. Nevertheless, it is hoped that the text will be both accessible to the reader who has only a general knowledge of the early Bourbon monarchy and at the same time of interest to the scholarly researcher, to students of the period and to historians working on other countries in the early modern centuries. Indeed, parts of the argument have necessitated the inclusion of much background material, and more importantly a summary of the latest research into French social and administrative history during the reigns of Louis XIII and his son. Therefore this section may serve as a convenient résumé of current scholarship as well as an essential element in the interpretative arguments which are expounded in these pages.

If the prime concern of the following chapters is the power structure during the personal rule of Louis XIV, from 1661 to 1715, a substantial discussion of selected themes and events in the history of the preceding fifty years is vital for three principal reasons. First it is important to demonstrate the extent of the continuity between the government of Louis XIII and that of his successor, and to examine the priorities of this aristocratically dominated society, many of whose values remained remarkably constant throughout the seventeenth century. Secondly this recent past, and especially the turbulent years of the Frondes, exerted a powerful influence on the thinking of the royal ministers and the social elites in the years after 1661. Many of them had been personally involved in, or affected by, these civil commotions which had brought more disadvantages than benefits to most leading figures at court and in the provinces. The conclusions that they drew from their experience of government under Richelieu and Mazarin were not always objective, but they inevitably served as a basis for judging the policies and achievements of the young king when he decided to take personal charge of affairs in 1661. As Louis and his advisers examined the lessons of the past and planned their strategy for the future, they privately admitted that some earlier governmental decisions had clearly been misguided, while others, though more sound, had been implemented tactlessly or at an inappropriate moment. They were keenly aware that such misjudgements and miscalculations must not be repeated because, although neither they nor the upper levels of French society wanted a return to the chaos of the Frondes, it was impossible to be certain that such disaffection would not return if the government once again seemed to be acting arbitrarily.

The third reason for studying in some detail the fifty years before the personal rule of Louis XIV is to consider, from the viewpoint of the historian, whether the Frondes were likely to have recurred in the second half of the seventeenth century. These civil wars have been accorded a major place in most historical analyses of *louis-quatorzien* government. Those who have designated this king as the supremely absolute monarch have used the weakness of the crown in the years 1648–53 to dramatize the contrast with the calm of the 1660s, when the dynamic young ruler is alleged to have crushed all his past, and therefore potential, opponents. Wiser scholars, unable to espouse this anachronistic portrait of totalitarian power but nevertheless aware that a decade of turmoil was followed by one of relative tranquillity, have stressed instead that the principal lesson of the Frondes for Louis XIV and his ministers was that caution and compromise would have to be their watchwords lest they too find themselves engulfed in a civil war. This second interpretation is undoubtedly more convincing historically, emphasizing as it does that many of those who had been at odds with the crown in the middle years of the century would, in other circumstances, have numerous reasons for making common cause with it in the pursuit of identical or compatible goals. There is, however, an additional conclusion to be drawn from an examination of the years 1610–61, and it has been thought necessary to discuss it at some length in these pages – namely that the Frondes resulted from a highly improbable coincidence of circumstances and were unlikely, according to the laws of chance alone, to recur. A few close advisers of

1. No Fronder because of ab. power
2.   "   "   Louis more prudent
3. Highly arbitrary to be any fronder in any case
4   *Introduction: Power and Faction*

Louis XIV were themselves inclined towards this analysis, although they accepted that outbreaks of localized provincial sedition were inevitable from time to time. Accordingly, they set a high priority on sowing division among those groups who had briefly come together in the civil wars, and on avoiding any action which might prompt them to put aside their differences and form a united opposition to royal policy.

The chapter on the years before 1661 is at times heavily dependent on the researches, gratefully acknowledged, of other scholars, although some new evidence is presented as well. Yet its inclusion is not justified solely by the fact that it is a résumé of current scholarship and demonstrates the degree of continuity between these early years and the personal rule of Louis XIV, nor even that it examines the uniqueness of the Frondes. It also seeks to create confusion, especially in its account of the 1650s, where there has hitherto been too much clarity. Many historians of this period, while producing admirable studies, have nevertheless concentrated on one or two aspects, whether governmental, financial, institutional, social, ecclesiastical or provincial. They have been able to assess the degree of continuity and the extent of change in each chosen field, charting long-term developments and ephemeral expedients. Unfortunately for the ministers and social elites of the seventeenth century, problems seldom arose singly, and few of them fell exclusively into just one of these categories. For example, the dispute about the cardinal de Retz not only came at a time of international and civil war, but itself raised questions of royal authority, papal power, theological orthodoxy and jurisdictional boundaries both within the church and between the secular and ecclesiastical courts. An attempt has therefore been made here to bring together all these diverse strands in order to demonstrate the complexity of the situation in which the government and the leaders of French society found themselves.

The two chapters on the personal rule of Louis XIV rely much more heavily on original archival research and on the massive collections of documents which were carefully compiled and published by nineteenth-century historians. Some of these sources have been used by other scholars, but not to sustain the arguments which are presented here. Similarly much familiar factual information is included, but again in the context of new, and hopefully convincing, analyses. There are fewer references to the recent work of other colleagues, simply because most of the latest books on seventeenth-century France focus on the years before 1661. There are some notable exceptions, although once more they tend to concentrate on specific themes during only a part of this long reign. It is indeed doubtful whether anyone could write a satisfactory history of a king who occupied the throne for seventy-two years, and ruled personally for fifty-four of them. Even more daunting is the amount of documentation which has survived, some of it being rediscovered only recently as historians pursue new lines of enquiry. This book therefore confines itself to those topics where it is possible to present some novel conclusions, based on an examination of certain kinds of archival evidence. These researches have sometimes merely added to existing knowledge, but more often have demonstrated the need to reinterpret the significance of better known facts and to challenge older generalizations. Where appropriate the arguments have been carried through the entire length of the personal rule, not least because, although circumstances might change and the priorities of the protagonists might alter as they entered old age, Louis XIV himself retained much of his original vision of kingship and continued to approach social and political problems with the same preconceptions.

If recent provincial, local, institutional and social studies have invalidated the traditional interpretation of Louis XIV as the supremely absolute monarch, they have not provided the foundation for an alternative analysis, equally sweeping in its claims. On the contrary, they have testified to the variety of experience in the different provinces of France and to the many conflicting tendencies within French society. Nevertheless, an attempt has been made here to weave some of these strands into a thread which is capable of bearing a little weight, so long as its inevitable limitations are recognized.

A number of factors have helped to determine the plan of this book, and it therefore seems wise to explain the rationale behind it. The first chapter makes some general observations about the history of seventeenth-century France as it has been and should be approached. As its starting point, it takes the old stereotype of the omnipotent Sun King. It could immediately be objected that, as for some thirty years scholars have been undermining this absurd and anachronistic portrait of totalitarian monarchy, it is perverse to resurrect it here. Unfortunately these pall bearers of absolutism have not succeeded in interring it satisfactorily, and the clichés about the all-powerful Louis XIV still persist both in the minds of sixth-formers and undergraduates as well as in the works of researchers in related disciplines such as literature and art history. This is scarcely surprising given the apparent indestructibility of some ancient text-books and the shortage of suitable modern equivalents by which to replace them. The task is made more difficult when a renowned academic press like that of Oxford can publish simultaneously, and in the same series, the highly perceptive work of Robin Briggs on *Early modern France, 1560–1715*, dating from 1977, and the *Louis XIV* of David Ogg, originating in 1933 and enshrining in its pages most of the interpretative evils which Briggs and others have been trying to combat. Similarly the two examples which are selected below, as a brief résumé of the absolutist case, are also firmly in print and continue to indoctrinate the unwary, for whom the creation of absolutism by Louis XIV, the westernization of Russia by the equally authoritarian Peter I, and the enlightened despotism of Frederick II and Joseph II are appealing and enduring concepts, despite the fact that they are all unhistorical. Dramatic change, especially at the behest of powerful individuals, has always attracted an applauding audience because, even when brutality has been a dominant quality of these great men, at least the enemies that they were fighting have been characterized, often most unfairly, as malign forces – religious tyranny, feudal privilege and selfish provincialism. It has allegedly been the story of 'progress' and 'modernization' triumphing over the satanic hordes of reaction.

If this book consigns such a caricature of Louis XIV to the fairy-tale world of good kings, bad kings and wicked barons, where it belongs, it does not seek to devalue the historical sources from which such erroneous conclusions were derived. Nor is it suggested that all these earlier writers were by any means unintelligent, and it will be shown that it was the limited range of their documentary evidence which frequently caused them to be misled. Intending to be objective historians, they unwittingly became governmental and social propagandists. Some of the archives on which subsequent revisions of their views have been based were either unknown or not easily accessible to them, while others were known to exist but seemed irrelevant to the aims of historical writing at the time. These might appear to be mitigating circumstances in any trial of the absolutist school of history, but there is one telling witness for the prosecution whose testimony is irrefutable. Norbert Elias published his *Die höfische Gesellschaft* in 1969, long before much recent research on Louis XIV had been reported to the reading public. He relied largely on the same source materials as the historians who created the myth of seventeenth-century French absolutism, but his own conclusions were very different. When his work became more generally available to English readers, on its translation in 1983,[1] it seemed to be compatible with the latest arguments about the structure of power in Bourbon France. He therefore demonstrated the value of those very sources which, in less

[1] As *The court society*, tr. Edmund Jephcott (Oxford); the 1969 edition was published in Darmstadt and Neuwied.

sensitive hands, had appeared to prove the existence of *la monarchie absolue.*

During the last twenty-five years, when diligent scholars have been sifting a mass of hitherto unknown archives and reinterpreting others, some of their fellows have become increasingly preoccupied with a very different debate, a quasi-philosophical investigation into the nature of French society and government. Absolutism, feudalism, capitalism, class, estates, orders, fidelities and many other concepts have been examined by historians who range across a spectrum from various shades of Marxist to the ultra-conservative institutionalists. These disputes have been admirably summarized and criticized by William Beik,[2] but that is not the only reason why the battle has not been joined in these pages. Although the often highly intelligent participants have posed many penetrating questions, which all historians should bear in mind, their conclusions belong more to political science and sociology than to history. The complex reality of the historical past is not suited to such theoretical categorization. The term 'absolutism', as used both in these intellectual debates and by the earlier writers who believed in an all-powerful Louis XIV, will therefore have no place here, and nor will an attempt be made to find an alternative adjective to which the suffix 'ism' might appropriately be attached. It is accepted, of course, that some contemporaries of Louis XIV uttered the words 'absolute monarchy' in their discussions of kingship and power, but the meaning that they gave to them depended on other seventeenth-century assumptions about the nature of society and government, which were very different from those of many modern historians.

On the positive side chapter 1 explains that, if the absolutist historians exaggerated both the power of the crown and the extent of its involvement in the daily routine of the kingdom, there were other ways in which the monarch could exert his influence over his subjects. The most important of these was the distribution of patronage and favour, emphasizing that the successes of Louis XIV and his ministers rested more on their skilful exploitation of the traditional values and priorities of French society than on the modernization of the administrative machinery and the creation of a new kind of royal official. It also warns against taking literally the public pronounce-ments of both the crown and the social elites, many of which were propaganda rather than descriptions of reality or statements of intent, and it stresses the need to identify the many issues on which there was

[2]*Absolutism and society in seventeenth-century France: state power and provincial aristocracy in Languedoc* (Cambridge, 1985).

agreement between the king and some of his principal subjects rather than to concentrate on those matters which led to confrontation. Finally it briefly considers the questions of centralization, which has too often been linked with the 'absolutism' of Louis XIV. It accepts that there were undoubtedly some centripetal tendencies in seventeenth-century France, but points out that the crown was neither the instigator nor the beneficiary of some of them.

Chapter 2 examines in greater detail the nature of government and the values of society. After a brief attempt to define 'the power of the crown' in the seventeenth century, it concentrates its attention on the royal court, that elaborate structure which was, at one and the same time, the personal household of the monarch, the seat of the central governmental machinery, and the place to which powerful subjects came in search of honours, offices and favours for themselves and for their clients. It was the principal social battlefield upon which rival factions jostled for position in the hierarchy of power and status, and the next section duly lists the various criteria by which this aristocratic society judged the success and failure of its member families. The chapter ends with three very different excursions into the recent history of France as Louis XIV himself would have perceived it on his assumption of personal power in 1661. The first considers the changing fortunes of the French crown under the childless Henri III, during the initially precarious rule of Henri IV, through the infancy and adult reign of Louis XIII and into his own childhood and tutelage under his Spanish mother and her Italian minister. The second describes the passionate debates about the idea of 'nobility' and the inviolability of privileges in the early seventeenth century, and the third charts the attempts of the monarchs to create their own enduring faction of loyal aristocratic houses. These aspects of the immediate past offered a number of lessons for the young Louis XIV, and his perception of them greatly influenced his policies throughout his long reign.

This second chapter elaborates the point that Louis, far from imposing a new kind of power structure on the country, worked within the constraints of a hierarchical and aristocratically dominated society, using the traditional powers of the monarchy to enlist the aid of some influential families and to reduce the obstructiveness of others – in an age when the crown never possessed sufficient strength to dominate all its subjects. Most leading social groups had much to gain from co-operating with the king, and some, like the judges of the *parlements*, depended on their position as senior agents of the royal government for their own exalted status in society. Although they felt compelled to oppose the illegal actions of Mazarin, they preferred to be on the same side as their sovereign and his ministers and therefore welcomed the initial indications that the personal rule of Louis XIV would mark a return to traditional methods of ruling, where harmonious relations with the crown could be resumed and overt opposition would not be necessary.

Chapter 3, for reasons which were explained above, analyses some of the tensions within French society and the principal problems facing the royal government in the period 1610–61. Such a perspective is essential to an understanding of social attitudes and political behaviour in the years when Louis took over the reins of power, not only because the experiences of the king and his subjects in these recent decades conditioned their reactions to subsequent events, but also because similar difficulties recurred during the personal rule, causing men to compare and contrast the present with the past in the hope of resolving them more satisfactorily. It considers the adverse effects of war on the crown and on the people, the chaotic state of the fiscal system, the role of financiers and tax-farmers, the exemptions of the privileged orders from direct taxation and the increasingly counterproductive efforts of the government to exploit the wealth of the office-holders. Then it examines the behaviour of leading social groups towards each other and towards the royal ministers, from the regency of Marie de Médicis, through the long ministry of Richelieu, to the minority of Louis XIV, the turbulent years of the Frondes and the confusion of the later 1650s. It assesses the extent to which the problems facing the crown were not of its own making, and how far ministerial misjudgements exacerbated an already difficult situation. Its conclusions, formulated from the point of view of the historian, are in many ways very similar to those which Louis XIV and his advisers derived from their own study of these years.

The fourth and fifth chapters discuss the mechanisms of social and political power during the years 1661–1715, when the king personally took responsibility for the actions of his government. They emphazise his determination to rule more traditionally, while at the same time cautiously introducing innovations in administrative methods and in policy. Such a seemingly paradoxical approach was possible because, while some initiatives might provoke a violent reaction from many influential groups and raise the spectre of another Fronde, others would gain support in certain quarters and incur hostility elsewhere. The crown was therefore often stimulating the rivalries which already existed among elites in the provinces and localities. The ministers had to weigh the advantages of implementing a particular policy and the strength of its supporters against the danger of seriously alien-ating other important citizens who might be useful allies in different circumstances. For Louis the ideal situation, which was not easy to create, was that relations among his principal subjects should be in a state of simmering tension and controlled instability. Then he could be sure that moderate governmental proposals would find favour with some Frenchmen, even if they upset others. Occasionally the local elites would close ranks in an attempt to thwart a particular policy, in which case the crown might retreat, but these liaisons were usually ephemeral because the various groups had few long-term interests in common and many more reasons for disliking each other. The king knew that reliable supporters were more likely to be found through the judicious dispensation of patronage to family and clientage networks than by seeking to forge permanent links with individual institutions or social strata. Although Louis and his ministers made some major misjudgements in their efforts to act upon these guidelines, at least their determination to respect the traditional values and priorities of French society prevented the recurrence of any opposition movement on the scale of the Frondes – even in the disastrous decades of war which ended the reign.

There is a good reason for dividing this analysis of the personal rule of Louis XIV into two chapters. The first, chapter 4, concentrates on those aspects of government which the king regarded as falling within his own prerogative – the restoration of the royal reputation and its propagation at home and abroad, the appointment of ministers and advisers, the making of foreign policy, the defence of the realm, and the assertion of the secular power of the crown against any religious movement which sought to place loyalty to God, to Rome or to the church above that owed to the sovereign. In order to attain these goals he had to restructure the central policy-making machinery, which was easy to reform because it was part of his own court and household, and to dispense favours and patronage to those who might assist him. In contrast, chapter 5 considers the internal administration of the kingdom, where Louis had little scope to alter the bureaucracy of hereditary office-holders and where the interests of powerful social and institutional elites had to be considered. Here the crown had to rule by negotiation rather than by Diktat, aware that the local notables could obstruct the execution of policies which they did not like. Moreover the central government had no wish to extend its influence into all aspects of domestic affairs, many of which were simply not suitable matters for royal attention. The king left much routine administration to the corporations, institutions and social elites which had traditionally been responsible for it – and which usually shared his desire for an orderly society where the laws were respected and enforced.

With his room for manoeuvre restricted by his determination to uphold the hierarchical traditions of French society and his need to respect the privileges, rights and liberties of his more influential subjects, the Louis XIV who emerges from these pages will also be seen to be conservative by temperament as well as through circumstance. Although he restructured the policy-making machinery at the centre, he did not make many changes in the personnel of the government nor in the group of aristocratic advisers on whom the crown had relied heavily in the years before 1661. Even in the prerogative areas of royal power he took careful account of powerful vested interests, not wishing to alienate men who, if they were treated honourably, would serve him well. From the beginning of the personal rule, he stressed that his best chance of retaining the loyalty of his realm was by being seen to be scrupulously fair, especially in the distribution of patronage and in the important royal role of mediator between rival groups who sought his arbitration. Yet, despite the best intentions of the king and his ministers, his government was soon to be a focus for much criticism and discontent, especially when the problems of war returned to plague it. The principal reason is a familiar one to historians of early modern France. Many ministerial initiatives, formulated after wide consultation, seemed eminently sensible at court where royal advisers were considering the whole range of domestic and international issues which currently affected the realm. In the provinces, where horizons were more geographically limited, such actions by a distant central government not only offered no benefit but often savoured of the arbitrary interference with local liberties which had characterized the ministries of Richelieu and Mazarin. France was a collection of very different provinces, many of which had little in common. It was therefore almost impossible to devise a policy which was in the best interests of the whole kingdom.

The conclusion accordingly looks briefly at the various forms of dissent which surfaced not infrequently during the personal rule of Louis XIV. French monarchs knew that from time to time there would be short seditious outbursts against their officials or against other administrative bodies in the localities, and they were more irritated than alarmed by these disturbances. Occasionally more serious and sustained revolts would occur, and then it would be vital for the crown to be seen to act in defence of its authority. In fact, as in so many aspects of government, the outcome was usually a compromise because the rebels often had legitimate grievances. The crown did not have the power to quell most kinds of insurrection, although it could enlist the aid of local notables and militias who were normally eager to repress disorder, especially if it became too prolonged. At least Louis

XIV could take comfort that, even during the 1690s and early 1700s, when France experienced the severest hardships, there was no sign that the leaders of Parisian and provincial society thought a civil war to be either desirable or possible. The reasons are not different to discover. The alliances of the *frondeurs*, the consequence of both arbitrary ministerial actions and a coincidence of circumstances, had already disintegrated before Louis assumed personal power in 1661. Long-term differences within these groups of temporary allies re-emerged, and the king stimulated these tensions while at the same time giving less cause for offence through his own cautious and traditional approach to government. When the Dutch War of 1672–9 compelled the royal ministers to act more imprudently in their urgent need to finance the conflict, a novel situation began to develop. The social and institutional elites, reluctant to challenge a king who was ruling personally, devised new methods of obstructing, rather than overtly defying, royal orders. They learned how to resist unpopular ministerial directives without the need for a resort to arms, and they soon discovered that such covert disobedience prompted expressions of kingly disapproval or merely sadness, but seldom wrath. In the 1690s therefore, they continued to use these evasive tactics, also finding that Louis XIV, confronted by apparently insoluble international problems, was making considerable efforts to be more conciliatory towards them. They therefore saw no advantage in insurrection and they feared that, with harvest failures inflicting dire distress on the rural and urban poor, those deprived elements of society might, if roused to revolt against governmental fiscal policy, turn against the wealthier members of their locality as well.

 This book attempts to show how the crown and other groups in French society defined their own best interests and set about the task of furthering them, how they evaluated their own position in the social hierarchy, and how they used their family and clientage networks in pursuit of their goals. The mechanisms and the structure of power had changed little since the sixteenth century, and there was certainly no evidence of an emerging 'absolute monarchy'. Social groups were adapting to new circumstances, but there was scarcely anything which could meaningfully be called 'modern' in the France of Louis XIV.

1

Historians and 'Absolutism':
The Illusion and the Reality

The illusion of strong monarchy, so carefully fostered by the kings and ministers of later Valois and early Bourbon France, was in some ways too convincing and rebounded upon its progenitors. There could be little comfort for Louis XIV when he found that this carefully projected image of steadily increasing royal power had led his foreign enemies so to overestimate the strength and misconceive the ambitions of France that, forgetting their differences one with another, they united against him and combined their armies into a force which considerably outnumbered his own troops. Likewise within the kingdom, his subjects, still prepared to oppose or obstruct many aspects of his government, had imbibed enough of this royalist propaganda that they now expected the king to take sole responsibility for the defence of the realm without their feeling obliged to contribute more generously towards the cost of his doing so. The increasing military role played by the crown in Europe and in France itself, at a time when the geographical scale and the financial demands of wars were expanding, meant that the central government was almost always living beyond its means and was forced into courses of action which went even further beyond its capabilities. War was the most disastrous effect of so-called 'absolutism' and, in the last years of Louis XIV, France was brought by these prolonged conflicts to its lowest ebb.

After this final decade of acute financial hardship, military defeats and tragic deaths among the younger members of his family, the king would have been astonished at the tributes paid by subsequent generations of historians to the myth of his absolute power. Such writers have identified a steady consolidation of royal authority in France from the early sixteenth century, so that, by the personal rule of Louis XIV, the French monarchy had acquired direct control over its kingdom to an extent which was unparalleled in seventeenth-century Europe, unheard of in preceding ages and rarely exceeded in later years. Even the aggressive dictatorships of the modern world appear less awe-inspiring than these posthumous portraits of Louis XIV. The twentieth-century totalitarian ruler may have greater brute force at his disposal, but the history of the *roi soleil* has been embellished by eulogistic generalizations about the destruction of privilege, the emergence of the modern state, the rise of the bourgeoisie and the patronage of the arts, which have added a corona of progress to this sun among monarchs. It became a historical truism that Louis XIV was the personification of absolutism, with the result that the precise implications of that word were seldom defined.

In recent years historical researches have begun to reveal a very different picture of the glorious reign. Where their predecessors saw innovation, change, progress and maximal royal power, these latest historians have discovered more repetition than novelty in the methods of royal ministers, and a recurrent pattern of advance, consolidation and retreat as the crown sought to increase its resources but had to acknowledge the effectiveness of the other powers which coexisted with it in the agglomeration of separatist provinces forming the kingdom of France. Change was sometimes illusory and often short-lived. It has also been made clear that, for all the bravura of its pronouncements about its supreme authority in the realm, the royal government was fully aware of the obstacles confronting it and of its limited scope for enhancing its own powers at the expense of the privileged orders and institutions, which were themselves confident that they could resist most attempts at unwarranted centralization by the ministers in Paris, or later at Versailles.

The image of Louis XIV which was current in the Europe of his own day was deliberately created by teams of expert propagandists, assembled through skilful royal and ministerial patronage, and by courtiers who, whether as a result of patriotism, loyalty to the king, sycophancy or simple myopia, allowed their enthusiasm to triumph over their sense of reality. Yet even in their writings and sayings, there was no attempt to use some of the more inflated claims which would be employed by the 'absolutist' historians of the nineteenth and early twentieth centuries. However shamelessly the contemporary publicists set out to deceive the Holy Roman Emperor and other monarchs into thinking that their master was indeed pre-eminent in Europe, it never occurred to them to claim that there were no limits to his control over the internal affairs of the kingdom, nor that it was even the business of the crown to concern itself with every aspect of the daily administration and life of France. Whereas some later historians have transposed a modern concept of all-pervasive central government into a seventeenth-century context, the contemporaries of Louis XIV would have made a clear distinction between those aspects of administration which were the concern of the monarch and those which were not. In asserting that the present government was more absolute than ever before, most of them were therefore saying only that the king was successfully resisting challenges to his authority in those kingly spheres of activity, and not that he had extended the power of the crown into new areas. Only a few ultra-royalists were advocating a greater degree of interference by the crown in the internal administration of the kingdom, and they were planning for the future, not commenting on the past or the present.

The crown remained chiefly concerned with the making of war and peace, the formulation of foreign policy, the defence of the realm and the maintenance of religious harmony. The taxes which it levied were primarily intended for the financing of these royal functions, and most of the judicial edicts which it promulgated were designed to facilitate the exercise of authority in these specific fields. Thus the lavish expenditure on the court was justified as much by the need to impress foreign powers and to lure skilled foreigners – scientists, political theorists, manufacturers of armaments and luxury goods, financiers, architects, artists – into the service of the king, as by the hope of overawing his own subjects. It was therefore a major element in diplomacy and in the fostering of French prestige abroad. Even the arbitrary regulations which the crown tried to impose on the economic life of the kingdom were almost entirely geared to these international purposes – the race for the colonies, the reduction in the import of luxury goods, the ban on the export of gold and silver, and the production within the kingdom of all necessary armaments and military supplies. The crown had to strive for self-sufficiency in finance and in weaponry, if it was satisfactorily to discharge its prime responsibility, that of defending the kingdom from attack. The routine economic life of the provinces was of no concern to the central government, and nor was most of the everyday administration within the towns and in the countryside. The sustenance of the poor and the weak, the policing of urban streets, fairs and markets, the maintenance of local road and river routes, the containing of vagabonds and other lawless elements, the prevention of epidemics and the resolution of petty legal disputes, these were not matters for the attention of royal ministers, unless some ambitious litigant or corporation decided to appeal directly to the king as arbiter. The monarch was the head of the judicial system, but he did not want to become too much involved in its daily activities at the lowest levels. The only local administration in which the crown showed an abiding interest was that of Paris, its own 'locality' and a city whose smooth running was essential to the government and to the court.

The most ardent royalist pamphleteer would therefore have assumed that, in parallel with the royal administration, there were other systems of control – seigneurial, municipal, ecclesiastical and provincial – which were largely free to administer their areas as they chose. The only requirement was that these bodies should not prevent the crown from carrying out its own role in the state, and that accordingly they should be prepared to contribute willingly to the revenues of the central government. These apologists for stronger monarchy were certainly eager both to exaggerate the ability of the crown to secure this fiscal support from its subjects, and to overstate the degree of enthusiasm felt by ordinary Frenchmen for royal policies, but neither they, nor the ministers themselves, would have thought of replacing the local networks of privileged elites with direct royal administrators. It would have been neither possible nor appropriate for the crown to do so.

The problem of raising adequate finance for its costly wars was made more difficult for the crown because it could not rely on the unquestioning loyalty of its own officials. Its financial and judicial agents, most of whom had bought their offices and acquired the right to pass on their posts to their heirs, frequently behaved less like royal servants and more as if they were yet another privileged elite group. They often carried out their administrative duties, for it was by this means that they acquired a sizable part of their income, but they not infrequently sided with other local bodies in refusing, or failing, to implement royal orders which did not seem to be for the good of themselves or their area. When Louis XIV came to personal power in 1661, many Frenchmen retained vivid memories of the Frondes which had rocked France a mere decade before. Then the royal officials had shown that they were even prepared to unleash civil war upon the kingdom, and had demonstrated that they, the agents of the central government, could bring that government to a halt.

LOUIS XIV AND ABSOLUTISM: THE TRADITIONAL VIEW
RE-EXAMINED

The royalist propaganda which misled contemporary foreign rulers and subsequent historians is a useful guide to the problems of government as the crown itself perceived them. The claims for the extent of royal success in a particular field of administration were often inversely proportionate to the degree of control which the royal ministers had actually managed to establish. Yet some historians have taken these statements at face value and, worse still, have added further generalizations about the reign of Louis XIV which are based on the misreading of the documentary evidence and on the endowing of words with meanings which no seventeenth-century writer would have intended. Whether or not this is the result of carelessness, lack of historical insight and imagination or even deliberate distortion, there is no doubt that the all-powerful monarchy which they created was both dramatic and appealing, often fitting conveniently into their wider interpretations of French history. For the historians of preceding reigns, the absolutism of Louis XIV was the culmination of a vigorous and successful centralizing process whose origins they attributed, anachronistically, to Richelieu, to Henri IV or even to François Ier. Similarly, chroniclers and analysts of the French Revolution, although they may postulate very different explanations for the cataclysmic decade after 1789, have shown a common desire to embrace the concept of an absolute Louis XIV as a suitable starting point for their various theories about the origins of the Revolution. Exaggerated characterizations of the eighteenth century too – for example as an age of aristocratic reaction – have been possible only because the period 1661–1715 has been so distorted.

Numerous instances of these historical misrepresentations could be quoted, beginning with Voltaire, whose *Siècle de Louis XIV* became very influential and persuaded many later writers to adopt its idealized account of the reign.[1] Nevertheless two extracts will suffice here to illustrate the tone of these writings and some of the obvious pitfalls which their authors failed to avoid. Georges Lefebvre, in the words of his English translator, declares that 'under Louis XIV the monarchy had become absolutistic, centralist and bureaucratic. Its supremacy was to all appearances firmly established; the nobility's submission seemed final', and adds that 'in so far as Louis XIV gave Colbert a free hand, the monarchy during his reign, already bourgeois in character, roughly sketched what was later to be called enlightened despotism'.[2] John Lough similarly chronicles dramatic government action and social change, asserting that:

[1]See the new edition of *Le siècle de Louis XIV*, eds S. S. B. Taylor et al, vols 11–13 of the complete *Oeuvres*, to be published shortly by the International Voltaire Foundation, Oxford: it contains an extended essay by Roger Mettam on 'Voltaire as historian of Louis XIV'.

[2]*The French Revolution*, tr. Elizabeth Moss Evanson (2 vols, London/New York, 1962–4), vol. I, p. 73.

except in war time . . . the great noblemen and princes of the blood now lost every shred of power. The new King ruled with members of the middle class which, thanks to its economic power, was already on the way to supplanting the nobility as the most important section of society. . . . The decisions of the central government were carried out in the provinces by the intendants, who, like the ministers, were of middle-class origin, and, since they were at any moment subject to recall, could be depended upon to fulfil loyally their role as agents of the royal authority. . . . In general the middle-classes were the firmest supporters of absolute monarchy in seventeenth-century France. . . . The nobles were now entirely disciplined. . . . To keep the nobles out of mischief, the King insisted on their coming to court. And the nobles came, not only because life at court suited their tastes for luxury and amusement, but because it was the only way of obtaining all the favours which the King had at his disposal.[3]

Many passages in the same vein can be found in the writings of other historians, but all are woefully far from the reality of *louis-quatorzienne* France. The fundamental error of these writers has been to assume that, because the Frondes were a time of turmoil and the 1660s a decade of peace, the crown had triumphed over all its opponents. They do not explain, of course, how this royal victory had been achieved, because no such explanation exists. The crown had neither the financial resources nor the physical strength to impose such a solution. More importantly, the royal ministers would not have seen the problem in the terms of a reforming and centralizing government versus reactionary and entrenched forces of opposition, subversion and privilege. Most of the *frondeurs*, and especially the office-holders, shared the royal desire for an orderly, well administered country. It was only the excessive aggression of Mazarin which had caused them to take drastic action against the ruling regime. After the collapse of the second Fronde, it was the leaders of the earlier parlementary rebellion who played a positive role in restoring order, although they contined to resist any arbitrary actions by the cardinal as he laboured to conclude the war with Spain.

The royal ministers and the majority of the more substantial levels of French society were all eager to avoid further civil strife, and there was therefore a positive attempt at co-operation and compromise in the first decade of the personal rule of Louis XIV, now that the international war had finally ended and the crown had been able to

---

[3] *An introduction to seventeenth-century France* (London, 1954), pp. 138, 140, 145–6, 149. That Lough has not in any way modified these views can be clearly seen in his *France observed in the seventeenth century by British travellers* (Stocksfield, 1984) — see the review by Roger Mettam, 'Ignorance abroad', *The Times Literary Supplement*, 8 March 1985.

withdraw the provocative wartime taxes and financial expedients which had been the main causes both of the Frondes and of the continuing tension in the later 1650s. The crown still hoped to extend its authority in the long term over certain limited areas of administration, and its most influential subjects were as committed as ever to preserving their privileges, but both sides were determined to avoid open confrontation whenever possible.

Thus, where compromises were reached and mutual provocation ceased, Lefebvre and Lough wrongly declare the dominance of absolute monarchy over submissive social groups. The very high nobles and princes of the blood, who had led the second Fronde, were undoubtedly brought to heel and kept at court, although their total subjection by the king was achieved only because their support in the country had evaporated. In this instance the crown did become more absolute because it had curbed the one group which had sought to take over the policy-making role of the royal ministers in the kingly sphere of foreign policy. Yet these men, from the loftiest echelons of French society, were untypical in that their ambition was to establish themselves in the innermost councils of the king. Most of them were legitimate or natural descendants of earlier Bourbon or Valois monarchs, or claimed descent from European sovereign houses which still, or had formerly, ruled territories beyond the frontiers of France. They emphasized their superiority over other nobles by continuing to marry into the ruling and princely families of other countries, the only group in the kingdom to do so and therefore the only men whose personal power base was affected by the international configuration of Europe. Accordingly it was vital for them to have a major influence on the foreign policy of the king.

The rest of the *frondeurs*, whose interests lay entirely within the kingdom and in most cases within one of its provinces, had no such ambition to dominate the central government and to dictate policy, nor to tell the king whom he should appoint as his ministers. They were simply concerned to resist any attempts by Mazarin to undermine local, social and institutional privileges. Accordingly they scrutinized royal policies and resisted those which they did not like. Although there were moments when all the *frondeurs* seemed to be united in shouting 'vive le roi, point de Mazarin!', it was only the princes who were determined to remove the Mazarinists and replace them with members of their own factions. The other rebels were perfectly prepared to reach an accord with the cardinal on more than one occasion, when he revoked the policies which had caused them such offence. Not even the *parlement* of Paris, that most vocal and critical of bodies, offered the king advice on how to exercise his prerogative powers. Therefore, in common with most Frenchmen, it commented not on his foreign policy as such, but on the taxes which were needed to finance it. As the supreme law court of the realm, the *parlement* was concerned with the legality of royal edicts, not with the details of diplomacy. Because it rejected the fiscal innovations necessitated by the demands of war, it obviously affected the ability of the government to carry out its military strategy, and the judges were therefore accused by the crown of meddling in affairs of state. Yet this is certainly not how they would have described their activities, because their concern was entirely with the law and not at all with politics.

If the princes of the second Fronde were reduced to political impotence, the leaders of the parlementary Fronde were far from being defeated by Mazarin. Having wrung many important concessions from him, they continued to thwart his attempts at further innovation until the end of his ministry. As in the Frondes, these subsequent confrontations all centred on the question of whether or not new fiscal measures were legal. Even during the personal rule of Louis XIV, when no one challenged the right of the king to appoint whomever he chose as ministers or to make foreign policy as he wished, the real limitation on royal power would always be the refusal of Frenchmen to give the government adequate financial resources to meet the growing costs of defending the kingdom and fighting wars.

As Louis took personal control of government during a period of peace, when his subjects were tired of both international and civil wars, the social and administrative elites were prepared to allow the new regime time to explain its style of government, and finding it much more to their taste, co-operated with it as long as there was no question of sacrificing their own interests and privileges. Prominent among these leaders of provincial society were thousands of nobles, all of whom, would appear to be included by Lefebvre and Lough in their generalizations about the 'submission' of that order, which was 'disciplined' so thoroughly. Not only was it impossible for the king to have 'insisted' that these men, whose power base lay firmly in their local areas, should permanently attend him at court, because they would most certainly not have answered his summons, but such a policy would have been counterproductive. The lesser nobles might at times oppose the royal government, but they were usually a force for stability and order in the localities and they still provided the officer corps of his armies. Moreover as the court was, until its establishment at Versailles in 1682, an itinerant institution, moving from one royal residence to another for the first twenty years of the personal rule, it is impossible to see how thousands of nobles could have been accommodated into the entourage of the king. Some aristocrats did undoubtedly spend much of their life at court, but many attended either infrequently or not at all. The king was certainly the principal source of favours and patronage, but personal attendance upon him or upon his ministers was not the only way of claiming a share in this beneficence. The aristocratic provincial governors, whose power has been underrated by these same historians, were a major channel by which requests for favours reached the king, as were other great nobles, bishops, senior office-holders and even *intendants*. An aspirant for patronage could usually find someone to champion his cause at court without himself having to leave his province.

Saint-Simon was perfectly accurate when he said that Louis had lured the *grands* to court and was determined to keep them there, because he was using the term *grand* in its specific and limited sense. So too, when Richelieu had declared that one of his three prime aims was 'ravaler l'orgueil des grands', he was not proposing an attack on the nobility in general. Both men understood the word *grands* to mean the grandees, the very high aristocrats and the princes of the blood – those men who had staged a series of attempted coups against Richelieu and went on to lead the second Fronde. Louis XIV was certainly intent on keeping such dangerous men at court, often appointing them to highly prestigious but purely ceremonial posts in the royal household. But when historians suggest that the nobility as a whole was enticed to the palace of the monarch, where it indulged its taste for luxury, amusement and the quest for favours, they are, of course, talking anachronistic nonsense.

There is a much more important aspect of this patronage system at which Lough does not even hint. If many Frenchmen eagerly sought favours from their sovereign, it was also vital for the king to have his clients in the localities. There were three principal ways of ruling France. The official channel was through the network of venal and hereditary office-holders, who balanced their loyalty to the king against their personal and local interests, and who on occasion had encouraged revolt and even joined the ranks of the *frondeurs*. A second alternative was the establishment of direct royal agents, such as *intendants*, but they were not always reliable, and excessive use of them provoked disturbances in the provinces. It was therefore vital to maintain a third and more informal system, which was not institutionalized but operated behind the scenes. The cement of this structure was royal patronage. Thus the king and his ministers either enlisted the aid of men they knew personally or asked trusted friends to recruit further potentially loyal agents from their own clients or from their local area. Many of those who were selected were from the old nobility, a number of them also being senior churchmen, but some were from the ranks of the office-holders. While it was essential that they be loyal to the king, it was equally imperative that they be influential and respected in their own locality or institution, because it was through their personal prestige that they would try to persuade others to obey the wishes of the central government. Just as those who served the king in the upper levels of this hierarchy were rewarded with offices, orders and pensions, so they in turn offered similar inducements to those lower down the scale. Some of these lesser men were, not surprisingly, prepared to support and publicize royal causes only in proportion to the rewards which they were likely to receive. Those closer to the king were usually of higher social rank and great integrity, which meant that they sometimes sincerely questioned the wisdom of certain royal decisions which they were being asked to promote. When an aristocratic governor or a bishop was trusted by the king, he was able to voice such reservations to a minister or even to the sovereign himself, and the governors in particular were able to convince the central government on many occasions that it should modify decisions which would inflict hardship on their province or would simply inflame the population against the crown.

If Lough, Lefebvre and many other historians have given the erroneous impression that all nobles posed the same threat to the crown and were accordingly dealt the same staggering blow by the government of Louis XIV, they have erred equally seriously when they have discussed the bourgeoisie, using that term to include anyone who was neither an aristocrat nor a peasant or humble urban worker. In the seventeenth century, these middle levels of society would certainly have disagreed with the suggestion that they formed a homogeneous bourgeois stratum. The venal office-holder, whether of the *noblesse de robe* or of humbler rank, would have felt that he had little in common with the merchant or the master craftsman, even though the money with which his family had purchased its first office, perhaps at a date long in the past, might well have come from the profits of trade or industry. Now, as an *officier*, he carefully cultivated all the habits of the old landed nobility, in whose circles he wished to be accepted. He might therefore have estates and peasants of his own, have even married his daughters to the scions of ancient noble houses, would have adorned his town house in the best aristocratic taste, and would have abandoned those middle-class economic pursuits which were forbidden by law to the nobility.

Lefebvre is correct in calling the monarchy bureaucratic during the personal rule of Louis XIV, but it was still the bureaucracy of hereditary office-holders, imbued with aristocratic values and ideals – the same men who had played a prominent role in the Frondes against the crown and who, in the early 1660s, chose to look favourably on its offer of co-operation. In some ways therefore these officials, perverse as it is to describe them as bourgeois, were indeed supporters of the monarchy. This is not, of course, what Lough and Lefebvre want us to believe. They are suggesting first that a new group of middle-class ministers and *intendants* had been installed at the core of the central government, giving the king a new kind of direct authority over his kingdom. These men, so it is claimed, were loyal, efficient and totally independent of previous forms of administration. The second assertion of the historians is that the wider middle class cheerfully supported the economic revival of France which was being masterminded by Jean-Baptiste Colbert. Unfortunately, both of these propositions obscure far more than they illuminate. An initial objection to the former is that, if it is misleading to designate the venal office-holders as bourgeois, it is equally unhelpful so to describe the ministers and *intendants*, because they too came from this same *officier* background. When Saint-Simon derided this period of government as a 'règne de vile bourgeoisie', he knew that his deliberate sneer was untrue. More important than this semantic point is the matter of the loyalty and effectiveness of these novel royal councillors and provincial agents. The ministers were undoubtedly loyal, or they would have been dismissed. Louis XIV ensured that he had total control over appointments to his inner councils, and no longer were princely factions able to challenge his freedom of choice. Thus the king, his ministers and a few trusted aristocratic advisers clearly had a monopoly of policy-making. Yet the effectiveness of these royal councils depended on whether they could persuade or force the venal officials to implement conciliar decisions in the localities – and this was far from self-evident.

The *intendants* had more scope for deception and disloyalty because, although they were instructed to supervise the administration of the venal *officiers* in the provinces, there was no superior royal agent to check that they themselves were carrying out their supervisory duties with energy, objectivity and integrity. Within the ranks of the *intendants* the historian can therefore find every kind of man from the loyal and effective, through the loyal but ineffectual to the plainly corrupt. Moreover, under the cautious Colbert, they were also to behave with greater circumspection than their predecessors had sometimes shown in the past, for the hatred they had inspired among the *frondeurs* was still a vivid and painful memory. Accordingly they were now to observe the workings of the administration in their *généralité*, and report their findings to the royal councils where decisions on possible action would be taken. They were also to respect local privileges, and they were to leave the task of executing royal orders to the venal office-holders and to elected bodies, such as the town councils. Lough is quite wrong in saying that 'the decisions of the central government were carried out in the provinces by the intendant', during these first decades of the personal rule. As a wiser historian has said, they were rather 'the eyes and ears of the ministers' in the provinces, and even in that capacity some of them could be selectively deaf or myopic.[4]

The true middle class – the entrepreneurs, merchants, craftsmen and industrialists – were far from being 'the firmest supporters of absolute monarchy', as they are characterized in Lough's dramatic portrait of political and social change. It was a source of perpetual sadness to Colbert that these men, on the basis of whose enterprises he was hoping to build a more prosperous France, were so unwilling to second his plans for reform. Many of them still preferred to purchase an office and aspire to nobility, when the minister wished them to plough back their financial resources into trade and manufactures. Nor did they welcome his *dirigiste* schemes for organizing colonial expansion, tariffs and customs dues on a national basis. All too often these ministerial directives seemed to threaten individual initiative, or to disrupt traditional trading patterns among provinces or with other countries, substituting in their place an arbitrary governmental system whose economic benefits were at best unproven. The commercial and industrial world accordingly resisted most of his reforms and welcomed but a few, and Colbert was therefore compelled to encourage foreigners to establish themselves in France in order to promote his programme of economic revival – a programme which, it must be said, was itself more limited in scope than some of his admiring biographers have suggested.

All these points will be elaborated in later chapters, but already one major historiographical point is emerging. When the history of France is studied from the centre – through government propaganda, diplomatic reports, the memoirs of courtiers, the writings of royal publicists, and the accounts by foreign travellers of their visits to the court and the capital – it looks very different from the picture which lies none too obscurely hidden in the provincial archives or in those Parisian collections of documents which record the day-to-day activities of the government. The declared intentions of the ministers and the publicity they engendered convey an impression of strong rule and drastic change. The daily reality was much less spectacular.

[1]An excellent account of the *intendants* and *officiers* is contained in *France in crisis, 1620–75*, selected, introduced and tr. P. J. Coveney (London, 1977), especially in the introduction by the editor and in the last of the three pieces by Roland Mousnier.

THE CURIAL AND DIPLOMATIC SOURCES: HISTORICAL
EVIDENCE OR PROPAGANDA?

Significantly, the bibliography appended by Lough is composed entirely of printed works, many of whose authors were deliberately or unconsciously exaggerating the power of the crown. Although the royal government had a somewhat tenuous hold on the kingdom in general, there is no doubt that Louis XIV seemed to be the unchallenged master of the court. As not only ministers, but also mistresses and favourites, rose to the heights of prestige and might then be cast down to the depths of disgrace, as the whole conciliar system was recast with a few strokes of the royal quill, and as favours, offices and pensions were granted or withheld by kingly whim, it truly seemed to those whose lives centred on the court that the king held the fortunes of his subjects in his hands, and that without his approval there could be no hope of advancement. Many writers eagerly lauded their sovereign in the hope of receiving such tangible signs of his approbation.

Those who were prepared to be more critical of the regime were hampered by the strict censorship laws and were hounded for their opinions. Even the frequently obstructive law courts and municipal authorities were not keen to encourage subversive literature. Subtle obstruction of the government and overt criticism of the king were very different matters. Such hostile works therefore often circulated clandestinely, frequently originating from disaffected Frenchmen in exile abroad, or at least bearing a foreign place of publication on the title page to disguise the fact that the author was secretly residing in the French provinces. So the royal publicists had all the advantages and the critics had every obstacle placed in their way. If a writer was widely acclaimed as a literary giant by his contemporaries, his writings receiving praise or his plays being performed at court and in the best Paris theatres, then it is likely that he will always have taken care to please the king. Later in the reign, criticism of the government and even of Louis himself would increase considerably, and some authors staked their hopes of success on the heir to the throne – for surely the old king must die soon! Yet in the 1660s and 1670s, when the monarch was still relatively young, adulation of this most powerful of patrons was the key to social recognition for the ambitious *littérateur*.

The memoirs and letters of courtiers, like the despatches of foreign diplomats, contain both deliberate and accidental distortions of the role played by the central government in the life of the kingdom. Some of the native aristocratic memorialists either visited the provinces or at least corresponded regularly with friends who resided there, but for many of them the court was their world. This was even more true of diplomats from abroad, who remained close to the king because it was in his immediate ministerial circle that they could best hope to carry out the tasks with which they had been entrusted. Both groups could not fail to be impressed by the celebration of the monarchical cult in architecture, sculpture, painting, theatre and music, and by the munificence of the king as revealed in the lavish gifts he distributed at sumptuous curial fêtes and in the pensions he bestowed on foreign artists and *savants* who were prepared to laud his wisdom and glory. This self-congratulatory regime must have seemed impressive enough when the court still moved from palace to palace in the 1660s and 1670s, but when it finally settled in the temple specially designed for the worship of the Sun King at Versailles in 1682, it would have been difficult for even the most well travelled diplomat to deny that this was the most astounding monarchy Europe had ever seen. (Only the magnificence of the palace built by Moulay Ismaïl at Meknès led French envoys to wonder whether they had not discovered a monarchy even more spectacular than their own.) The courtiers of Louis XIV basked in the radiance of these splendours, and foreign rulers read about them in the reports of their envoys with amazement, envy and more than a little alarm. On the international scene, the claims made by the king for his rights of precedence over other monarchs had the *hauteur* of the greatest kind of emperor.

No opportunity was lost by the ministers to publicize and exaggerate the achievements of the government and to minimize its weaknesses. Foreign diplomats had little or no opportunity to visit the provinces in order to test the veracity of these claims, and, if some courtiers were certain that they themselves were being fed with propaganda rather than with information, it was both unpatriotic and risky to enlighten foreigners about such matters and it was often unwise to commit their doubts to paper, especially in letters written for transmission by a postal system in which government spies were hard at work. Even in the last years of the reign, when a group of French nobles did pen political tracts which were extremely critical of the king and included drastic proposals for governmental and social reform, the gulf between Versailles and the localities is clearly visible. Although writers like Saint-Simon and Boulainvilliers tried to solve the problems of the whole kingdom, the former, who had spent his life at court, was chiefly concerned to restructure the policy-making system of the central government. Boulainvilliers, whose experience had been largely acquired in a provincial context, concentrated more on reforming the lower levels of the administration and on aiding the humbler members of society. The court and the country remained very different worlds.

The only topic on which foreign diplomats were much better informed than the court nobles was the progress of French armies in wartime. The crown took great care to publicize their victories, celebrating them with fireworks and services of thanksgiving, but failed to report major reversals in the field. The agents of other monarchs often received more objective information from international sources, but courtiers had to wait until news of these disasters filtered back through less official channels. On matters of French internal government, the diplomats were often victims of their own pride, ambition or insecurity. Many of their despatches boast of the confidences which had been entrusted to them by ministers or by court nobles who had the royal ear. Sometimes the king himself had spoken a few flattering words to them or given them a small token of his goodwill. If many of these reports of confidences and courtesies were true, the envoys often overestimated the veracity of the information they had received or the deeper significance of the courteous gesture, and they sometimes revealed too much of their own thinking during these encounters, so that they gave away more than they had learned. They too easily convinced themselves that they had been singled out for royal or governmental approval, at a court where suitors were prepared to wait for days in ministerial antechambers or patiently follow the king in the hope of a glance or a word. Sometimes these ambassadors restorted to pure invention, as they sought to reassure their sovereigns that they had mastered and entered the inner networks of power and patronage when many of them had done no such thing. If they gave excessive credence to ministerial confidences, they also frequently placed too much reliance on the titbits of information passed on to them by courtiers. Here again their informants might be deliberately misleading them, but often they too were merely trying to give the impression that they had personal access to the centre of power. As these purveyors of deception, rumour or progaganda might be in contact with more than one diplomat, it is not uncommon for the historian to find that the same piece of misinformation is repeated by a number of envoys in their despatches, but it is an unwise scholar who mistakes the repetition of falsehood for truth, as too many have done in the past. At the same time, the diplomatic agents of Louis XIV were publicizing the achievements of their master in the courts of Europe to which they were accredited, although these French agents were no more successful than their foreign counterparts in reading the minds of other kings and their ministers. Even allied powers did not exchange intelligence with anything approaching frankness. Allies were business partners rather than friends, and those envoys charged with seeking supporters for the policies of their ruler were frequently guilty of overestimating their own progress towards this end.

The relationships between nations were therefore based on much erroneous evidence. In the case of Louis XIV, it led to the formation against him of mighty European coalitions, made by countries which underestimated his internal difficulties and saw instead a nation of unparalleled strength, orientated towards conquest and the aggressive pursuit of glory. Although many of these enemy rulers were being forced to engage in expensive modern warfare from a fiscal base which had changed little since the Middle Ages, and accordingly had regular recourse to short-term financial expedients and to loans at extortionate rates of interest from bankers and financiers, they failed to realize that the mighty king of France was in exactly the same position, desperately wondering how long he could sustain a massive military involvement that his own inflated reputation had helped to cause.

A final and perhaps more excusable explanation of these diplomatic misconceptions is that foreign envoys tended to judge the effectiveness of another government by the presence or absence of the limitations which restricted their own sovereign at home. Thus the agents of Charles II of England noted the good fortune of Louis in having no parliament to restrict his powers of decision, but they failed to recognize that he was limited in other ways which were not to be found across the Channel. Indeed the later French critics of Louis XIV would also add that the lack of such a national representative institution, through which the government could consult and liaise with the country as a whole, was a major reason for the endless misunderstandings and confrontations between the crown and the provincial elites.

Literary, curial and diplomatic sources therefore provide only one facet of the reign – the image of monarchy as devised for public, and especially for international, consumption. Unfortunately the royal ministers, with very few exceptions, have not bequeathed their personal reminiscences and reflections to the historian, an omission perhaps to be explained by both pressure of work and prudence. Not only might couriers be ambushed and letters fall into the wrong hands, but it was possible that a private secretary might have been bribed by hostile forces at court. On matters of high policy, it was safer to commit as little as possible to paper, especially when such observations included explicit or implied criticism of other ministers, or contained an admission that the realistic expectations of the government for the success of a particular policy were much more modest than the publicized claims for it suggested. It was better to keep sensitive information *in petto* or destroy any records as soon as they were no longer needed. If a minister were to fall from power, the less incriminating evidence he had left, the better for him and for his family. More than one recent holder of such high office had been condemned largely on the basis of statements made indiscreetly in his own hand.

It is only when the provincial archives and documents relating to the daily routine of government are examined that the power of the crown can be accurately estimated, and the grandiose plans of Colbert and his fellow ministers can be seen in a true context.

THE CROWN AND THE PROVINCES: BLUFF AND REALITY

In the edicts and letters addressed by the crown to its provincial subjects there was much bravura, boasting and propaganda, and in their replies the localities included much special pleading and even downright deception. Some of the most audacious royal proposals for sweeping change were very unlikely to be implemented in the near or the distant future, but a major reason for formulating such ambitious projects were to convey the impression that this was a monarch who could do anything. No scheme was too bold to be included in his vision of a reformed and prosperous France. Many of the preambles to royal edicts were written in this vein, although the specific provisions contained in the text which followed were usually much more modest. Often a minister would berate a group of provincial officials for failing to co-operate in carrying out a government policy, when so many other provinces had been both helpful and responsive – an assertion which was, needless to say, frequently untrue. As there was relatively little contact among the officials of different provinces, those who received the ministerial rebuke were never certain that they were not unique in their disobedience, although they suspected that other areas of the kingdom would have felt as they did. They were definitely not to be intimidated by such psychological pressure from above. Nor were they merely motivated by separatist stubbornness, resisting desirable change simply because it was proposed by distant Paris or Versailles. It could be argued, and the political reformers of the later personal rule did indeed proclaim it, that some of the plans for the rationalization of the kingdom, its laws, taxes and resources, were plainly inappropriate for such a variegated collection of provinces, each proud of its local liberties and distinctive traditions.

Although Colbert and his fellow ministers were convinced of their

own rectitude in postulating such reforms, they were not surprised at
the reception accorded to some of their directives by the provincial
elites. They knew that autocratic methods were not available to them,
and that they must therefore persuade Frenchmen that these were the
right courses to follow. In some aspects of government they would
undoubtedly have liked to increase the power of the centre at the
expense of local privileges and jurisdictions, but they knew that for the
time being they had no alternative to working with these traditional
groups and institutions – nobles, officials, town councils, gilds and, in
the *pays d'états*, the representative Estates. Yet in his letters to friends
and to *intendants*, Colbert at times showed feelings of intense frustration
that his schemes, particularly those for economic revival which seemed
to him to be so self-evidently desirable when one regarded the
kingdom as a unit and considered its role in a Europe which was
expanding into new continents, were unappealing to provincial
worthies whose prime concern was for the best interests of the only
effective geographical unit they comprehended – their province, or
even their immediate locality.

In the face of such persistent, if often subtle, provincial opposition to
any policy which savoured of change or reform, the crown would
periodically make a spectacular gesture in order to give an impression
of great strength. The arrest of a great noble or of a minister like
Foucquet was designed to demonstrate that no one was too prestigious
to be immune from prosecution. Equally startling was the dispatch of
a Grand Assize into the notoriously lawless province of Auvergne in
1665, where it arrested, tried and in some cases executed men of the
highest social rank. Yet these assertive acts were possible only at court,
in the capital or in the jurisdiction of the *parlement* of Paris. Elsewhere
in the kingdom, the forces of law and order seemed often to be on the
side of the lawbreaker – although the local judges would have been in
no doubt that it was the royal edicts, ordinances and fiscal demands
which savoured of illegality, violating as they did the liberties of the
province. Thus the leaders of local revolts frequently went unpunished,
because the judicial officials in the immediate area, and the police
forces under their control, sympathized with the aims of the
insurrection.

At the same time as it was trying to impress its subjects by drastic
actions at the centre and by the unveiling of extensive plans for reform,
the crown was also taking more covert steps to extend its authority.
The strategy here was to make small and rather tentative inroads into
local liberties, in the hope that at a later date these advances could be
cited as precedents for slightly stronger acts. The provinces were quick
to comprehend the reasoning of the government, and were determined

that no such innovations should be permitted to succeed. Thus a royal attempt to impose a minimal direct peacetime tax, a complete novelty, on the Boulonnais in 1662 provoked a revolt of the entire area – an insurrection totally disproportionate to the size of the proposed levy but wholly appropriate for the magnitude of the principle which was at stake.

In its efforts to justify these encroachments on provincial privilege, the crown needed lucid theorists and jurists who would argue its case, while the privileged orders, whether ancient nobles or venal *officiers*, assembled their own teams of counter-propagandists. Both sides were prepared to engage, through the printed word and through verbal argument, in a passionate battle where the weapons were historical precedents, laws, customs, traditions, grants of privilege, and various philosophical theories about the nature of sovereignty, the constitution of France and the very origins of the state – although criticism of Louis XIV himself was avoided, at least until the 1680s. The near and distant past was ransacked for supporting evidence by both sides. As it was innovations by the ministers which usually caused these confrontations, the crown was less successful than its opponents in finding historical justifications for its actions, and it had therefore to rely more heavily on recent philosophical ideas about the ways in which societies should be reformed, rationalized and reorganized. The psychological advantage undoubtedly lay with the conservative defenders of privilege, especially as the worst disputes usually erupted in wartime, when hard-pressed ministers had no time to engage in measured debate.

One danger which awaits the historian who examines these passionate quarrels is that he may be led to exaggerate the scale of the royal actions which had given rise to them. For example the vehemence of the outcry against the *intendants* at the time of the Frondes might convince the unwary researcher that a novel group of powerful officials had been created, and that they were already threatening the security of the venal office-holders. In reality, their power was much less spectacular. What brought every *officier* to his feet, baying for the abolition of the *intendants*, was the danger of a precedent and the threat to the future liberties of the administrative caste if the crown were now to be allowed to make these new royal *commissaires*, sent out from the centre to spy on and interfere with traditional local hierarchies, into a permanent agency of the state machine. Again, a vital principle was at stake, and pre-emptive measures were being taken.

The lengthy works of seventeenth-century jurists, who substantiated their arguments for and against administrative change by writing apparently exhaustive descriptions of the French institutional structure, have also been accepted too uncritically by many historians. The sheer volume of detail they contain and the authoritative air of their pronouncements may conceal, from the uninitiated reader, their underlying polemic purpose. A number of relatively recent historians, most of them Frenchmen, have fallen into this very trap and have produced magisterial histories of French institutions, which are as misleading in their overall interpretation of the subject as they are useful for yielding fragments of factual information about obscure local taxes and privileges. These works fall short of historical objectivity in two principal ways. First, they describe the whole hierarchy of institutions in an excessively clinical and cellular manner. This is the system as it ought to have functioned, each component part obeying the rules prescribed for it and acting within its own clearly designated sphere of influence. Such an orderly pattern is, of course, far removed from the chaotic historical reality of seventeenth-century France. There, it was possible to find a host of conflicting regulations, which had been issued or revised haphazardly over preceding decades, although on some practical points which gave rise to regular disputes these legal codes remained obstinately silent. In consequence jurisdictions overlapped, and officials spent many hours seeking to deny their rivals the right to exercise contentious functions. Nor did the institutions themselves invariably behave in the way the jurists claimed.[5]

Secondly, these modern historians make too much of attempts to reform the administrative system, falling victim to the special pleading of royal publicists and failing to perceive the substantial degree of continuity which is the true hallmark of *ancien régime* bureaucracy. Roland Mousnier can confidently delineate four successive and clearly distinct ages – those of the military nobility, the office-holding nobility, the *commissaires* and the *fonctionnaires*. A less legalistic historian would notice, in contrast, how quickly the office-holders joined some of the causes which were championed by the old nobility, and how these parvenus copied the life style of this more ancient elite, some even seeking to marry their daughters into its ranks; how the *commissaires* and *intendants* were given only a very restricted sphere in which to exercise their novel powers, how tentatively they approached their task and how rapidly some of their number also associated themselves with the aspirations and attitudes of the new intermingled hierarchies of military and office-holding nobles; and that, if Mousnier can find

[5]See Roger Mettam, 'Two-dimensional history: Mousnier and the ancien régime', *History*, lxvi.

some men in the eighteenth century to whom the term *fonctionnaire* can be not inappropriately applied, the striking fact is that they were so few, not so many, in number. It is undeniable that on occasions institutions acted in a corporate spirit to defend their rights and jurisdictions, and that a man who progressed from one such body to another changed his institutional allegiance accordingly, but here again there is a further complicating factor. In an age of patrimonial politics, loyalty to an institution had to be balanced against duty to the family, which would have placed its members in many different areas of the bureaucracy. Thus, while jurisdictions had to be defended, the rivalry of kinship and patronage networks was an even more dominant consideration. Difficult dilemmas could arise when two institutions were locked in jurisdictional wrangles, and a family had members or clients within both of them.

Now that the monolithic 'absolutism' of Louis XIV, so carefully created by three centuries of historians, has recently been shown to have been built on sand, it may be asked why the improbability of such a dramatic historical synthesis did not occur to earlier scholars. The answer to this question, as to so many others in French history, lies in the dichotomy of a centralizing national state and a series of fiercely independent separatist provinces. Accordingly historians, since the eighteenth century, have themselves been divided into two camps. Some have studied France as a whole, or so they claim, but they have usually concentrated on the central government, have overstressed the growth of centralized power and of a sense of national identity, and have often sought to make history conform to preconceived ideas of bureaucratic development, social mobility and processes of change. At the same time, in the provincial archives, painstaking scholars have been producing histories of parts of France, frequently their own native area, and confining themselves to a single province or even a town over a shorter or longer period, or examining the workings of a single institution, or tracing the life and administration of a noteworthy bishop or the history of a local aristocratic or office-holding family. Many of these fine works of scholarship, especially those of the last century, are admirably in tune with the most recent histories of France, explaining the character and strength of provincial feeling, and showing the considerable success of the localities in resisting a central authority which tried to undermine traditional privileges and seemed to sacrifice local interests to what it claimed to be the greater good of the state. Yet although these volumes are preserved upon the shelves of major libraries, the 'national' historians of the nineteenth century and some of their successors nearer to the present day have ignored their conclusions. Their bibliographies barely refer to them. The local academies and societies in which the scholars of the area met, discussed and published their conclusions were dismissed by the Parisian historical elite as dens, not of fellow historians, but of bumbling antiquarians. No description could be less just, but such prejudices prevented the two sides from engaging in debate about their respective interpretations of *ancien régime* France.

LA MONARCHIE ABSOLUE IN THEORY AND PRACTICE

If an investigation into the realities of seventeenth-century France will raise grave doubts about the wisdom of employing the term 'absolute monarchy', with its modern overtones of omnipotence, it is nevertheless true that some of the subjects of Louis XIV did discuss the concept of *la monarchie absolue*, using it in a much more specific and limited sense. The same cannot be said of the word 'absolutism'. That, like 'mercantilism', is an anachronism coined by later scholars who wished to suggest a much more dynamic, thoroughgoing and systematic change in the government of France than had actually occurred. It should therefore have no place in a discussion of the power of the crown in early modern France.

'Absolute monarchy', like 'gallicanism' and the 'fundamental laws' of the realm, was not a precise concept. The implications and emphases associated with it varied according to the circumstances and issues of each debate in which it was employed. Many Frenchmen accepted that Louis XIV was *absolu* in most of those prerogative areas of government which were generally accepted as the responsibility of the monarchy, and during his personal rule no further princely *frondeurs* would challenge him. Only in religious affairs was he sometimes unable to exercise his authority over a 'gallican' church in the way that he and many others thought proper, because Rome was able to intervene effectively on more than one occasion, and some of his subjects, both Protestant and Catholic, showed at times that they preferred to follow their faith rather than their sovereign. Such religious disputes might therefore take on an international aspect, even causing some Frenchmen to associate with the enemies of the king. Then the royal prerogative in both religious and foreign policy would be challenged at one and the same time.

Those of his contemporaries who readily supported the idea that Louis was absolute, or should be, in these kingly areas of government did not mean by this adjective that his power should be totally unlimited or arbitrary. There was a theoretical limitation contained in the term *monarchie absolue* – a moral prescription that the monarch should work for the greater good of the kingdom. Otherwise it was *monarchie arbitraire*. Louis undoubtedly tried to obey this requirement as best he could, and was genuinely concerned to give legitimacy to his foreign policy and international interventions, not only by respecting treaties and fulfilling his moral obligations, as in his support of the exiled James II, but by demonstrating to his subjects that he was acting in their best interests as well. Unfortunately for him, just as other rulers seldom believed these protestations of rectitude and saw only a lust for conquest and aggrandizement, so too his provincial subjects were frequently sceptical that royal demands for heavier taxation in wartime were really designed to promote their own safety and welfare. These international entanglements often seemed to be nothing more than episodes in the dynastic power game which European ruling houses had played for centuries. How many Frenchmen in the first decade of the eighteenth century would have borne their poverty more cheerfully because they knew it to be a consequence of maintaining the grandson of Louis XIV on the throne of Spain? It was therefore virtually impossible to define the 'best interests of the state' in terms which made sense both to the royal ministers, who saw the whole spectrum of international problems facing the realm, and to the inhabitants of these varied and geographically dispersed provinces, who judged policies by their relevance to the needs of their immediate area. The line between *absolu* and *arbitraire* was thus impossible to draw in practice.

In the debates about the internal administration of the kingdom, no one claimed that the monarchy was already absolute. A few governmental supporters hoped that it might become increasingly so, but the majority of the population felt that the ambitions of the royal ministers were excessive and should be curtailed. In 1661, when Louis XIV declared his intention to rule personally, the crown lacked the mechanisms of absolute government and it was an inappropriate time to introduce them. After the unpopular ministries of Richelieu and Mazarin, the violent disruption of the Frondes and the impoverishment of the royal treasury by years of war, the only course was to build upon the general desire for prolonged peace and internal order, and to co-operate with other powerful groups, whether hereditary as in the case of the nobility, elective as with the town councils and the provincial Estates, or both hereditary and venal as in the bureaucracy. So, although total harmony between subjects and monarch was never possible, the 1660s began in an atmosphere of co-operation and caution, as displayed by almost all of those involved in the administration of the kingdom on the one hand and by the royal ministers on the other. The 1662 revolt in the Boulonnais was one of the very few serious interruptions in this general period of calm.

The king and his ministers not only lacked the physical force to subject the whole country to their will, but never entertained ideas of doing so. They merely hoped to tilt the balance of powers within France towards the centre, although in reality little short-term and no long-term success attended their efforts. Except in the city of Paris, the urban militias and local police forces remained under the control of the provincial officials, who would usually take the side of their locality in any dispute with the crown. The army was of little more use as a means of implementing unpopular royal orders within the kingdom. Most serious disturbances occurred in wartime, because of heavy taxation, and in war the troops could seldom be spared from the battlefronts. Moreover, as the payment of wages to the soldiery was often seriously in arrears, an attempt to use them for the maintenance of internal order would have been an open invitation for them to loot and pillage. Such brutality was ideal for terrorizing an enemy, but it was not a method for ruling one's own realm. Also, although in the 1620s there might have been many Catholic soldiers and officers willing to fight the treacherous Protestants of La Rochelle who had allied with the English against their own king, it was a very different matter to require that noble captains should unleash their companies against fellow Frenchmen, some of them nobles like themselves, whose only offence had been to resist arbitrary governmental encroachment on traditional privileges. Thus, throughout the machinery of the state, except in the ministerial circle at the very centre, all loyalty was conditional and therefore the effective forces of *la monarchie absolue* were undoubtedly lacking.

The only satisfactory way in which the crown could hope to free itself from some of the restrictions imposed upon it by the hierarchy of privilege was to purchase its freedom, generously compensating those who were prepared to surrender some of their liberties and immunities. To attempt to suppress them without compensation would have been to risk rebellion or even another Fronde. Unfortunately for the ministers, the royal treasury, although it was in a healthier state in the mid-1660s than it had been for many decades, still did not have surplus funds for such enterprises. All too soon wars broke out again, and the government was quickly in the position of having insufficient resources to meet its most pressing needs. Not merely being unable to buy out existing venal offices and privileges, it now had to create more of them in its desperate search for funds. Thus, while ministers remained vulnerable and could be dismissed from their posts, the office-holders knew that the rest of the bureaucracy was secure; their investments in these hereditary positions were safe. Only if they could be convicted of a criminal offence would their office be declared forfeit, and a serious crime would have to be committed before judges and officials would take steps to arraign one of their own number. Nevertheless, most of these bureaucrats had no intention of breaking the law. They regularly came into conflict with other groups of officials or with the ministers about the interpretation of certain laws or even about their very legality, but this was because the whole system was in disarray, riddled with loopholes, conflicting provisions and provincial variations. Colbert was not the only man who wished to bring order to this confusion, for leading judges were equally concerned about the time wasted in internecine legal disputes, in which the real losers were the litigants who could not obtain justice, or only at an exorbitant cost. However, as in so many aspects of government and administration during this period, the identification of a problem brought its solution no nearer.

To the politically conscious members of seventeenth-century French society, the term *la monarchie absolue*, whether applied to the theory or to the practice of government, did not describe the system as it was presently constituted. It was rather a direction in which the royal ministers were hoping to proceed. No one thought that the ultimate goal had been reached, but a few hoped, and many more feared, that it was on the distant horizon. The advocates of this stronger monarchy knew that their path was a difficult one and that caution was essential. As long as the crown ruled traditionally, it commanded much support from the elite strata in society. When it introduced innovations into the domestic administration, it risked provoking the many influential subjects whose main preoccupation was the preservation of the status quo. The royalist writers accordingly stressed, loudly and unceasingly, that, in trying to free the crown from the restrictions on its power, they had the best interests of the state at heart. Their opponents, convinced that the king was seeking to extend his authority into wholly new areas of everyday administration, emphasized exactly the opposite viewpoint. To them it was the sanctity of privilege and the whole corpus of local rights and liberties which protected the interests of the people. A very powerful monarchy was more likely to be an oppressor than a friend.

At a superficial glance it might seem that the ministers of Louis XIV were doing what every government attempts to do, namely to acquire greater freedom in policy-making and in its ability to act. Yet there were certain guiding principles in the thinking of these architects of more absolute monarchy which are not common to all regimes and all ages. Their most remarkable characteristic is that they passionately

believed in a limited programme of reforms which did not seem to
have the support of any sizable group within the population. Most of
these plans were not formulated in response to any pressure from
below, and the crown consequently had no opportunity to present
itself as the mediator between those who wished for change and those
who opposed it. The crown was the sole instigator of almost all these
proposals, and its inspiration was not the demands of its subjects but
the tenets of a rationalist and scientific philosophy, which was
Cartesian in its obsession with order, unity, oneness, uniformity and
absolute standards. Appealing in its certainty and logic, its deductive
principles suggested policies which were ill-suited to the kingdom as it
would have appeared through the inductive eyes of the empiricist.
Thus, although the ministers recognized that they must proceed
slowly and would ultimately have to persuade the population of the
wisdom which underlay their policies, they set themselves an
impossible task by embarking on reforms which were never likely to
commend themselves to the people as a whole.[6] The criticism of the
government which erupted in the 1690s was therefore all the more
vigorous because by then the fundamental presuppositions of Cartesian
philosophy were also under attack. The most striking attempts at
drastic reform had not only failed but began to seem doubly
misconceived in the light of new philosophical explanations about the
nature of society and the state, and about the role the government
should play towards its subjects and in promoting international
harmony.

The ministers realised from the outset that, if their reforms were to
be implemented at all, new kinds of royal administrators would have
to be created, not to supersede but to supplement the existing
bureaucracy. Most of their plans envisaged the improvement of
current practices, and therefore a new stratum of royal inspectors was
needed to report back to the central government about the willingness,
or more often the reluctance, of local officials to comply with these
directives. A few proposals involved the assumption by the crown of
powers and administrative functions which had never been shouldered
by any level of the bureaucracy, central or local, and accordingly
required the invention of a wholly new group of officials. Yet past
experience showed that such innovations in the bureaucratic hierarchy,
especially the addition of non-venal officials, were very unpopular, and
even more so when they were associated with novel policies. Moreover
there was a growing chorus of complaints that the crown seemed to be

---

[6]See E. H. Kossmann, 'The singularity of absolutism', and G. Durand, 'What is
absolutism?', in Ragnhild Hatton (ed.), *Louis XIV and absolutism* (London, 1976).

increasingly enclosed within an intimate circle of ministers, where policies were evolved without wider consultation and where the selfish family interests of the ministerial clique were the paramount consideration. If it made obvious sense to Colbert, both philosophically and politically, that the kingdom should be a legal and economic unit – one code of laws, one standard of weights and measures, a single customs unit to replace the mass of internal tariff barriers – it made no such sense to the provinces, whose traditions and economic activities were based on the existing system, in which relations with other countries might be closer than those with either court or capital. France was not a unit in many significant ways and had little inclination to become one. The only enthusiasm for some of these reforms came from the elites of Paris, pleased that the rest of the kingdom was to be brought into line with their own practices and standards.

Thus, behind their realism about the difficulty of effecting their plans for unification, the royal policy-makers had a conviction of their own rectitude which was based largely on abstract reasoning. Most striking was their claim that the state had an independent existence and rationale, above and beyond the totality of its subjects. There was no shortage of publicists and theorists to champion the royal cause, their arguments bristling with abstractions, although the opponents of their ideas began to evolve new ways of refuting them as the personal rule of Louis XIV progressed. In the first three quarters of the seventeenth century, their objections were founded on the assertion that privileges and traditions were being violated, a clarion call for the preservation of the past. During those years the royalists made much of the hereditary nature of kingship, the principle of divine right to rule, and the idea of the king as the father of his people, while the opposing camp stressed the obligation of the crown, the sanctity of the constitution and the immutability of the fundamental laws of France. (Ironically, many of the weapons in this struggle to define the balance of secular power in the state had been borrowed from a previous and very different quarrel, namely the prolonged battle about the distribution of power in the church of Rome.) It was only in the 1680s, and particularly after 1690 when Fénelon and his circle espoused some of the theories which would later become corner-stones of the Enlightenment, that a number of these critics began to offer an alternative road, leading to a reformed future rather than a restored past. These later writers made many specific proposals on points of detail, unlike the absolutist and traditionalist theorists who, in their earlier confrontations, had confined themselves to the polarized extremes and made no attempt to draw a precise dividing line between royal power and privilege in the disputed middle ground.

Although both sides in these earlier debates sought some historical validation for their fundamental principles, as they did when specific rights and privileges were at issue, their arguments tended to be dubious in their historicity. Moreover, as the more general concepts were employed only during short periods of crisis, usually fiscal or religious, they retained the character of shibboleths rather than acquiring the substance of sustained theories. Most of the controversial royal innovations, the consequences of wartime expenditure, were abandoned in peacetime when the dominant desire was to restore the co-operation of crown and local elites. Similarly religious conflicts were often resolved by a compromise, albeit a temporary one. Therefore a concept like the *lois fondamentales*, or that most elusive doctrine, 'gallicanism', was introduced into the forum of political debate at these moments of stress, but it was not expounded in a consistent way over long periods of time. How the slogan would be used would depend on the precise points of dispute in each crisis. Most of the vigorous disagreements between the crown and its subjects centred on detailed issues of law and privilege, and these more general theories were invoked so that each side could claim that it was acting in the best interests of the whole kingdom.

For the advocates of more absolute monarchy, there was one major contradiction within their own corpus of beliefs which was impossible to resolve, and it was a reflection of a dilemma which preoccupied the disciples of Descartes at the purely philosophical level. On the one hand there was the need to reform, which was a synonym for to rationalize. Against this, there was the assumption, prompted by the conviction that the world was hastening downhill towards chaos, that order should be firmly established and that all change was likely to cause greater instability. The ministers of Louis XIV certainly applied this latter principle to their social policy, insisting on preserving the hierarchy and discouraging social mobility within it. Yet at the same time, and especially in the field of economics, they embarked on policies of rationalization and therefore of change which, although they seemed to the crown to be self-evidently desirable, were resisted by many members of society, causing tension and undermining that very stability which it was thought so important to maintain. Historians used to portray this situation in terms of a progressive and reforming government, hampered by selfish, separatist and reactionary elites, but it is no longer possible to use such emotive adjectives. Each side was responding to events in the way which seemed most appropriate, and the lack of agreement arose because of the gulf between the centre and the provinces. Nevertheless, if the ministers balanced their reforming zeal against their conservative social attitudes, it is hard to avoid sympathizing to an extent with Fénelon, when he designates them as the real culprits in this drama because it was they who blindly pursued aggressive national unity and failed to consider the interests of the people as a whole.

THE SHIFT TOWARDS THE CENTRE, 1500–1660

As the crown shared the general desire to preserve the hierarchical nature of French society, and as its few drastic attempts at reform in the seventeenth century met with little success, there is not surprisingly a strong feeling of continuity to be found in the social and bureaucratic history of early modern France. The same elites, institutions and many of the same families continued to play a dominant role. Yet under the later Valois and the first three Bourbons there was a slow shift towards the centre. This was partly engineered by the crown, though without the aggressiveness which was associated with its more overtly centralizing policies, but it was also stimulated by some influential groups in the localities which felt it advantageous either to co-operate more closely with the king while continuing to live in their province, or in some cases to move themselves and their ambitions to the court itself. This did not mean that they wished to see any overall increase in the independent power of the crown, but they did seek the aid of their sovereign in order to boost their own position within the existing social hierarchy.

The first example of this increased central activity in the provinces is the most ambiguous. Although the royal ministers often regarded the venal office-holders as the most serious threat to the effective exercise of governmental power in the kingdom, there is no doubt that the creation of this large bureaucracy had seemed to many in the provinces as an extension of monarchical authority throughout France at the expense of more traditional forms of administration, whether seigneurial, municipal, ecclesiastical or provincial. As the purchasers of these new posts consolidated their position by making them hereditary, the older elites strove unceasingly to defend their own jurisdictions against attacks by these intruders, pausing only to ally with them on occasions when the crown itself uttered threats to local privileges. Then all provincial notables, venal, elected and hereditary, might briefly present a united front to the central government. Those who bought the new royal offices were themselves men of wealth and substance in their locality, and saw that entry into the service of the crown would enhance their status in society. Thus, while they did not always obey their new master, they did depend on their relationship with the crown in that it alone entitled them to claim such a degree of social superiority. They might therefore frequently ignore ministerial instructions when they disapproved of them, but they tried to avoid open defiance of the king whenever possible.

If the crown could never rely on the unswerving loyalty of these officials, at least their presence as royal agents in the provinces was soon accepted by most of the population. Moreover there was an increasing resort to the royal law courts by aggrieved parties, and the extra-judicial family feuding and private vengeance of the past began to decline. Seigneurial courts still survived in their thousands, but the role of the king as the fount of justice seemed to be more welcomed than resisted. This was partly because the judges themselves acted as a brake on any excessive zeal by the ministers to legislate in ways that would have been unpopular in the provinces. The most dramatic example of the manner in which the members of this venal bureaucracy could be both the agents and the opponents of the crown at one and the same time is provided by the right of the *parlement* of Paris to refuse to register royal edicts and to remonstrate against them. This fundamental privilege had been accorded to the sovereign courts by the monarch himself, and yet it could easily be used to thwart his wishes. The quarrels between the king and the Paris judges could never last too long, of course, because they depended upon him for their very position as the most senior dispensers of royal justice, and he needed their approval of his edicts which would be of immense psychological importance when he was trying to enforce them.

A further shift from locality to centre involved the increasing recognition by Frenchmen that there was only one army in the kingdom, that of the king himself. This transition from a host of small armies to a single royal force was not complete when Louis XIV began his personal rule, but considerable progress had been made. Some of these bands of personal retainers had been technically under ultimate royal control, others had been in private hands, but all owed loyalty to their immediate patron rather than to the sovereign. Particularly important and dangerous in the private sphere were the armed followers of the aristocracy, especially those of very high and prestigious nobles, and these forces were being steadily emasculated both by royal initiative and by effective pressure from other influential groups in the localities, further evidence that effective reform was possible only when the crown had considerable support from some of the local elites. Yet during the personal rule of Louis XIV there were still complaints that a few nobles were tyrannizing the countryside with the aid of lawless bands of armed men. Of the companies of soldiery, which were technically the agents of the king himself in the sixteenth century, the most vigorous and efficient were those of the *gendarmerie*, but they too owed their prime allegiance to a more immediate master, the provincial governor. As the governors under the later Valois were usually powerful but were not always loyal, and as both the governorships and the senior positions in the *gendarmerie* were normally hereditary, these troops were the carefully created products of private patronage and could therefore pose a great threat to the crown, the more so as they claimed to be acting in its name.[7] By the reign of Louis XIV these companies had lost their right to a permanent existence, and the governorships had either been entrusted to more reliable nobles or had been made into virtual sinecures. Lastly, at the very top of the army hierarchy, posts like those of *connétable* and *colonel-général de l'infanterie* had been allowed to lapse, again preventing great aristocrats from exercising too much patronage over the personnel of the military. It is true that the posts of *colonel* and *capitaine* remained venal, though not hereditary, until the end of the seventeenth century and beyond, and that these officers had close personal links with the men under their command, being responsible for recruiting and maintaining them. Such loyalty as soldiers felt would therefore be to these immediate officers, rather than to distant generals and royal ministers, which meant that companies would still support their leaders in their frequent reluctance to put down revolts and in return officers might condone the brutality of their men at times when their pay was seriously in arrears. Yet at least the threat of hereditary aristocratic domination over substantial sections of the army had been removed. By 1661 a large amount of military patronage was in the hands of the secretary of state for war – a shift of emphasis which was important not least for its symbolic implication that the crown was now in direct control of its troops – and civil bureaucrats were now responsible for much routine military adminstration.

While accepting the extension of royal judicial and military powers, the local elites were well aware that it was possible to resist those aspects of the new administration which they did not like. Disobedience, obstruction and even rebellion were effective weapons in the provincial armoury. Yet royal authority seemed increasingly preferable to the capricious power of the great nobles, and therefore these illustrious houses found that there was declining support in the localities for their ambition to maintain virtual dominance, transmitted

[7]The *gendarmerie* in the sixteenth century is well described in Robert R. Harding, *Anatomy of a power elite: the provincial governors of early modern France* (New Haven/London, 1978).

by heredity, over entire provinces. Accordingly, they now abandoned their earlier power bases and concentrated their activities on the court, caballing and intriguing in their efforts to dislodge ministers and substitute members of their own factions in the highest stratum of the government.

These centripetal tendencies cannot helpfully be called centralization, and certainly not absolute monarchy, as these terms have commonly been used to describe the assertion of royal power at the expense of the traditional elites. Here those elites were hoping to enlist the aid of the king in order to preserve and enhance their social stratum and their individual families. Of these prestigious groups, only the princes wished to dominate government at the centre, to which end they also sought to abolish the venal bureaucracy because it would limit the power which they sought. Such ambitions were therefore anathema, not only to the king and to his ministers, but to the office-holders as well. Those lower down the social scale, who sought civil or military office, were also forced to focus their attention on the court, at which an increasing amount of all important patronage originated, but they could do so without sacrificing their status in provincial society and without compromising their vested interests. While the princes actually had to reside at court, in order to plan and attempt to execute their plots against ministers and to compete with other comparable families for the highest curial offices, the lesser suitors for royal favour remained in their locality, channelling their requests through the governor or some other high ranking patronage broker, who would convey them, personally or by letter, to the court.

Thus, as the seventeenth century progressed, the political or social ambitions of an increasing number of people depended, at least in part, on the influence wielded by individual courtiers and ministers. Any examination of the nature of power in France at this time must therefore begin in the turbulent society which immediately surrounded the monarch, and must consider the success of the various kings in playing off the rival factions, ministerial as well as aristocratic, which sought an excessive share of royal favours for their own families and for their wider network of clients. It was because of their greater skill in balancing and manipulating power groups, and not through any extension of their own absolute authority, that Henri IV and Louis XIV created the reputation which some later historians have described as strong monarchy. Moreover, for all their talents, their successes were possible only because certain factors beyond their control had taken a propitious turn.

2

King, Court, Aristocracy
and Faction

THE POWER OF THE CROWN

An essential preliminary to the argument which follows must be to define 'the power of the crown'. This is a difficult problem because, as the challenge to the royal government during the Frondes came partly from its own officials, it is unhelpful in such situations to regard them as participants in the exercise of monarchical authority. They were quite clearly taking a stand against it. Yet at other times they self-evidently did carry out many of the instructions given them by the ministers and proceeded with the routine administrative tasks associated with their posts. Other municipal and provincial officials undoubtedly considered them to be the agents of the king, and yet to Richelieu and Mazarin this venal and hereditary bureaucracy seemed to be one of the principal obstacles to effective government, thwarting more policies than it implemented. The two cardinals would dearly have liked to undermine this administrative structure which their predecessors had created.

In this present discussion therefore, the power of the crown will be taken to mean that of the king and his intimate circle of ministers and advisers, to which was linked the network of royal and ministerial clients and dependants which fanned out from the court into the provinces. The venal bureaucracy is better regarded as a separate force in the kingdom, sometimes working for the crown, sometimes against it, and often distracted by the endless squabbles and divisions within its own ranks. This is the distinction which is in the mind of a recent historian when he states that 'in 1659, the crown could not be said to be in control of the kingdom'. He means by this assertion that the royal government was unable to act independently of its venal

officials, who were still successfully preventing Mazarin from introducing fiscal reforms. Yet those same officials had restored a
considerable degree of order and administrative routine since the
Frondes.[1] Having wrung concessions from the minister by fomenting
civil war, their interests were now best served by calming the country
and administering it in an orderly and traditional way. Indeed most of
the other social elites, who encouraged not only the Frondes but the
innumerable localized revolts of the early seventeenth century, would
have had the same priorities. Revolt was a useful weapon by which to
combat arbitrary governmental innovations, but prolonged disturbances began to harm the locality itself and the rebels might sometimes
turn against local notables as well as the royal agents who were the
original target. Revolts should therefore be closely supervised and
short! The government was well aware of this attitude, of course, and
knew that, even though it could not suppress most of these rebellions,
the disorder was unlikely to last very long – the leaders of local society
would see to that. The Frondes were not as well organized as these
lesser insurrections. Too many parts of France were involved, too
many issues were in contention, and there was no undisputed
leadership. It was really a coincidence of separate revolts. By 1653
most Frenchmen agreed that the disorder had lasted too long and
welcomed an accommodation with the royal government, although
they would still not permit it to exercise its power in an arbitrary way.

It was rare for the crown to be at odds with the whole nation at once
and for it to have virtually no freedom to act independently, but such
was its position during parts of the Frondes and the immediately
subsequent years. Usually its influential clients were able to rally some
support in the provinces, whether by subtle intervention in the
disputes between local power groups or by distributing royal favours.
It was impossible to please everyone at once, because generosity
towards one man or group might be regarded by others as a slight to
themselves. Nevertheless, as long as the king ruled traditionally and
respected privileges, his government was unlikely to become the target
for major discontent. Such prudence was less easy during periods of
war, and, as each international confrontation seemed more expensive
than the last, the clamour of opposition to wartime expedients grew
correspondingly louder. Thus at the very moment when the king
wanted a united kingdom in order that he might concentrate on the

[1]The *parlement* of Paris had already an effective mediating role in 1650 – see A. Lloyd
Moote, *The revolt of the judges: the Parlement of Paris and the Fronde, 1643–1652* (Princeton,
1971), pp. 271–8. The behaviour of the *parlement* in the years 1653–60 is thoroughly
examined in Albert N. Hamscher, *The parlement of Paris after the Fronde, 1653–1673*
(Pittsburgh, 1976), pp. 82–118.

foreign enemy, his realm was disrupted by protests, disobedience and even insurrection. This also provided a pretext for the princes to attempt one of their palace revolutions, as they could claim to be freeing the country from the ministers who were responsible for both the war and the emergency fiscal measures. In 1659, when peace was finally signed with Spain, the crown needed a breathing space to recover from the doubly disastrous effects of the international conflict and the internal civil wars. Some stability would have to be restored to the royal finances, but drastic reforms and innovations were out of the question. Traditional methods would have to be used, and then, hopefully, some provincial support would be forthcoming.

Much of the routine administration in the localities therefore resumed its regular rhythm, enlivened by local jurisdictional and social squabbles but undisturbed by threatening gestures from the ministers. The crown concentrated on persuading its subjects to part with sufficient money for it to improve the army, maintain its foreign policy and accumulate some reserves in case a future war could not be avoided. The historians of 'absolutism' have asserted that the central government was highly successful in achieving these goals, and they have also insisted that it acquired a much greater degree of control over the daily administration of the country. Neither of these conclusions will be accepted here. Instead it will be argued that the crown still left much of the country to run itself, and that in the limited spheres of kingly activity its achievements were much more modest. They would not be enough to sustain it in the years of warfare which were not far off in the future. Soon, it would once again be lurching from crisis to crisis and, although not all the problems would be of its own making, some would stem from the unforced errors of its ministers.

Whereas the absolutist historians have searched for, isolated and exaggerated the signs of an emergent 'modern state' or of modern economic structures, it is the intention here to begin by examining the extent to which French government and society had not changed in the last two centuries of Valois and Bourbon rule, so that any novel developments can be seen in the context of this wider canvas. If this seems an obvious and sensible approach, it is certainly not one which has appealed to those historians who search only for change or who chronicle and idealize the actions and influence of 'great men'.

THE COURT

The royal court was at the heart of the political system. In the seventeenth century it was organized, as in past ages, in the form of a household, in which governmental and domestic functions were intertwined. A minister or a secretary of state was as much a royal servant, attending personally on the king, as were the first gentlemen of the bedchamber, the chamberlain, the captain of the Swiss guards and the master of the horse. The principal difference was that, while the ministers usually owed everything to their sovereign master, were held by him in high esteem and could be cast into political oblivion if they displeased him, the courtiers who filled the great ceremonial posts were mostly from leading aristocratic families and therefore, although they could be deprived by the king of their curial offices, they could not be made to forfeit their hereditary noble rank and the considerable prestige which was associated with it. The Bourbon monarchs had no choice but to accept the existence of a powerful aristocracy within their dominions, and to devise ways of restraining its most seditious members. Fortunately for them, whereas that other hereditary elite, the venal bureaucracy, pursued its social advantage by the purchase of further offices and did not therefore require direct and regular intervention from the king, this older nobility was more heavily dependent on royal favours and military posts and accordingly needed to maintain permanent links with the court through the network of patronage. The leading families of the *noblesse d'épée*, with the greatest prestige and the highest ambitions, gravitated physically towards the royal household, residing there for at least part of the year, because it was within its confines that they could best hope to advance the power and fortunes of their houses and clients.

Thus it was from the ranks of his extended domestic entourage that the king sought to select those whom he could trust, while trying to identify and outwit any members who cherished subversive designs against his authority. A substantial number of loyal nobles from prestigious houses was essential for the government of the country. From no other social group could he choose his provincial governors, diplomats and senior army commanders. A governor had to be of high rank so that he did not have to defer socially to any of the subjects over whom he had been given authority. Moreover, as one of his chief methods of gaining influential supporters for his administration was by agreeing to convey to the king the requests of local worthies for royal patronage, those who aspired to these favours had to be confident that the prestige of their champion at court was great enough for his nominations to be sympathetically received. An advocate with direct access to the king and his ministers could achieve much more than a letter, sent by a provincial notable to the office of a secretary of state where it might rest for weeks on the desk of a subordinate. The governor was bound to be at court for part of the year, when he could personally approach the dispensers of patronage, but even during his months in the province his letters would be scrutinized rapidly and at the very highest level.

Diplomacy was still an aristocratic monopoly throughout much of Europe and, once again, it was essential that a French envoy should not be at a social disadvantage when he encountered the negotiators or ministers of another sovereign power. Such embassies could be very costly for the ambassador, but diplomatic success often brought lavish rewards, perhaps in the form of titles from his own or from foreign rulers, and gave him added strength when he petitioned his government for favours to be accorded to his family. There was also the satisfaction both of displaying his personal splendour and of being fêted at the courts of other monarchs, and courtiers, writers of memoirs and the ambassadors themselves chronicled these ceremonies with the eye for minute detail which a precedence-conscious age required.

The army officer corps was also the preserve of the nobility, and here too it was preferable for high authority to be accompanied by a correspondingly superior family background. The king could, of course, promote successful officers to the upper ranks of the aristocracy, as everyone accepted that valour in battle was a legitimate reason for initial or further ennoblement, although the deeds would have to be outstanding if other great families were not to take offence. The nobility was the military estate, and not only would it have been impossible to undermine its domination of the army, but it did not occur to the king that he should do so. All that he could attempt was to ensure that, as with provincial governorships, military posts did not remain or become the hereditary property of families, and that only loyal aristocrats should be appointed to them. In practice son would still often succeed father, because a family association with an office enhanced the position of the present holder, but at least undesirable heirs could be excluded from the succession, and in very rare cases the link between a noble house and a particular post was permanently broken.

The king understood and accepted these aristocratic preoccupations and priorities because he himself was an aristocrat by birth and breeding, although he had also been invested with the mantle of monarchy which placed him at the apex of the social pyramid. Nevertheless his pleasures, friends and companions were all noble, as was his attitude to the problems of government. Sharing the disdain felt by all members of this military and landed class for the bourgeois world of finance and economics, the king was happiest when he was reviewing troops, attending the capitulation of besieged towns, supervising his latest architectural schemes, hunting, dancing and entertaining lavishly. Although he well knew that a full treasury was essential for all his enterprises, he left the details to his ministers and showed interest only in the final balance sheets. Thus Colbert found it very difficult to persuade Louis XIV that royal visits to his new manufactures would greatly encourage the workers, because the king knew that these occasions would not be amusing for him and his entourage. An uncomfortable progress across the muddy terrain and along the tortuous roads of France to visit the battlefields was much more to his taste, although some of the grand ladies of the court were less than convinced about the delights of these outings.

The court, whether travelling or stationary, was the society in which the life of the monarch unfolded, and it was the only world of which he had direct experience. From it went out the royal and ministerial edicts and letters which were usually designed to order, exhort or cajole the subjects of the king to pay more into his treasury. To it in return came letters, reports and petitions which showed how co-operative, or more often how unco-operative, the French people were being. The provincial governors, spending some months of each year at court but visiting their *gouvernements* for at least one extended period, were familiar with the thinking of both the central government and the local elites. Yet there were effective governors only in certain provinces, largely those which were more distant from the capital. In other areas of the kingdom, the crown had no comparable agent on whom to rely for advice about local susceptibilities, and there its decisions consequently often appeared to be more arbitrary because the ministers tended to see every problem from the royal point of view. As a result they frequently underrated the strength of local feeling on certain issues, and sent out instructions which sometimes provoked an unforeseen outcry. Even the *intendants* seldom showed much sympathy for the concerns of their *généralités*, because they too remained government men at heart. Only the governors and some of the bishops shuttled to and fro, trying to create a more constructive dialogue. It was their experience of this system which would lead Fénelon and his friends, in the last decades of the reign of Louis XIV, to call for an increase in the number of governors and the institution of regular national and regional representative assemblies, in order that better mutual understanding might be established between the centre and the periphery.

Beneath a veneer of courtesy and elegance, the royal court was a turbulent place. Everyone who resided there was ambitious. Some sought political power at the highest level, and worked unceasingly to dislodge ministers or to persuade the king that they themselves should be included among his innermost circle of advisers. Others were in search of pensions, higher titles, grants of revenues, military and ecclesiastical positions, and other favours. One of the motives for this unending quest was financial, as some of these gifts and positions offered aristocratically acceptable ways of replenishing depleted family resources. The other principal reason was a desire to outdo rival noble houses. The courtier was not just acting on behalf of himself and his immediate family circle, because he too had his clients in the parts of France where he possessed estates and, no doubt, in the capital and court as well. His ability to obtain patronage from the king was a means of cementing his control over his own clientele.

In this world of self-advancement, it was not possible to act alone. Allies were essential, and the court was accordingly filled with factions, each seeking to gain the ear of the king or of a minister and thereby obtain favours at the expense of its rivals. A principal task for the monarch was therefore to find out who was in league with whom, and then to balance these groups against each other. If one clique became too powerful, it had to be destabilized by sowing discord among its members. Frequently disagreements broke out without royal intervention because these ambitious fortune-hunters were working partners, not friends, and they often decided that a particular alliance had served its purpose. Although at all levels of society, at court and in the provinces, such business arrangements lasted only as long as they positively furthered the ambitions of all the participants, this fluidity was most marked among those who wished to exercise high political power at the centre. In the half-century before the collapse of the second Fronde, it was relatively easy for the princes to organize a conspiracy against a minister, but it was much more difficult for the conspirators to agree on which of their number should succeed him. The ministers too needed their own factions and supporters in high places, because they had to safeguard themselves not only against aristocratic plotters but against a change of heart by the king himself. It was therefore essential to be on good terms with some of the other men whom the monarch trusted and consulted regularly. Thus factions were based on personal relationships, whether friendships, family ties, strategic marriages or the bond between client and patron. Yet none of these liaisons could be guaranteed to save a man who was falling from favour, either because he had displeased the king or was proving to be a nuisance to his allies. His disgrace would not necessarily harm those of his relatives who held posts of their own, and they too might not feel that it was a propitious moment to mount a campaign on behalf of their discredited kinsman. It was better to consider the interests of the family as a whole. Loyalty and gratitude were not dominant qualities in courtly society, and those who were no longer useful were discarded. Conversely, a courtier who had gravely offended the monarch might be restored to favour without mention being made of his past misdeeds. A striking example is that of the prince de Condé, who had led the French army against the Spanish, fallen foul of Mazarin during the Frondes, then led the Spanish against the French, returned to France when the two countries made peace, and during the personal rule of Louis XIV was once more an outstanding French general and an effective governor of Burgundy.

As the memoirs of any courtier will reveal, the principal skill required by the successful aristocrat, minister or even monarch was the ability to dissimulate.[2] With everyone engaged in increasing his own influence, gaining friends in high places and enlarging the ranks of his own clients, it was essential to chart the progress of rival power groups. Every sign of favour shown by the king, the ministers or the great nobles towards those below them was an indicator of the shifting fortunes of the various court factions. When the staff of a courtier appeared to be rising, it was for each man to decide whether his own ends were better served by aiding or thwarting this process. No one wanted any faction to be too powerful, unless it was his own. It was therefore as vital to disguise the strategems of your own clique as it was to uncover those of others. The result was a society dominated by bluff and counterbluff, in which it was imperative to be a step ahead of everyone else. Accordingly, the king and his ministers had their spies throughout the court, as they did in the provinces where similar power struggles had to be identified. The courtiers, particularly the princes, had their own networks of informants. Such a mistrustful world was a paradise for 'double-agents', because all loyalty depended on tangible rewards for the services rendered, and it was not difficult for one spymaster to outbid another. The king and the ministers were attractive patrons in the sense that they had at their disposal many forms of desirable patronage, but many men still chose to give their prime allegiance to other leading courtiers. Yet a minister might be deserted by his spies and other clients if his power appeared to be waning, and even an aging king lost some of his royal charisma because a dauphin or a future regent might provide a better focus for those who sought positions of influence in the longer term.

A successful monarch was therefore one who managed to keep all

---

[2] It is impossible to give brief references to these memoirs, because the manoeuverings of court factions are seldom discussed *in extenso*; they were a permanent and principal feature of curial life. The task of charting their progress is achieved only by piecing together thousands of asides and specific items of information. For the advice of a contemporary on dissimulation at court, see Jean de La Fontaine, 'La cour du lion', *Fables*, VII, 7.

the volatile elements at court, and by extension in the country, in a state of equilibrium. Accordingly the most important quality for the ruler was an ability to judge whether or not a minister or a courtier could be trusted. Louis XIV had great faith in his own judgement and was only infrequently proved to have been mistaken, whereas his father and his great-grandson were less resolute both in choosing and in continuing to stand by their advisers. This unpredictability on the part of kings inevitably encouraged the conspiratorial spirit in their most influential subjects, because there was the chance that a single faction might achieve total dominance of the government. Such a situation would never have been permitted during the personal rule of Louis XIV. The realization that this monarch did not intend to give excessive power to any one group was an encouragement to many nobles, who knew that their requests for patronage would at least receive a just and sympathetic hearing. Louis positively furthered this competitive atmosphere by introducing new subtleties into the daily routine of court life, so that his every gesture might be seen as a sign of his favour, his displeasure or his indifference. Courtiers took care to respond by eagerly petitioning him for lodgings in the palace or for some small part in this carefully choreographed pageant, and the king either granted the requests or answered with one of the non-committal phrases for which he became famous. He therefore took care to live almost his entire life in public, every moment organized by strict etiquette in which his own superiority to everyone, and the rigidity of the hierarchy beneath him, were formally restated. Occasionally he slipped away to the freer world of Marly, but even then his choice of companions was a major preoccupation of the court. Although in his old age he spent many more hours in private, in the room of the marquise de Maintenon, he never allowed himself the truly 'private apartments' which Louis XV would favour. There was always some political or social advantage to be gained by being in the full view of the court, where his most important subjects could see him and he could keep watch over them.

Despite the great differences in attitudes and priorities which distinguished provincial France from the governmental and courtly centre of the kingdom, the king tried to control the whole of his dominions as if they were an extension of the court, and he treated both the provincial elites and the factions of courtiers in basically the same way. Such tactics were far from unsuccessful for, in their geographically distant societies, the local and courtly factions behaved in very similar ways. All were competing for increased power and social prestige against their immediate rivals, and Louis XIV tried to distribute his patronage in the provinces with the same care that he employed at court, giving encouragement to many family and clientage groups, but favouring none to an excessive degree. He could never hope to manipulate provincial society as effectively as he could manage his own household, because some of the most cherished prizes sought by the local elites were not in his gift, but at least the experience of trying to balance courtly factions was a valuable training for making the best and the subtlest use of royal authority in the realm as a whole.

If the king and his ministers were therefore eager to chart factional rivalries in all areas of the realm, because they had to govern these lands, the average courtier had a more ambivalent view of the provinces. Although many of them had clients in distant parts of France, and indeed some court factions depended for their prestige on the extent of their influence in particular regions, the public pronouncements of those at court or in the fashionable salons of Paris included much sneering at and contempt for anything provincial. Apart from the genuine problem that the best interests of the kingdom would be defined very differently by the courtier, the Parisian citizen and the provincial notable, high society in the capital gratuitously disparaged everything which originated outside the Ile de France, especially in the cultural field, where it was amusing to jeer at regional attempts to ape the artistic achievements of the leading city in the realm. In return the leaders of local society bitterly resented and castigated the arrogance of these supercilious, self-appointed arbiters of taste and their overlavish Parisian world. Although the provincial notables sought royal patronage through intermediaries, many of them seldom or never went either to Paris or to the palace of the monarch. Moreover the royal favours they sought were also designed to increase their prestige within their own locality, not in other parts of the kingdom. Admittedly some of these pillars of the community, especially the wives, copied the social mannerisms of the court and the salons, a piece of rustic impertinence which caused endless mirth and satirical comment in truly *haute société*. For the Paris audiences of Molière, the out-of-town absurdities of the *précieuses ridicules* were just as entertaining as the pretensions of Parisian bourgeois like Monsieur Jourdain. Both served to demonstrate that high society was the only place to be, and that outsiders could have no place within it. This judgement became increasingly unfair as the seventeenth century progressed because a number of provincial cities could soon boast a flourishing cultural tradition of their own, with artistic and literary figures of great talent, and certainly no mere copy of life in the capital.

THE COURTLY LIFE STYLE AND THE CRITERIA OF
SOCIAL SUCCESS

At court, as in Parisian and provincial society, there were three tests by which to assess the prestige and influence of a noble or office-holder, or even of that greatest aristocrat, the king himself. The first of these was the social status of the man and of his family, the second the extent of his clientele and the importance of his patrons, and the third was the manner in which he lived. Whether they were applied to an old landed and military noble house or to one of the new dynasties of *officiers*, the criteria of social status were the same. Great antiquity of lineage was highly prized, and the establishment of an impeccable pedigree was of vital importance. Within the *noblesse d'épée* there were a few men who frankly admitted that their genealogy, or those aspects of it which reflected credit upon them, could be dated only from the preceding century, but most could trace back a direct line into the later Middle Ages. The year 1400 was of especial significance, and over three-quarters of the non-royal peerages which were in existence during the personal rule of Louis XIV could boast that their family origins lay in the fourteenth or earlier centuries. Royal blood added additional lustre, whether Bourbon, Valois or foreign, legitimate or bastard. The *robe* nobility of office could adduce no such ancient or illustrious forbears, but its members too were eager to prove how long ago their ancestors had left the bourgeois world of industry and commerce and entered the superior strata of the bureaucracy. Some of these genealogical claims were, of course, a little exaggerated, but crude deception was unwise in a competitive world where there were plenty of rivals who would gleefully unmask or satirize such pretence. Colbert suffered doubly from these attentions, being accused of having a bourgeois father, which was untrue, and at same time being ridiculed for allegedly claiming direct descent from the medieval kings of Scotland.

As important as the respectability accorded by age was the prestige of the posts which had been held by former members of the family, whether at court, in the army and the church, or, for the office-holders, in the bureaucracy. Equally significant was the length of time that hereditary titles had been part of the patrimony of a noble house. There was no exact way of comparing age, position and title, because each family argued in the way best suited to the glorification of its own genealogy. To the memorialist, the duc de Saint-Simon, rank was of supreme importance, because he held no influential posts and his family had been relatively insignificant until his father had been created the first *duc et pair* by Louis XIII. Another noble house, which had the more humble title of *comte* but had possessed it for hundreds of years, might lay greater emphasis on antiquity and less on the hierarchy of rank.

Most families, of the robe and the sword, were able to provide a pedigree which contained a mixture of age, rank and positions of influence, and all earnestly sought to advance themselves further. One method of doing so was by strategic marriages into other clans which offered any or all of these qualifications to an equal or greater degree, although there was a mass of legislation to prevent one family from exploiting the wealth and property which the other had already accumulated. Only the children of the marriage, as direct heirs of both houses, could do that. These liaisons were for the mutual advantage of the two groups of kin, and the laws saw to it that the relatives of the bride and the groom had equal rights in the negotiations, even if one side could claim greater status and resources than the other.[3] Another method of advancement was to seek more posts for the present members of the family circle, because the personal prestige of an individual depended partly on his own role in society, but also on the whole range of titles and positions held by his relatives. In this quest the family once again acted as a unit, some members lobbying on behalf of others and the major decisions being taken by a council of its principal figures. This dynastic approach to social mobility was accentuated by the fact that many posts could be passed on from father to son, or to some other person in the kinship group, in the same way that land and titles could be inherited.

The monarch could do little to influence the fortunes of the office-holders, because the purchase of an office was a straightforward transaction between buyer and seller, subject only to the laws of the market-place. Yet he had much to offer the *noblesse d'épée*, in the form of chivalric orders, ceremonial positions in his household, places in wealthy abbeys and convents, grants of revenues and pensions, military commands, higher aristocratic titles, and, when he really trusted someone, bishoprics, embassies and governorships. Louis XIV was particularly skilful in focusing attention upon himself as the fount of patronage, because of his evenhanded distribution of his favours. All aspirants knew that, although an influential advocate at court would advance their request, the merits of their claim would be seriously considered. That was not the feeling under Henri III, Louis XIII and

---

[3]The clearest extended account of marriage and inheritance law is to be found in Barbara B. Diefendorf, *Paris city councillors in the sixteenth century: the politics of patrimony* (Princeton, 1983), pp. 213–97. She also gives, earlier in the book, an excellent picture of the stratified society in the capital.

Louis XV, when it seemed to many that favourites around the throne were clouding the judgement of the king. Louis XIV had advisers, but appeared to be enslaved by none of them. Certainly no single man or group held total sway over the political and social decisions of the sovereign. Only in his passionate devotion to his mistresses and to his illegitimate children, did the king, of his own volition, offend against the social rules of high society by distributing excessive largesse, although he was still careful to allow them no political role in the state. On balance therefore, the nobles felt that this monarch was a supporter of the traditional order, and noted with pleasure that lesser families were no longer given positions which ought to have been the preserve of the true nobility, the *noblesse d'épée*.

Although these ancient families might sneer at the parvenus of the *noblesse de robe*, with their recent or more distant bourgeois ancestors, the office-holders were undoubtedly respected members of society. They came into regular contact with the landed nobility, professionally and even socially, and individual clientage systems embraced representatives of both groups. A senior judge, a municipal mayor or councillor, a receiver-general of the taxes, all were men of account, and their posts were eagerly sought by lesser *officiers*. The hierarchy of offices therefore had its own associated scale of social status and prestige, and these less tangible rewards were as important to the purchaser of a post as the administrative influence and the financial return which it would bring. Although the *robe* and *épée* paths to advancement were distinct, seldom even touching, the same methods and the same criteria of success were applicable to both. It was just as vital for the office-holder, as for the ancient noble, to demonstrate the strength of his family, through its genealogy, its wealth, property and titles, the range and the rank of all the offices held by its members now and in the past, the number of its clients and the influence of its patrons. Thus it would earn the respect of fellow critizens and of rival clans. As administrative offices were hereditary and were regarded as investments, they were passed on to the next generation in the same way that family estates and military commands were bequeathed in more ancient noble houses, and with these legacies went that elusive but highly prized bequest, the reputation which had been carefully built up over the years. In Paris and in the provinces there were, as a consequence of strategic marriages and opportunism in purchasing offices, many veritable dynasties within the bureaucracy. If the crown could not control the actual sale of posts, it could sometimes mediate in disputes between these family groups, just as it could intervene in jurisdictional squabbles, between the judiciary and the municipality, the higher and lower courts, the clerical and secular jurisdictions – the permutations were nearly endless. Here was a chance for the royal ministers to acquire some supporters, if usually only in the short term. More effective mechanisms for controlling the purchase of offices were evolved by the local officials themselves. Again the actual sale was difficult to prevent, but there were ways of either making the post unsaleable or of persuading a purchaser that he was not welcome. The most extreme methods were normally reserved for newly created offices, when would-be buyers might be threatened with death, and there were occasions when someone who did not heed this warning was actually murdered, which did dissuade others from seeking the same fate. When an office had been purchased, it was still possible for it to be rendered virtually useless, because more senior colleagues could make sure that they allocated no profitable business to the new incumbent, in which case he would soon accept his defeat and sell his position.[4]

If the estimated worth of an individual depended partly on the pedigree of his family and the positions held by himself and by his relatives, the extent of his clientele and the prestige of his patrons were no less important factors.[5] Moreover, for the king, as for every one of his socially or politically ambitious subjects, it was vital to know who depended on, or could be influenced by, whom. Each man had to be placed in context within the elaborate network of social inter-dependence, for it was by the manipulation of this system that allies could be found and strategies implemented. This is clearly demon-strated in the reports on the personnel of the *parlements*, which Colbert required the *intendants* to compile in 1663.[6] These royal observers described not only the character of each judge, and what they could discover about his financial resources, but also his friends and those who had influence over him, whether other judges, local officials or nobles. The minister knew that it might be easier to ask a noble to use his powers of persuasion than to approach a member of a *parlement* directly. Thus, either through such third parties, or by direct contact once suitable candidates had been identified by the ministers, the

[1]For some reservations on these points, see Moote, *The revolt of the judges*, p. 18, including note 26. See also Colin R. E. Kaiser, *The masters of requests: an extraordinary judicial company in an age of centralisation, 1589–1648* (London PhD. thesis, 1976), pp. 425–94.

[5]A good introduction to the workings and priorities of the clientage system is provided by Sharon Kettering, *Patrons, brokers and clients in seventeenth-century France* (New York, 1986), pp. 3–39.

[6]G. B. Depping (ed.), *Correspondance administrative sous le règne de Louis XIV*, 'Collection des documents inédits sur l'histoire de France' (4 vols, Paris, 1850–5), vol. II, pp. 33–98.

intendant, the governor, the bishop or a trusted noble, the crown sought to acquire clients within the institutional structure, thereby compensating for its inability to dictate who should or should not purchase the offices. As there was no question of drastically reforming the bureaucracy after the recent turbulence of the Frondes, this search for temporary or permanent supporters had the highest priority. Thus throughout the kingdom, as well as at court, an informal mesh of personal allegiances was interwoven with the formal hierarchy of office and rank, and the power of a individual was assessed as much by the 'company he kept' as by the office he held. Yet, while the dependants of ministers, governors and bishops were supposedly working to further royal policy, there were still many great magnates, with loyal followers, who had very different goals.

The third test of personal and social prestige was based on the life style of the individual courtier, noble or office-holder, although the rigid rules of prescribed behaviour were occasionally breached. The aristocratic disdain for money and for the debasing bourgeois world of commerce and trade received practical expression in the lavishness of their daily lives. A high noble lived more spectacularly and wastefully than a lesser one, and the king had to outshine everyone in the splendour of his household, his prodigality and his generosity. All levels of society were quick to notice when an inferior tried to adopt the life style of a higher stratum to which he did not have the right to belong. Simply by knowing the rank and lineage of a courtier, it should have been possible accurately to guess the size of his town house in Paris, the number of his servants, the ornamentation on his carriage and the degree of ostentation he would adopt in his manner of dress. The aristocratic *hôtels* in the capital were themselves courts in miniature, deliberately copying the royal prototype, and within them the host and hostess received people of equal and lesser rank. The higher very seldom visited the lower, just as the king very rarely consented to be entertained by anyone other than a member of his own intimate family. The *nobles d'épée*, for all their general dislike of the idea of a *noblesse de robe*, did not object to receiving prestigious officials from the judicial and municipal hierarchies. They shared some common civic and social concerns, and they were not in competition for the same posts and patronage. Thus many leading *parlementaires* and city councillors were regular and intelligent contributors to the intellectual salon society of the capital, and seem to have been regarded as amiable companions by members of even the oldest noble families. Yet, despite the role of the aristocratic *hôtels* in Parisian high society, their owners did not really feel themselves to be citizens of the city. It was rather a place where they sometimes resided, when they were not at court or

visiting their country estates. It was the office-holders and the municipal officials who formed the uppermost stratum of the citizenry proper.
   The only people whom it was impossible to place within the strict
social hierarchy of life style were the royal ministers. Under Louis
XIV they were not integrated into the elaborate etiquette of
ceremonial court life, and they were not permitted to acquire any of
the positions which were reserved for the higher aristocratic courtiers.
The great nobles did not therefore regard them as direct rivals, but
they bitterly resented that these royal advisers, of relatively humble
origin, were frequently addressed and treated in a manner more fitting
for a duke. The office-holders, from whose ranks their families had
come, also disliked them, because they had abandoned the concerns of
the *robe*, had become 'king's men' and were even party to the
undermining of the very bureaucratic privileges which, for patrimonial
reasons, they ought to have been defending. Yet the political power of
the ministers and their influence with the king seems to have
compensated in some ways for their inferior birth, and Madame
Foucquet was able to hold a glittering salon to which her social
superiors thronged. Nevertheless, whatever the other faults of her
husband as a minister, there is no doubt that the ostentation displayed
by Foucquet at Vaux-le-Vicomte, especially in the lavish fête at which
he entertained Louis XIV, was becoming offensive to the true
aristocracy. Nor was the king pleased to see such an almost royal
display of prodigality. While many Frenchmen believed that the king
was working for the good of the kingdom, even if they did not always
agree with his definition of their collective best interests, it was easy to
conclude, however unfairly, that these wealthy ministers were striving
to enhance the position and resources of their families out of state
revenues and hence at the expense of the ordinary people.
   In this ceremonial age, the visible aspects of daily life were therefore
clear indications of social and political ambitions beneath the surface.
The obsession with privilege, etiquette, display, precedence and forms
of address was an integral part of the wider struggle for advancement
which was the permanent preoccupation of the French social elites. If
the king could help to speed the upward mobility, within the limits
imposed by the hierarchy of rank, of those he liked, trusted, or wished
to enlist because they were already powerful and therefore better as
friends than as enemies, he could never deprive a noble he disliked of
his hereditary prestige, his titles and his network of clients. When a
minister was dismissed, it was a different matter. His relatives would
doubtless keep the positions which he had obtained for them, but his
own enormous influence would cease and he would henceforth be
merely a member of his wider family group, which would be judged

according to the usual social criteria. Also he would find that his clients melted away, because their relationship with him had been one of expediency rather than loyalty. The ultimate dependence of the mighty secretary of state on the whim of the monarch who had raised him from relative obscurity made him a powerful but possibly ephemeral patron, and it was an unwise client who committed all his fortunes entirely to a single minister. In the words of the maréchal de Villeroy, as reported by Saint-Simon, 'when a minister is in power you hold his chamber pot for him, but as soon as you see that his feet are beginning to slide, you empty it over his head'.[7] In the case of great aristocrats, the bond with their dependants might be much more durable, especially in a province where their ancestors had resided for centuries. To exile a noble from court and to deprive him of posts which had been in his family for generations might be to encourage him to rebel. It was better to keep the possibly subversive within the ranks of the courtiers, where they were under surveillance, and to prevent them from building up too large a faction by making it worth while for some of their supporters to desert them. Here again Louis XIV was more successful than many other monarchs in using his patronage to neutralize the power of his most ambitious subjects.

The largesse required of the aristocrat as part of his inevitable life style was beyond the means of some families, who accordingly fell increasingly into debt. The king, quick to seize every opportunity to win the gratitude of individual nobles at court and in the provinces, was thereby offered many chances to do so. If the titles and posts which he alone could bestow were always in demand, how much more desperately did some great families need his financial help. Ideas like 'balancing the budget' and 'living within one's means' were bourgeois preoccupations which had no place in the noble ethic. All responsibility for domestic finance was accordingly delegated to household officials, who were simply required to keep the family financially afloat by whatever methods they could devise. Louis XIV expected Colbert to play the same kind of role in the royal court and in the government, and even that minister, renowned for his prudent housekeeping, never dared to criticize the massive expenditure on fêtes and on the extension of Versailles because these were the essential trappings of monarchical superiority. As the later seventeenth-century court was deliberately made increasingly lavish, so in consequence did the life styles of the aristocrats become more elaborate, and at a time when their traditional forms of income were often yielding diminished

[7]The duc de Saint-Simon, *Mémoires*, ed. A. de Boislisle (45 vols, Paris, 1879–1930), vol. XII, p. 124.

returns. The household officials found it even more difficult to keep their masters solvent. Therefore royal generosity was more keenly sought, longer spells were spent at court by those nobles who desired a share of it, and such sojourns further increased their outgoings. But *noblesse oblige*, and the extravagance had to be sustained if the family were to hold up its head in public. When debts finally and irrevocably overwhelmed an aristocratic house, there was no alternative but to retire from court and from Parisian society. It was possible for a noble to live beyond his means for a time, if his creditors permitted it, but he could never be seen to live in a style below his rank.

Withdrawal from society was the final remedy when all accepted methods of replenishing dwindling resources had failed. Even if the king ignored requests for pensions, gifts and grants of revenues, it was usually possible to avert disaster by one or more palliatives. Least painful socially was for the impoverished noble to marry one of his scions to the daughter of another *épée* house. Many members of the old landed nobility were still extremely wealthy, and a minority of them, through prudence and foresight, had further supplemented their fortunes by playing the money-markets and investing in bourgeois enterprises, preserving their social integrity by using false names and employing middle men to act on their behalf. If the poorer of the parties to such marriages was of higher rank, then the genealogical benefits more than compensated the wealthier house for the dowry it had to provide. Alternative cures for insolvency included direct borrowing from the financiers, a short-term form of relief which was only possible if the aristocrat was considered to be creditworthy, and marriages with the wealthy but socially inferior families of the *noblesse de robe*. No one liked the financiers, but they were a necessary evil and even kings regularly enlisted their aid. *Robe-épée* marriages, like royal largesse, were much more controversial, because both might affect the balance of political power or social influence. The marriages were therefore disparaged by almost everybody, the largesse by all those who did not receive a share of it – and a little more must be said about both of these remedies for poverty.

The liaisons between old and new noble houses add a further note of ambivalence to the relations between the two elites. The *épée* never ceased to complain about the *robe* in general, whose *noblesse* was in no way comparable with that based on antiquity, heredity or outstanding military valour. Members of each nobility frequently appealed to the king to uphold their rights against the claims or encroachments of the other, thereby giving the monarch the chance for some ostentatiously evenhanded mediation which kept the tensions between them gently simmering. Yet that did not prevent them from meeting each other socially, nor from working together when their personal and local interests coincided. It was certainly preferable for the poor aristocrat to select a rich daughter-in-law from the *robe* than from the more inferior ranks of the bourgeois and the financiers. The *robin* father of the bride would welcome such an alliance because, not only did it extend his network of clients and patrons, but it meant that his grandchildren by the marriage would be *noblesse d'épée* in their own right. Such *mésalliances*, as their detractors called them, therefore satisfied the financial needs of the older, and the social aspirations of the newer, house. Nevertheless they were frowned on – by more solvent members of the *épée* who regarded them as socially demeaning, by other office-holders who resented the social advancement they brought to individuals within their own ranks, and above all by the king and his ministers who considered them to be highly dangerous. If elite groups, at court and in the country, were to be kept in a state of equilibrium, it was essential that they all remain separate and distinct. Alliances of *robe* and *épée* might produce excessively powerful provincial dynasties, and they encouraged social mobility and personal ambition in an undesirable manner. Whereas a financially hard-pressed Louis XIII had been unable to prevent all these marriages, Louis XIV was determined to do so, and was always ready to offer sums of money to the impoverished family in the hope of averting a *mésalliance*. As a result there were fewer of them during his personal rule than the violent tirades against the practice might suggest. Such payments were thus an essential aspect of social control, even when the treasury could ill afford to make them, and the king, aristocrat that he was by training, never minded living beyond his means if by doing so he could preserve the static hierarchy which was vital to the stability of the kingdom. He could be sure that the resourceful finance ministers would somehow find the appropriate funds, an increasingly difficult task in the expensive wartime years of the 1670s and an impossible one in the two later wars. Louis XV not only abandoned the policy of social stability, but was actually prepared to receive financiers at court, thereby both alienating his noble courtiers and giving these parvenus excessive opportunities for influence which they eagerly seized. The crowing insult came when the daughter of a financier family became the royal mistress, with the title of the marquise de Pompadour, and was allowed to play an important role in the faction politics of the court. Never had Louis XIV selected a mistress from such inferior stock nor permitted one to meddle in the high affairs of state.

If most of the old and new nobles joined the king in deploring *mésalliances*, they were no less displeased by the general implications of the direct gifts in money and revenues which the monarch himself and his ministers dispensed. They were aware that such generosity sometimes saved an ancient house from destitution and loss of face, but it was also used to recruit men who would be useful to the government. This strategy enabled the crown to build up too large a clientele at court and in the provinces, which alarmed other elite groups in society. Most dangerous of all, many of these payments were made *sub rosa*, by means of *ordonnances de comptant* in which the beneficiary was not named. On numerous occasions therefore, the office-holders clamoured for a reduction in royal expenditure on pensions and gifts, together with the cessation of all secret transactions of this kind. Louis XIV did insist in 1661 that henceforth the name of the recipient should be stated on the *ordonnances* and that he should have a personal record of every one which had been issued, but this was to ensure that he knew whom his ministers were favouring and was not a response to the demands of *officiers* that such patronage should be open to general scrutiny. It should not, of course, be thought that gifts of money emanated solely from the king and from lesser or rival patrons. Much came in the reverse direction, as institutions, social groups and individuals were prepared to pay substantial gratifications to their patrons and to the royal ministers for favours received and, most importantly, for the preservation and extension of their privileges.[8]

Where the historians of absolutism imagined that they had identified a period of rapid social change, with a rising bourgeoisie, recent scholars have stressed instead that French society was largely static and stratified in the seventeenth century, even before Louis XIV assumed personal power and voiced his own continuing opposition to a socially mobile population. A few individuals and families rose or fell dramatically, and there were occasional instances of marriages which linked houses of different social status. The more usual pattern was one of slow advancement, as nobles were granted the next highest rank of nobility in return for outstanding service, or as bureaucrats managed to climb a further rung on the office-holding ladder. Even there it was commoner for a father to obtain a more prestigious post for his son, rather than to improve his own position in the hierarchy. Although patronage networks included men of varying social backgrounds, the marriages contracted by the member families seldom involved spouses of differing strata. Not only did a *noble d'épée* try to seek his sons- and daughters-in-law within the sword nobility, but a

---

[8]For example the decisions of the Mâconnais Estates to send gifts to Colbert and to other influential men at court and in the province – Pierre Clément, (ed.), *Lettres, instructions et mémoires de Colbert* (8 vols, Paris, 1861–82), vol. IV, pp. 596–8.

ducal house would endeavour to choose the offspring of a fellow duke. Similarly, in a great city, where some of the municipal elite came from lawyer stock and others were from the commercial world, the two groups did not intermarry, although marriages were common within each of them. The dominant principle in society seems to have been that, while it was very important to advance one's own family and clientele, it was much more vital to prevent the destabilizing effects of very rapid mobility by others. Most men accepted a self-denying ordinance that modest ambition on the part of everyone meant greater stability for all.

INSTABILITY AND EQUILIBRIUM: FRENCH SOCIETY FROM HENRI III TO LOUIS XIV

In their unceasing efforts to advance their fortunes, the various groups in early modern French society – whether families, clientage networks or institutions – planned their strategy with great care. It was accepted that on occasion an individual might find it impossible to reconcile the best interests of his family with the obligations imposed on him by his office, and at such times a compromise would be reached. Everyone would understand the dilemma. Yet there were some periods of more general instability in the kingdom, where these carefully prepared plans were put at risk by extraneous factors and it seemed that the whole fabric of society was being threatened. At such times the desire for a restoration of order was stronger than the wish to gain further influence, and the local notables therefore abandoned their jurisdictional or family squabbles, closing ranks in an attempt to restore calm. Such a mood was evident during the later stages of the sixteenth-century civil wars and again after the Frondes, both Henri IV and Louis XIV being quick to capitalize upon it. The two monarchs wished to establish a greater degree of equilibrium among the various social groupings, and the people, exhausted by years of disruption, seemed willing to acquiesce.[9] Local leaders continued to be vigilant lest the king seize the opportunity afforded by this mood of co-operation to encroach upon their liberties and privileges, but these two rulers were too wise to take such risks. The population also withdrew its support from the great nobles who had played a leading part in these insurrections, because in each period of conflict they had revealed themselves to be selfish, quarrelsome and hungry for personal power, showing no thought for the misfortunes of lesser men.

[9]The establishment of social equilibrium is discussed in a stimulating, if sometimes provocative, way by Norbert Elias, *The court society* (Oxford, 1983), chapter 7.

Ironically, the Henri IV who was to recreate an atmosphere of stability in France had himself been one of the aristocratic faction leaders whose fierce rivalry had prolonged the state of civil war, and had deprived the Valois monarch of any effective authority in large areas of his kingdom. Henri de Navarre had a strong but not an undisputed claim to the throne, especially as, according to the fundamental laws of France, his Protestant religion seemed to bar him from the succession. Yet by 1589 many Frenchmen were ready for peace. During the instability of the civil wars, local assemblies and councils had grown up and had become increasingly formalized, as the provincial elites sought to restore order in their area at a time when the crown was too weak to give them a lead. The governor was often the central figure in these new administrative configurations, but he maintained this position more by his willingness to compromise than by his ability to direct.[10] A few unscrupulous governors exploited this confusion for their own ends, but many sought to serve the crown as best they could. Neither they, nor the king whose principal representatives they were, had the power to command in these rebellious decades. The crown accordingly did not issue them with detailed orders, but rather gave them *carte blanche* to do anything which would preserve their own appearance of superiority and hence that of their royal master. They accordingly tried to play off the local elites as a king might balance court factions, and made full use of the general desire for a return to order. They still had their powers of patronage, but these were less effective when the ultimate giver of favours, the Valois monarch, was in such an unstable position, dominated by favourites and by courtiers who might be hostile to many of the governors. The balance of power and influence at court had been temporarily destroyed, and patronage was being distributed for capricious reasons, favouring the claims of some families and ignoring those of others. So the governor had to temporize, even changing his religion if that seemed appropriate to the mood of his province, but at least it meant that the localities could profess their loyalty to the king and to his chief local agent, while lamenting that this particular monarch had fallen victim to the selfish designs of unscrupulous aristocrats at court. The governors were still the 'king in the provinces', and a wise and cunning one was able to do much to preserve the respect in which the crown was held.

When Henri III died, many Frenchmen were ready to welcome a monarch who would respect their privileges but would emancipate

---

[10]See Robert R. Harding, *Anatomy of a power elite: the provincial governors of early modern France* (New Haven/London, 1978) esp. chapter 4.

himself from the tyranny of high aristocratic faction and concentrate on the defence of the realm. In 1589 it was not yet clear to everyone that Henri IV could, or even should, be that man, and other candidates were favoured by those who disapproved of his religious beliefs, questioned his integrity, or lived in a part of France which had been staunchly anti-Bourbon during the civil wars. Only as Henri consolidated his hold on the kingdom did these doubters begin to swing round towards his cause. Even less enthusiastic were some of the most powerful aristocrats and officials who had wielded great influence at the court of Henri III or who were members of the mighty institutions in the capital city of Paris, especially the *parlement* which claimed to be the custodian of the fundamental laws of France and was determined to exclude a heretic king. Other high nobles saw this as the moment to dislodge the favourites of the late king and establish their own houses in similarly dominant positions under one or other of the candidates for the succession.

The leading courtiers and Parisians shared few common grievances or ambitions, but many of them were prepared to maintain a temporary unity against the Bourbon claimant and to support the candidate of the Catholic League, who was actually proclaimed Charles X by the *parlement* of Paris. Even Villeroy, a loyal secretary of state under Henri III and subsequently a devoted servant of Henri IV, was a supporter of the League in these early days of a disputed kingship. A principal reason why he and the Paris judges favoured the *ligueur* cause was that this disparate alliance was presenting itself as the party of financial reform, determined to sweep away the fiscal corruption and the lavish expenditure of the preceding reign. Although many factors aided Henri IV in his consolidation of power – especially his abjuration of Protestantism, the war weariness of the provinces and the internal divisions among the leaders of the Ligue – it was only when he acceded to *parlementaire* demands for fiscal reform and agreed to pursue some of the other policies championed by the office-holders that the influential upper levels of the bureaucracy finally deserted the party of Charles X and accepted a Bourbon monarch. Although some of these concessions were forced upon Henri, others were more freely agreed, and there is clear archival evidence to justify the assertion that the new king was consciously trying to break up the alliances against him by appealing to the different priorities of their various component groups, and in general to make his rule partly acceptable to as many of his subjects as possible. It was also vital for him, as the former head of an aristocratic faction, to seek an accommodation with his erstwhile princely enemies within the kingdom. If this was not feasible in every case, it became easier to achieve as he gained greater acceptance as the true king of France. Even so he had to purchase the loyalty of some great nobles, expending large sums of money in the process, which involved the crown in borrowing heavily from French financiers and also from the foreign creditors to whom Henri was already deeply indebted because of the cost of fighting the civil wars. He was therefore deliberately seeking to establish an equilibrium among the elites in French society by playing them off against each other, and by offering something to everyone without showing excessive favour to any. He was not wholly successful, and his reign was not the glorious triumph to which later royal publicists would look back with nostalgia. Moreover he dared not renegue on many of the promises which had enabled him to widen the basis of his support. Most Frenchmen, especially the office-holders, remained suspicious of his sincerity in converting to Catholic-ism, and were watching for signs of a recantation. The cautious middle course of his religious policy pleased no one, because it seemed to lack any positive conviction or direction. Yet many of his subjects did welcome the end of the civil wars and the making of international peace, preferring some assertion of royal authority to the preceding power vacuum at the centre, when Valois, Guise, Bourbon and Montmorency had nearly torn the realm asunder.

Given the newness of the Bourbon monarchy and the turbulent times during which it had been born and established, it was a national disaster when Henri IV was assassinated in 1610 and a small child ascended the throne. The declaration of a regency was always a signal for internal disorder, as every ambitious subject could then claim to be fighting for the king against the government of inept regents and corrupt ministers. The *parlement* of Paris would be able to maintain that a regent was not permitted to exercise total royal power and that it, as the guardian of the fundamental laws, was the watchdog charged with preventing such abuses of authority. This prestigious court insisted that she could not hold a *lit de justice*, in order to enforce the registration of unpopular royal edicts when its own members were unwilling to endorse them. That, it claimed, could be done only by an adult king, although there were royalist pamphleteers who were prepared to sustain the counterargument that the regent was invested with the totality of monarchical power and could therefore issue and enforce edicts on any subject. Certainly the government would have ensured that any such controversial document bore the hallmarks of monarchy, as the chancellor would have affixed the seal and perhaps the infant king might have appended his 'Louis' in childish hand-writing.

When the king was of age, the fiction of protecting the sovereign against evil counsellors was a hollow argument. The enemies of a minister could still vilify him, but ultimately they would have to persuade the king himself to authorize his dismissal. Only he who had appointed the minister could dispense with his services. During regencies it was therefore easier to topple leading members of the government from office, because loyalty to the person of the king was compatible with disloyalty to the trustees of his authority. If a royal minority accordingly gave greater freedom to the opponents of the central government, in one important respect it also offered the ministers more room for manoeuvre. In the first Fronde, for example, Mazarin could risk totally alienating the *parlements* without prejudicing the power and reputation of the crown. Similarly the *parlementaires* could flatly defy the cardinal without compromising their relations with the king on whom their entire authority as judges depended. Only ministerial power was at stake. Monarchy not only remained free from attack, but the opponents of Mazarin voiced their longing for the day when the king would take over the reins of power and free them from ministerial tyranny. An adult monarch unquestionably held the final responsibility for the actions of his government, and this imposed caution on both sides. The king dared not force his judiciary, so vital for the administration of the kingdom, into open rebellion, but nor did the judges dare overtly to disobey him and thereby throw away the very foundation of their power, perhaps provoking a constitutional crisis into the bargain. The son and the grandson of Henri IV chose to deal with this problem in different ways. Louis XIII took care to remain in the background for much of the time, allowing Richelieu to take the blame for policies of which the minister, not the king, appeared to be the author. Louis XIV in contrast made it abundantly clear that every governmental decision had his personal approval. Thus, both his ministers and his opponents were compelled to behave with caution, after such an explicit declaration which directly exposed the royal authority and deprived it of any ministerial shield.

The death of Henri IV, like that of François II in 1560 and of Louis XIII in 1643, brought a foreign-born Queen Mother to power as regent. The choice of international brides for kings and dauphins often made excellent dynastic and diplomatic sense, but if a queen subsequently became regent she might soon find herself accused of furthering the best interests of her ancestral family and her native land, rather than those of her adopted country. When Marie, prematurely widowed by the assassination of Henri IV, took charge of the government on behalf of the young Louis XIII, it seemed politically sensible for this impoverished kingdom to seek friendlier relations with Spain and thus prevent another costly war. Yet some

Frenchmen saw this amity towards the principal enemy of her late husband as a betrayal of France, especially as it implied an enthusiam for ultra-catholicism which contrasted dramatically with the tolerant religious settlement achieved only a few years before. She also bore the name of Medici, which evoked memories of the last regent, Catherine, from that same illustrious Italian house, who had skilfully preserved the Valois monarchy throughout the recent civil wars but had been far from universally liked or trusted. Marie, like Anne of Austria some thirty years later, also counted foreigners among her intimate circle of advisers, which distressed the xenophobic French, although she did not allow them to exercise the influence which her daughter-in-law would accord to her Italian minister, Mazarin.

Recent historians have rescued Marie de Médicis from the ignominious reputation which she has long had to bear, her period of power sandwiched between the reign of the mighty Henri IV and the ministry of the masterly Richelieu. It is not only that the actual achievements of Henri-le-Grand have now been separated from the posthumous aura he acquired, and that the memoirs of his minister, Sully, have been acknowledged to be a mixture of chronicle and eulogy, in which he exaggerated the successes in government of his master and of himself while denigrating the queen regent who had dismissed him from office. It is also recognized that Marie and her ministers showed considerable skill in tackling the financial and other administrative problems which confronted them, some of which were the legacy of the preceding reign. Undoubtedly many Frenchmen did not want a return to overt civil hostilities, but there were plenty of influential groups in society which sought to advance themselves during these years when there was no adult king. Her government deserves considerable credit for its part in maintaining a kind of equilibrium in the kingdom, even if the oscillation of forces was wilder than under Henri and Sully or during the personal rule of Louis XIV.

Only in the 1630s did tension dramatically increase between the crown and the elites in provincial and Parisian society, as France overtly entered the Thirty Years War. At the topmost social level there was an additional cause of instability because, as late as the twenty-eighth year of his reign, Louis XIII had no direct heir of his own body. His brother, Gaston d'Orléans, the prince next in line to the throne, therefore possessed enormous prestige and attracted a following of highly ambitious fellow nobles. Even when he became involved in conspiracies designed to oust Richelieu, it was difficult to take severe punitive action against him, lest he become the future king. The cardinal handled Gaston with care because he had no wish to be the first casualty of the new reign, should they both outlive the present monarch.

Lower down the social scale, hostility to the royal ministers was growing because of their fiscal policies, some of them plainly misconceived but most following from the impossibility of financing a prolonged war on the basis of inadequate revenues. It was not surprising therefore that Louis XIII deemed it prudent to keep out of sight and allow his political advisers to become the targets of provincial rebellions, princely revolts and scurrilous pamphlets. Once again, as under Henri III, the aspirants for patronage complained that the balance of influence at the centre had been upset, in this case because the faction of Richelieu seemed to be predominant and his *créatures* occupied too many positions of importance.[11] With the deaths of the cardinal and Louis XIII, the situation deteriorated for a number of reasons. Although the policies of Mazarin were in some ways less provocative than those of his predecessor, the cumulative problems of financing the war were now insoluble and yet international hostilities could not be ended swiftly. Worse still, it was again a period of regency under a foreign queen, and the new minister was that most hated of figures, the foreign cleric. Moreover this one had made his reputation in the diplomatic service of the Roman pontiffs, themselves no friends of France. As an outsider, Mazarin lacked the family connections within the kingdom which might have enabled him to manipulate the wheels of patronage and build himself a network of clients, in order to counter the factions and clientage systems of his princely and office-holding opponents. His only real patron was the now deceased Richelieu. All these factors help to explain why hatred of the Italian cardinal grew to such an intensity that a variety of different opposition groups, with much mutual hostility and few common aims, combined briefly on two occasions during the Frondes in order to remove him from his supreme ministerial position. Although their periods of alliance were short, turbulence and disruption continued throughout the rest of the 1650s, and it is all the more remarkable that Louis XIV managed to re-establish social and political equilibrium in France so soon after declaring his personal monarchy in 1661.

Throughout the decade between the attainment of his majority, following his thirteenth birthday in 1651, and his decision to rule in

[11]Richelieu's very traditional ways of extending his own influence and that of his family and clientele have been well examined by Joseph Bergin, *Cardinal Richelieu: power and the pursuit of wealth* (London, 1985), although there is still much useful information in the more conventional and narrowly conceived study by Orest Ranum of *Richelieu and the councillors of Louis XIII: a study of the secretaries of state and superintendents of finance in the ministry of Richelieu, 1633–1642* (Oxford, 1963).

person at the age of twenty-two, Louis had been called upon by many pamphleteers to dismiss Mazarin and become 'the new Henri IV', by which they meant the idealized and posthumous Henri created by Sully and others. When the young king did finally decide to assert himself, there was sufficient goodwill towards him – and his initial policies seemed so moderate and reasonable – that his rule was largely welcomed. Accordingly, any mishaps or mistakes were still blamed on ministers and secretaries of state, despite the royal assurance that every one of their decisions and pronouncements was personally approved by him. Even in war the monarch was allowed to claim the successes, while ministers and generals bore the stigma of the defeats. Not until the 1680s did Louis begin to attract the criticism on to his own head, and from then the clamour steadily increased until, at his death in 1715, there were few Frenchmen prepared to defend him. Thus in the 1680s 'monarchy' once again became an issue in French political theory, with a discussion of the origins, nature and obligations of kingship. For the preceding eighty years Sully, Richelieu, Mazarin, two queens regent, Colbert and Louvois had shielded their sovereign from attack, and during that time the theorists had concentrated on the claims and counterclaims of regents, ministers, office-holders, nobles and other elite groups, all of whom professed loyalty to the king.

THE DEBATES ABOUT THE DEFINITION OF *NOBLESSE* AND THE NATURE OF PRIVILEGE

Unlike the princes, whose aim was to secure a major role in policy-making at the centre and who therefore had to prove that they had a hereditary and time-honoured place within the French constitution, the rest of the nobility concentrated on justifying the social position of the noble order in society. As they sought to extend their local influence and to outwit their rivals, they laid stress on their privileges, rights and liberties, and ignored the niceties of the constitutional debate about the balance of power in the central government. Yet many of the *nobles d'épée* seem to have felt that their whole estate was in crisis, as is clearly shown by the preoccupation with the idea of *noblesse* in the literature of the period and in the discussions held at the leading Parisian salons. The economic resources of some nobles were undoubtedly dwindling, but this investigation into the very origins and nature of nobility was prompted by a much wider unease. The chief enemies of the *noblesse d'épée*, as identified in these pamphlets and *conversazioni*, were the royal ministers from above and the rising ranks of office-holders from below. This did not mean that the average noble supported the princes in their attempts to oust the present policy-makers and in their promise to abolish the venal bureaucracy. A government of princes was likely to be more factious, more self-seeking and therefore a great deal worse. Yet, if ministers and venal bureaucrats could be allowed to remain, the slow encroachment by both groups on the right of the nobility had to be arrested at once, before the erosion became too serious to contain.

The dispute about the fundamental nature of *noblesse* subsumed all the more specific quarrels between the old nobles and the office-holders about jurisdictions and liberties. To the *épée*, a *noblesse de robe* was plainly a contradiction in terms. A robe of office could not confer nobility. Only military valour justified the creation of noble titles, and all those who inherited them had to ensure that they too were prepared for courageous service in the field when it was required. Otherwise they would tarnish the reputation of their family, and would betray their whole calling because the Second Estate was the military class. A *noble d'épée* who served in a high bureaucratic office did not thereby join the *robe*. The holding of such a post did not lower his social standing, and neither therefore could it elevate a bourgeois into a noble. The office-holders could honestly argue in their turn that the king himself had authorized the conferment of nobility on senior officials, to which their opponents retorted than no monarch had the right to decree any such thing. Tension increased because the *officiers* missed no opportunity for claiming that the two kinds of *noblesse* were on a par, and at the same time they were subtly infiltrating the *épée* by means of *mésalliances.* There was no doubt that a distinguished royal judge of the *parlement* of Paris was a man of great social prestige and position. The question was whether, as his fellow *officiers* claimed, he was a senior member of the noble hierarchy, or was not part of the nobility at all and owed his status solely to his being a judicial officer of the king. As the publicists of the noble cause never failed to point out, the *noblesse de robe* had no right of entry into the Second Estate at the infrequent meetings of the *Etats-généraux*. They did attend the equally irregular *assemblées des notables*, but there too they were not included among the members of the nobility and sat as a separate corps of office-holders. When the three tests of *noblesse* were applied to the members of the *robe* – military origins and continuing valour, great antiquity of lineage, and inherited nobility – they were found wanting on all counts. They were not of the fighting elite, their short genealogies led straight back into the bourgeoisie, and their inheritance consisted of an office which had been purchased in the market-place by one of their ancestors, probably with money made in commerce.

The principal purpose of the *nobles d'épée* was to prove that they were the sole hereditary elite in French society. They and their propagandists accordingly stressed those aspects of the aristocratic ethic which could not possibly apply to an office-holding nobility, and especially to one of recently bourgeois origins. They insisted that every true noble could trace the origin of his privileged status to a conjunction of two essential elements, an act of military valour and a decision by the monarch, who alone could elevate a family into the Second Estate, to honour that act by making a grant of hereditary nobility as a permanent memorial to the man and his deeds. From that moment all his descendants were expected to subscribe to the time-honoured code of aristocratic values, out of respect both for their valiant forbear and for the *noblesse* as a whole. It was truly a privilege to be among their illustrious ranks and every member must labour unceasingly to be worthy of his title. Those who fell short of this ideal should be harshly treated. A family which found a 'black sheep' in its midst should cast him out and cut him off from his patrimony, and it was accepted that a noble who committed a crime should be more severely punished than a lesser mortal found guilty of the identical offence. He had erred more greatly because the moral standards expected of him were higher and his rejection of them was less excusable. The publicists of the noble cause maintained that, when an aristocratic house took pains to live according to these demanding ethical principles, it accumulated a store of *vertu*, which continued to grow over the years and could be bequeathed to subsequent generations in the same way as more tangible bequests of titles, estates and wealth. These writers constantly reiterated that nobility of birth and nobility of sentiment were two parts of an indivisible whole.[12]

What, they enquired, could members of recently bourgeois houses know of such lofty ideals? Whether in their middle-class past or in their office-holding present, these men were engaged in making money through their own labour, a totally alien concept for any true aristocrat. The image of true *noblesse* was so remote from the base concerns of the world that wealth and poverty in no way enhanced or tarnished it. Even Antoine L'Oisel, a jurist who strongly supported the power of the crown and was no apologist for the nobility, merely stated as a matter of fact in 1607 that 'pauvreté n'est point vice, et ne désanoblit point'.[13] Thus, although it was impossible to play an active part in the world of high society without the resources necessary to

[12]An excellent guide to these debates is provided by F. E. Sutcliffe, *Guez de Balzac et son temps: littérature et politique* (Paris, 1959).
[13]*Institutes coutumières . . .*, ed. Claude Joly (Paris, 1679), I, 1, xvi (15).

sustain the life style appropriate to the gradations of rank, an impoverished aristocrat who had been forced to abandon this expensive way of living could at least reassure himself that he had lost none of his nobility.

The aristocratic disdain for the idea of working for financial gain posed a problem for the crown. The nobility was the military class, and it was vital that it be sufficiently solvent to play its hereditary role in the defence of the kingdom. *Mésalliances* were undesirable, and royal pensions or gifts were very costly. An obvious solution was for the ministers to persuade these illustrious families that some ways of making money were not incompatible with their birthright. Hitherto it had been illegal for nobles to trade, but under Louis XIII and Louis XIV the central government amended the law on more than one occasion, and then tried to convince them that colonial and wholesale trade in no way derogated from *noblesse*. Colbert made particularly vigorous efforts in this direction, hoping that it would also further his schemes for economic expansion. It was only retail transactions, with their vulgar overtones of market-place haggling, which were obviously suited to the bourgeoisie and no one else. Yet nobles, with very few exceptions, remained unconvinced. They were a landed elite, and they preferred to be poor rather than debased.

The nobles and their publicists, merely contemptuous of these ruses to lure them into the degrading world of trade, were much more concerned about certain other trends in government policy which boded very ill. Here they found, albeit with some distaste, that they they had some allies among the office-holders. The central government valued the nobility as the military class, but some of the numerous privileges enjoyed by the Second Estate were major obstacles to ministerial plans for the administrative unification and economic rationalization of the kingdom. The nobles were not only exempt from direct taxation, but their right to impose their own dues upon the peasantry further diminished the yield of the royal taxes. The peasant, burdened with fiscal demands from both the crown and the *seigneur*, tended to prefer to pay his immediate lord who at least gave him some services in return, rather than the distant central government which demanded so much but apparently showed no interest in his welfare. In times of crisis, the *seigneur* would actually help to defend him against the rapacious agents of the Paris ministers. Certainly no humble provincial subject would have thought of appealing to the crown for protection against his landlord. In addition to their dominance of the army officer corps, the nobles also preserved their considerable rights of seigneurial jurisdiction, outside and in parallel to the lower levels of the royal judicial system. Yet their most dangerous power was also the most elusive – the sheer influence they could exert over the locality because of their hereditary and prestigious position in society. The office-holders did not regard all these rights and privileges with equal enthusiasm because some of them conflicted with their own bureaucratic functions, but they, as members of the *noblesse de robe* or as aspirants for entry into its ranks, did not want to see a general attack on noble liberties and immunities. They wished to enjoy many of these advantages which were associated with both *robe* and *épée* nobility, and some *officiers* had also become *seigneurs* in their own right. Moreover there was the perpetual concern that, if one privilege were successfully abrogated by the crown, then all the others would become more vulnerable.

One highly emotive and symbolic issue in the quarrel between the royal ministers and the old nobility was the right to duel. There were a number of edicts against this practice during the reigns of the first three Bourbons, and none was effective in stamping it out. Nor did any royal minister expect such an outcome. These regulations were designed rather to assert a principle, namely that the king was the sole fount of justice in the realm and that all disputes among his subjects should be brought before his judges. No one had the right to decide cases by the sword. Yet the nobles were not prepared to be classed as mere subjects. Their obligation to defend their own honour was a chivalrous duty which could not be taken from them. They belonged to a social group whose very name stressed this point, the *noblesse d'épée*, underlining the fact that it was their inalienable privilege to carry the *épée* and to use it in defence of their personal reputation and integrity. The 1626 edict of Richelieu on duelling caused particular offence. The cardinal himself valued the nobles as army officers and as a force for order in the localities, except when they briefly chose to foment revolt, but he was determined to assert the all-pervasive nature of royal justice. A fierce war developed, fought not with arms but with literary arguments and pamphlets. The nobles were further annoyed by the provocative action of the minister in arresting and executing a duellist of the highly prestigious Montmorency clan. They were not alarmed, because they knew that such drastic methods were possible only at or in the vicinity of the court, where royal guards could be summoned, and could never be effectively extended to the provinces on a regular basis. It was the principle which mattered, embracing as it did the whole question of whether an aristocrat should prefer to preserve his honour and follow his conscience or to obey a dishonourable command of his sovereign.

Le Cid, by Corneille, was one literary work which was adopted by the champions of the aristocratic cause, and to such good effect that a counterattack in defence of royal supremacy had to be mounted. This riposte – *Roxane* by Desmarets de Saint-Sorlin – was given full support by Richelieu, and there is evidence to suggest that he may actually have commissioned it. Other distinguished writers, such as Guez de Balzac and La Mothe le Vayer, lent their weight to the noble camp, while a more cynical note was sounded by Pascal and the duc de La Rochefoucauld.[14] These two sceptics denied that there was any intrinsic moral worth in inherited *noblesse* but pointed out that, as the populace believed this to be so, it was still a useful concept to invoke in the maintenance of social control. Most of these writers met and debated their conflicting views in the Parisian salons, but the fact that the discussions were conducted in a civilized drawing-room atmosphere did not mean that their beliefs were any less sincerely, even passionately, held. So the nobles were defending the military virtues and the honourable ethic of their order in courtly debate. Less than one hundred years before, Henri II had been killed in a tournament which was devised to celebrate the peace of Câteau-Cambrésis, but such knightly displays, with their unnecessary risks, were now out of fashion. Only the duel and the occasional foray by dwindling bands of aristocratic retainers remained as reminders of a chivalrous and feudal past. Although nobles might be involved from time to time in armed revolts, it was more by verbal plotting at court and by forging powerful alliances, rather than by physical violence, that the ambitious aristocrat sought to demonstrate his influence and to advance his family fortunes. As one of the two main enemies of the *épée*, the *noblesse de robe*, was not a social group which was adept at using force, the old nobility was prepared to accept its choice of weapons – theoretical treatises and the invocation of legal precedents.

The concept of privilege was at the heart of all the disputes between the crown and the social elites, and those which erupted between different strata of society as well. Yet while the royal ministers tried unceasingly to reduce the most obstructive liberties of the people, hoping thereby to increase the access of the treasury to the financial resources of the kingdom, both crown and subjects accepted that privileges were legally established rights. The few ministers who failed to respect this legality, either through misjudgement or because

[11]See: (Guez de Balzac), *Les oeuvres de Monsieur de Balzac* (2 vols, Paris, 1665), François de La Mothe Le Vayer, 'De la noblesse', *Oeuvres* (2 vols, Paris, 1656), vol. II, esp. pp. 191–2, 197–8; Blaise Pascal, 'Trois discours sur la condition des grands (1659/ 60)', *Opuscules et lettres* (Paris, 1955), pp. 164–71, and the expansion of his ideas by Pierre Nicole, *De l'éducation d'un prince* (Paris, 1670), esp. pp. 189–221, 252; the duc de La Rochefoucauld, *Reflexions ou sentences et maximes morales* (Paris, 1671), for example p. 90, no. 239.

wartime expenditure called for drastic action, provoked a counter-productive reaction of which the Frondes were the most spectacular examples. It has already been noted that, although a few individuals might be prepared to surrender one of these liberties in return for substantial compensation, the crown was seldom sufficiently solvent to take advantage of these offers. It was sometimes possible to accord the holder an alternative privilege, which he would find more prestigious and the government would regard as less constraining, but this sort of exchange might provoke a reaction from other families who objected to the enhancement of a rival house. Although this was a way of eroding specific municipal, seigneurial, economic and judicial rights – like that of a town or a noble to collect a toll on a certain road or river route – the privilege which most restricted the government remained intact, the exemption of all nobles from the payment of direct taxes. Because it applied throughout the realm, there was no hope of abolishing it by a policy of reimbursement, and its legality had been confirmed many times over the centuries. As late as 1690 no ministers, not even Colbert, had thought of challenging it. It was a fact of life which had to be accepted. The nobles could be taxed more heavily by increasing indirect levies, always an unpopular step, but only one bold reformer of the finances, Marillac, had suggested, and quickly abandoned, the idea of a permanent wealth tax in the 1620s.

It was only in the 1690s that a tentative move was made in the direction of universal taxation with the institution of the *capitation*, carefully publicized as a temporary wartime expedient which in no way violated traditional noble immunities. At the same time a group of reformers, themselves aristocrats but untypical of their social order, were beginning to question the very principle of exemption from direct taxation solely on the grounds of heredity and rank, although they were also advocating a totally novel kind of role for the aristocracy in government.[15] Yet these writers were eager to curb the lavishness of life in high society, where the funds which it was now proposed to tax were being squandered on mere show. Responsible use of power under the crown, not vain display, should be the hallmark of the successful noble. These fiscal ideas, part of a wider programme for reforming French society and government, were the opening moves in a vigorous debate which was to continue throughout the eighteenth century. When Colbert died in 1683, such a fundamental attack on the very nature of privilege had not been voiced at all. Certainly the views of

[15]For a full discussion of their reforms, see Roger Mettam, *The role of the higher aristocracy in France under Louis XIV, with special reference to the 'faction of the duke of Burgundy' and the provincial governors* (Cambridge PhD thesis, 1967), pp. 67–114.

these later reformers on the central role that the aristocracy should play in politics were worlds away from the early seventeenth-century debate on *noblesse*, *honneur* and *vertu*. That had been concerned with the social and military superiority of the nobility, and there was no suggestion then that the nobility as a whole should claim to be the sole governing class in the state.

During the years when Louis XIII and the young Louis XIV were safely screened from attack by the ostentatious presence in the firing line of the two cardinals, the pamphleteers of the aristocratic cause did not discuss the desirability of, or the alternatives to, monarchy, nor whether any new limitations should be devised which would restrict the power of the crown. The existing and time-honoured restraints on royal authority were enunciated regularly, but in the most general terms. Thus the nobles declared the sanctity of privilege in the same way that the *parlementaires* championed the woolly fundamental laws of France, and the royal publicists stressed the unlimited authority of the sovereign. None of them discussed what should be done in specific situations, when these opposing views might be in open conflict. Even *Le Cid* and *Roxane* were concerned with basic principles and not with precise definitions or actual confrontations, and Corneille would have insisted that he was totally loyal to the king.

If the nobles were quick to combat any advocacy of *la monarchie absolue*, they showed no alarm at a different, but nevertheless prolific and popular, stream of royalist literature. This took the form of numerous pamphlets, too crude to be described as works of political theory, whose aim was to praise the monarch and the new stability which the Bourbon rulers had imposed on the chaos of later Valois France. The writers avoided contentious social issues, and merely included vague assumptions that the king would, of course, respect the liberties of his subjects. Many nobles would have agreed that monarchy was better than anarchy, and they would have supported the pamphleteers of the 1650s who called on the young Louis to become the 'new Henri IV'. Anything would be better than Mazarin!

More worrying for the defenders of aristocracy were the economic theorists, of whom the most celebrated was Antoine de Montchrétien.[16] Their prime purpose was to promote a revival and an expansion of the French economy which, they believed, necessitated the creation of a national economic unit and a self-sufficient kingdom. Such a process required strong action from the centre to override the provincial tolls

[16] *Traicté de la'oeconomie politique*, with introduction and notes by Th. Funck-Brentano, (Paris, 1889). An admirable résumé of Montchrétien's ideas and those of other early seventeenth-century French economic theorists is given by Charles Woolsey Cole, *French mercantilist doctrines before Colbert*, (New York, 1931).

and tariff barriers which were a major disincentive to trade within the country. It was these doctrines which formed the foundation for the only aspect of ministerial reform where the government tried to be truly and drastically innovative, even though it approached its task with caution and persuasion. The nobles treated this enthusiasm for economic growth with the contempt they showed towards all such 'bourgeois' activities, but two arguments did cause them some concern. The first was the suggestion that the crown should sweep away inconvenient local levies, and this raised the wider issue of the inviolability of provincial rights and liberties. The second affected them even more personally. The theorists deplored waste, and therefore condemned expenditure on luxury goods, advocating the promulgation of sumptuary laws which would forbid this extravagance. Yet such displays of wealth were the very stuff of aristocratic life, and each noble adopted the degree of ostentation appropriate to his rank. These economists were calling for a uniformly dowdy society, and that could not be tolerated.

One missing element in the debates of seventeenth-century social and political theorists was the idea of 'social contract', which may at first glance seem surprising in view of its vigorous history during the civil wars of the preceding century. Then there had been talk of popular sovereignty, of breaking the contract with the king and even of tyrannicide, revolutionary ideas which found favour with extremists at both ends of the politico-religious spectrum – the militant Huguenots and the ultra-catholics.[17] The achievement of Henri IV in ending the conflict was sufficient to silence most overt criticism of the king, and at least a religious *modus vivendi* had been created by the Edict of Nantes in 1598. The assassination of the monarch by a fanatical Catholic further reduced support for the ultramontane cause, while many Huguenots also abandoned their extreme republican stance, even during the renewed persecution which preceded the final attack on La Rochelle in 1627–9. Their enemies still accused them of cherishing such seditious notions, but the idea of social contract had lost its dynamism in France. It was for the English to nurture it during the seventeenth century. Even in the 1690s, when Louis XIV became a target for sharp personal criticism, after the decades in which ministers had shielded the crown from blame, the contractual

---

[17]For a summary of these writings, see William Farr Church, *Constitutional thought in sixteenth-century France: a study in the evolution of ideas* (Cambridge, Mass, 1941), although recently some scholars have stressed that many of these writers were not so revolutionary as their detractors at the time and subsequent historians have chosen to claim.

argument was not revived. Great care was also taken to avoid any of the theories which the English had used to justify the murder of their divinely anointed sovereign. Thus, under the first three Bourbons, there was no attack on the actual institution of the monarchy, but only a debate about how the powers of the crown should be exercised. The fiction of ministerial responsibility and royal innocence was more easily preserved because of the aristocratic disdain for financial and commercial matters, and the well-known fact that the king was an aristocrat in his interests, pleasures and choice of companions. As most of the grievances against the central government were fiscal, it seemed very probable that Sully, Richelieu, Marillac, Mazarin and Colbert were the culprits and that the king had not known exactly what was happening. Certainly no great noble would have looked deeply into the ways by which his household financial officials planned to keep the family 'in the black', and he could reasonably expect that the monarch would behave in the same way. As the Bourbons did run their court and their country in much the same way as a noble ran his household and his estates, this was a plausible assumption.

POWER STRUGGLES AT COURT AND IN THE PROVINCES – THE 'KING'S FACTION'

In this competitive world, where political, military, ecclesiastical, ceremonial, institutional and social rewards were keenly sought, families were continually rising and falling. Often their changes of fortune were gradual, but sometimes, usually for financial reasons or because of unexpected mortality, a house might disappear into temporary or permanent oblivion. The history of early modern France reveals some examples of individuals and their kin who spent a very short period at the peak of the social or the political pyramid and then vanished from view, sometimes to re-emerge at a later date, but it also shows that there were some dynasties who, through a mixture of skill and chance, exercised considerable influence for decades or even centuries. From this second group came both the most dangerous enemies of the crown and the men whom the crown enlisted as its most intimate and trusted advisers. When Louis XIV assumed personal power in 1661, he could take comfort from the fact that the high aristocrats who had regularly challenged Richelieu and Mazarin were in considerable disarray after the collapse of the princely Fronde. Their increasing concentration on court politics and conspiracies had lost them much regular provincial support in the first half of the seventeenth century, and their brief period of leadership in the early

1650s was founded on the general hatred of Mazarin rather than on any revival of their own long-term popularity. Moreover their proximity to power had stimulated rivalry within their own ambitious ranks. Yet Louis could also identify a number of powerful families, both aristocratic and ministerial, on whom he could rely, because they had served his father, and in some cases his grandfather too, with consistent loyalty and often with considerable talent. These men were far from uncritical of government policy on occasion, but they voiced their complaints to the ministers in private and did not seek to arouse popular hostility to the regime. Indeed in their public pronouncements they never ceased to advocate greater obedience to the monarch and his policies. Such a group had been assembled through wise judgement and the judicious use of patronage by Henri IV and Louis XIII, so that they were truly the 'king's own faction' in the power struggles of the seventeenth century. As with all such groups, it was not prudent for the members to flaunt this political allegiance too brazenly, especially in the case of provincial governors and bishops when it was essential that they should retain the respect of their province or diocese, and should not appear to be 'king's men' in all things. As most of them did sympathize both with genuine local grievances and with the problems facing the government, this was not a difficult image to present.

It should first be remarked that during the seventeenth century the king himself became less itinerant. Although the court still travelled regularly from place to place until its permanent establishment at Versailles in 1682, it increasingly confined its peregrinations to palaces in the immediate vicinity of the capital or in the city of Paris itself. Visits to provinces and battlefronts became rarer, although some royal ministers went on frequent tours through the regions in order to inspect the workings of government at first hand. *Intendants* and other officials were also to be found throughout the kingdom, sending back information of frequently questionable veracity, but here an important change was taking place. There was a growing tendency for the personnel of the royal administration to be drawn from the north of France, a very small proportion originating in lands to the south of the line from Saint-Malo to Geneva. The almost permanent establishment of the court in the Ile-de-France and the presence of officials whose accents immediately betrayed them as northerners confirmed the belief of the proud and separatist peripheral provinces that the government at the centre was remote and uncaring. It was therefore all the more vital for the crown to find, in these distant areas, some senior agents who were loyal and highly intelligent, but who were natives of the area and came from respected families. Such a local connection was essential in the selection of provincial governors, and useful in the choosing of bishops.

In seeking trustworthy nobles for appointment to provincial governorships, the Bourbon kings had to accept that they were nominating, not just an individual, but a family group which would expect to pass on the office to succeeding generations and to acquire further positions of influence in the area and perhaps at court. It was the hereditary possession of offices which gave the holders an added aura of prestige and respect. A flagrantly unsuitable heir could be offered a socially desirable but administratively less dangerous post in order to prevent him from directly succeeding his father, in which case another close relative would be appointed as the new governor, but the total exclusion of the whole family from the succession was virtually impossible to achieve. An additional consideration was that other dynasties of administrators, of whatever rank, became restive when they saw such royal interference with patrimonial strategy, for it was in everyone's interest that hereditary transmission of offices be preserved.

The advantages and the dangers of powerful hereditary governorships had been clearly demonstrated during the civil wars of the sixteenth century. Most governors had tried, using family connections and their networks of patronage, to keep their *gouvernements* in a state of obedience and calm, some having done so in order to advance, others to obstruct, the policies of the crown. Fortunately for Henri IV, as he sought to establish and then to strengthen his position, some of these key posts were already in the hands of the Bourbon faction, and there were a number of vacancies caused by casualties in battle. The same was true of other high military and civil posts. In a few cases, an aristocratic house could offer no obvious successor, thus enabling the king to insert one of his trusted followers into the hierarchy. Another tactic was to persuade a family whose loyalty was questionable to exchange its governorship for a vacant one elsewhere. If its new province were larger and the post therefore more prestigious, it could not say it had been slighted and indeed its reputation might be much enhanced. The advantage for Henri IV was that a potentially dangerous governor was now administering an area in which his was not the traditional ruling clan and therefore could not command the popular support which often grew up around such local dynasties. Some great noble houses could not be dislodged from their provincial strongholds, but the king did not expect to achieve an immediate and total victory over all these most powerful subjects. He seized opportunities as they arose and Richelieu continued his policy, so that slowly these pivotal administrative positions fell into loyal hands.

Moreover, the kings and ministers never forgot to show continuing favour to those who did support them, because loyalty could dwindle if it were not regularly recharged from above.

It would have been unwise for the crown to remove a governor from a province which was staunchly devoted to him and his family, because the local elites might show their displeasure by obstructing the royal government in other ways. Again fortune favoured the king, because in some areas the traditional ruling houses were losing popularity in the last years of the civil wars. As the prospect of a peaceful France drew closer, and the new monarch gained increasing acceptance, local worthies became disillusioned with the behaviour of many high aristocrats at court and in the provinces. They seemed to be prolonging the disturbances for no other reason than selfish opportunism. Some of those who were moved to other posts were therefore not greatly mourned by those whom they had formerly governed.

If some governors, bishops and senior military officers collectively formed the provincial arm of the 'king's faction', the competition for their posts, as for other high positions, took place at court. Moreover many of the families whom the crown began to trust soon acquired a range of offices in the provinces, at court, in the church, in the army and in diplomacy. A single member might serve in a number of these roles, either successively or sometimes concurrently. The emergence of such newly powerful houses further incensed those aristocrats whom Henri IV had dispossessed of their governorships, and those who had been too strong for him to humiliate. They planned, conspired and waited their chance to raise their families to positions of greater influence. Although many of them could no longer incite the provinces to rebellion on their behalf, that did not make them less dangerous at court, where all that was needed for a victory over rival factions was to persuade the king or a minister to change his mind about their respective merits, or even to murder the minister himself. Many of these plots nearly succeeded under Louis XIII, although few courtiers, apart from the conspirators themselves, thought that these attempted *coups* would usher in a better, and certainly not a more stable, government.

A major cause of this reaction on the part of high aristocracy against the new appointments made by Henri IV and Louis XIII was that men of lesser social standing were being given posts which were traditionally the preserve of the upper stratum of the nobility. The two kings knew that governors and other such senior officials had to be of high rank, but they sometimes selected a man of inferior status who had served them well in another role and then conferred a substantial noble title upon him in order that he should now have the social status appropriate to his new post. Louis XIV, with his greater insistence on the preservation of a strict hierarchy, did not continue this practice. When he needed to fill a vacant governorship, he chose a man who had possessed ducal rank for some time or had a suitably ancient lineage, so that he was already socially qualified for the office and no one could object to him on the grounds that he was a parvenu.

As the century progressed, new ruses were devised for replacing senior officials of dubious loyalty with men from the royal circle of trusted advisers. One such method was, on the death of a provincial governor, to appoint a member of the royal family as his successor. The family of the deceased found it difficult to resist such a decision, especially as they would have been offered a prestigious post at court in compensation. A loyal noble from another house would then be given the task of running the province on behalf of the new governor, who might well be a child or a dowager queen, and who would remain at court, performing ceremonial duties. The noble would be given the title of *lieutenant-général*, but would be *de facto* governor. The effective power had therefore been transferred from one family to another, but without administering a social snub to the initial holder. The post of *lieutenant-général* might itself become hereditary, as with the ducs de Noailles in Languedoc, though the fictional aspect of this kind of transaction is underlined by the fact that the ministers, in their private correspondence, frequently referred to the Noailles as 'the governor'.[18]

Despite the efforts of Henri IV and Louis XIII, not all governorships were in friendly hands when Louis XIV became an adult ruler. Most dangerous was that of Normandy, where the duc de Longueville, now revealed as a leading *frondeur*, held sway. Mazarin and Louis dared not dispossess him of his post, for this would have sent tremors of alarm through the whole nobility at a time when the crown was eager to calm the kingdom after the turmoil of the Frondes. Accordingly a compromise was reached whereby the king promised to recognize the Longueville family, a bastard line of the house of Valois, as princes of the blood royal, thus fulfilling a similar commitment which had been made, but never effected, by Charles IX. In return the duke, who was still to retain his governorship, would allow his powers in Normandy to be exercised by a *commandant-du-roi*, the duc de Montausier, a man who had proved his loyalty and his ability as a provincial administrator in Saintonge and the Angoumois during the

---

[18]See, for example, the abbé Millot, *Mémoires politiques et militaires . . . composés sur les pièces originales recueillies par Adrien-Maurice, duc de Noailles, maréchal de France & ministre d'état* (6 vols, Lausanne/Yverdon, 1778), vol. I, pp. 8–9.

Frondes. Louis showed his good intentions by creating a *duché-pairie* for the Longueville, who were *ducs non pairs*, in 1656, and the duke responded by relinquishing his role in his *gouvernement*. Yet Louis never found time to declare them to be princes of the blood, and the duke must have been enraged when he discovered that, in a subsequent *Etat de la France*,[19] the *commandant* was given precedence over the governor, which never happened when a *lieutenant-général* was the *de facto* administrator of a province. By this time Longueville and his family had been detached from Normandy for too long, and there was no question of their raising support there. The only course for them was to join the faction struggle at court, and see if any prizes could be obtained.

The historian who seeks to discover which aristocrats belonged to the intimate circle of close advisers to Louis XIV will have little difficulty in identifying those who also held office as governors or *lieutenants-généraux*. Apart from evidence concerning the actual circumstances of their appointment to these posts, their long sojourns in the provinces caused them to write regularly and frankly to the king or to his ministers, often continuing a discussion which had begun, unrecorded, in verbal exchanges at court. The archives contain both sides of many such collections of correspondence.[20] More elusive are the nobles who spent most of their time in personal attendance on their sovereign, because much of their conversation with the monarch and with his councillors took place behind closed doors, or out of earshot during promenades in the gardens, and no written record was kept. Nor was possession of a particular ceremonial office a reliable guide to the influence of the holder in the innermost group around the king. The elaboration of ceremony and etiquette under Louis XIV was undoubtedly part of his deliberate plan to keep the various noble factions in a state of equilibrium, but he had no intention of announcing who were his closest advisers. He would honour them in public because of their rank or their known services to the crown, but he did not wish openly to record his debt to them as counsellors.

As Louis was determined to preserve the hierarchy and to discourage social mobility, he could not reward all of his secret advisers by bestowing high noble titles upon them. Some of them were socially unqualified for such honours. To have ignored this fact would

[19]The *Etats de la France* were the official published lists of all those who held positions in the social and institutional hierarchies.

[20]Most extant letters from the governors to Colbert have been preserved in the 'Mélanges Colbert' collection of the Bibliothèque nationale, for which vast series there is a detailed printed index. Many examples of this correspondence are discussed in Mettam, *The role of the higher aristocracy*, pp. 209–343.

have been both to alienate other courtiers and to reveal too much about the realities of power close to the throne. Thus one of the clerics who was nearest to him, Bossuet, had to remain bishop of Meaux, because his relatively humble social background made it unthinkable that he should be raised to one of the great archiepiscopal sees. The son of a secretary of state could become a *marquis*, but a higher title was out of the question. In fact most of the courtiers who formed the small group which enjoyed the complete confidence of the king were already members of the high aristocracy. They held 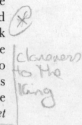 important ceremonial posts, but these were appropriate to their rank and would have raised no social disquiet among other members of the court. Thus, although the offices held by an individual gave a guide to his social standing, they did not give any clear indication of his influence with the monarch. A minor bishop might be close to the king, but an archbishop of distinguished family might not. Some *ducs et pairs* were royal confidants, but others were not.

Historians who are obsessed with the formal institutional structure, or who look only for the rise of 'new men' like the secretaries of state, have therefore failed to notice that some senior aristocrats were among the close advisers of the king. Certainly their informal and private contacts with their royal master were very different from the more overt discussions of Louis and his ministers. There the content was still secret, but at least the court knew when they were taking place. A monarch could not fraternize socially with members of the ministerial cadre. He either met them in the formality of the council, or summoned them individually, in which case the courtiers could see the secretaries of state scurrying towards the royal apartments with their files of papers. No one knew how momentous was the substance of conversations between the king and his aristocratic friends, and even the ministers were not always told of everything that was said, but perceptive courtiers had a shrewd idea of where Louis regularly turned for advice. By studying their letters and memoirs, a patient researcher can discover some of the hidden power structures which lay behind the façade of courtly life. Such documents can never be taken at face value, because the writers were often partial and sometimes vindictive, but a wide-ranging examination of many collections penned by different courtiers does yield up more reliable information. Certain nobles are repeatedly identified as men of great influence, whether as confidants of the king or as leading subversives in court intrigues, and these assertions become even more probable when they are uttered by both admirers and opponents. Slowly more corroborative evidence can be gathered, and the factions of which these individuals formed a part can be revealed. There is no shortage of such documentation in public and private archives, and yet it is only recently that scholars have devoted serious attention to it. Even today most of them prefer the more comprehensive and superficially more reliable documents of the bureaucracy and the provinces. Unfortunately, the historian who has not understood the nature of power at the centre will only partly comprehend the workings of his chosen bureaucratic and local institutions. He will see the formal structure, but may miss the pressures, patronage and influence which operated behind the scenes.

The surest sign that a courtier belonged to the inner circle of royal counsellors is to be found in the willingness of Louis XIV to waive a principle which was normally fundamental to his social policy. Determined to prevent marriages between *robe* and *épée*, and even between high and lower sword nobles, the king positively encouraged the intermarriage of ministerial houses with some old aristocratic families, he and the queen often consenting to be godparents to the offspring of these liaisons. The rest of the court regarded these arrangements as *mésalliances* of the worst kind, but for Louis they were part of a deliberate attempt to create tightly knit groups of advisers, bound together both socially and politically. Then it would be in their best personal and family interests to show solidarity with each other and to work together, although Louis took care to ensure that there was more than one such grouping in order to prevent a single faction from attaining total dominance of policy-making. Moreover, these marriages ensured that the descendants of a minister would, by the second generation, be high nobles in their own right, compensating the ministerial family for the persistent refusal of the king to elevate the ministers themselves into the peerage. A few examples will serve to illustrate this royal strategy. The duc de Beauvillier, the only royal confidant who was both a *duc et pair* by birth and was also accorded the title of *ministre*, married one daughter of Colbert. Her sister became the wife of the duc de Chevreuse, who was also held in high regard as an adviser by the king, was the direct descendant of the duc de Luynes – the minister of Louis XIII – and was also the nephew of the duc de Chaulnes, the powerful governor of Brittany. Indeed the monarch made it plain in a letter to Chaulnes that the marriage was partly a recompense for all these services, as well as a sign of his current esteem for the bridegroom.[21] Yet these trusted nobles were not merely pawns in the hands of the king, and some were reluctant to link their fortunes with only one ministerial faction lest that minister should subsequently displease his royal master. Thus the ducal house of d'Estrées married

[21]Louis XIV, *Oeuvres*, eds P. A. Grouvelle and P. H. de Grimoard (6 vols, Paris, 1806), vol. V, pp. 402–3.

into three such clans, the Colbert, the Le Tellier and the Lionne, and also into another much favoured aristocractic dynasty, the Noailles. The ducs de Noailles, themselves both counsellors at court and also governors and *lieutenants-généraux* respectively in the troublesome frontier provinces of Roussillon and Languedoc, welcomed a link with the d'Estrées and made further marriages with the ducal family of Gramont and with the Le Tellier, all three of which were represented in this inner circle around the king. Louis continued to honour the Noailles by arranging two matches which the court knew to be a sign of his highest approbation – one with his beloved illegitimate son, the comte de Toulouse, the other with a niece of Madame de Maintenon, a girl for whom he felt almost paternal affection. With such a spectacularly expanding genealogy, it is not surprising that the Noailles acquired additional prestigious and influential positions, as when the brother of the second duke became bishop and ecclesiastical peer of Laon and later archbishop of Paris.

Other noble houses singled out for special royal trust and favour included the Villeroy, governors of Lyon since the reign of Henri IV and now given added governmental and military responsibilities, the Rouannais-La Feuillade who excelled as governors of Dauphiné, and the d'Aumont who governed the strategically vital area around Boulogne. The governors of another sensitive frontier region, Béarn, were the ducs de Gramont, and the king positively approved of the marriage which linked them to the Noailles, who were in charge of the eastern end of the same Pyrenean mountain chain. Four of these dukes – Beauvillier, a Noailles and two Villeroy – received one of the highest royal accolades when they were appointed *gouverneurs* in a very different sense, being made responsible for educating the younger members of the direct Bourbon line. The elder Villeroy held this position when Louis XIV was himself a child, the younger subsequently taking charge of the young Louis XV. Beauvillier was responsible for all three grandsons of Louis XIV, any of whom might have become king in these days of capricious mortality, while the task of Noailles was to prepare the duchesse de Bourgogne for the position of queen which death was ultimately to deny her. It was vital to instil the kingly virtues into future sovereigns, but also to encourage sentiments of unwavering loyalty in impressionable young princes of the blood lest they follow the rebellious example set by some of their predecessors. As a further precaution Louis XIV did not permit his favoured aristocrats to marry into the ranks of the legitimate Bourbon princes. This was not to avert any likely threat to his own power, but was a preparation for a possible regency or succession crisis in the future. Then the princes would doubtless play their usual disruptive role, and it was undesirable that they should be closely associated with noble houses which had enormous influence in particular provinces. Such anticipation of possible disaster, a major preoccupation for the head of any aristocratic house as well as for the monarchy, seemed rather over-cautious during the personal rule of Louis XIV. After the twenty-eight worrying years in which Louis XIII had no direct heir, the supporters of the crown could rejoice that the new king had sired a healthy progeny and assured a stable succession. Suddenly, in a few death-dominated months during 1711 and 1712, the confidence evaporated and a sickly two-year-old became the heir to his great-grandfather. A regency would almost inevitably follow, because the king was in the seventieth year of his reign and must surely die before the dauphin reached the age of majority. If this infant were also to die, there would be a major succession crisis as well. Monarchy was an impressive superstructure on the hull of the state, but it was remarkably vulnerable to the winds of chance.

The inner circle of aristocrats, and the ministerial families to whom they were more and more closely tied by marriage, were at the very centre of policy-making under Louis XIV and spearheaded his attempts to make the authority of the crown more effective throughout the kingdom. The ministers spent most of their time at court, working daily with the king. The careers of the nobles were more varied. The duc de Chevreuse was primarily a courtier. The duc de Villeroy also spent much of his time in the immediate entourage of the monarch, while his very able brother, the archbishop of Lyon, carried out his duties as governor of the Lyonnais. The duc de Chaulnes, in addition to ruling Brittany so successfully, was also an effective military commander and a subtle diplomat. He, together with a fellow *duc et pair*, d'Estrées, proved extremely skilful in that most difficult area of foreign affairs, the relations of France with the Holy See. Many other examples could be given, all proving that during the personal rule of Louis XIV the same ministerial and noble surnames recurred frequently in these positions of real power.[22]

Untypically for men of their high social background, many of these aristocratic advisers shared the expansionist economic aims of Colbert, and as provincial governors were prepared to devote much detailed attention to the commercial and industrial life of their *gouvernements*. Often their personal relations with the ministers seem to have been extremely cordial and close, despite the gulf between their respective social origins. This amity may have been the affability of

[22]For an analysis of the influence of all the individual peerage families, see Mettam, *The role of the higher aristocracy*, pp. 132–85.

business partners, rather than the warmth of true friends, even though some of their houses were now more closely linked by marriages, but there is at least plenty of evidence that the whole group functioned as an effective governing clique. It may therefore seem surprising that some of these favoured nobles were also members of the so-called 'faction of the duc de Bourgogne', from which circle originated some of the sharpest criticisms of Louis XIV in the last decades of the reign, penned by Fénelon, Saint-Simon and their friends. In fact this apparently unholy alliance of both trusted advisers and virulent critics is largely a consequence of distortions perpetrated by the historians of 'absolutism'.

It must first be said that Saint-Simon was indeed bitter that he had been given no position of trust in the government, and that can be seen in a number of his writings. Yet historians have erred in their frequently stated assumption that the king was fiercely antipathetic towards this group of critics. Certainly some of their pronouncements were unflattering to the sovereign, but Louis himself regretted some of his earlier decisions, the consequences of which were now being reaped in these terrible years of war and hardship. Nor have historians been fair in describing the Bourgogne circle as reactionary aristocrats who advocated the resuscitation of the feudal past, because a detailed study of their ideas reveals that some were very similar to current ministerial thinking and others anticipated the theories of the Enlightenment. The nobility was undoubtedly still a potent force in French society, and the regret of these reformers was that most members of the Second Estate continued to cherish outdated beliefs and social values. They proposed a more constructive role for the *noblesse* in the running of the state, but it was unfortunately not a role which the average noble wished to play. These ideas will be discussed in a later chapter, but the important point for the present argument is that this was not, as most historians have assumed, merely a group of embittered and powerless thinkers, playing no part in the current political life of France. It was a circle of friends which contained not only writers, but also some men at the very centre of power who agreed with this proposed programme of reforms and sought to put some of them into practice. Among them were the ducs de Beauvillier, de Chevreuse and de Noailles, who were members of this reforming group at the same time as they were at the height of their influence as royal advisers. These men had little time to write extended works themselves, leaving that task to friends like Saint-Simon in his enforced idleness, but one trenchant series of proposals by Fénelon is headed 'Plans de gouvernement concertés avec le duc de Chevreuse pour être proposés au duc de Bourgogne', and it was compiled at Chaulnes, the country house of the governor of

Brittany.[23] Once again we see some of the now familiar aristocratic names. Louis XIV therefore felt a variety of emotions towards the Bourgogne circle. They were educating the future king of France, and they counterbalanced the circle around the dauphin. Moreover, in these decades of war and misery, Louis confided more than once to his close advisers that a different kind of education might have prevented him from making some of the mistakes that he now regretted. Thus even when their criticisms were really stinging, the king did not force these writers to break off their close contacts with their protégé, and Fénelon from his distant diocese of Cambrai, to which he had been sent for very different reasons, kept up his correspondence with the prince who was destined never to become the king of France.

The trusted aristocratic advisers of the king were often given one of the ceremonial posts at the summit of the court hierarchy. Their duties would bring them into regular contact with the monarch, often in private, when he would be able to discuss matters of great importance with them without alerting other courtiers. For example, the duc d'Aumont, the effective governor of Boulogne and a regular counsellor on policy-making, was also *premier gentilhomme de la chambre du roi*, a position which involved constant close attendance on the king. Yet, like most other high officers of the inner household, d'Aumont shared his tasks with three other dukes, the four serving in rotation, a device which ensured that the king came into close contact with a larger group of nobles, whether he trusted, mistrusted or simply wished to reward them. Periods of duty might be as little as three months or as long as a year, after which the next name on the rota took over. Thus a governor had plenty of opportunities to visit and administer his province, as well as a lengthy spell in the immediate royal entourage. At the end of the 1660s, the four *premiers gentilshommes* were the ducs d'Aumont, de Créquy, de Gêvres and de Saint-Aignan, and of these only the first was a true confidant of Louis XIV. The rest were all being rewarded for past services, civil or military, performed by themselves or by their families.

An analysis of the personnel in other senior courtly positions reveals the same variety of reasons for these appointments. Some were given to members of the inner circle of advisers, others were for past or present services in the army or in administration, a few were bestowed simply because they had been in specific families for many years, and yet another group went to men whom the king mistrusted or wished to win over to his cause. A casual observer might assume that the

---

[23]Printed in François de Pons de Salignac de La Motte Fénelon, *Ecrits et lettres politiques*, ed. Charles Urbain (Paris, 1920, reprinted Geneva, 1981), pp. 92–124.

creation of a new high office, that of *grand-maître de la garderobe*, for the duc de La Rochefoucauld in 1669, and his elevation after a decade to the post of *grand veneur de France*, which in the past had been occupied by princes of either French or foreign royal blood, were marks of the greatest royal esteem. Furthermore, he was a provincial governor and married his son to the daughter of the war minister, Louvois. The ancestors of the duke had served earlier French monarchs and regents, and the family was regarded by many contemporaries as perhaps the most prestigious non-royal and non-foreign noble house in the kingdom. Yet the king did not trust some of its current members. He thought that they had shown dubious loyalty during the Frondes, and continued to exhibit unsuitable religious, possibly even Jansenist, tendencies. Therefore he offered the duke lofty ceremonial positions at court which were of such prestige that he could not refuse them. The La Rochefoucauld claimed to be princes in their own right, through their inheritance of the principality of Marcillac, but the French kings had not recognised them as *princes étrangers*, with precedence over the native peerage. Louis also refused to do so but he did appoint the duke to an office normally reserved for princely houses, and one which was near the top of the courtly hierarchy. La Rochefoucauld thus found himself among princes through the seniority of his post, even though he was not able to be there on grounds of birth. The king ensured that, first as *grand-maître de la garderobe* and then as *grand veneur*, the duke did not share his position with other courtiers, serving in rotation. He was the sole holder, and his duties therefore kept him permanently in attendance on his master. Louis could keep a close watch on him, and the duke could hope that, if he gave devoted service, it might one day bring his family the recognition as princes in their own right which he so much desired. Having no alternative but to pursue these ambitions at court, his provincial governorship effectively became a sinecure and he no longer wielded significant influence in his *gouvernement*. His marriage with a member of the Le Tellier family led to more royal patronage but to no posts of political importance. The duke was a very reluctant partner to this liaison with a mere ministerial house, but he was persuaded to agree by Louis XIV who wished to give Le Tellier and Louvois some socially desirable recompense after rejecting their candidate for the secretaryship of state for foreign affairs and preferring that of Colbert.

The list of those who held high court offices or provincial governorships – all of them illustrious nobles, under the hierarchically minded Louis XIV – provides a starting point for the historian of patronage and no more than that. The name of every member in the circle of royal confidants, provided that his rank was sufficiently elevated, appears in this table of dignitaries, some of whom held a number of offices simultaneously. Conversely, others on the same list, whether they had a single post or a plurality, had no influence on policy-making, although some of them were held in high enough regard by the king for him to grant their requests that pensions and posts which carried financial benefits or social prestige be given to themselves, their relatives and their clients. Politically sensitive offices were a very different matter, and went only to the chosen few.

By making a series of interrelated investigations – estimating the actual power associated with each office, assessing the influence which did or did not accrue from strategic marriages, examining correspondence and memoirs, evaluating gossip – the historian can slowly identify the aristocratic members of the 'king's own faction'. In contrast the naming of ministers in this inner circle requires no such complex sleuthing. Among the nobility prestige might not be accompanied by real power or influence, but in the ministeriat they were inseparable qualities. The secretaries of state had been raised to their position of pre-eminence solely because of their political talents, which had usually been brought to the notice of the king by another minister. They could claim no rightful social place in the upper echelons of the court, although their political influence compensated for their lack of breeding. Yet their period of office might be short-lived, and they therefore busied themselves with obtaining offices for their relatives, the arrangement of socially advantageous marriages and the acquisition of clients and patrons. In this strictly hierarchical society, the ministers were unique in that they advanced the fortunes of their families solely through their personal power and their favour with the king, without reference to the usual criteria of rank, antiquity, cumulative past service to the crown and hereditary claims to office. In every way therefore, their detractors saw them as parvenus.

Whatever the motives of Louis XIV in permitting marriages between trusted ministerial and aristocratic families, the ministers themselves welcomed them for both social and political reasons. Such liaisons could bring extraordinary upward mobility, as with the Colbert, where the father of the celebrated Jean-Baptiste was only a middle-ranking administrator and yet there were three duchesses among his grandchildren.[24] For this minister these marriages had two other important purposes. His new sons-in-law came from houses

[21] Only two of the three marriages were into ducal houses of great influence. The third was to the Mortemart family, also ducal and socially prestigious, but not favoured with the close confidence of the king. Indeed the Mortemart hoped that Colbert might help them to remedy this situation — see Mettam, *The role of the higher aristocracy*, pp. 161–3.

which were close to the king, and he could therefore hope to have some supporters in this inner circle if ever his royal master began to be disenchanted with his services. Moreover Beauvillier, Chevreuse and the uncle of the latter, Chaulnes, were sincerely trying to pursue the same policies as himself for the revival of the economy and the restoration of the royal finances. These matches were therefore desirable for personal, family and political reasons.

Despite their considerable power and their attempts to build themselves into secure networks of patronage, many ministers were brusquely and dramatically dismissed by the seventeenth-century Bourbons or by the regents ruling on their behalf. Sully, Marillac and Foucquet were all disgraced, while La Vieuville was arrested in 1624 and re-emerged only in 1651. Others found that their ambitions were curtailed by the frequent changes in the machinery of ministerial government, some of which were drastic. After the death of Mazarin, there was to be no *premier ministre,* and the arrest of Foucquet ended the long line of *surintendants des finances.* Councils were remodelled, suppressed or created, usually at the wish of the king or his advisers, but occasionally, in times of crisis, because of princely pressure. Most of the men who sat on these policy-making conciliar bodies were indeed loyal and devoted servants of the king, and those who fell from favour usually did so because of rivalries within the ranks of the ministeriat. Sometimes their disgrace followed from a clash of personalities, but more often from genuine disagreements about policy. Discussion of alternative courses of action was welcomed by the king, provided that it took place behind the closed doors of the council chamber and that a united front could then be presented to the country at large. When a minister made his reservations more widely known and began to canvass outside support, it was time for him, or his opponents, to be removed from office. Sometimes a secretary of state, or even a *premier ministre,* was so closely associated with a particular policy that he had to sustain it, even when a change of heart might have been more prudent. His own reputation, the interests of those who depended on him and the need to foil his rivals left him no alternative but to persist and pray for success in the face of increasingly unfavourable omens. Backing down would bring him as much discredit as ultimately failing to achieve his aims. In its public face, the conciliar government of the first three Bourbons rarely gave any hint of such disputes over policy. It usually seemed to be both united and resolute, and this appearance of harmony, together with the ability of the crown to restructure its councils and dismiss its ministers at will, has led unwary historians of absolutism to assume that the king could similarly impose his wishes on the realm at large.

In fact, as the ministers knew, it was so difficult to persuade the hereditary bureaucracy to implement many government policies that it was vital for the immediate circle of royal councillors to be of one mind in proposing them.

Although some of these close advisers fell from grace, leaving only the wide range of offices and marriages they had obtained for their relatives as a reminder of their former influence, others belonged to veritable dynasties of ministers which held office at the centre over many generations. The Phélypeaux family provided secretaries of state from Henri IV to Louis XVI, most of whom are known to historians by the seigneurial or lower noble titles they acquired – La Vrillière, Pontchartrain, Châteauneuf, Saint-Florentin and Maurepas. Moreover, within each generation, a minister would not only seek to promote his relatives to socially prestigious positions, but would also select the more trustworthy among them for important governmental tasks. Thus, under Colbert, the posts of *intendant* in Alsace, *intendant* of the navy at Rochefort, bishop of Auxerre and many others were in Colbertian hands. Not that these grants of office were invitations to relax in sinecures, because the minister demanded a higher degree of service from members of his family than he could reasonably expect from his other appointees. Yet there is another factor to be noticed here, if the historian is not to fall prey to anachronism. It is tempting, at first glance, to conclude that a secretary of state placed many of his relatives and clients within his own department in order to ensure that his subordinates would be of his own faction and would therefore be more loyal. Certainly most of the *intendants de l'armée* and *commissaires de guerre* came from the Le Tellier clientele during the early personal rule of Louis XIV. Nevertheless an examination of ministerial patronage over a longer period suggests a different explanation. A relatively new minister placed his clients in his own department because he had no other form of patronage at his disposal. As he grew in royal favour he was able to procure higher positions for them, whether civil, military or ecclesiastical. Thus, although it was useful to have a trusted client in a key post, the majority of appointments represented, not a decision by a minister to pack his department with friends, but the highest positions that he could obtain at that moment for his dependants and kinsmen.[25]

If Louis XIV was the most successful of the Bourbon monarchs in maintaining an equilibrium among aristocratic court factions and among the provincial elites, he was equally skilful in preserving a

[25] This point is well demonstrated on a number of occasions in André Corvisier, *Louvois* (Paris, 1983).

balance within the ranks of the ministeriat. He permitted no *premier ministre* to fill the councils with his own *créatures*, as had happened in the past, and he was careful to show no marked preference for any one ministerial group. His two successors would be more easily swayed, first in favour of one, then of another, cabal, and that would encourage a dangerously competitive spirit in the corridors of power. The Colbert and Le Tellier families, and to a lesser extent the Phélypeaux, undoubtedly dominated the councils during the personal rule of Louis XIV, although there were secretaries of state who came from other clans and there was the small circle of trusted aristocratic advisers as well. Yet Colbert, Le Tellier and Louvois quickly realized that the king would never allow one single family to dominate the central government. On the death of Lionne in 1671, the Le Tellier hoped that their client, Courtin, would take over the portfolio for foreign affairs. The king appointed Pomponne instead, a man of neither clan. When he was dismissed in 1679, Le Tellier had recently become chancellor and Louvois was still war minister, and father and son hoped once more to secure the appointment of Courtin. Louis appointed Colbert de Croissy instead, to maintain the balance. After the death of Jean-Baptiste Colbert in 1683, the Louvois faction seemed briefly to be triumphant, with only Croissy representing the opposing side in the *conseil du roi*. The balance was redressed in 1689 when the son of Jean-Baptiste, the marquis de Seignelay, was admitted to the council, having been a secretary of state for some years, and Pontchartrain, from the Phélypeaux clan, became *contrôleur-général des finances*. Yet neither the family interests nor the policies of Colbert were neglected in the years 1683–9, as the imbalance in the *conseil* seems to imply, because they had two effective champions in the aristocratic inner circle – the ducs de Beauvillier and de Chevreuse, the sons-in-law of the deceased minister. It must be added that many past historians have exaggerated the hostility between the Colbert and Le Tellier families. Certainly each clique was trying to extend its influence, in these days when dynastic rivalry was everywhere. But many of their disagreements resulted from genuine arguments about policy, often arising because their members held different government portfolios. Colbert was trying to fill the coffers of the treasury in order to reform the internal administration, and Louvois was demanding more and more of these precious resources so as to enlarge the army and pursue a satisfactory foreign policy. Each therefore found that the other was undermining his political strategy.

The post of secretary of state was a venal office, but, although the king could seldom designate the purchaser of an office in the wider bureaucracy, here at court he could demand that a secretary should now vacate his post and sell it to the chosen royal candidate. Very rarely did Louis XIV make a major misjudgement when appointing or dismissing ministers, and in the two most celebrated cases, the arrest of Foucquet in 1661 and the disgracing of Pomponne in 1679, his decision was made on the basis of extremely dubious advice from other close counsellors. The prospect of Foucquet becoming the successor to Mazarin dismayed many ambitious men in governmental circles, and they determined that it should not come to pass, while in 1679 Colbert and Louvois worked together to dislodge Pomponne, each hoping that his own candidate, respectively Croissy and Courtin, would be chosen. Louis acknowledged that this second dismissal had been a grievous mistake when he restored Pomponne to the foreign ministry in the 1690s. Only the war minister, Barbézieux, who succeeded his father Louvois in 1691, was an almost unmitigated disaster. The king did not want to dismiss him because of the supreme service which his father had rendered to the crown, but he often merely ignored his advice and wrote instead directly to men like the duc de Noailles, who were near to the battlefronts, and preferred their counsel to that of his own secretary of state.

The most thorny problem for the historian is to assess the role of Louis XIV himself in the formulation of policy. The secrecy surrounding the discussions at the *conseil*, the privacy of royal conversations with individual ministers or aristocratic friends, the paucity of ministerial memoirs and the fact that those which do survive were often written with the benefit of hindsight or with a desire for self-justification – all these factors mask the precise role played by the king. Yet it is known that on many occasions the ministers were not unanimous in the advice they offered, and at such times Louis could choose which course he would follow. As he made plain in a celebrated letter to Colbert in April 1671, which seems to be a very rare rebuke to this most loyal servant, 'do not take the risk of angering me again, because, when I have listened to the advice of you and your colleagues, and have made my decision on the course to be followed, I do not wish that subject to be raised again. . . . After I have given my judgement, I do not wish to hear a single complaint'.[26] Although Louis might stand on his royal dignity in this way, it was nevertheless virtually impossible for him to obtain a totally independent evaluation of the counsel given to him by his ministers and advisers. He could not discuss affairs of state outside his most trusted circle of counsellors, and even his aristocratic friends would usually be in accord with the

[26]Champollion Figeac, M. (ed.), *Documents historiques inédits* (4 vols, Paris, 1841–8), vol. II, p. 519.

viewpoint of some of his ministers. If they were all united on a single plan of action, the king had no room at all in which to exercise his own judgement. Very seldom does he seem to have been at odds with almost all his advisers, and then the dispute was almost always about the very nature of kingship. Such a situation arose over the decision to recognize the Stuart pretender as James III of England. To anyone with political sense, including Louis himself, this was unwise, but how could one divinely anointed Catholic king disown the legitimate heir of another, a brother monarch? There is also evidence to suggest that, especially in the later years of the reign, Louis took care to reject some of the advice given to him by each minister, so as to underline the point that he was the master. In order to counter this tendency, the wily Colbert de Torcy tried to ensure that the ministers resolved their differences before the meetings of the council, so that the king was given very little opportunity to play off one adviser against another.[27]

There was one other influence at work behind the scenes at court which is very difficult for the historian to evaluate, that of Madame de Maintenon. Nor could the courtiers be sure of her precise role, which seemed to be very different from that of former royal mistresses. They knew that it was in his amorous relations with beautiful women that the king most clearly showed himself to be human and fallible. Yet, although he had showered ceremonial and social honours on their relatives and clients, he had not allowed them or their cliques to invade the domain of high politics. Once their feminine charms had faded or they had displeased him in other ways, he continued to ensure that their families were provided for, financially and socially. Moreover many of their clients had been careful not to commit themselves totally to the patronage of a single mistress, being aware that her complete dependence on the royal whim made her even more insecure than a minister. Louis also seemed to lack prudence in the affection he showed towards his illegitimate children, the product of these liaisons, and he bestowed upon them positions of the highest prestige. His last gift to them, the right of succession to the French throne after the other male heirs of his own body, should not be included in this list of prodigality, at least not without qualification. It undoubtedly infuriated the nobility, especially the d'Orléans and the Condé who saw the throne receding from them, but for the king it was a desperate attempt to strengthen the Bourbon succession after the tragic deaths of two successive dauphins in 1711 and 1712.

[27]See John C. Rule, 'Colbert de Torcy, an emergent bureaucracy, and the formulation of French foreign policy, 1698–1715', in Ragnhild Hatton (ed.), *Louis XIV and Europe* (London, 1976), pp. 261–88.

Against the background of the 1660s and 1670s, when the amorous young monarch had celebrated each new love by holding fêtes and bestowing lavish gifts on her, the austere Madame de Maintenon could not seem other than an enigmatic figure. She was, and she remained, a simple *marquise*, because Louis had no wish to provoke a repetition of the social outrage which had accompanied his creation of the duchy of Vaujours for an earlier mistress, Louise de La Vallière. Yet it was rumoured that the king had married her in secret, although she certainly did not become queen. The questions about her were endless. The monarch was now more pious, and her devotion to the faith was well known. Had she engineered or merely encouraged this revival of royal devotion? Was she in league with the Jesuits? Had she played a major part in the increased persecution of the Huguenots? Was she a significant influence in fostering the *rapprochement* of France and Rome in the 1690s? No one knew, but when her period of favour extended from years into decades she was considered by many to be a very useful channel through which to petition the king for favours. As the aging Louis spent more and more time in her apartments, and as he held his discussions with his ministers and advisers there, within her hearing, it was obvious that she was privy to much state business, even though she always protested that she could not speak to the king about such matters. It is nevertheless undeniable that many of the favoured royal counsellors during the last years of the reign were also to be counted among her own personal friends. The duc de Noailles, whose son had married her niece, his brother, who became archbishop of Paris, the duc de Beauvillier and the finance minister, Chamillart, were of this company.

If the king had to take on trust much of the advice which he received from his ministers and aristocratic friends, they in turn were heavily dependent on the reports of *intendants* and other provincial agents whose veracity they could not check. Even when the royal advisers had agreed on a policy, they then faced the problem of persuading the hereditary bureaucracy and the provincial elites to implement and accept it. Far from being a place where, as older historians would have it, everything depended on the king, French society was rather a complex network of interdependent relationships. The monarch needed his courtiers as much as they had need of him. Certainly he had something of value to offer almost every social group, but it was impossible to please everyone at once. Moreover the options open to the central government in 1661, the year when Louis decided to rule personally, were further limited because of experience gained under, and the legacy bequeathed by, the two preceding ministries, as well as the memory of the Frondes. Heavy-handed attempts at centralization were out of the question. Therefore, behind an overt policy of caution and respect for both privilege and legality, the young monarch played off the various groups at the centre and in the localities, one against another, and at the same time laboured to build up an effective network of royal clients. These men, placed in high administrative positions, would at least promote the royal cause at court and in the provinces, even if they could not ensure that the will of the sovereign would always be obeyed. The creation of such a clientele was of necessity a slow process because it depended on offices falling vacant, either because the holder had died and his family had been persuaded to waive their claim to hereditary succession or because he had accepted the offer of a socially more prestigious post. Fortunately for Louis XIV, both Henri IV and Richelieu had begun to assemble this royal 'faction', and he was therefore able to continue along the same path. If past historians have eagerly stressed the modernity of Colbertian France, in this respect at least the crown was employing the oldest weapons of all – the ties of family, patrimony, clientage and patronage, together with the lure of higher offices, titles and rank.

The present chapter has considered the attitudes and priorities of seventeenth-century society, and some of the ways by which the crown hoped to assert itself over the kingdom. The crucial problem in 1661 was to devise means of keeping the various social groups in a state of balance. In order to understand the dilemmas facing the royal advisers at the beginning of the personal rule, it is essential to examine in some detail the issues which had united or divided Frenchmen in the first sixty years of the century. Such an investigation will also reveal whether the Frondes were the consequence of an extraordinary coincidence of circumstances which was never likely to recur, or whether, as the ministers of the late 1650s feared, a recurrence was always possible.

3

Social and Political Tensions, 1610–1661

WAR AND PEACE

In an examination of the tensions within seventeenth-century French society, whether between the crown and its subjects or among the various local elites, war emerges as a principal cause. A short period of hostilities, like the War of Devolution in 1667–8, might create few problems and even be welcomed by some Frenchmen, but the longer struggles – against the Dutch in 1672–9, and against most of Europe in 1688–97 and in 1702–13 – brought almost total disaster to both the government and the kingdom. Yet, if the prolongation of international conflict had been a factor of considerable importance in the outbreak and the course of the Frondes, there was no such general insurrection during the last two foreign wars of Louis XIV. Most historians have been reluctant to offer any sustained explanation for this absence of concerted opposition, although a few have resorted, not surprisingly, to all-purpose generalizations about 'absolutism'.

Scarcely less turbulent than the years of war were those which followed immediately upon the making of peace. At such times, the people expected rapid relief from the burdens which had been imposed upon them and were unwilling to allow the ministers any respite in which to restore the depleted royal finances. Nearly as worrying for the treasury were the lengthy periods when the crown was either spending heavily on building up its defences in preparation for an apparently inevitable confrontation or was paying huge subsidies to allies who were acting on its behalf. Only in peacetime could the central government hope to restore stability and order to its budgeting and housekeeping. Unhappily for the first three Bourbons, the international configuration of Europe and the unpredictability of events permitted them few spells of calm in which to embark upon a systematic reform of their finances. For most of the time the monarchy lived from hand to mouth, desperately trying new short-term expedients, and wondering how long it could sustain its military expenditure.

Even when not at war, the crown always had to rely on extraordinary sources of income, to supplement the woefully inadequate receipts from the direct and indirect taxes. Borrowing on the money-markets and, from the sixteenth century, the sale of offices were accepted ways of supplementing the resources of the government but, like the taxes themselves, both were very unpopular with certain sections of the community. In war, all these methods had to be exploited to the full, and the outcry against them grew correspondingly greater. As so many of the higher social groups were partially or totally exempt from direct taxation, it was the poorest members of society who had to bear most of the increases in the *taille* and other similar levies. In an age when privilege was regarded as a legal fact, it did not occur to them that tax liability might properly be related to wealth. Their grievance was against the crown, which had raised its demands unreasonably. Far from resenting the exemptions enjoyed by their social superiors, they looked to the nobles and office-holders for support, which was often forthcoming, in resisting the collection of these inflated sums. Landlords were also much concerned that the peasants should not beggar themselves in order to satisfy the appetite of the finance ministers, because they had their own dues to collect from their tenants, and the meagre resources of the average husbandman would not meet both seigneurial and royal requirements, not to mention the municipal market dues and the tithe to the church. The peasant preferred to honour his obligations to the seigneur and to local bodies, because he at least received some protection and services from them in return. The crown took a great deal, but gave him nothing of value in compensation. Thus, although he accepted that there would always be some royal taxation, he reacted with fierce hostility to the greatly increased assessment which he received in time of war.

For the crown, there could be no question of seeking to obtain the consent of the taxpayers to higher direct taxation, because they had no voice in any of the representative institutions which existed in the kingdom. Occasionally, higher members of society would speak on their behalf at the provincial Estates or at one of the infrequent meetings of the *Etats-généraux*, but the royal ministers had no formal means of persuading them as a group to look with favour on their requests for extra funds. The crown published plenty of propaganda, dramatizing the danger facing the realm and the expenditure which was needed to defend it, but such pleas had little appeal for provincial

Frenchmen unless they lived in a region which was close to the battlefront. Having no contact with the international policy-making of the distant central government, the provinces were concerned with their own security and best interests. As the crown sometimes made war on countries which they regarded as friends or trading partners, and as the presence of French troops in their locality was likely to be almost as costly and disruptive as the arrival of an invading enemy, it was easy for the local population to convince itself that the king was fighting a personal dynastic war which they should do nothing to further. Even when a province did feel threatened by a neighbouring power, it was reluctant to give generously to the treasury, although that did not prevent it from calling on the king to defend his subjects. It was the monarch who, increasingly as the seventeenth century progressed, told his people that he was their protector, and at moments when danger loomed they insisted that he should substantiate his boast.

Behind these general attitudes, there were, of course, variations governed by time and place. Particularly during periods of economic hardship, some men regarded conscription into the army as preferable to the poverty in which they found themselves, although the south and west of the kingdom were more reluctant than the north and east to provide members of the soldiery. If a war was prolonged, then many men deserted because of the appalling conditions or the arrears in their pay, and others were sent home because of their wounds or their deteriorating health, all of them returning to be burdens on their native community. Here was yet another of the horrors associated in the peasant mind with the word 'war'.

In the early stages of an international conflict, particularly when it followed a long period of peace, the increase in taxation might not seem too crippling. The crown was able to rely on its reserves and on other sources of income. It was even possible to inspire the taxpayers with some short-term feelings of patriotism, and the nobles might encourage their tenants to help the king in his difficulties. Such support was never universal and wholehearted, and it was always ephemeral. The frequency of economic crises, the escalation of government tax demands as its alternative ways of raising funds became less productive, the effect of troop movements and the refusal of the landlords to continue to waive seigneurial dues in favour of the royal treasury soon sowed discontent throughout the kingdom. Taxes were not paid in full, and revolts erupted at the very moment when the crown needed to concentrate all its energies on the foreign enemy. Some dissident frontier regions might even look favourably at alien powers whose lands bordered their own. Troops could not be spared from the battlefronts to combat all these dissenting movements, and it therefore seemed to many opponents of the new levels of taxation that resistance paid off. The crown followed up its threats with inaction. The impression of royal weakness was reinforced after the making of peace when the king, as a gesture of goodwill which was designed to defuse the tensions in society, would not only lower the taxes but would write off the outstanding sums which had not been collected during the preceding years. A further problem was that, while it was essential for the monarchy to boast of its triumphs and minimize its defeats, the announcement of major victories by the royal armies made the people less inclined to give more money to the treasury. The widespread publicity given to the success of Condé over the Spanish at Rocroi in 1643 was especially notable for its counterproductive fiscal consequences. An added complication for Mazarin was that the Peace of Westphalia of 1648 seemed to many Frenchmen to be the end of the war and they accordingly demanded immediate relief from wartime burdens, although the conflict with Spain was to last for eleven more years. When the final peace was made in 1659, France had suffered from twenty-four years of open hostilities, and many more if the earlier period of expensive war by proxy is included. The population was in no mood to give the impoverished crown any respite in which to order its finances.

It is a historical irony that it should have been Mazarin, and not Richelieu, who had to bear the full rage of the French people during the Frondes, because the Italian cardinal was more of a conciliator in foreign policy than his predecessor. In this he had to be circumspect, because enemies would be quick to regard a French willingness to accelerate peace negotiations as a sign of weakness and approaching defeat. Yet his main difficulty was that by 1642, the year when Richelieu died, the principal ways of raising extra money had been pushed to their limits. The taxes could go higher on paper, but they would not be paid. Offices had been created and sold in such large numbers during the 1630s that existing office-holders were incensed and any new creations would be rendered unsaleable. Worst of all, the crown was so lacking in creditworthiness that it could borrow on the money-markets only at the most unfavourable rates. Such were the problems of government in wartime, and they left the new ministers of Louis XIV with a very limited range of options in 1659. One course of action seemed unavoidable. The tensions between the crown and its subjects had to be defused, and conciliation substituted for confrontation. The introduction of any long-term reforms, which had been totally impossible in wartime, would have to be implemented with the greatest caution.

THE ROYAL FINANCES, 1610–1661[1]

The period between the assassination of Henri IV in 1610 and the overt entry of France into the Thirty Years War in 1635 was technically one of international peace for the French. The spectre of Habsburg encirclement and aggression still hovered over the kingdom, and much money had to be spent on preparing adequate defences for the conflict which seemed inevitable. In the 1620s there was also the expensive problem of the Huguenot rebels and the need to subsidize the foreign powers who were engaging the emperor and deflecting his attention from France. Yet the crown had some room for financial manoeuvre in these years, because many powerful elements in French society were busily occupied in confronting each other and devoted only part of their energies to attacks on royal policy. Moreover there was considerable disagreement about governmental actions, most of which found favour with at least one social group and aroused the ire of others.

Even in peacetime the peasants continued to be heavily burdened by royal, seigneurial and ecclesiastical taxes, but many of their social superiors were also far from solvent. A substantial number of municipalities had become deeply indebted, not least because their officials spent enormous amounts on lengthy law suits in order to challenge other jurisdictions which rivalled their own. A significant proportion of nobles had fallen on hard times, and were eager therefore to make profitable marriages and to seek royal pensions or favours. Indeed the only groups which seemed to be prospering were the more substantial office-holders, the tax-farmers and the financiers. Of these, the *officiers* might at least play some constructive role in local society and therefore not be totally loathed by the population, but the other two categories were passionately hated. Yet to the crown both were essential. When compared to the collection of revenues by royal officials, the farming of taxes produced a swifter and surer flow of revenue into the treasury, and it was left to the farmer to coerce reluctant taxpayers by whatever means he chose in order to recoup the

[1]Some excellent research by other scholars on the period 1500–1661 has been indispensable in the preparation of this section: Michael Wolfe, *The fiscal system of Renaissance France* (New Haven/London, 1972); J. H. M. Salmon, *Society in crisis: France in the sixteenth century* (London, 1975); and, most importantly of all, Richard Bonney, *The king's debts: finance and politics in France, 1589–1661* (Oxford, 1981). There are also many brilliant flashes of insight in David Parker, *The making of French absolutism* (London, 1983), its conclusions often very similar to those expressed here but frequently reached through studying different aspects of the social and administrative systems.

sums he had advanced to the central government. His victims loudly denounced the brutality of the methods used by the collectors and the fact that all those involved in the process of collection were clearly making a substantial profit. The financiers were hated for two reasons. First, many Frenchmen were personally indebted to these grasping opportunists and knew how cruelly they exploited their hapless clients. Secondly it was widely believed that, if the king could escape from their clutches, taxes would come down and everyone would reap the benefits. They were accused of being 'sangsues', leeches, upon the body politic, the source of both the misfortunes of the crown and the miseries of the people. Such attacks on them became more violent in years of crisis, the very moment when the treasury was most heavily dependent on their services. Sometimes the crown was forced to heed this clamour, and make scapegoats of certain financiers. Its usual method for doing so was to institute a special tribunal, a *chambre de justice*, and the creation of such a body was a prominent item in the demands made of the crown by the office-holders on a number of occasions – from the days of the Catholic League in its opposition to Henri IV, to the early personal rule of Louis XIV when the *surintendant des finances*, Foucquet, and a number of financiers were tried and found guilty by the *chambre* of 1661–9.

In the deepening crisis of the 1640s and the subsequent upheavals of the Frondes, the tax-farmers and other financiers did desert the crown for short periods. The tax-farm contracts became so costly that it was impossible for a potential purchaser to be certain of recouping his investment, especially as years of war and high taxes had lowered the ability and the willingness of the population to pay, no matter what savage methods of collection were used. It was more than likely that the collector would find himself the victim of an angry mob. The financiers also felt that Mazarin was an unreliable debtor, because the treasury simply could not meet the terms of the loans they had advanced. It could not afford the interest, let alone the repayment of the capital. On two occasions, in 1648 and 1661, the crown did indeed default on its debts, an action which was easily within its power but presented the ministers with the difficult problem of how to raise funds on the money-markets thereafter. In more normal times, the financiers were organized into rival consortia, each eager to profit from the discomfiture of its competitors. At moments of royal bankruptcy, they drew together, and refused to lend any more money, in the same way that the tax-farmers also united and would not pay the inflated price of the contracts. Such a situation could not last, because the government and financiers had mutual need of each other. Many consortia were clients of a particular minister, from whom they hoped to obtain a variety of favours, as well as a guarantee that they would receive the interest due to them and the ultimate return of their capital. Some therefore suffered drastic reversals as their patron himself fell from power. Foucquet, who had been able to borrow funds on the money-markets and then lend them to the crown, at a time when the government had not been considered creditworthy, was summarily dismissed and the sums he had obtained were consequently not repaid. Yet, after each crisis, the crown and the money-markets had to rebuild their bridges and restore a working partnership, thus demonstrating the degree of their interdependence. In the process, the financiers would demand considerable assurances from the government, and the royal ministers knew that declarations of bankruptcy could be made only very rarely or they might find themselves permanently shunned by the world of credit.

Except in these brief periods of total royal poverty, the king could normally appease the critics of the 'sangsues' and at the same time retain the co-operation of the moneylenders. When the demands of the office-holders for an investigation into financial malpractice became dangerously strident, the king would reluctantly agree to create the *chambre de justice* which they desired. It would begin to examine specific charges of malversation, often imposing severe penalties on certain financiers. The mood of the *officiers* then became more friendly towards the crown, but their victims now began to exert pressure on the ministers, pointing out that, if this was the only reward they received for their labours and for the risks they took, they might be much less ready to lend to the government in the future. This would prompt the king to extend a conciliatory hand towards them, commuting severe sentences into more moderate punishments and reducing the size of fines. As soon as it was tactful to do so, he would suspend the *chambre*, loudly proclaiming that it had completed its work, had performed its functions splendidly and had stamped out corruption.[2] Such a typically *ancien régime* compromise was the best solution that the various parties could hope to achieve. The office-holders had made their point and had shown that they could not be ignored, the financiers had won through although they had been reminded that excessive greed would not be tolerated, and the king had defused the tension. Calm would then return until the next crisis, when the whole process might have to be repeated once again.

[2]On the earlier *chambres*, see the many references in Bonney, *The king's debts*; on that of 1661–9, see Pierre Clément (ed.), *Lettres, instructions et mémoires de Colbert*, (8 vols, Paris, 1861–82), vol. II. pp. 751–2, 758, 764–6; on the *chambre* of 1661–9 and that established in 1716, see Daniel Dessert, *Argent, pouvoir et société au grand siècle* (Paris, 1984), pp. 238–73.

The enemies of the financiers – whether *officiers* or humbler members of the population, or even great nobles like Saint-Simon who denounced them as the worst of the evils which were parasitic upon the French state[3] – all gave the impression that the object of their hatred was a group of speculators who thought only of themselves, lived for greed and played no constructive role in French society. They were a self-contained band of leeches. Recent prosopographical studies of these men have revealed a very different picture. Of those who lent money to the crown, very few were engaged in commerce and industry. For men in those occupations, funds were better employed in furthering their enterprises and in buying the offices and land which would enable them to forsake the world of the bourgeoisie for the socially superior ranks of the *officiers*. It was from the men who had already reached the higher social levels, whether through the purchase of office or by their inheritance of rank, that the government obtained most of its credit. The lenders therefore included office-holders, lawyers, nobles, clerics and army officers – men who had resources to spare and did not wish to invest in the socially demeaning practices of trade and manufactures. Venal *officiers* and their relatives formed the largest group, many of them working in the financial administration where they had a vested interest in ensuring that the taxes were collected because it was from these revenues that their loans would be repaid. Such families regularly advanced money to the treasury over many generations. The surnames of secretaries of state also feature on the list of royal creditors, either the secretary himself or members of his kin. Indeed Colbert, in his reform of the finances, used his influence not to end treasury dependence on the financiers as a whole, but to promote the fortunes of his own family and reduce the role of rival clans.[4] Similarly, some of the office-holders who clamoured for a *chambre de justice* were only pretending to demand a major onslaught on all financiers, because many of them would have been among those called to account. They hoped instead that the *chambre* could be manipulated so that their rivals were investigated and punished, leaving them free to continue their speculative activities without so much competition.

As it was chiefly the office-holders who considered the financing of the royal deficit to be an appealing form of investment, there were few

[3]The duc de Saint-Simon, *Projets de gouvernement du duc de Bourgogne* (Paris, 1860), p. 3, where he attributes the greater wealth of England and the Dutch Republic to the absence of financiers.

[4]See: Dessert, *Argent, pouvoir et société*; D. Dessert and J.-L. Journet, 'Le lobby Colbert: un royaume ou une affaire de famille?', *Annales, ESC*, xxx, 6, pp. 1303–36; and on the years before 1661, J. Dent, *Crisis in finance: crown, financiers and society in seventeenth-century France* (New York, 1973).

Huguenots among the financiers. Their religion excluded them from most official positions, and they, in common with socially comparable Catholic bourgeois, invested their spare funds in their commercial and industrial activities. Of the small group of Protestants who did lend, a minority were foreigners, and indeed foreign involvement in crown finance was minimal for much of the seventeenth century. Henri IV had borrowed heavily from abroad in order to gain his kingdom, and Mazarin, whose connections in Italy were as strong as those he had forged in his adopted country, also looked beyond the frontiers of France for the means to solve the terrible financial crises of the 1640s and 1650s. Yet in more usual times, the machinery of royal borrowing was in the hands of competing French families, each using its role in maintaining the solvency of the government as a bargaining counter for obtaining favours and offices for its members. Colbert tried to persuade foreigners to purchase new issues of *rentes*[5] and to invest in native industries, but he too was unwilling to be as heavily dependent on outside funds as his mentor, Mazarin, had been. Fortunately the 1660s were years of peace, and the new finance minister was able to confine himself to borrowing from those families he trusted. Among their number were some at the very peak of court society, including that of the ducs de Chevreuse and de Chaulnes, two members of the favoured aristocratic inner circle. Here loyalty was a vital factor, because a provincial governor like Chaulnes would aid the royal finances by purchasing the right to collect certain taxes in his *gouvernement* and advancing the potential yield, at a discount, to the treasury. Such a personal involvement in the raising of local revenues was highly desirable when the governor was loyal, but would be disastrous if he were not. When war did return to plague the ministers in the 1670s, the families which had been out of favour in the preceding decade had their opportunity for revenge. The hard-pressed crown could no longer choose its lenders, and those who now rejoined the ranks of the royal creditors made it clear to the ministers that their renewed participation was conditional upon the favours they would receive in return.

Close examination of the financiers by recent historians has revealed that many of them made only infrequent loans to the government, while some twenty-five per cent offered substantial sums on numerous occasions. Almost all of them came from northern France, especially from Picardy, Champagne and Burgundy, which reinforced the views of southerners that the royal administration was a northern conspiracy. They consolidated their power by strategic marriages and were truly

[5]For example Clément, vol. II (i), p. 102, note 1.

the mainstay of the state. Not until the time when wider use would be made of paper transactions in government finance would their services be less than essential. The heavy reliance on precious metals throughout the seventeenth century meant that the role of the financier remained crucial. They helped the crown to anticipate the yield of both direct and indirect taxes, aided it in selling new issues of *rentes* by purchasing large numbers at a discount and then bearing the financial burden until further purchasers could be found, and in every way allowed the crown to live beyond its means. Many of them had invested other funds in office-holding as well, so that their personal wealth was closely tied to the fortunes of the central government. Some among them had to borrow heavily in order to lend, and there were therefore many men whose names did not appear on the actual contracts made between financiers and ministers, but who had advanced large sums to fellow financiers on the strict understanding that it was to be used for a royal loan. Also many of those in high society who were prepared to participate in this unsavoury world of credit were not eager to use their own reputable family names, and so some of the signatories to these transactions were mere intermediaries, shielding the real sources of the money from public view.

Daniel Dessert has described the relations between the crown and the financiers as 'amours tumultueuses', turbulent love-affairs, in which the two sides were so mutually dependent that passionate quarrels and ruptures had to be followed by periods of 'making up'. The same metaphor can also be extended to include the office-holders in general. They enjoyed the status and power associated with their posts, and the king needed them to administer the country. The Frondes showed how violently the two sides could quarrel, but some accommodation would have to be reached. The *officiers* had invested a great deal of money in the venal system, and an office was regarded as a piece of property, to be passed on to subsequent generations as if it were a parcel of land. Moreover investment in the government was the only way of gaining a good return, without the social stigma associated with commerce and industry. As they or their ancestors had worked hard to lift their families out of the bourgeoisie into the more respectable ranks of the bureaucracy, they were not eager to tarnish their new reputations by dabbling in the economy of the market-place.

It was generally assumed in seventeenth-century France that all governments regularly borrowed money by various means, and the only important consideration was whether the royal treasury was passing through a period of crisis and might default on its obligations. If so, it could be difficult to sell *rentes* or raise loans. So too in periods of more general hardship, it might not be easy to find willing tax-farmers.

The financiers would wait for better days to return. Yet the purchase of an office was a longer-term investment, and royal attempts to manipulate this aspect of the financial system were doubly resented, because the investors could not withdraw temporarily until the crisis was over. The whole range of their family offices was a tribute to careful patrimonial planning over the generations, and could not be abandoned. If royal ministers tried to undermine the power, privileges or income associated with any particular post, then they would have to be prevented from succeeding. Other *officiers* would offer to help in such a situation, because it was vital to all of them that the rules of the system be observed by the ministers and by the king. Yet, as so much money could be obtained from the sale of new offices and the exploitation of existing ones, the central government was regularly tempted to tap this ever flowing source.

Under Henri IV, the office-holders and the ministers were on reasonably amicable terms. The institution of the *paulette* in 1604 had advantages for both groups. Although many offices had been passed on to relatives in sixteenth century, this new legislation now guaranteed the heredity of venal posts provided that an annual payment was made to the crown. Apart from the greater security which was thus given to the holders, and the additional revenue which was received by the treasury, the *paulette* made it much more difficult for powerful nobles to insert their own clients into the bureaucracy. Some historians have insisted, and others have denied, that the undermining of this aristocratic patronage over the *robe* was a major motive in the decision of the minister, Sully, to introduce this reform, and it is undeniable that many subsequent opponents of the *paulette* assumed this to be so.[6] Yet many earlier decisions to create new strata of venal offices and expand the number of others had been similarly regarded as an attack on existing elites, when the aim of the crown had simply been to increase revenue. This financial reason is the most likely explanation of the 1604 edict, although the possible social and political consequences were fiercely debated in the two years between the first formulation of this plan and its final implementation. In fact the wider disadvantages for the royal government appeared to be fewer than the compensations. On the negative side, the office-holders would henceforward be a hereditary and more closed caste, so that it would be difficult to influence them directly, although the king still had the useful weapon of royal patronage in his armoury. Moreover

[6]See, among many others who have discussed this point: Bonney, *The king's debts*, pp. 61–2; J. Russell Major, 'Henry IV and Guyenne: a study concerning the origins of royal absolutism', *French Historical Studies*, iv, 4, 1965–6, pp. 363–83; J. Michael Hayden, *France and the estates general of 1614* (Cambridge, 1974), p. 12.

noble networks of clientage within the bureaucracy would also be undermined, and the crown was always seeking aristocrats and other men of prestige in the locality who did have influence over the *officiers*. Yet, if the task of loyal notables, who discreetly used these subtle social pressures in order to implement the royal will, was made more difficult by the new exclusiveness of the *paulette*, this restriction was more than counterbalanced by the fact that the great magnates, often disloyal to the central government, would now find it less easy to build themselves a faction which had many members within the administrative hierarchy of the office-holders. In addition it seemed likely that the new security provided by the hereditary transmission of offices would make the bureaucrats more, rather than less, grateful to the crown. In 1604 there was no intimation of the massive creation of new posts which would cause so many of them to become disaffected in the 1630s, leading ultimately to their revolt during the Frondes.

Abhorring the base world of commerce and industry from which many of their ancestors originally or even recently came, and taking care instead to 'live nobly', the office-holders were very willing to invest their surplus wealth in government financial enterprises – always provided that the royal treasury was in a condition to honour its part of the bargain. Thus, they purchased *rentes* when the rate of interest was satisfactory, and were prepared to pay additional sums in return for the promise of higher salaries in the future or for the confirmation that their privileges would be maintained in years to come. They were also willing to act as financiers, and advance money in anticipation of revenues which had not yet been collected. If these investments were more risky than those in the safer world of land-holding, they could yield high profits and might give the investor the opportunity to extract favours for his family from a grateful government. Such dealings emphasize how intertwined were the worlds of public and private finance, because the advantages of lending money to the royal treasury were assessed by the *officier* primarily in terms of the benefit to himself and to his relatives, without any considerations of patriotically aiding his sovereign. Although the crown might default on many or all of these contractual obligations in wartime, provoking an outcry from its creditors, their fiercest denunciations of the royal ministers were prompted by the creation of additional offices. Some new posts were welcomed and found eager buyers in families which wished to elevate more of their members into the bureaucracy, and it was not uncommon for office-holders and other financiers to act as middlemen, purchasing the new creations *en bloc* from the government and then seeking men who would pay a higher price for the individual offices. Here was yet another way by which the skilful entrepreneur could make some money for himself through advancing funds to the treasury. The rage of the *officiers* was reserved chiefly for those new posts which undermined the position of existing office-holders. A venal office was regarded as a piece of property, increasingly so after its hereditary transmission was formalized by the *paulette* legislation, and associated with it was a guaranteed income from the duties carried out by its holder. If the crown now created one, two or, in some instances, three further posts where a single office had previously existed, the incumbent would either have to share the administrative tasks with the new purchasers, who would divide up the income which had formerly been his alone, or he would have to buy up the novel creations in order to retain his monopoly over his area of the administration and thus keep his income intact. It was as if a man had bought a piece of land only to find either that part of its yield had been assigned to someone else or that he had to pay the purchase price yet again in order to retain his property. Although it has already been pointed out that there were ways of dissuading would-be buyers from taking on a new office, that did not lessen the resentment felt towards ministers who had violated the fundamental principle of ownership.

Scarcely less objectionable to the *officiers* were threats to abolish the *annuel*, the yearly levy by which the *paulette* legislation assured the hereditary transmission of office. Sometimes these were the result of pressure from the enemies of the office-holders, and the crown would make it known discreetly that the proposal would be dropped once the crisis had passed. On other occasions they were part of an attempt by the ministers to extract money from the *officiers*, who were being asked to pay once more for a right which they supposedly possessed already. The whole issue was usually a matter for negotiation, because it might be possible for the office-holders to extract further guarantees from the king in return for this extra payment. Yet in the 1640s, when the venal officials had suffered a series of affronts at the hands of the crown – in the form of new offices, manipulation of the *rentes* and defaulting on the terms of loans – the threat by Mazarin to abolish the *annuel* was the insult which finally prompted them to abandon all co-operation with the minister and to stage what was effectively an administrative 'strike'. Their fury was fuelled by the knowledge that the cardinal urgently needed the funds provided by this levy, and was therefore playing politics rather than seriously intending to abolish it. As they, the executive arm of the crown, suspended their administrative activities, Mazarin had no choice but to seek an accommodation and concede many of their demands at the peace of Rueil, early in 1649.

A crown so heavily dependent on venal officers and financiers, and so frequently impoverished by the burdens of war, could hardly hope to move far along the path to 'absolutism'. When Louis XIV declared his personal rule in 1661, the treasury was desperately trying to recover from a long war, and the memory of the Frondes was still vivid. The crown needed help from the financial world now, as always, but Colbert hoped that in a few years, provided that a further war could be avoided, the government could go to the money-markets from a position of strength and not as a supplicant. During the years 1589–1661, the total yield of both the direct and indirect taxes seldom amounted to a third of royal needs,[7] and there was no attempt by the ministers to introduce a fundamental reform of the system. The crown increased its demands by raising these existing levies, especially in wartime, but its expenditure usually rose by equally large or even greater sums. The indirect duties were always farmed to the financiers, but the direct taxes too were often advanced by the collectors who bore the burden until they could reimburse themselves from the taxpayers. The second principal source of royal revenue, the venal office-holding system, offered further opportunities for moneylenders to make a profit by helping the king to anticipate his receipts. The *annuel* was particularly suitable for farming to the financiers, because it was a stable form of royal income and the farmer could therefore be assured that he would recoup his investment. The final means of raising money for the treasury was through the whole range of direct loans, *rentes* and other short-term expedients, where the risk was greater for the lenders as the crown might default, but the profits were larger if it kept its side of the contract. The best tactic for the ministers, and one which was impossible in years of crisis, was to play off each group of creditors against another, so that, if any became too importunate in the conditions it wished to impose, the government could find others who were eager to lend.

Although the critics of Henri III exaggerated the extent of his financial mismanagement, the royal finances were in disarray at the accession of Henri IV. In order to gain the allegiance of his kingdom, the new king had no choice but to expend enormous sums and was also forced to agree to a reform of the financial system. When he at last gained the recognition of the majority of Frenchmen, he dared not alienate some of this hard-won support by imprudent action. Accordingly, he decided that he must not declare a bankruptcy and refuse to honour the debts of his predecessor, nor abandon his pledge to reform the finances. Moreover the treasury had been deprived of much revenue during the civil wars because the money had passed

[7]The details of the crown's finances and its attempts to ameliorate them have been exhaustively researched and expounded by Bonney, in *The king's debts*.

into the hands of the magnates who controlled large areas of the kingdom. Henri IV had already sold off many of his patrimonial lands to provide funds for his campaign, and was heavily indebted to foreign bankers and rulers. Here at least was one avenue which led towards solvency. By changing his religion he was able to default on his debts to Protestant creditors outside France and to arrange new loans from Catholic countries. From such a difficult beginning, it would have been little short of miraculous if Sully had managed by 1610 to accumulate the surplus resources of which he boasts in his own account of the reign.[8] In fact the condition of the treasury at the accession of Louis XIII was far from healthy. Revenues had been anticipated, and many contracts had been made with the financiers, not only for the collection of taxes but for the long-term resumption of crown lands and rights which has been alienated during the civil wars. The wealth of the government therefore was much more impressive on paper than in reality, and a prolonged period of international peace and internal stability was essential if these interim measures were to be turned into permanent financial gain. The sudden death of Henri IV in 1610 seemed to end any hope of implementing these schemes.

During the later years of the reign there had been a number of unsuccessful princely conspiracies, and a long regency would surely give greater encouragement to ambitious magnates. It was true that many Frenchmen were growing increasingly hostile to these high aristocratic plotters, preferring the return of peace to the realm which Henri IV had ultimately engineered, but now there was no adult king and it remained to be seen whether the government would again fall into the hands of the princes and their factions. Lower down the social scale, tension was growing between the lesser nobility of the sword and the office-holders. In the earlier sixteenth century, it was not uncommon to find members of ancient families in bureaucratic positions, but by 1610 such posts were the virtual monopoly of the venal *officiers*, whether *noblesse de robe* or of lesser rank. Similarly the administrative families were being increasingly excluded from access to positions which had originally been, and were now to be once again, staffed exclusively from the ranks of the *noblesse d'épée*. The crossing of social barriers, which had become less unusual in the sixteenth century, was now to be prevented. The formalization of the rules for acquiring and passing on an office, especially the *paulette* legislation,

[8]His memoirs, the *Sages et royales oeconomies d'estat*, have appeared in many editions, which vary considerably; the variations are conveniently described in David Buisseret, *Sully and the growth of centralized government in France 1598–1610*, (London, 1968), pp. 17–21.

had given the *officiers* greater security and had assured them that they would be the group through which the crown would administer the kingdom. As their dynasties consolidated their hold on the locality, the nobles in the area resented the consequent curtailment of their own powers of patronage. *Robe* and *épée* therefore waited with apprehension to see whether the policies of Henri IV would be continued. The various parties were not, of course, totally distinct. It was still possible for local robe and sword to combine in an attack on a central government policy, and the lesser *épée* and the magnates might unite against the pretensions of the office-holders. A principal task for the regent was to prevent such alliances and keep the various groups in a state of tension. One further major problem awaited Marie de Médicis, when she took over the government on the death of her husband. His religious compromise had satisfied no one. The Protestants waited fearfully, and the Catholics more hopefully, to see what she would do.

CONFLICTS, COMPROMISE AND CONSULTATION, 1610–1626

A good opportunity for the historian to sample the mood of the various elite groups in French society, albeit in a somewhat artificial and self-conscious form, is provided by the meeting of the *Etats-généraux* in 1614, because both during its debates and in the electioneering and pamphleteering which preceded it a whole range of views and grievances was clearly expressed. Some of these pronouncements made it plain that the great princely families had very little support in the country, except among their own clients. The situation in the civil wars of the sixteenth century, when the monarchy was both weak and unpopular in the eyes of many Frenchmen, no longer obtained. At that time some of the magnates had seemed to offer the best hope of restoring order, at least in the part of the kingdom where they had constructed their power base. Now it was the Bourbons who seemed most likely to maintain stability, and therefore the government of Marie de Médicis commanded a degree of loyalty. She would, of course, have to respect liberties and privileges, but at least she appeared to be determined to avoid a further war. Thus, when a princely revolt was mounted against the regency in 1614, and its leaders exploited their links with other European ruling houses in a manner which threatened to unleash internal chaos and international conflict, many subjects of the young Louis XIII denounced these magnates for what they were – factious schemers who were putting family interests above the good of the kingdom. Even the majority of

Huguenots could not be persuaded to join Condé and his band of rebels.

Nevertheless, if the princes were the only group with international connections and therefore were alone in introducing a European dimension into their disagreements with the government, there were many other members of society who had their own grievances. The forthcoming *Etats-généraux* would not be an easy assembly for the crown to control. Its meetings always involved a calculated risk for any monarch or regent, but Marie had summoned it because she hoped, rightly as it turned out, that it would condemn the princely agitators who were undoubtedly the most serious threat to her government. Beyond that, she had to pray that other criticisms of her regime could be deflected or defused. Many of the deputies who were elected did seem to be reasonably favourable towards the monarchy and its current caretaker, and a sizable proportion of these were royal office-holders who had profited from the policies of Henri IV and Sully. The princes also had their supporters in the assembly, so that the whole spectrum of opinion was represented there – high aristocracy, lesser nobility, clergy, *officiers* and other leading members of the Third Estate. The groups were not all of equal strength, but at least they had their spokesmen, and it can be seen how the various issues were supported or rejected by individual deputies in a flexible pattern of alliances.

The details of proceedings in the *Etats-généraux* have been so well examined and analysed by J. M. Hayden[9] that they need not be rehearsed here. Yet, as a starting point for a discussion of social tensions under Louis XIII and Mazarin, the historian will find some of the attitudes adopted by members of the assembly to be particularly relevant. Although the toleration of Huguenots was confirmed by the regent, and was reiterated by the young king when his majority was declared only a few weeks before the opening of the assembly, spokesmen for the clergy quickly demanded the extension of Catholicism throughout the realm. Some of them also called for the reform of the church and insisted that the decrees of the Council of Trent be admitted into France. Passing beyond the ecclesiastical sphere, they insisted that reductions be made in the excessive levels of taxation, they criticized the increase in the number of office-holders and they castigated the unruly lives of the nobility. The poor, they maintained, were the principal victims of all these disorders. The Second Estate, the *noblesse d'épée*, also singled out high taxes and the plethora of judicial and financial officials as major evils, and went on to demand

[9]*France and the estates general*, pp. 74–218.

the confirmation of their own privileges and freedom of access to certain offices. The Third Estate, in its turn, called for the reform of the church, the lowering of taxes and the re-establishment of justice. This last demand necessitated an attack on venal offices, although this estate also felt no affection for seigneurial and ecclesiastical officials. The three orders did not each speak with a single voice, of course, because some clergy had no wish to be reformed and the *officiers* within the Third Estate were not in favour of condemning or abolishing themselves. Yet a substantial number of members in all three chambers had spoken out against the very institution of venality, the number of officials and the crippling nature of taxation. They were therefore demanding a major reorganization of the royal finances. Worst of all from the point of view of the regent, they decided to put aside those grievances which were particular to one or two estates, and concentrate on these matters which were the common concern of all three. The *officiers* were prominent on their list of culprits, but the real villains were the financiers, who took advantage of the difficulties which the venal system caused for the crown, and made themselves a healthy living by acting as financial middlemen, tax-farmers and straightforward lenders. The deputies clearly seemed to regard them as a distinct group, which has already been shown to be an erroneous assumption, and their hostility to them was so great that, by the end of the session, the king had agreed to hold a *chambre de justice* in order to investigate their activities.

Many of the grievances voiced in the 1614 *Etats-généraux* were not new, but it is strikingly clear that the venal office-holders had no friends and had become a major focus for opposition. Fortunately for them, the lack of negotiating expertise among the deputies, the divisions within each estate and the determination of all three to retain the initiative and stand on their social dignity together prevented the launching of a united and sustained onslaught against venality. The *officiers* would have supported some of the other grievances of the deputies had it not been for these violent attacks on their own positions. They too sought reform of the royal finances, and deplored the worst excesses of certain financiers. In its own palace, a short distance away from the meeting-place of the three estates, the *parlement* of Paris was also much exercised by these financial irregularities, but it was even more passionately concerned about the ecclesiastical debates in the assembly. Never a friend of heterodoxy, unless its own jurisdiction was best served by championing dissidents in the short term, this great secular court was ever on the watch for ecclesiastical attempts to usurp its powers. The demand for the admission of the Tridentine decrees savoured of the most dangerous clerical ultramontanism, and some deputies of the Third Estate felt bound to support the judges on this issue. Yet, in the face of the wide-ranging criticism of venality within the *Etats-généraux*, the proud *parlement* had no intention of involving itself in the religious debates of that body, through the agency of deputies who were themselves *officiers*. The court could speak for itself, and could address the outside world directly. After all, it had a permanent existence, which the *Etats-généraux* did not. So the Paris judges launched their own attack on ecclesiastical pretensions and, as the assembly drew to a close, issued their own severe criticisms of the present state of the royal finances.

Marie now decided that the best course of action was to remain on good terms with the *parlements* and the *officiers*. For most of the time they had shown reasonably steady loyalty to Henri IV and to the regency, and she therefore decided to extend the *paulette* and to preserve the hereditary venal system. As a result the judges ceased to press their demand for financial reform with such vigour. Seeing that, on venality as on other matters, the grievances of the *Etats-généraux* were being ignored by the crown, Condé and his princely friends staged a further rebellion, and discovered once again that the country was not prepared to rise in support of them. Thus, in the years 1614–16, there was no sign that the *parlement* of Paris would one day be hailed by the French people as their saviour in the first Fronde, and the princes regarded briefly as national heroes in the second. The historian must find out whether society had undergone lasting change between the early days of Louis XIII and the minority of his son, or whether the years 1643–53 were untypical and unlikely to recur. Certainly those many complaints of the clerical, noble and Third estates in 1614, which were not directed against the crown or the *officiers* but arose out of their own rivalries, were still subjects of contention during the Frondes and long afterwards.

The social atmosphere in France can readily be tested again in 1626, when a meeting of the *assemblée des notables* prompted many groups to express their attitudes, grievances and opinions of government policy at some length.[10] Conveniently for the historian, that year also saw another princely revolt. As the crown had thought that many of the proposals made by the deputies of 1614 were highly undesirable, it had not implemented them. Others had seemed more appealing, but the government had not been able to introduce them. Thus little had changed at the centre, and therefore any marked difference between the opinions of the 1614 deputies and those of the 1626 notables is of

---

[10]The debates of the *assemblée* are summarized by A. D. Lublinskaya, *French absolutism: the crucial phase, 1620–1629*, tr. Brian Pearce (Cambridge, 1968), pp. 289–326.

considerable scholarly interest. In the intervening years, tensions within the localities had simmered, and there had been revolts against the royal ministers. The high nobles had continued their subversive designs, and a new faction had emerged under the leadership of the former regent, Marie du Médicis. She and her younger son, Gaston, the heir to the childless king, were attractive patrons for dissident aristocrats. In contrast many towns had aided the armies of the king in combating both princely and local disturbances, because disorder could easily become uncontrollable and all such upheavals were harmful to trade. Even in the areas where the crown was attempting to convert or repress the Huguenots and restore the true faith, the administrative and commercial elites of the Protestant towns were less than eager to adopt a military stance, and certainly rejected the plan for an alliance with the English against their sovereign.[11] Conversely, a number of the greater nobles who supported these treacherous negotiations with a foreign power were not convinced Huguenots. They merely seized this opportunity to embarrass the government and sow further discord. The ministers were able to persuade some of the lesser nobles to join the royalist side, and even a few of the greatest magnates were prepared to remain loyal if the king would pay a high enough price. Still more money had to be expended on those who were already in the monarchical camp, because others might be trying to tempt them away.

Thus expenditure on the court and on the dispensing of secret sums rose enormously. Only La Vieuville, the finance minister from January 1623 until August 1624, tried to economize on these outgoings, but he was quickly dismissed. Whatever the other charges made against him, both real and imaginary, there is no doubt that the purchase and maintenance of loyalty were two costs on which no government could economize at these dangerous moments. The Thirty Years War was raging, even though France was not yet overtly involved, and the Huguenot problem was not solved. The enemies within the realm could find plenty of supporters among the international community, because Louis XIII was clearly seen to be involved by proxy in the European conflict, and to a degree which placed a further heavy burden on his treasury. It was not so much the religious beliefs, but more the foreign links, of the Huguenots which determined Louis to bring these rebellious subjects to heel. Accordingly

[11]The conflicts of allegiance facing the merchants, the municipal elite, the bureaucrats and the nobles during the royal campaign against La Rochelle form a major theme throughout the text of David Parker, *La Rochelle and the French monarchy: conflict and order in seventeenth-century France* (London, 1980).

he sent troops against them on a scale which would never have seemed appropriate for an ordinary local revolt. At least Catholic soldiers might be willing to put down Protestant rebels, whereas they could not be relied upon to repress insurrections by fellow Catholics whose only crime was to resist taxes which the officers and men themselves detested. By 1629 the independent power of the Huguenots would finally be broken, and they would alarm the crown no more, although Richelieu did not insist on their mass conversion to Catholicism because the merchants among them, who were less rebellious by nature because of their business interests, could and indeed did become effective partners in promoting his economic policies. One compensating factor for the treasury, in these expensive years of buying loyalty and destroying the military strength of the treacherous heretics, was that the church, on the direction of the pope himself, agreed to give considerable funds to the king in order that his crusade against heterodoxy could be sustained.

When the *assemblée des notables* met in 1626, the crown had temporarily slowed down its attack on the Protestants. Before the final onslaught, Richelieu felt that it was necessary to attempt a more lasting solution for royal financial problems. He was planning an extensive scheme for the expansion of the navy and, associated with it, for the development of colonial trade. The cardinal was but one of many ministers during the seventeenth century who felt that an increase in overseas commerce could generate considerable wealth, both for the government and for the mercantile community. Unfortunately, the means by which they hoped to achieve this economic growth owed too much to 'absolutist' and mercantilist theorists. Thus the merchants were to be regimented in state companies, and in wartime their ships would be organized into convoys, protected by naval vessels. Such methods were not well received in the business quarters of the major ports. Many of those who were making a profitable living from international trade were doing so in order to buy themselves out of the bourgeoisie and into the ranks of the *officiers*, while those who planned to continue their commercial enterprises for some time were convinced that excessive *dirigisme* by the crown would reduce their profits. The secret of success was to berth a single ship, carrying rare and desirable cargo, in a port where high prices could be demanded, and not to arrive in convoy on an established trade route.

Although these plans, including those for the colonies, fell within the traditional royal monopoly of all international and military affairs, their fiscal ramifications were such that Richelieu felt it essential to have them endorsed by the French people. He accordingly summoned the notables, hoping that they might be easier to convince than the larger and more unwieldy *Etats-généraux*. Yet, before they could meet, the princes at court organized a conspiracy which was intended to oust the cardinal from office, the immediate pretext being that, in his attempts to consolidate his hold over the navy and ultimately to reform it, he had steadily reduced the powers of the duc de Montmorency in his high position as *amiral-général de France*. If the motives of the minister were more financial than political or social, the great aristocrats regarded this attack on one of their number as further evidence that Richelieu was trying to concentrate all patronage in his own hands and to replace them with his own *créatures* in positions which their families had held for many years. The magnates did not seek to achieve their goal by raising large areas of the kingdom in revolt, because recent experience had shown that their following in the country was minimal. They preferred to attempt a *coup d'état* at court, which simply involved the gaining of the royal ear, in order to persuade the king that his cause was harmed by retaining the cardinal in office. Nevertheless they did try to whip up some support for their conspiracy among the lesser nobility and were unsuccessful in doing so. Not only did their plot fail at court, but the experience of 1614 and 1616 was repeated once again. Whatever the faults of Richelieu, many Frenchmen did not think that a royal council, dominated by factious magnates, would be an improvement. The conspirators were exposed and severely punished, although Gaston, the heir to the throne, had to be treated leniently. The post of *amiral*, and very soon that of *connétable* as well, were left vacant, thus depriving two powerful nobles of enormous opportunities for naval and military patronage. Henceforth, the crown would decide how to fill the senior posts in the royal armed forces.

The rest of French society, for all its antipathy to princely plotters, was nevertheless far from amenable to the programme of reforms which the cardinal hoped to introduce, and the *assemblée* was quick to point this out. Unlike the elected *Etats-généraux*, the notables were chosen by the king and invited to attend the assembly. His freedom of choice was not unlimited, because there were some who assumed that they had a right to be called and, as a principal purpose of the meeting was to gain support for royal policies, there was no point in packing the gathering with men who were loyal to the crown but carried no weight in the country. In 1626 Louis XIII summoned twelve archbishops and bishops, ten court nobles, the *premiers présidents* and *procureurs-généraux* of the sovereign courts, and the *prévôt des marchands* – who was effectively the mayor – of Paris. The members of the clergy and the nobility could express opinions on the matters placed before them, but could clearly not bind the whole of their respective estates to subscribe to their views. Nor could the mayor of Paris speak for the Third Estate. The judicial representatives, in contrast, were regarded as spokesmen for their courts, and therefore the debates of the assembly provide a useful insight into the attitudes of the upper judiciary at this moment.

One burning issue of the 1614 *Etats-généraux* was not present in 1626. The royal ministers now relied heavily on the payment of the *annuel* and on the sale of offices for the provision of regular funds, and therefore had no intention of making a direct attack on the *paulette*. Nor did the nobles make any general onslaught on the whole venal system. They confined themselves to demanding that certain offices be restricted to the *noblesse d'épée*. It seemed that a hereditary bureaucracy had now become an accepted part of the French administration, if only for the practical reason that the more the *officiers* had to pay for their privileges, the less was the fiscal burden on other social groups. The *épée* still denied that the *robe* was a true *noblesse*, but that issue was debated in the salons rather than in the *assemblée*. Richelieu had anticipated another problem of 1614, which might well have recurred in 1626, by summoning the *chambre de justice* which had been promised to the *Etats-généraux*. As always the crown did not allow it too much freedom to investigate the role of the financiers, but a few of them were made scapegoats and heavily fined, so that it seemed as though the cardinal was willing to purge corruption from the government. It was therefore to a wary, but not overtly hostile, assembly that the ministers presented their proposals for reform. The notables were asked to discuss and approve the plans for the extension of the navy, the establishment of trading companies on overseas routes, the strengthening of certain economic protectionist measures, a reduction in expenditure on both the court and the army, a review of interest rates on loans, the redeeming of the royal demesne and the establishment of new taxes which would not fall heavily on the more humble levels of the population. Care was taken by the government spokesmen to emphasize that nothing would be done arbitrarily. For example it was explained that proper compensation would be paid for the redemption of royal lands, and that there was no suggestion of their simply being confiscated. The whole programme was presented in a manner which, it was hoped, would inspire confidence in the goodwill of the crown toward its subjects. Richelieu knew that he could quickly alienate them if any of the ministerial decisions savoured of despotism.

In the ensuing debates, social tensions rapidly surfaced. When the old nobility demanded that it should have a monopoly over most court offices, the venal *officiers* protested at once, because some of these curial posts were the highly prized rewards for members of their own ranks. They reinforced this counterattack by welcoming the reduction in court expenditure, adding that this could obviously best be achieved by reducing the enormous amount spent on pensions and gifts, which went almost entirely to princes of the blood and to the *noblesse d'épée*. Although they did not openly say so in the assembly, they also knew that this largesse was the means by which the king maintained his personal patronage, often secretly by means of unrecorded payments. The office-holders wished to ensure that all administration was carried out by themselves, through the formal channels of the bureaucracy and without external interference. They therefore wanted royal and aristocratic clientage kept to a minimum. The nobles wished to see no such reduction in kingly generosity, because the expensive life style which their social position dictated often led them into financial hardship and made them heavily reliant upon these funds.

The notables were also soon in disarray about the manner in which the assembly should vote. If each estate expressed its own corporate opinion, the nobility and the clergy could always defeat the judiciary. If each member voted as an individual, the numerically superior *officiers* could achieve domination over the combined strength of the sword and the mitre. It was assumed that most contentious issues would divide the assembly into two groups, with the judges on one side and the First and Second Estates on the other. An uneasy compromise was devised, after which the ministers presented a more specific series of proposals, in the hope of starting the debate in earnest. They suggested that henceforth a proportion of the royal troops should be maintained financially by the provinces; that the notables should list the fortresses which they wished to see demolished, and say how the rest should be garrisoned, the cost of this also being levied upon the provinces in a manner which the assembly should select; that they should decide on the appropriate punishments for great nobles and Huguenots who had led rebellions, although it is significant that popular revolts in the localities were not mentioned; that it was also for them to say whether wise nobles should be brought into the royal council; that they should define *lèse-majesté*, considering in this regard the maintenace of private armies and fortifications, negotiating with foreign powers, the holding of popular assemblies and the publishing of seditious political pamphlets; that they should propose means for preventing the levying by powerful men of unauthorized taxes; and that they should decide whether a permanent system of grand assizes, *grands jours*, ought to be instituted in order to arraign powerful miscreants whose own locality dared not bring them to book. Furthermore they should put forward ways of restributing the *tailles*, so that the poor would receive some relief; they should draw up regulations for the grain trade; they should also consider whether some petty offices should be suppressed at once and should give an opinion on how many more of these posts should vanish in the future; and lastly they should say how expenditure could best be cut, pensions and salaries reduced, the demesne redeemed and the interest on debts lowered. Richelieu also promised that, where the assembly devised economies in the royal finances, the money thus saved would be used for purposes which had been agreed by the ministers and the notables. This was a necessary promise, because past experience had shown that the government could not be trusted to spend its resources in the ways it had previously undertaken to do, and the cardinal was now overtly committing the crown to keeping its word on this occasion.

The reactions of the notables to this lengthy series of propositions are very revealing. There was strong feeling on all sides against both religious heterodoxy and high aristocratic ambition. Huguenot rebels and seditious magnates were to merit very severe punishment, while the maintenance of private armies and fortifications, the negotiating by nobles with foreign powers and the domination by individual aristocrats of high offices of state like those of *connétable* and *amiral-général* were all condemned by the assembly. It also deplored the levying of unauthorized taxes by powerful men. The notables, whether clerical, noble or judicial, were clearly of the opinion that, in those kingly areas of war, peace, foreign policy and the defence of the realm, the responsibility should rest with the king and with ministers of his own choosing, and that in such matters the great nobles were more likely to be tyrants than protectors of the people. The assembly accordingly allowed the crown to expand the navy and approved the plans for a better disciplined army – although taking care to preserve their own exemptions from the billeting of troops. They also endorsed the proposal to set up colonial companies, but then insisted that the edicts creating these new commercial bodies should be registered by the *parlements*. This rider effectively negated their initial approval, because it was the well-known hostility of the sovereign courts to all such companies which had prompted Richelieu to consult the notables on this matter in the first place.

On the royal proposals which touched upon the internal administration of the kingdom, there was less agreement. They did not object to the suppression of lesser offices, because even the judicial representatives were prepared to acknowledge that the bureaucracy had become too large. Nevertheless, they did insist that the holders of these posts should be reimbursed on terms which were very favourable to them and unsatisfactory for the government. They had no intention of establishing a bad precedent which might be used against higher

offices at a later date. Nor did they quibble about the fairer
distribution of the *taille*; no member of the assembly paid this tax
anyway and it was not being proposed that they should do so. It was at
this point that one judicial member suggested that the *taille réelle*
should be extended to the whole of France, on the grounds that it was
fairer and that it offered an opportunity for increasing royal revenue.
The rest of the *officiers* quickly rejected this suggestion. In the areas of
taille réelle a man was exempt from paying tax on land which had noble
status, whereas elsewhere, under the *taille personnelle*, exemption was
granted when the person himself was noble. If the *personnelle* form were
to be replaced by a *réelle* assessment, a noble who held some non-noble
land would find that his personal exemption from the whole levy was
now changed into an obligation to pay tax on these commoner estates.
As it was largely the office-holding nobles, eager to become landed
seigneurs, who had purchased non-noble lands, it was they who now
spoke vigorously against a reform which would have had serious
financial consequences for their families. At the same time, the sword
nobles bitterly complained of the poverty to which their Estate had
been reduced as a result of the advent and rise of the new office-
holding nobility.

Further disagreements between *épée* and *robe* erupted over the
suggestion that sword nobles should be brought into the royal council,
and the plan for provincial contributions towards the cost of the army.
In fact the members were all hostile towards this increased burden on
the provinces, but they managed to quarrel about the details of the
scheme, even though they intended to reject it totally. The problem
turned on how these funds would be administered, in the hypothetical
situation that the assembly had accepted the general principle. The
aristocratic governor, the *parlements* and the *intendants* were possible
candidates for this task, and none of these was acceptable to all the
groups within the notables. The judicial members were also exercised
about the proposal for regular grand assizes. The courts were always
suspicious of such special royal tribunals, which threatened the
fundamental basis of their own jurisdictions, but they would sometimes
accept them if their purpose was desirable and if they were staffed by
suitable personnel. On this occasion they therefore insisted that the
grand assizes should be staffed entirely by *parlementaires*, which would
have immediately deprived these courts of their directly royal
character, and would ensure that certain kinds of malefactors, the
leading office-holders in fact, would escape punishment. Thus the
prime purpose of Richelieu – to create an independent series of courts,
immediately under the crown, which would investigate all crimes
without favour towards any social group – was thwarted. The officials

also demanded a formal confirmation of their right to amend royal edicts which were submitted to them for registration, and that they should have total control over all procedures concerned with resumption of the royal demesne. They also petitioned that all tax-farm contracts should be submitted to the *parlements* for registration, that those courts should take charge of municipal elections and that the *intendants* should be abolished.

Some of the later grievances of the Frondeurs were clearly present, therefore, in the debates of the notables in 1626, and the office-holders were becoming more vociferous in opposing ministerial attempts to extend the direct authority of the central government at the expense of traditional institutions. Yet the hostility of the *épée* towards the *robe* seemed little diminished, even though there was no longer a campaign for the abolition of the *paulette* and the whole venal system, and the mistrust felt by the whole assembly for the great magnates was very strong indeed. There was still no sign that within thirty years the *parlement* of Paris and the princes would have emerged as 'national' leaders in two Frondes.

INTERNAL REVOLTS, INTERNATIONAL CONFLICT AND CIVIL WAR, 1626–1653

After 1626 the government did not again consult the representatives of the kingdom, although a meeting of the *Etats-généraux* was mooted during the Frondes and in the War of the Spanish Succession. Richelieu had hoped for some positive support from the *assemblée des notables* for many of his reforms, but little had been forthcoming. The members had helped him in his desire 'ravaler l'orgueil des grands',[12] and they had not rejected his plan for a larger navy, although they had omitted to suggest any ways of financing this extended fleet. Indeed in all respects they had blocked his attempts to put the royal finances on a sounder footing. Accordingly, he abandoned many of his proposals. They would have been too provocative and therefore would not have been implemented by the *officiers*. Soon compelled to spend heavily on defeating the Huguenots, and then to take France openly into the Thirty Years War, he pursued as cautious a policy as the desperate state of the revenues in the treasury would permit. Having failed to

[12]This desire to crush the pride of the grandees, together with his determination to ruin the power of the Huguenots and his intention to pursue a successful European war in order to establish a lasting peace, are the three main goals which Richelieu set himself in his *Testament politique* — see the edition with an introduction and notes by Louis André (Paris, 1947).

reform the system, he was forced to exploit the financial expedients which had kept the government afloat in past crises, especially the use of financiers and the manipulation of the venal office system.

It has already been noted that, during these difficult years, the cardinal protected the king either by taking the blame himself for unpopular decisions, or by making one of his fellow ministers into a scapegoat. Occasionally the king might hold a *lit de justice*, to coerce a difficult *parlement*, but Richelieu was not fond of this procedure because it had two distinct dangers. The first was that the Paris judges had many ways of delaying or waiving the provisions of edicts which they had been forced to register, in which case the authority of the monarch was being flouted in a scarcely veiled manner. Even worse, they might overtly voice their objections in public or might add some extra provisions to the edict, thus modifying the intentions of the crown. That was open defiance and, as the cardinal knew that the *parlement* was vital to the effective running of the judicial system, it was unwise to provoke its disobedience unless there was no alternative course of action.

The 1630s were fraught with dangers for the government and for the minister himself. The decade had begun with the *journée des dupes*, the attempted *coup* in which Richelieu had nearly become the victim of princely plotters, and there was a continuing threat of conspiracy against him until his death in 1642. Yet his victory over his enemies in the 1630 plot led to further difficulties, because he now filled most of the high governmental posts with his *créatures*. There were still some disagreements about policy, but basically he was administering with the aid of his trusted advisers. It was therefore more difficult to find someone to sacrifice if an unforeseen disaster occurred, but more importantly the monopoly of power by one faction enraged, and encouraged co-operation among, other groups who were excluded from influence. Here was the reverse of the approach taken by Henri IV. Where he had sought to balance rival patronage networks, the cardinal tried to assert the dominance of his own clientele over all others.

For most of this troublesome decade there was still the problem that the king had no direct heir, and even when the future Louis XIV was born in 1638 it seemed probable that his father would not live long enough to ensure a direct transfer of power from one adult king to another. As the war had already caused increasing tensions and strains in French society, a period of regency was to be dreaded. These years were also punctuated by much provincial disobedience and open revolt, about which the crown could do little. By the end of the reign, almost every financial expedient had been pushed to the limit, and

Mazarin would have hardly any room for manoeuvre. Moreover those factions which Richelieu had excluded from the government would seek their revenge, not just out of family pride, but because some of them genuinely believed that the extensive involvement in war had not been necessary. Historians no longer accuse the elder cardinal of pursuing *gloire* for its own sake, and accept that his foreign policy was designed to strengthen the defences of the realm by the means that he thought best. Yet many of his enemies, including his attackers in the *journée des dupes*, did not believe that such overt involvement in the war was either necessary or desirable, and they therefore blamed him and his *créatures* for the disastrous consequences of this policy.

The financial methods used by the crown in the 1630s admirably demonstrate the seriousness of the crisis facing the treasury. The ministers turned first to one quarter, then to another, in their search for funds, and found increasingly that they could obtain only short-term relief. By 1642 the direct and indirect taxes had become so heavy that it was fruitless to raise them further, and they had been mortgaged to financiers in order to anticipate the yield of future years. The levies were now so high that some would not, and many could not, pay. The poorer taxpayers always lived dangerously close to the bare level of survival, and one bad harvest could push them below it. There was no point in seizing the means of livelihood, especially the livestock, of these men as payment for outstanding taxes, because this virtually guaranteed that they would soon be dead, and therefore totally useless as a source of revenue. It was better to have a living taxpayer, even if he were in arrears. Although the royal collectors were therefore exhorted not to take such drastic action, the more un-scrupulous tax-farmers were not above these cruelties as they sought to recoup their investment in tax contracts. Yet by 1642 they too were often reluctant to offer their services to the treasury, because the chances of making a profit were declining year by year. Some found that their receipts fell so far short of the sums they had advanced to the crown that the finance minister, Bullion, remitted some of their initial outlay, in order to encourage them to continue as farmers in years to come.

It was during this disastrous decade that the *parlements* and other office-holders began to emerge as the loudest and most persistent critics of royal policy. Not only were some of them also involved in tax-farming and in lending directly to the crown, and many more were investors in the *rentes* which were also being manipulated by the ministers, but this was the time when the exploitation of the venal office system reached its height. There were numerous creations of new posts, and a series of attempts to extract further sums from those who already possessed an office. In 1629 the government had proposed that *officiers* should pay one quarter of the value of their office as a loan to the treasury in return for the renewal of the *annuel*. The clamour against this suggestion had been so great that the finance minister modified his demands almost at once, but in fact most office-holders were granted their continuation of the *annuel* without having to pay any part of the loan. The same offensive tactics were tried once more when the next nine-yearly renewal of the *paulette* fell due in 1638, arousing even greater ire among the bureaucrats. Like the direct and indirect taxes, this was another source of royal income which Bullion pushed to unacceptable lengths, and therefore it could not be increased, or even sustained at the same level, by Mazarin. He would not be able to set such a high price on the next renewal of the *annuel* in 1647, on the very eve of the first Fronde. In every way Bullion emerged as the villain of French finance. Demanding increased amounts from all parts of the fiscal, bureaucratic and financial systems, he further alienated those who had lent money to the crown, or who were owed salaries and other sums, by reimbursing them not in cash but with pieces of paper which could be redeemed against future revenues. As those revenues were themselves unlikely to materialize in full, these credit notes were of dubious value. Soon many of the newly created offices could not be sold either, as the price was too high and the likelihood of a secure income for the purchaser was conjectural. This also affected the financiers, who had bought up these posts *en bloc* and could not now dispose of them. Also, the existing bureaucrats were effective as saboteurs of these government expedients, challenging new offices and tax contracts in the courts and employing delaying tactics which were enough to deter would-be buyers and investors.

One consequence of the financial distress in the royal treasury was particularly offensive to the office-holders – the increased use of the *intendants*.[13] These direct royal agents were no novelty, whether called by this or by other names, and they had never been welcomed by the venal officials because they were outside the formal, hereditary bureaucracy. Whereas a provincial governor was a great aristocrat who was integrated into the society of his *gouvernement* and understood local problems, the *intendant* always seemed like a royal spy, an outsider who came to do the will of the king but had no sympathy for the areas he visited. Very often, this popular view was remarkably

[13]This subject has been examined at length by Richard Bonney in his first book, *Political change in France under Richelieu and Mazarin, 1624–1661* (Oxford, 1978), where the *intendants* are at the core of the entire text; see also Roland Mousnier, 'Research into the popular uprisings before the Fronde', in P. J. Coveney (ed.), *France in crisis, 1620–75* (London, 1977), esp. pp. 144–60.

near to the truth. Local *officiers* never liked the idea of royal commissioners on principle, although, as with the creation of *chambres de justice* and the *grands jours*, they would agree to them if they approved of the purpose for which they had been appointed, for example, the investigation of the financiers and their malpractice. Then office-holders would even consent to serve on these special commissions, hoping to play a dominant role. In contrast, the *intendant* had none of these redeeming qualities. He always seemed to oppose their interests and was totally without friends or supporters.

The judicial representatives had asked at the *assemblée des notables* in 1626 for the abolition of the *intendants*, but their request had not been granted, although it must be noted that the use made of these officials in the later 1620s was spasmodic and not particularly offensive on the practical level. The problem for the historian is therefore to consider why these *commissaires* became a major focus of hatred during the Frondes and yet were accepted more readily under Colbert in the 1660s, when they were used more regularly and systematically. The unwise scholar would say that it was the establishment of 'absolutism' which silenced such criticism, and would add that, during the personal rule of Louis XIV, these officials became the very cornerstones of the new authoritarianism. While these explanations are obviously as anachronistic and unrealistic as the assertions that the Sun King crushed the nobles and the *parlements*, there is certainly a need to account for this change in the reputation enjoyed by the *intendants*.

The hostility of the *parlementaires* and other office-holders to the increased use of these direct royal agents stemmed from a variety of different causes. One prime objection of the Paris judges concerned the social standing of these new men. They came, not from the bourgeoisie as the 'absolutist' historians used to claim, but from the *noblesse de robe*, and many of them had spent part of their working life within the *parlement* or the other sovereign courts before becoming *maîtres des requêtes*, the cadre of judges from which almost all *intendants* were selected. The *maîtres* exercised certain functions within the *parlement* but in most ways were distinct from it, and there had been many acrimonious disputes between them and the *parlementaires* about their respective jurisdictions. On a number of occasions, kings had tried to remove the cognizance of certain crimes from the sovereign courts and hand them to the *maîtres* instead.[14] Indeed it seemed to many judges that these men, even though some of them were former colleagues, had betrayed the *robe* and were working for the extension of royal power at

[11]See Colin R. E. Kaiser, *The master of requests: an extraordinary judicial company in an age of centralisation, 1589–1648* (London PhD thesis, 1976), esp. pp. 352–419.

the expense of the traditional bureaucracy. Worse still, they were passing their posts down through their families and were intermarrying, thus forming dynasties and clienteles which were theoretically part of the *robe* hierarchy but in practice were associated with royal and ministerial patronage. These therefore were reasons for hating the *intendants*, regardless of the tasks which were entrusted to them.

It was not until the 1660s that the commissions of the *intendants* took on any consistent format, although the list of their duties would lengthen as the personal rule of Louis XIV progressed. Under Richelieu and Mazarin their instructions were much more haphazard. They were sent out to deal with specific crises, and their brief was tailored to meet a particular short-term situation. In the 1620s it was thus impossible to define the powers of *intendants* in general, but only to describe those which has been assigned to one individual for a single spell of duty. In the 1630s there appeared to be a greater degree of uniformity because the burning problem for the crown in all parts of the kingdom was the same – how to raise extra money for the war. Accordingly, their visits to the provinces became increasingly frequent, and they began to be associated chiefly with the raising of extra taxation, the exploitation of extraordinary sources of revenue and the organization of the military. Certainly a principal objection to them in 1648 was that, with the signing of the Peace of Westphalia, the only conceivable justification for their existence – French participation in the Thirty Years War – was now removed.

Despite the virulence with which the *intendants* were attacked by *officiers* and other local notables, their powers had never been very great even in theory, let alone in practice. Many of their duties were purely investigative, which involved their prying into the activities of the local administration and reporting back to the crown. They did not take over the functions of other officials, but were sometimes instructed to supervise their activities. Occasionally they were given powers of judgment, but these were usually of a temporary and summary kind, and appeals against their decisions could then be taken to the regular courts where the *intendant* was very frequently overruled. Only rarely did this royal *commissaire* attempt actually to usurp the powers of other institutions or individuals, and then he sometimes encountered effective resistance. Yet he and his fellows became bogeymen for the office-holders, symbols of attempts by the crown to extend its power at the expense of traditional privileges and jurisdictions. Although they were used rather more moderately by Mazarin, the reputation they had acquired in the 1630s continued to grow, and the outcry against them forced the regent to abolish them during the first Fronde. The *intendants* must therefore join the whole range of problems to be examined below, concerning the restoration of royal authority after the turbulent years of civil war.

At the death of Richelieu in 1642, most subjects of Louis XIII were discontented with the government. The wider citizenry shared the hatred felt by the office-holders for the finance ministers and their oppressive policies, the country was impoverished by the costs of war and the effects of troop movements, revolts were frequent and the princes were awaiting their chance for revenge. It was scarcely the moment for a child to ascend the throne, and certainly not the ideal time for a regent whose own family was currently the principal French enemy, with a foreign cardinal as chief minister whose training had been in the papal service and who lacked a clientele within the kingdom. Even the clergy, who were not averse to a churchman being *premier ministre*, were not pleased by his Italian and Roman background. Recent historians have credited Mazarin with greater skill in international affairs than his earlier biographers allowed, and even his internal policies in the years before the Frondes have now been rescued from total condemnation. The situation which he inherited was an impossible one. The main financial remedies for royal poverty had been exploited to the limit by Bullion, and yet France was still engaged in the most expensive war which she had ever fought, with no sign of an imminent end to the hostilities. Moreover, there were always plenty of influential groups in the kingdom who would claim that a regency government had very limited powers, could not change policy and could not initiate legislation.

If tensions abounded in France on the death of Louis XIII, it was still by no means clear that a civil war was only six years away. Many people voiced grievances against the royal government, but there were also disputes within the localities. Not all the numerous revolts of the 1630s had been concerned solely with ministerial excesses. Some had been directed against local nobles, office-holders or municipal officials. Nor was there any shortage of jurisdictional disputes between rival elites. Moreover, although the war was costly and the troops became ever more unruly as the years went by, at least many potential troublemakers in the provinces were away at the battlefront, serving as officers and even as generals. Some of the greatest magnates were occupied in this way and, unless they decided to defect to the enemy, as a number were to do, they were less dangerous there than at court. Nor were the various sovereign courts closely united, and they could certainly not rely on the support of lesser *officiers*, because many of their complaints were relevant only to their own part of the bureaucratic hierarchy. The ministers of the early 1660s, a number of whom had served the crown during the Frondes, were therefore very

assiduous in analysing the events of the years 1643–8, because they felt
that it was vital to identify the factors which had transformed tension
and disorder into civil war. If they could discover the extent to which
ministerial errors had inflamed the situation, then they could avoid the
same mistakes in future.

When he succeeded Richelieu as *premier ministre*, Mazarin undoubtedly tried to be less provocative than his predecessor, and also
embarked on a more conciliatory foreign policy. He stressed the need
to accelerate the peace negotiations, but knew that France must not
seem desperate to reach an agreement, nor to be in any way pro-
Habsburg which might have implied that the queen was putting her
family before her adopted country. The great princes, at the top of the
French social hierarchy, found that the new regime looked more
friendly. Some of them had long been intimates of the queen, and the
hostility shown towards them by Richelieu was now replaced by signs
of royal favour and social rewards. Yet this was the only group in the
state which wanted a major political role in the councils of the crown,
and here Mazarin was more wary. He did accept the presence of
Condé and d'Orléans on the *conseil d'état*, but was careful to be
imprecise about their exact role in the government. It nevertheless
soon became clear to other magnates that the cardinal had no
intention of bringing them all into the corridors of power, and they
accordingly planned the first conspiracy of the new reign, the *cabale des
importants*. This plot was unmasked in time, and Mazarin could hope
that he had staved off the princely danger. D'Orléans and Condé were
still being co-operative, and it was known that the *grands* had no great
support among the populace in general.

Towards other leading members of society, that is to say towards
those groups which often resisted the crown but, unlike the princes,
did not actually wish to enter and dominate the royal council, Mazarin
also extended the hand of friendship whenever he saw an opportunity
to do so. The *parlement* of Paris was flattered to be asked by the queen
to set aside the testament of Louis XIII, in order to secure her power
as regent, and she underlined this tribute to its authority by asking it
to advise her on the problems facing her government and to criticize
past actions. As a further sign of her goodwill towards the *parlement*,
she chose one of its *présidents* as a *surintendant des finances*. The judges
were not only pleased by these overtures, but they preferred there to be
a single regent, with a monopoly of power, whom they could challenge
when the need arose, rather than a council of squabbling and factious
princes. The Italian cardinal was determined to draw his immediate
advisers from different backgrounds and patronage groupings, aware
that the heavy reliance of Richelieu on his own *créatures* had alienated

many important people. One powerful interest which had to be represented was that of the financiers, so vital to the crown and yet deeply disillusioned by the treatment they had received at the hands of Bullion. For the post of *contrôleur-général des finances*, Mazarin therefore chose an experienced financier, Particelli d'Emeri, a man whom he could trust because he had known him for many years, originally in the diplomatic sphere when d'Emeri had been the French ambassador to Savoy. Mazarin shared the view of Richelieu that the *premier ministre*, although he might interest himself in major proposals for financial reform, should leave the everyday finance of the kingdom to a lesser minister and be free to concentrate his own attention on war and foreign affairs. That was one reason why Bullion had been able to mismanage royal money matters for so long without being called to account by Richelieu. Mazarin knew that his *contrôleur* could be trusted to do his job well, and this confidence seemed justified. D'Emeri was not widely disliked or mistrusted at first, and it was only when he was less successful that he began to be called the Italian lackey of an Italian master. He was in fact much more French than the cardinal, as his father had become a naturalized Frenchman in 1595.

The first actions of the new *premier ministre* were therefore designed to placate as many important groups as possible, and d'Emeri initially pursued this policy in his administration of the finances. Knowing that Bullion had increased the direct and indirect taxes to the point where they could neither be raised nor farmed, he now reduced the *tailles* and the price of the tax contracts. As Bullion had saturated the market with *rentes* and newly created offices, there was no further revenue to be obtained by these means. Nor would existing *officiers* be persuaded to advance more money to the crown, and he accordingly did not even raise the matter. The most likely way to obtain financial relief was to borrow directly from the money-markets, and d'Emeri was able to reassure fellow financiers that the government would keep faith as a debtor, and that it would never allow them to be arraigned and punished by a *chambre de justice*. As a result of these assurances, d'Emeri retained the confidence of many lenders until 1647. Unfortunately for Mazarin, the peace negotiations remained inconclusive, the costs of war rose still further, and the harassed finance minister was forced into less wise courses of action. Already the crown was anticipating its revenues for two years ahead, and drastic measures were needed. D'Emeri was still reluctant to raise the extra money he needed from taxpayers and office-holders, although he did introduce some new levies, chiefly on Paris and on the lessees of the royal demesne, which yielded little but caused great discontent. Instead he preferred to reduce the outgoings from the treasury, regarding that as one of the swifter ways of closing the gap between the income and expenditure. The two most obvious economies which he could make were a reduction in the interest due on the *rentes* and a cut in the salaries of *officiers*.

Historians have frequently censured the finance minister in the strongest terms for this apparent stupidity, but that is too simple a judgement. It may be that Mazarin and Anne were not sufficiently French to understand the subtleties of the bureaucratic *mentalité*, but d'Emeri cannot be accused of that. He also fully comprehended the mind of the typical financier, from his own first-hand experience. There were plenty of men in the money-markets who were prepared to lend to the crown, as long as this able minister was in charge, but they were putting pressure upon him to cut royal expenditure lest the treasury should become so impoverished that it would have to default on its debts. It had done so in the past, and both the lenders and d'Emeri himself knew that a repetition of such an arbitrary act had to be avoided at all costs. No one could prevent the king from renouncing such loans, but the consequence of his doing so was always to make the crown totally uncreditworthy and therefore unable to borrow further. Yet the fact that this minister came from the financial world and relied so heavily upon it was beginning to provoke an outcry among the office-holders, who claimed that all would be well if the government were not enslaved by these 'sangsues'.

Cuts in salaries and interest payments were always provocative, but in earlier days such measures had not caused a Fronde. For the major revolt of 1648 to break out, there had to be a coincidence of other factors. Very importantly, the ministeriat itself was not united. Some of its members were clients of d'Orléans and Condé, and were therefore supporters of Mazarin only as long as he and the two princes agreed on policy, and that harmony was soon under strain. Also the presence of these senior magnates in the government, and the conciliatory tone adopted by the regent and the cardinal in 1643, had led the office-holders to expect that the most unpopular decisions of Richelieu would be reversed. In particular they hoped for an end to the *intendants*. Mazarin had no intention of extending the use of these officials, but they had proved their worth as military organizers and as a channel of communication between the court and the provinces. So the system continued, with the aristocratic governors and the specially commissioned *maîtres des requêtes* working side by side. The really provocative new decision was that complaints against the *intendants*, and against certain other financial innovations, were to be sent directly to the royal council, by-passing the *parlements* and the *cours des aides*. Those two sets of sovereign courts had no love for each other, and the provincial *parlements* frequently resented the arrogance of their Parisian confrères, but all these courts had a common interest in resisting encroachments by the royal council on their respective jurisdictions. They were furious that they were denied their right of judicial review over these new levies. They were further outraged by the insistence of the regent that she could hold a *lit de justice* in the *parlement* and could enforce the registration of fiscal edicts in the *chambre des comptes* and the *cour des aides*. Not only was she offending against the theoretical argument, denied by the crown, that there could be no *lit de justice* during a royal minority and that the *parlementaires*, as the senior judges and the guardians of the *lois fondamentales*, had a duty to ensure that no such abuse of monarchical power took place. There was the added insult that d'Orléans and Condé were sent to force the fiscal edicts through the other two sovereign courts. The judges detested all the princes of the blood, because they were the authors of the frequent court conspiracies which threatened to return the kingdom to a state of factious division, and because a major item on the princely agenda had always been the destruction of venality and hereditary bureaucracy.

Thus the office-holders had become increasingly incensed in the mid 1640s, and when d'Emeri finally had to resort to additional tax increases and to demanding more money from the *officiers* themselves, the two things which he had hoped to avoid, they unleashed their full fury upon him. Mazarin was equally angry because he was sure that the militancy of the judges was encouraging Spain to be more grasping in the peace negotiations. It was for such reasons that the crown felt the *parlement* to be meddling in affairs of state, as it was affecting the kingly area of foreign policy, although the judges would have said that they were simply concerned with legal rights, privileges and jurisdictions. D'Emeri not only demanded a forced loan from the office-holders as a condition for renewing the *paulette*, which expired in 1647, but he also tried to divert the municipal taxes into the royal treasury. Town councillors and royal *officiers* often squabbled about their conflicting jurisdictions, but here were some arbitrary actions to unite them against the finance minister. With the government near to bankruptcy and the financiers very uneasy, and with widespread hostility in the country to the high levels of taxes, one further problem made its appearance, a disastrous harvest.

The news that the Dutch had made a separate peace with Spain took away the very last shred of credibility from the beleaguered cardinal. Even his foreign policy had failed. D'Emeri now made his final mistake. In April 1648 he announced that the renunciation of their salaries for four years would be the price which the officials of the sovereign courts would have to pay for the renewal of the *paulette*, although he made an exception for members of the *parlement* of Paris. If the minister thought that this was a way of dividing the sovereign courts and other *officiers* – of maintaining equilibrium among factions – he was wrong. Not only were the *parlementaires* outraged by the implication that they would simply look after their own interests and ignore the wider illegality of this action, but they also had their relatives to consider, who actually served in these lesser posts. Thus the sovereign courts issued their *arrêt d'union*, the financiers refused further loans and the first Fronde had begun.

Generations of historians have written at great length and reached very different conclusions about the *fronde parlementaire*, and it is therefore important to assess the role of the *parlement* in that rebellion because for these few months it seemed to have the support of many groups, some of whom normally felt little affection for it.[15] The cause of this new unity was the assignment by the regent of more power to the council at the expense of traditional regulating bodies. Some of its supporters were primarily concerned with this usurpation of their jurisdictions and rights, while others were directly affected by the actual import of these conciliar and ministerial decisions which had been promulgated without the usual consultations. Therefore the *parlement* of Paris made the jurisdictional point that the council was behaving arbitrarily, and the victims of the new royal exactions appealed to the sovereign court for protection. At the same time as the *parlement* was not asked to verify the novel tariff levied on Paris, the tax on illegal house building in the capital and the extra levy on lessees of the royal demesne, the *chambre des comptes* and the *cour des aides* were told that they could not examine current contracts for tax-farming – all of which they were traditionally entitled to do. The *trésoriers de France* were also denied their role in arranging the farming of certain taxes. By carrying out their negotiations without the usual checks and intermediaries, the crown and the financiers did not have to reveal the terms of their agreements, and everyone suspected that the money lenders were making enormous profits at the expense of the people of France. The increasing use of secret *ordonnances de comptant* for payments by the treasury further fuelled these suspicions. The sovereign courts supported the *trésoriers de France* and the *élus* in their

[15]The most detailed, and in some ways the best, book is A. Lloyd Moote, *The revolt of the judges: the Parlement of Paris and the Fronde, 1643–1652* (Princeton, 1971), which stresses the primarily legal concerns of the *parlement*, although it is less good on the decades before the Frondes because it presents an excessively dramatic view of Richelieu's achivements. The most stimulating study remains the much older but enduring book by E. H. Kossmann, *La Fronde* (Leiden, 1954).

growing chorus of protest against the *intendants*, and at the height of the troubles the *maîtres des requêtes* themselves appealed to the *parlement* for a decision against the reduction of their duties and the creation of many new offices within their *compagnie*.

Outside the ranks of the bureaucracy, with its unaccustomed unity of purpose, there were many citizens of Paris who now saw the *parlement* as their champion against tyranny. The merchants, craftsmen and the lower levels of society demanded an end to the new levies, although it had been largely impossible to collect them, and even gathered outside the *palais de justice* in great numbers at the time of the *lit de justice* in order to show the judges that the city was behind them. In fact such manifestations of popular support alarmed the *parlementaires* into taking a more aggressive line, as they feared that the citizenry might turn against their heroes if they were irresolute and seemed ready for a compromise. There were also frequent demonstrations throughout the capital, involving bourgeois as well as humble workers, because a vigorous campaign by broadsheets and word-of-mouth reports ensured that every Parisian had access to the latest developments in the confrontation with the regent. Faced with the growing unity of the citizenry against them, the ministers did withdraw some of the offending levies for brief periods, but reimposed them again as their search for alternatives proved fruitless. Even the tax-collectors and *intendants* were not daring to demand payments of more familiar taxes, so hostile was the mood in Paris and the provinces.

If Paris rallied to the *parlement* for a variety of short-term reasons, the provinces were less certain that this court should be their spokesman.[16] Hatred of taxes, *intendants* and financiers, as well as the increase in the billeting of troops and the requisitioning of supplies, had led to much rioting and disorder, but the local elites did not want to be too closely associated with the arguments in Paris, lest it prevent them from negotiating some concessions which were of more particular and more urgent benefit for their area. Nevertheless they watched the developing chaos closely, for it was from this confusion at the centre that they hoped to profit in their dealings with the ministers. In the summer of 1648 the crown became convinced that an alliance of all the *parlements* was imminent, when the provincial judges still had no such intentions, and the governors spent much time in trying to detach their local

---

[16]For example that of Provence — see Sharon Kettering, *Judicial politics and urban revolt in seventeenth-century France: the parlement of Aix, 1629–1659* (Princeton, 1978), pp. 251–97, esp. pp. 270–7.

parlement from an alliance which it had not actually joined. This was fortunate for the provincial judges, who were offered concessions which they had not demanded. One interesting aspect of this action by the governors is that not only Condé and d'Orléans, but also Longueville, were still carrying out their duties on behalf of the regent and Mazarin, without any overt sign of their future *frondeur* sentiments.

When the Parisian sovereign courts issued their *arrêt d'union* on 13 May 1648, they were not taking a revolutionary step, because the four bodies had met in plenary session at times of past crisis. Yet the crown was very much alarmed for two reasons. Not only had the various courts put aside their rivalry, but the *parlement* itself was more united than usual. Within that most senior tribunal, there was a range of opinions from the radical to the very conservative. During the early months of 1648, the various groups among the *parlementaires* had agreed to take a middle course, rather radical in its policy but conservative in its methods. It had decided to remonstrate against, rather than to alter, the royal edicts of the *lit de justice*, which was the more legal way of proceeding, but it did expect its remonstrances to be heeded and their content was sometimes very critical. As the regent alternated between inaction and further provocation, the conservatives found it difficult to maintain that a negotiated outcome could be achieved, and either submitted to radical pressures or even spoke out spontaneously in more aggressive tones. Far from backing down, the government took the offensive, but the judges would not retreat and the people were on the streets in support of their stance.

Yet it was only in June that the united courts and their *Chambre de Saint-Louis* took up the grievances which had prompted many of their supporters outside to appeal for their help. From January to March they had concentrated on the fiscal edicts of the *lit de justice*. In April and May they had turned to the *paulette*, the one issue on which their radical and conservative members had much in common. Now they began to demand an investigation of the royal finances, an end to the *intendants*, a restoration of all the traditional powers of the office-holders and a massive reduction in the burden of taxation. These new concerns were initially debated by the separate courts, but with the threat to convoke a *Chambre* of all four very much in their minds. By the end of the month there was nothing to be gained from further delay, and on 30 June the *Chambre de Saint-Louis* began a month of deliberations, during which the representatives of all the sovereign courts worked rapidly and harmoniously on their proposals for reform. They took care to look after the interests of other groups, especially the *maîtres des requêtes* and the *trésoriers de France*, who had not been allowed to send some of their own number to the *Chambre*. Now that the body was in session, lesser *officiers* lobbied the *parlement* to ensure that they were not forgotten. They need not have worried, because the *Chambre* was careful to formulate its proposals in such broad terms that all the office-holders would benefit. If their movement had arisen out of their particular concerns, there was no doubt that the sovereign courts were enjoying their role as spokesmen for the people of France. As these deliberations continued, the *parlement* took action to implement the reforms. It did not intend to wait for the conclusion of the *Chambre* because urgent action was needed as soon as the delegates reached agreement on each point. The *parlementaires* still acted legally. When the crown had used its own powers unwisely, they sent a remonstrance demanding redress, but where their own authority had been by-passed, they took matters into their own hands. Thus they quickly abolished the *intendants*, because their commissions had not been registered in the *parlement* and were accordingly void.

In the provinces other sovereign courts were following the example of Paris, and were extending the scope of their demands in order to include the grievances of the wider populace. They were not working with the Parisian courts, but were simply pursuing similar courses. It was the government which gave a greater semblance of unity to their disparate efforts because the regent felt that, if she were to make any concessions to the judges in the capital, she would be wise to consult the provincial courts as well, lest her failure to do so provoke an outburst from those more distant institutions. The first concessions came at a *lit de justice* of 31 July, where she pledged the crown to the cause of reform, but in very vague terms, and pleaded that the wartime situation prevented her from taking rapid action. The *parlement* responded by adding the specific reform proposals which the royal decree lacked. Although not all the *parlementaires* were equally popular in Paris, and some conservatives were thought to be delaying the reforms, in general the court was being hailed as the champion of fiscal reductions and therefore of the oppressed. Massive popular demonstrations in its favour confirmed the judges in their feeling that they should continue to present themselves in this light, or they might become targets of the discontent.

After the brief arrest of Broussel and the radical judges, and the two days of the barricades, some of the *grands* decided that this was the moment to join in the confusion, in the hope of ousting Mazarin and either replacing him or at least joining the royal council. They had nothing in common with the judges except their hatred of the cardinal, but some of the radicals, like Broussel himself, believed that the magnates could be useful in removing him from power. Certainly Mazarin thought this might be so, because he overestimated the danger to such an extent that he took the royal family away from Paris on 13 September.

Already, therefore, it is clear that the first Fronde was an extremely improbable alliance of groups which were often at odds – the various sovereign courts, the *maîtres des requêtes*, many other office-holders, the people of Paris, the elites and populace of many provinces, and now some of the great aristocrats. Moreover the government had provoked moderates into becoming more militant, and had taken decisions which were so wide-ranging that they gave a common grievance to many different sorts of people. The ministers of the 1660s would take careful note of all these matters, knowing that there must be no repetition of what were quite clearly governmental mistakes. The subsequent history of the Frondes showed how fragile were these alliances, but also how rapidly they could revive if the crown made further unforced errors.

The demands of the *Chambre de Saint-Louis* had been very comprehensive. The only obvious omission was the renewal of the *paulette*, because the members knew that it would be conceded by the regent as a compromise, which indeed it was. They did demand the restoration of the salary payments to office-holders; the abolition of recent creations and the promise that any new offices would have to be approved by the appropriate courts; an end to all special commissions which had not been similarly verified; no further farming of the *taille*; and no usurpation by the royal council of the jurisdictions which rightfully belonged to other bodies. Some of these bland statements were extremely far reaching, because most of the unpopular actions by the regency had involved the abuse of at least one of these principles, and many levels of society would benefit from them. The judges also insisted on an end to arbitrary arrest, which would prevent a repetition of the detention of Broussel but would also apply to the kingdom at large. On fiscal matters, some of which were already covered by their earlier general demands, they sought a reduction in the *taille*, a close examination of the tax-farmers and an end to recent innovations. The *rentes* were not to be manipulated, and *ordonnances de comptant* were not to be used for the secret reimbursement of royal creditors. These and other reforms appalled the regent and the cardinal, but she had to make some rapid concessions. Ironically, had it been peacetime, an astute minister like Colbert would have readily agreed that much of this programme for reform was highly desirable and he would indeed implement some of its provisions in the 1660s; but the late 1640s were years of war, and Mazarin had neither the understanding of the financial system nor the room for manoeuvre to do anything more than procrastinate. As any feasible compromise eluded him and the government became more desperate, the *grands* continued to cabal. On 5 January 1649 the royal family again left the capital, the regent this time threatening to besiege the city with troops under the command of the still loyal Condé. She also intemperately accused her opponents of treachery and of Spanish sympathies, which gave the judges the resolve to fight, united most of Paris behind them and prompted the great princes and magnates to throw themselves into the battle against Mazarin. Already revolts were erupting in the provinces, certainly stimulated by the events in Paris but not caused by them, and both judges and magnates now used their persuasion and influence to raise even more support throughout the kingdom for the Parisian cause.

The co-operation of the judges and magnates was too improbable to last. The former insisted on acting legally, the latter were even in favour of a Spanish alliance and, with their long experience of international family politics, knew how to organize such an association. Yet the *parlement* did retain the confidence of most Parisians, and it resisted the flattering overtures of provincial courts who asked it annul royal decisions which they did not like. It knew that the legality of its stance would be destroyed if it intervened in matters which were rightfully within the jurisdictions of other *parlements*. In return the provincial judges declined to implement in their areas all the decisions made by the court in the capital. Nevertheless Parisian and provincial judges spoke warmly in support of each other's struggles. With trouble abroad and throughout the realm, Mazarin and the regent had eventually to negotiate. As everyone except the magnates wanted a return to normality, the negotiations at Rueil were swift, and the agreement which resulted was soon registered by the Paris courts and the *parlements* of Aix and Rouen in April 1649. The burning problem, which has long been debated by historians and was vigorously addressed by contemporaries, was to decide who was the winner of the first Fronde.

The terms agreed at Rueil were undoubtedly regarded by the judges as a victory, and by the magnates as a total betrayal. The extreme posturings of both the regent and the *parlement* were abandoned, and the settlement was based on the more specific grievances which had given rise to the *Chambre de Saint-Louis*. In particular the Parisian magistrature dropped its demand for the total exclusion of Mazarin, which continued to be a principal goal of the aristocratic *frondeurs*. On her side, the regent ceased to insist that the judges should come to Saint-Germain-en-Laye and submit formally to her authority. Yet in the detailed negotiations she had been forced to concede a very great many important points and principles. The judges had agreed to a brief anticipation of the *taille* but not to one of the size that the government required, and they had insisted that this tax should not be farmed. It was to be collected by the traditional officials, and any loans designed to anticipate its yield were to be scrutinized by the *chambre des comptes*. It was also insisted that the lenders should not be reimbursed by secret *ordonnances de comptant*. Henceforth, all government borrowing should be open to examination by the sovereign courts. If the Paris judges therefore stood by the other officials in the capital and upheld the rights of the *trésoriers de France* and other tax-collectors, they did not forget their provincial confrères. They obtained fiscal concessions not only for the Paris area but for the lands within the jurisdictions of the *parlements* in Provence and Normandy, and they forced the crown to rescind the creation of new judgeships at Aix and Rouen. Thus they spoke up for the provincial *parlements* without actually having to take action on their behalf in the Paris courts. Although these provisions were fiscally disastrous for the treasury, the *parlementaire* success was such that the impoverished government did not dare to renegue on its promises, nor to introduce fresh levies by enforcing edicts at a *lit de justice*. The innovations of the past twenty years, including the new role of the *intendants*, were all brought to an end, although Mazarin hoped that in the not too immediate future some of them could be reintroduced. As for the regent, she could take some comfort from the fact that the *parlementaire* negotiators had allowed her to present some of these concessions as voluntary decisions of her own, rather than forcing her to accede to demands presented by them.

At least the *parlement* and the crown were agreed on the undesirability of the aristocratic *frondeurs* becoming members of the government, and at the time of the Rueil settlement Condé and Longueville, who had powerful provincial followings in their *gouvernements*, were still loyal to the regent, although the attempts of Longueville to placate Normandy by compromise caused Mazarin to question his sincerity. Nor was the cardinal any more favourably inclined towards Condé. That brave general was undoubtedly a devoted servant of the child king but he was voicing many reservations about the policies of the ministry, albeit behind closed doors at the court. In two years, it would be time to declare the majority of the young Louis and then Condé, according to established custom, would have a strong claim to head the council of the adolescent monarch, because the senior adult prince of the blood always presided over the royal advisers during the years of tutelage in which the king was technically a major but not old enough to rule unaided. In 1649, Mazarin could nevertheless derive some comfort from the hostility of both Condé and Longueville to the aristocratic *frondeurs*, the two men considering these seditious magnates not only as dangerous enemies of the young king but as personal rivals in the battle for the control of the royal council.

Unlike Condé and Longueville, the leaders of the high aristocratic party in the first Fronde did not have a secure power base in the provinces, although some of them were held in considerable esteem by the Parisians, and the judges feared that they might persuade the citizenry to rise against the new accord with the regent. Fortunately for the *parlementaires* and for the government, the magnates were divided on what course to follow. Gondi, the future cardinal de Retz, wanted to infiltrate his men into the councils of the king without the need for an armed struggle, whereas the ducs de Beaufort and d'Elbeuf wanted to raise the mob and attack the treacherous *parlement*. As Mazarin was coming under criticism from his fellow ministers, he did admit some supporters of Gondi into his inner circle, in the hope of playing them off against d'Orléans, Le Tellier and the increasingly discontented Condé. He also tried to pay arrears in salaries to the *officiers* and to honour interest payments to the *rentiers*, hoping the Paris judges would believe that he genuinely desired to implement the Rueil agreement. As further provincial unrest erupted in the later months of 1649 and in 1650, the *parlement* at least resisted the appeals from these distant regions that it should champion, and therefore legitimize, their cause. The Paris *parlementaires* were fully occupied in keeping the capital in a state of relative calm, and did not wish to take up cudgels on issues which did not personally involve them. Very soon there would be an outcry against them, their accusers saying that this most prestigious court of law was interested only in its own powers, and merely masqueraded as the guardian of the general rights of the kingdom. If these accusations were largely true, it was not the Paris judges who had changed. They had never asked to be invested with this heroic mantle, and were simply continuing to scrutinize the legality of edicts and to hear appeal cases as their judicial duty required of them. It was coincidental that some of the recent controversial decisions by the crown had both savoured of illegality and had affected a large part of the population, thereby giving the *parlement* massive support in the kingdom, and the principal lesson of 1648 for Mazarin was that such an alliance of diverse groups must never be provoked again.

Even before the financially restrictive clauses of the Rueil agreement, the months of the first Fronde had witnessed a deepening crisis in the fortunes of the royal treasury. The crown had to default on its loans and, as the office-holders were laying most of the blame for fiscal mismanagement at the door of d'Emeri and his financier friends, Mazarin dismissed the minister and announced that a *chambre de justice* would investigate corruption by the speculators of the money-markets. Thus ended any hope of immediate co-operation with the financiers, although they too were very alarmed at the demands of the *Chambre de Saint-Louis* which threatened to deal a permanent blow to their role in financing the state. The siege of Paris was a costly enterprise and, if the peace treaty with the emperor in October 1648 gave some cause for hope, the expensive war with Spain dragged on. Not until the accord was signed at Rueil would the financiers be prepared to consider a *rapprochement* with the government, and then only if the cardinal would give them guarantees which were scarcely more palatable to him than those which the *parlement* had just exacted. The *premier ministre* had no choice but to give the required undertakings.

It was against this background of turmoil that Jean-Baptiste Colbert began to work for Mazarin, learning at first hand how unforeseen happenings and ill-considered decisions by a variety of different individuals or groups could change the flexible alliances within French society. The first major miscalculation by the cardinal after the Rueil agreement was the arrest of Condé, Conti and Longueville. Condé now sincerely believed that the policies of Mazarin were harmful to the kingdom, and therefore found no difficulty in both protesting his loyalty to the king and demanding the dismissal of the cardinal. Longueville, like d'Orléans, had shown a willingness to modify royal decisions in his own province, but that too was for the best of reasons. Their arrest ensured that, as long as Mazarin was in power, they and their followers would be at odds with the government. Conti had been one of the *frondeur* princes in 1648 and 1649, and had looked to Spain for support, hoping to bring the *parlement* into this international alliance. The judges therefore disliked him for his treachery and for suggesting that they might join him, and they had no love for Condé, who had led the royalist siege of Paris, had been a staunch supporter of Mazarin until recently, and had forced the cardinal to give him wide-ranging powers over many areas of central government, especially over new appointments where his opportunities for extending and consolidating his clientele would have very dangerous implications. The princely *frondeurs* of the Gondi and Beaufort circles felt no greater warmth for Condé, and it was valuable experience for the young Colbert to observe not only how the Condéens and the great aristocrats drew closer together, but also why the *parlement* of Paris and other groups once again found themselves on the same side as these magnates whom they detested.

The nine months between the Rueil agreement and the arrest of Condé were punctuated by serious provincial revolts, and by renewed demands from some *parlements* that the reforms of 1648 be fully implemented. In Paris the judges continued along their moderate course, trying to prevent the *frondeur* aristocrats from inflaming the citizenry and giving the minimum of support to the grievances of the provinces. They also gave advice to the government behind the scenes on how to defuse the tension in certain parts of the kingdom, and the cardinal recognized that their ideas were constructive although he lacked the financial resources to act upon most of them. Yet he did make some of the concessions which they suggested, and at least the relations between the crown and the *parlement* of Bordeaux were improved by this means. Mazarin then made the serious mistake of asking the apparently co-operative Paris judges to hear the cases against Gondi, Beaufort and Broussel, which were based on extremely unreliable evidence. The *parlementaires* were appalled at such a suggestion, as it made a mockery of their professional integrity, and they rejected it curtly. One consequence of their refusal to act was a rapid resurgence of popular support for the *frondeur* nobles, and to such an extent that the minister now had to make overtures to them. At least the Gondi faction shared his loathing for Condé, and was delighted at his arrest. The judges were very worried by these events, not just because they regarded the high nobles as dangerous but because the arrest of the three Condéen princes violated the freedoms of the *Chambre de Saint-Louis* and showed that the government was still prepared to act arbitrarily. As the crown subtly tried to sidestep other aspects of its obligations under the Rueil agreement, and office-holders appealed to the *parlement* for justice, the judges increasingly felt that they must speak out in defence of the law. Meanwhile, in the provinces the imprisoned Condé was becoming the hero of many aggrieved Frenchmen, who were demonstrating their hostility to the government in ever more violent ways. Mazarin was also discovering that the *frondeur* aristocrats could not be won over as a group, because their unity of purpose disguised the fact that each one was out to advance his own family, and to favour one with a high governmental post was merely to inflame the ambitions and demands of the others.

   In the summer of 1650 the Paris *parlement* decided, despite the differences of opinion among its radical, moderate and conservative members, to act as a mediator between the crown and some of the discontented provincial elites, and by October the *parlements* of Bordeaux, Toulouse and Paris were able to ratify the terms of the agreement which had been reached. Mazarin felt strongly that the mediators had given too much away to the provinces, but at least calm had been restored to a greater degree. Yet the cardinal still had two urgent problems to solve – what to do with the imprisoned princes and how to contain the ambitions of the aristocratic *frondeurs*. His decision to employ delaying tactics and his refusal to make even moderate concessions to either of them forced these two groups, each disliking the other, into an alliance. The Paris *parlement* was now being bombarded with appeals from provincial officials against arbitrary actions by royal agents, and with petitions from Condéens asking the judges to release the princes. The clergy joined in the clamour, and their assembly refused to pay its subsidy until the crown gave Conti his freedom, because he was a member of the First Estate as well as a prince. A number of social groups also began to call for a meeting of the *Etats-généraux*.

The Paris judges were still reluctant to become too much involved in the grievances of provinces which were outside their own jurisdiction, but they did make a great show of investigating the complaints. They decided that it was better to concentrate on the case of Condé, where the point at issue was certainly within the competence of their court. Although the outcome of their debate would almost inevitably be a condemnation of the arbitrary arrest, the *parlementaires* proceeded with their customary care and legalism. As during the battles of 1648, the moderates insisted that the decision should be sent to the regent as a remonstrance, and the court declined to release the princes on its own authority. Then came the defection of d'Orléans to the Condéen-*frondeur* alliance, and it was only a few days later that the regent bowed to the inevitable, signing the order for the release of the princes as Mazarin began his slow journey into his first exile. Thus the *parlement* had achieved what the princes and *frondeurs* could not. They had caused a minister to be dismissed, and by purely legal arguments. They had not sought this leading role for themselves, but they nevertheless emerged with credit and popularity in Paris and in the wider kingdom.

No sooner had Mazarin departed than tensions reappeared among the various groups which had opposed him, although the crown had little opportunity to exploit them because of its continuing poverty. Moreover Condé, Conti and Longueville were now at liberty, depriving the opposition of another focus for its discontent. The *parlement* speeded the process of disintegration by asking the regent for a law which excluded the clergy from high offices of state. This request was designed not only to prevent the return to power of Mazarin, but also to thwart the ambitions of Gondi and Châteauneuf, two *frondeurs* who were demanding entry into the Sacred College. The judges never liked the presence of cardinals in the government, because their rank gave them precedence over nobles of both sword and robe. The assembly of clergy reacted sharply to this challenge, and received support from the lesser nobility, who were also holding an assembly.

The hostility of the *épée* to the office-holders quickly emerged once more, partly because the *parlement* had not shown much eagerness to support their cause during recent years. The sovereign courts, in their turn, disliked the demands for a meeting of the *Etats-généraux*, preferring to speak for themselves outside the forum of the three estates, as they had done in 1614. It was evident too that the First and the Second were prepared to unite in a further attack on venality and office-holding. Condé and Gondi were uneasy allies, because they had identical ministerial ambitions, but they were prepared to work together for the moment. That became impossible when Anne appointed a number of Condéens to her reorganized administration and acceded to the *parlementaire* request for the exclusion of clerical ministers. She nevertheless kept the support of the clergy by secretly making it known that this would be reversed when the time was right.

The rift between Anne and Condé came in July 1651, and the prince then left the capital because of numerous threats to his life. By now his faction possessed a number of important provincial governorships, and so the Condéens once again based their power in the wider kingdom while the Gondi clique concentrated on Paris. The *parlement* was rapidly caught up in this dispute, because the regent and Condé were both determined to win the support of the prestigious court which had been so influential in recent years. Appeals also poured in against the excesses of soldiers and tax-farmers, so that once again the judges found themselves negotiating settlements of these quarrels in many parts of the kingdom. They usually took the side of the traditional officials while their old enemy, the royal council, tried to sustain the tax-farmers and the special commissioners for the army, whom the judges suspected of behaving like *intendants*. The *parlements* of Bordeaux and Toulouse quickly condemned Mazarin, thereby standing firm with their provincial governors, who were respectively Condé and d'Orléans. Other sovereign courts away from the capital preferred to temporize, because many of them were negotiating quite different concessions from the regent, and wanted to take no stand on the subject of Condé. They therefore, in the summer of 1651, deemed it prudent to avoid any contact with the Paris *parlement*, although this did not mean that there was overt hostility between the provincial and the Paris judges. All were still committed to the reforms of the *Chambre de Saint-Louis*, and the officials in the localities had recent evidence that the courts in the capital were prepared to uphold their appeals against royal excesses.

The declaration of September 1651 that Louis XIV was now of age, although he was only thirteen, presented the office-holders, and particularly the *parlements*, with a new tactical problem. No longer could they confidently claim to be defending the throne against evil ministers, and nor could they deny the right to hold a *lit de justice*, because the young monarch was now directly responsible for his advisers and could enforce his edicts on the sovereign courts. It was accepted that he was in tutelage, but the royal authority was nevertheless active in a way that it was not during a regency. Fortunately the government seemed to be eager to please the Paris judges. It purged the ministry of the Condéens, at a time when the prince appeared to be on the point of raising a major provincial revolt, and appointed more acceptable ministers in their place. One was Molé, who became keeper of the seals but remained *premier président* of the Paris *parlement*. He had been a conservative, but had never been subservient to the regent in the crises of the first Fronde. He was one of many who were both royalist and anti-Mazarinist. The new finance minister was to be La Vieuville, recalled to power after twenty-seven years, and he also commanded some respect in the sovereign courts. More important he was trusted by the financiers, who had shown no desire to help the crown since the collapse of confidence in the policies of d'Emeri on the eve of the 1648 revolt. The real danger came from the new chief minister, Châteauneuf, whose appointment was a concession, and hopefully a temporary one, to the Gondi party. He was no friend of Condé, Mazarin and the *parlements*. As the agents of the exiled cardinal worked stealthily to lure senior army commanders and their troops into his camp, Condé was finding it difficult to rally support. Many provincial *parlements* and officials wanted to see a rapid restoration of order after these troubled years, and the new government of the young king certainly showed no overt sign of Mazarinist influence. With the condemnation of Condé by the Paris judges on 4 December 1651, calm seemed to be on the point of returning to the kingdom. Even Gondi was preserving a neutral position, partly because he had now been nominated for the Sacred College but more importantly because he, like Condé, discovered that princely conspiracies had been discredited. The last three years had shown Frenchmen that these great houses were solely concerned with their own advancement, and felt no concern for those who had at times been their allies.

A few weeks later, all had changed. Mazarin had returned, many supporters of Gondi had joined Condé, who now had stronger Spanish backing, and the office-holders were in disarray. The Paris judges, not knowing what to do, quarrelled among themselves, although they did preserve their common hostility to Mazarin. Their provincial counterparts presented no united front, as they had to assess the strength of the royalists and the rebels in their own area, and to make as few long-term commitments as possible lest the balance of power should change. This led many other citizens to condemn the judges of both Paris and the provinces for their vacillation. The capital city was in total confusion, as Condé and Mazarin each sought its support. Before the return of the cardinal, Anne had removed the royal court to Poitiers, and so in April 1652 it was Condé who entered the city first in his final bid for its allegiance. Yet his demands were excessive, and the sovereign courts, the municipal councillors and the gilds preserved their moderate neutrality. It was then that the mob took over and Condé began his brief period of triumph, while many judges left the city for the safety of the countryside. Ironically, it was this bloody day on the streets of Paris which convinced the substantial citizens that the prince should be removed from their city as soon as possible, and this was the last time that they would encourage such unbridled ambition. They had disliked the conspiracies against Richelieu, and it was only the excesses of Mazarin which had promised them to consider supporting Condé, Beaufort, Gondi or any other great magnate. They would never make this mistake again, but most of them were no more pleased to welcome Mazarin, not least because his presence in France was likely to prolong the disorder indefinitely.

Despite its temporary loss of face when Condé aroused the mob of Paris, the *parlement* was soon back in the forefront of the peace negotiations with the crown. Those judges who had remained in the capital continued to demand a compromise settlement, but they insisted on the departure of Mazarin. When the cardinal persuaded some of their fellows to join an alternative *parlement* at the royal residence of Pontoise, promising that they too could send him into exile for a while if that would help to restore stability, they eagerly took up his offer and he departed for his second exile on 18 August 1652. The Pontoise judges were very cautious, because they knew that the Paris tribunal was the legitimate body, and they were still members of it. At least the focus of hatred was once again beyond the frontiers of the realm, and all moderate men, including both groups of judges, hoped that unity and calm could now be achieved.

The settlement of differences in 1652 was undoubtedly no victory for the crown, and it also marked the virtual end of princely anarchy. The excessive demands of Condé found no support in Paris, and the prince returned to his *gouvernement*, where his attempts to prolong a provincial rebellion foundered during the following year. He accordingly left for Spain and put his great military talents at the disposal of the Spanish forces. Gondi, who had now become the cardinal de Retz, was imprisoned, a royal action which was to cause much trouble in the very near future. For the judges of the Paris *parlement*, the outcome of the negotiations was highly satisfactory. They had to submit to a *lit de justice*, which the king was perfectly entitled to hold, and at that meeting they had to endure some stern words from the throne. Yet this was not the first stage in the restoration of strong monarchy, as the 'absolutist' historians have tried to maintain. The *parlementaires* were told that they must never again interfere in affairs of state – something that they, seeing everything from their legalist viewpoint, would claim not to have done. The court was also forbidden to make common cause with great magnates, a step that it had taken only with the greatest reluctance. These proscriptions, therefore, were no great cause for alarm. A few radical judges were to be removed from office, which was not too displeasing to some of the moderates and conservatives. Moreover their moderation had lain in their methods rather than in their aims, because the whole court was opposed to illegal royal innovations, and the only difference had been on whether to annul the decisions of the crown or to remonstrate and then allow the regent to make the changes. Soon a new radical group emerged, and the balance of opinions in the *parlement* was much the same as before the purge. The real victory for the judges lay in the fact that nothing was done to modify the concessions they had negotiated at Rueil, on the basis of the demands put forward by the *Chambre de Saint-Louis*.

With peace restored in the capital, and the king once more in residence there, Mazarin was able to re-enter the city in February 1653 and rejoin his master. As in 1649, the *parlementaires* did not object to the presence of the cardinal in the government. Then as now, they had obtained their concessions, and it was undeniably the prerogative of the king to choose his ministers. It was only when the hated Italian had seemed to be an obstacle to any peace settlement that they had joined the chorus clamouring for his exile. Yet they had no intention of allowing him to ride roughshod over them in the future, and they had shown during the two Frondes that they could act as a very effective brake on ministerial tyranny. In one important respect, the cardinal was useful to the judges. As the war was continuing and the royal finances were still in disarray, it was probable that the crown would have to introduce arbitrary measures in the future. If that were to happen, it would be very convenient for them to claim that Mazarin had the young Louis in tutelage, and that although royal orders now came from an adult king, they could be resisted because they were really the decisions of an evil minister. This was a tactic they would employ on more than one occasion during the remaining years of the turbulent 1650s.

The royal government, on the second restoration of Mazarin, was therefore very weak and beset by continuing problems. The queen had been forced to concede a great deal to her opponents, and the Frondes were fresh in the minds of everyone. Where past historians saw a dramatic resurgence of royal authority after 1653, leading to full-blooded absolutism in 1661, it is now generally recognized that the crown remained enfeebled until the end of the war in 1659, and that a third Fronde seemed to be imminent. Indeed some scholars have claimed that the later 1650s do merit that title, so strong was the opposition to the government.[17] The crown had very little freedom of action in these financially disastrous years, and if some degree of order prevailed in the localities, it was because the local elites, who had supported the Frondes, had decided that calm should be restored and preserved. That did not imply a change in their attitude to the government of Mazarin. The *officiers* had fought hard to preserve the system of venality and hereditary office, and they had succeeded in doing so. The slightest sign that the crown was resorting to the illegal tactics of d'Emeri once again would have been enough to inflame them. The Frondes had shown that the office-holders could effectively resist such challenges, and without the help of the princes. Their revolts had added to the confusion, but it was the legally constituted powers of the courts and the other officials which had given the bureaucracy its victory.

The royal ministers understood the situation all too well. They had made some major misjudgements during the Frondes, and they had learned from their mistakes. Their approach to government would therefore be as cautious as the desperate plight of the royal treasury permitted. Yet there was also greater circumspection to be seen among some of the elites. The Paris *parlementaires* had been alarmed by the recent rising of the lower citizenry in support of Condé, and the notables of Bordeaux had only just restored calm after the Ormée in which they had become the victims of popular unrest.[18] In Aix, and in other provincial centres, the leaders of opposition to Mazarin had found that they too had lost the confidence of the populace, which accused them of being excessively moderate and concerned only with

[17]For example Richard M. Golden, *The godly rebellion: Parisian curés and the religious Fronde, 1652–62* (Chapel Hill, NC, 1981). The turbulent events of the recent past and the threat of a further Fronde were frequently mentioned throughout the years 1653–9: see Albert N. Hamscher, *The parlement of Paris after the Fronde, 1653–1673* (Pittsburgh, 1976), pp. 88–117. In the uproar about the *rentes* in 1664, one royal spokesman actually told the meeting of *rentiers* in the Paris *hôtel de ville* that this was indeed another Fronde, 'to which no one made any reply' – Olivier Lefèvre d'Ormesson, *Journal*, 'Collection des documents inédits sur l'histoire de France' (2 vols, Paris, 1860–1), the entry for Tuesday, 10 June 1664.

[18]S. A. Westrich, *The Ormée of Bordeaux: a revolution during the Fronde* (Baltimore, 1972).

furthering the interests of their own social group.[19] Moreover, throughout the Frondes there had been no serious attack on the monarchy. The republican arguments of the extreme Huguenots had not been heard for nearly fifty years, and there was a widespread feeling of revulsion among well informed Frenchmen against the recent barbarities of the English who had savagely murdered their king. In France it was on the young Louis, the 'new Henri IV', that many were pinning their hopes for the future.

The government was determined to widen the rifts which already existed among the notables, and to do so in such a way that it would not incur blame from other quarters. It therefore confirmed the traditional rights of the *chambre des comptes* and the *cour des aides* of Paris, hoping to detach them from the *parlement* whose judges could hardly complain about this reaffirmation of long-established functions. The *trésoriers de France* and the *élus*, united in 1648 against the *intendants*, were now quarrelling again about their own respective roles, and here too there was the opportunity for subtle intervention from the centre. Local law courts, provincial *parlements*, municipal councils, gilds and other bodies who were frequently in dispute would perhaps resume their appeals for royal arbitration, and the demands for royal favour would increase, especially from those who had been loyal during the Frondes and now sought their reward. All these opportunities for earning the gratitude of groups or individuals would nevertheless be worthless unless the ministers could avoid further arbitrary actions of the kind which had provoked the Frondes. If the crown could rule traditionally – through the governors, bishops and office-holders – then a restoration of equilibrium was possible. The *officiers* wished for a return to normality, so that they could again enjoy a secure income and have the chance to acquire further offices at the expense of rival families. They also had a high sense of professional duty, which they passed on to the relatives who were to succeed them under the hereditary system. They would therefore welcome a resumption of orderly government so that they could concentrate their attentions on carrying out their administrative tasks. The crucial factor was therefore finance. Could the treasury continue to fund a war of unknown duration on the basis of the traditional revenues, supplemented by the good offices of the financiers?

AFTER THE FRONDES – THE TURMOIL CONTINUES, 1653–1661

La Vieuville died in the month before the return of Mazarin from his second exile. He had not been able to restore the confidence of the

[19]Kettering, *Judicial politics*, pp. 298–328.

money-markets in the crown as a borrower, and many financiers had suffered further harm from his manipulation of the royal debts. Yet he had persuaded some of them to help the government, by treating them more honourably than the others, and he was thus able to bequeath to the cardinal a group which was prepared to lend further sums. On the negative side, the tax returns were disastrous. Evasion was widespread, much money had been diverted into local levies for the maintenance of troops, and in those provinces where the Condéens had raised their standard it had found its way into princely coffers instead. There was no point in demanding higher taxes and trying to collect them directly, because the poverty and reluctance of the people would make this a fruitless exercise. The only course open to the crown in 1653 was to win over many more of the financiers, and persuade them to lend money either as straightforward loans or as anticipations of the *taille* and the indirect taxes. If this was inevitable, it was also to risk provoking discontent because these very methods had been sternly condemned by the office-holders during the Frondes.

Although Mazarin was frequently satirized by his detractors for his relatively humble Sicilian origins, he had spent enough time in the princely Roman world of the Colonna and the Barberini, and subsequently in the entourage of Richelieu, to have an aristocratic and courtly disdain for money matters. Like his predecessor, he felt that *premiers ministres* and kings should concentrate on war, the army and foreign affairs, leaving national and personal housekeeping to lesser men. He followed the example of Richelieu in that he interfered in financial affairs from time to time, but it was usually to propose major changes which others were then supposed to develop and implement, if possible. The royal finances were therefore largely entrusted to his chosen advisers, who had both to devise the methods of raising funds and to bear the responsibility for the consequences. His choice of ministers was made with care and cunning, because the financiers had refused to work with the caretakers who were in charge, pending the appointment of a successor to La Vieuville. His decision to divide the task among three men, Abel Servien, Nicolas Foucquet and Barthélemy Hervart, had a multiple purpose. First, as he impressed on the young Louis XIV, it was wise to have some rivalry within the ministry. Healthy competition encouraged hard and more honest work, as each minister was eager both to stress his own worth and to report his rivals for their misdeeds. Secondly, it was important to have continuity in such a crucial area of government, for great disruption had been caused in the past when a single minister, like Particelli d'Emeri or La Vieuville, had either been dismissed or had died. It was also useful, given the unpopularity of many past financial advisers, to be able to lay all the blame on one of them and yet have no hiatus in the running of the department. This ruse was employment by Mazarin in 1654–5 when Servien was blamed for recent mistakes, not all of his own making of course, while Foucquet both continued in office and yet appeared to be a new man at the helm.

Foucquet was a useful choice for many reasons, and it is only proper to discard the calumnies which were heaped on his allegedly corrupt administration at the time of his arrest and trial in the early 1660s. He was undoubtedly able, had close ties with the world of finance in which he was also respected, and was already, and remained, *procureur-général* in the *parlement* of Paris. If anyone could introduce financial expedients, and then prevent the *parlementaires* from opposing them, it was he. He was also successful, as the creditworthiness of the crown declined in the last years of the war, in raising loans from other financiers and then lending these sums to the treasury in his own name. As the amounts were very considerable, his enemies were quick to point out that he must therefore have an enormous fortune, probably acquired dishonestly, and they failed to mention that he had borrowed in order to lend. He began his task in 1653 with the immediate intention of reassuring the money-markets. Not disguising the poverty of the crown, he made it plain that those who had lost money, when the government had defaulted on its debts in 1648, would be reimbursed when the funds were available. As a token of his good faith, he also continued to make contracts with the men who had lent sums and acted as tax-farmers in the past. The treasury was standing by its friends, who were in addition the most experienced investors. He was quickly successful, through these open tactics, in finding lessees for the indirect taxes and for the *taille*. After a brief period of faltering confidence in 1654, for which Servien was made the scapegoat, these amicable relations resumed, and there is no doubt that the financiers were able to enrich themselves substantially at the same time. So too did Foucquet, even if his accusers exaggerated the actual amount.

If this source of royal finance was always vital in the seventeenth century, it could not meet the entire burden of government. Yet, in trying to exploit alternative means of raising revenue, the ministers had to take great care lest the *frondeur* spirit revive. At least the princes seemed to be a largely spent force when it came to starting an insurrection. Not that the crown had defeated all of them. In some instances it had overlooked their misdeeds and had made it worth while for them to return to the government side. The only crime of men like Bouillon and Turenne was to have supported Condé, who had been among the losers in the second Fronde. At the time when these great nobles had pledged their loyalty to the Condéen cause, it would have been possible to see their action as one of devotion to the king. Mazarin was then generally regarded as the source of every ill within the realm, and Condé seemed to be perhaps the only man who could have saved France. He had a long history of distinguished military service to the crown, and membership of his faction was therefore not initially an act of rebellion. Now that the outcome of the Frondes was known and Mazarin was back in power, under an adult king, Condé was deemed to be not only a rebel but a traitor, and both Bouillon and Turenne were pleased to seek an accommodation with the cardinal because they had never wished to take up arms against their sovereign. Others also accepted that, if one group had won the battle for power at the very centre, then it was wise to be on its side. Mazarin was careful not to humiliate such influential subjects, and took pains to treat them in a manner appropriate to their rank. Some of them received largely ceremonial posts, which were none the less prestigious, but others continued in positions of real authority. Turenne became one of the leading commanders of the army, and even Condé would be allowed to exercise considerable power after his restoration to favour in 1659.

One important constraint on the crown in dealing with the *frondeurs* was that a whole family could not be disgraced simply because one or two of its members had misbehaved. In this age of patrimonial politics, offices had been acquired to honour a lineage, and it was accepted that they would remain in the family as part of its inheritance. Also, in positions such as provincial governor, these great nobles did have considerable influence over their area. During a civil war, they might use it against the government, but now internal calm had been restored, and it was to be hoped that some of them would work with the royal ministers once again. Thus d'Elbeuf retained Picardy, La Rochefoucauld stayed in Poitou, Longueville continued to hold Normandy with his loyalty hopefully guaranteed by the royal promise to recognize his line as princes of the blood, and d'Orléans remained in Provence. When Condé returned to France after the 1659 peace, he too was restored to active control of Burgundy. It was of course possible to find military, diplomatic or courtly tasks which would keep such men away from their *gouvernement*, but that was certainly not done in every case. Condé would be very deeply involved in the daily running of Burgundy, where only someone of his prestige could manage the difficult provincial Estates.

In 1653, this turbulent prince was outside the realm, but he was not out of mind as far as Mazarin was concerned. Throughout the years 1653–9, the *premier ministre* was haunted by the fear that the exiled

Condé, supported by his Spanish hosts, might ally with the only other *frondeur* who remained a serious threat – Paul de Gondi, cardinal de Retz and, from March 1654, archbishop de Paris. Religion had played little part in the Frondes, except for clerical excitement at the arrest of Conti and at the attempt of the *parlement* to exclude clerics from ministerial office. The Huguenots had been docile, and had denounced the regicidal actions of their fellow Protestants in England. Now religious issues came to the fore, and to such an extent that one recent historian has described the years 1652–7 as 'the religious Fronde'.[20] The most disastrous aspect of the continuing conflict with Retz, from the point of view of the crown, was that the *parlement* and other institutions became involved in it, at a time when the ministers were having enough difficulties with the Paris judges over matters of secular government. If the Frondes had taught the young Colbert how it was possible to provoke, and therefore how to avoid, civil war, the remainder of the 1650s schooled him in further aspects of government. He learnt about the issues which aroused explosive feelings in various corporate and social groups, with the result that, in the 1660s, he would become highly skilled at identifying the concerns which a particular body shared with the crown, and at avoiding those where there was a major conflict of interest.

Although Mazarin recognized, after his return to the court in February 1653, that he must take care not to antagonize his recent opponents, the problems facing the government were too severe to permit excessive delay. On some matters emergency action was essential, and he therefore needed to circumnavigate a number of the obstacles erected by the *Chambre de Saint-Louis*, the Peace of Rueil and the settlement of 1652. This would be a very difficult course to follow, because the office-holders were expecting such trickery and were constantly on the watch. Fortunately for the minister some of the *officiers* were locked in combat with each other, especially the *trésoriers de France* and the *élus*, who were fiercely arguing about their respective roles in collecting the direct taxes. As Mazarin urgently needed these revenues, and was prepared to lower the total sum demanded by the crown in the hope that the taxpayers might be more willing to pay, it was vital to have a direct royal agent to oversee the allocation and collection of these levies. Yet he dared not re-create the *intendants*. He therefore sent out *maîtres des requêtes* but without giving them that additional and highly offensive title. After all, the *maîtres* had rallied behind the *parlement* during the Fronde of 1648–9, and had even

---

[20]Golden, *The godly rebellion*, which examines many aspects of these events in great detail.

subscribed to the demand for the removal of the *intendants*. Perhaps they would also cause less offence if they did not spend too long in the provinces and if they did not have special troops at their disposal, as *intendants* had done on occasions in the past. Above all Mazarin hoped that the use of these long-established officials would not appear to be a flagrant violation of the compromise agreed at Rueil, because the *Chambre de Saint-Louis* had denounced *intendants* as such, but had not attacked the *maîtres*. Accordingly the cardinal began to issue commissions to selected *maîtres*, and waited to see the reaction. The sovereign courts in the provinces were quick to sense the danger to their own authority, and began to protest vigorously or to negate the actions of the new commissioners through the use of their own judicial powers. Yet some lesser courts, in conflict themselves with these higher tribunals, began to see in these new agents a possible champion of their claims at the royal council. The *maîtres* were able therefore to have some influence on events in the localities, but throughout the later 1650s they were unable to carry out many of the missions entrusted to them by the ministers. Only in the administration of the army was the presence of a direct royal agent accepted by the populace, because the king was entitled to control his troops in whatever way he chose, and these commissioners were at least charged with trying to restrain the worst brutality of the soldiers towards the areas in which they were quartered.[21] The years between the end of the Frondes and the Peace of the Pyrenees were therefore still years of disobedience and even spasmodic revolt, and the crown frequently had to accept these reversals because it had no alternative. The only consolation for the cardinal was that the forces of opposition were no longer united, and unlikely to join together against him. Even the *parlement* of Paris was too much preoccupied with its own grievances to offer its leadership to other groups. Moreover it was regarded by many *officiers* and Parisians as a selfish ally, prepared to co-operate only as long as the personal interests of its members were being served. If this was unfair, these were suspicious times when everyone seemed to be out for himself.

One of the first decisions by the newly restored Mazarin was to resist demands for the summoning of an *Etats-généraux*. He knew that this assembly might be dangerously outspoken, and that the sovereign courts would welcome the news that it was not to meet. Yet he also declined to set up a *chambre de justice* to investigate financial

---

[21]On these *intendants de l'armée*, see Bonney, *Political change*, pp. 263–7; the caution which had to characterize their dealings with other levels of the military administration is well described in André Corvisier, *Louvois* (Paris, 1983), pp. 78–112.

improprieties, thereby pleasing the financiers but annoying the courts, which had called for such a tribunal in the demands of the *Chambre de Saint-Louis*. On his return, the minister was immediately embroiled in a major controversy, as a consequence of the new fiscal edicts which the king forced through at a *lit de justice* in December 1652, some of which went directly against the concessions of 1649. Thus, only two months after the settlement, in which the *parlement* had been rebuked but had been left with its powers intact, the crown was reverting to its old arbitrary methods. The judges were reluctant to challenge the power of the adult monarch by amending these edicts, a gentility they would not show in the very near future, and approached Mazarin with a request that they should be allowed to debate them. The cardinal, sensing a possible confrontation on fundamental principles, refused to allow them to do so but quickly suspended those edicts which were causing the greatest offence – and not just to the judges, because *rentiers*, gildsmen and other citizens of Paris were equally incensed. The *premier ministre* had received his first warning that the spirit of the Frondes had not been exorcized.

During the rest of 1653 and throughout 1654, there were continuing skirmishes as the crown tried to introduce other financial expedients, the courts protested and compromises were reached. The *parlement* had considerable support from groups of citizens on some of these issues, especially from the *rentiers* who saw that the government was making new and devious attempts to defraud them of their rightful interest payments. The next stage in the legal confrontation came in March 1655, when Louis XIV held a further *lit de justice* to enforce more fiscal edicts, and justified himself by pleading that his pressing needs made extraordinary measures unavoidable until an international peace could be signed. It took the judges some days to decide on their next action, and their decision was highly dangerous for the crown. They would examine the contents of the edicts, thus openly defying the authority of the sovereign. Mazarin uttered threats and played for time, and the judges accordingly decided to summon the *maîtres des requêtes*, some suggesting that the chancellor himself be called, to investigate abuses of power by the royal council at the expense of the traditional jurisdictions. A compromise was duly reached, and was presented as an assertion of royal will over submissive judges. Yet some of the edicts had been modified, and the crown had guaranteed that the council would not exceed its authority in future. The judges were most satisfied with the result of this confrontation, having proved that they could force the government to make concessions, even after a *lit de justice*.

Meanwhile the religious problem was growing daily, and embraced an increasing number of issues. The most urgent question concerned the status of Huguenots. They had been loyal during the Frondes, but the fear of a Protestant rising preoccupied Mazarin because the Condéen revolt was strongest in those provinces where heterodoxy was most firmly established. He accordingly published a declaration in 1652 which restated the original intentions of the Edict of Nantes, thereby appearing to remove the restrictions which had slowly been added by Richelieu and other ministers. Such a step immediately infuriated many Catholics, although they regarded with equal suspicion the attempts by Mazarin in later years to modify the tone of the 1652 document. Yet, where the Catholics saw duplicity, the Huguenots took these subsequent modifications at their face value and accused him of betraying them. So neither side was content with this cardinal of the Roman church, who seemed to put politics above religion.

If the Protestant issue was a tiresome undercurrent, the arrest of Retz in December 1652 was rapidly becoming a cause célèbre. First, it violated the amnesty to the *frondeurs* which had been conceded in the settlement of the preceding October. More importantly, it united a number of religious groups which were normally more renowned for their disputes. As in the hierarchy of office-holders, there were many tensions among the members of the clergy, some of them jurisdictional, others concerned with morality or matters of faith. There were also grounds for conflict with the government, and above all with the secular law courts. At the top was the supreme pontiff, an international prince with the power to intervene in the internal affairs of the kingdom, and there was a group of French churchmen which strongly supported this traditional Roman authority. The majority of the episcopate were more ambivalent. They wanted to retain their loyalty to the Holy See, but they wished to exercise their authority without too much interference, whether it came from Rome, from the king or, most offensive of all, from the *parlement* of Paris. They were prepared to be gallican or ultramontane, as the problems of the moment seemed to require. The parish clergy, who frequently enjoyed the warm support of their parishioners, often showed loyalty to their bishop, but that might depend on his willingness to espouse the cause of reform. The episcopate in France had shown itself less than eager to adopt many of the reforms stemming from the Council of Trent and from the subsequent stages of the Catholic Reformation, so that the gulf between the wealthy prelate on the one hand and the poor priest with his poorer flock on the other had given rise to strident calls for greater equality. Charitable members of higher society had given their support to these grievances, forming associations like the Compagnies du Saint-Sacrement[22] whose secrecy worried the government. Then there were the Jansenists, who shared the desire for a reformed and more moral church, even though their theological beliefs appeared to divide them from other Catholics. The presence of the regular orders of monks and friars added further ambiguities, for their prime allegiances were to international institutions and to Rome, and they insisted on immunity from certain secular and episcopal controls. The divines of the theological faculty at the Sorbonne formed another group which jealously guarded its privileges, especially against attacks by the *parlement*, and could be gallican or pro-Roman as the occasion demanded. Finally there were the Jesuits, who were theoretically too ultramontane, frequently seemed to be too royalist, openly resisted demands for moral rigorism and were mistrusted by almost everyone.

Depending on the precise jurisdictional, theological, moral or political point at issue, these groups could ally in a variety of ways, sometimes suddenly changing sides as a wily ecclesiastical or secular politician introduced a new and confusing element into the debate. The shifting alliances of the two Frondes therefore soon had their counterpart in the church. The main difference was that the clergy had largely avoided interference in the events of 1648–53, whereas the Paris judges would soon become involved in the drama of the cardinal de Retz. The gallicanism of the sovereign courts has been much misunderstood by historians until very recent days, but it is now accepted by perceptive scholars that, like so many of the stances adopted by the judges, it was primarily concerned with matters of legal jurisdiction. By temperament the *parlementaires* disliked the disruptive effects of heterodoxy, whether Huguenot, Jansenist or any other kind. More importantly, they detested the international power of Rome, whether it took the form of direct commands in the form of Bulls, or of the subtle infiltration associated with the Jesuits and the regular orders. Scarcely less offensive to them was the authority of the

[22]These charitable groups were motivated by Christian compassion, and the anonymity of their members was a device to ensure that no personal merit accrued to them for their good works and also to obliterate differences of rank and precedence among people who were drawn from the nobility and the bourgeoisie. Secret societies always worried the crown, especially when they were working with that potentially most seditious element in the population, the poor, and were inspired by a kind of religious faith which the church hierarchy suspected of being unorthodox, as it gave too much weight to personal initiative and perhaps therefore insufficient respect to the ecclesiastical authorities — especially as their very activities implied that the episcopate was neglecting these pastoral activities. See: Raoul Allier, *Une société secrète au XVIIᵉ siècle: la compagnie du trés-saint-sacrement de l'autel à Toulouse* . . . (Paris, 1914); Georges Guigue (ed.), *Les papiers des dévots de Lyon: recueil de textes sur la compagnie secrète du saint-sacrement* . . . , *1630–1731* (Lyon, 1922).

bishops and the ecclesiastical courts, because they believed that the secular judiciary should have a monopoly of justice within the kingdom. As the *parlementaires* were quick to challenge any encroachments on their preserves by the agencies of the church, it was not unusual for one party in a clerical dispute to appeal to the *parlement* for justice, while its opponents submitted themselves to the verdict of an ecclesiastical tribunal. Thus the judges sometimes found themselves defending heterodox groups simply because they could assert their jurisdictional rights by doing so. Such alliances were usually brief, but they added an important secular dimension to many religious disputes.

The arrest of Retz had a remarkable and dangerously unifying effect on the church. The pope, his nuncio, the bishops residing in Paris, the chapter of Notre-Dame, the faculty of the Sorbonne, the majority of the parish clergy in the capital and their parishioners all deplored this act. Of these lesser priests, some were Jansenist, others were simply advocates of reform, and many more were neither, but on the issue of the cardinal they were as one. The archbishop of Paris, who was uncle to Retz, had kept his clergy calm during the Frondes, and even now he was still a firm royalist and was therefore very mild in his defence of his nephew, who had been designated as his successor almost exactly ten years earlier. The affection in which the aged prelate was held nevertheless failed to restrain the widespread sense of outrage at the incarceration of Retz. Mazarin was inundated with protests from the Parisian clergy, drawn from all levels of the hierarchy, while Rome, whose help was vital to him in his international peace negotiations, also issued the direst threats. Innocent X was only just dissuaded from removing the *premier ministre* from the Sacred College, an act which would have deprived him of his only major claim to precedence over the leading nobles of the realm.

The situation now took a confusing turn. Mazarin had been trained in papal diplomacy, and both he and the pro-French party in the Roman curia knew how to defuse an explosive issue. Thus Innocent was reassured that he would have the full backing of France if he were to promulgate a Bull against the Jansenists, which was duly published on 31 May 1653. The *parlement*, whose members had been delighted by the decision to try Retz in a secular court, now became uneasy at the arrival of a Bull which demonstrated the right of Rome to prescribe on internal matters within the kingdom. A compensating factor for Mazarin was that it at least placed the Jansenist supporters of Retz in a dilemma, or so he hoped. Yet the accession of the imprisoned cardinal to the see of Paris, on the death of his uncle in March 1654, found his extensive body of supporters still united. Now there was the additional problem of whether the new archbishop or the crown should appoint vicars-general to administer the diocese. Each naturally claimed the right to do so, and a major jurisdictional conflict was thus inevitable. As the enthusiasm for Retz reached further heights, after the news of his escape from prison in August 1654, Mazarin feared that there would be an uprising in the city, and at exactly the moment when the *rentiers* were at their most vocal against government attempts to defraud them. Yet the minister did have the support of the judicial and municipal authorities when he took action against some of the Retzian clergy, as this asserted the rights of the crown over the church and promised an end to a dangerous current of popular discontent. In fact the leaders of the opposition merely went into hiding, their ideas bursting forth in pamphlets and in inflammatory sermons, as Mazarin and the *parlement* were preparing for the trial of Retz on a charge of *lèse-majesté*.

The year 1655 brought severe reversals to the ecclesiastical policy of Mazarin, at the same time as the *parlement* was defying the *lit de justice* of March. The new pope, Alexander VII, was no friend of France and he now unmistakably recognized Retz as archbishop by personally investing him with the pallium on 14 May. To the embarrassment of the crown, it could not actually find the Retzian vicar-general, who remained in hiding within the walls of Paris, gaining a heroic reputation and publishing instructions on the running of the diocese, together with letters from Retz himself. One such missive forbade two bishops of Mazarinist persuasion to carry out any duties in Paris because they had not been licensed to do so by the legitimate vicar-general of the true archbishop. This was a serious matter because the bishops had ordained clergy in Paris, and those ordinations and the subsequent acts of the priests were therefore null and void. It became much more serious when François de Harlay, archbishop of Rouen and one of the six *pairs ecclésiastiques*, gave his support. At the *assemblée du clergé* in October, the question of the two bishops was resolved by a compromise, but the assembled prelates took a more dangerous step. They declared that the see of Paris was not vacant, thereby acknowledging the legitimacy of the claims of Retz, and further they applied to the Retzian vicar-general for permission to hold their opening Mass. Mazarin was now left with no choice. The *assemblée* was a vital source of royal revenue, and the rebellious mutterings of the Retzians in Paris were a continuing cause for alarm. He accordingly recognized the vicar-general, and therefore the position of Retz, and he also permitted some of the exiled clergy who had supported the cardinal to return.

The following year, 1656, saw a further deterioration in the relations of Mazarin with both the clergy and the *parlement* of Paris. The judges were incensed by the ministerial attempt to devalue the coinage, which was registered at the fourth sovereign court, the *cour des monnaies*, in December 1655. Plenary sessions were held, normal judicial business was suspended, the other courts began to rally behind the *parlementaires*, merchants, *rentiers* and other groups affected by the devaluation began to petition the judges for justice, provincial support started to flow in, and there were rumours that a rising of the Parisian citizenry was imminent. The ministers hoped that the basis of this dispute was a judges showed that they were very much concerned with the subject which prompted them to concede the right of registering the controversial edict to the senior court in June, after six months of stalemate. Yet this concession did not solve the problem, because the judges showed that they were very much concerned witt the subject matter of the document, and began to uphold a series of appeals from litigants against its provisions. The popular support for these actions was so great that the crown simply abandoned the attempt to impose the new monetary values, and the judges had once again defeated the government. Moreover a number of ministers and royal agents in the *parlement* disapproved of the manner in which Mazarin had handled the whole affair, causing needless provocation for minimal results.

Yet the *premier ministre* was concerned by another aspect of this confrontation. He was convinced that the *parlementaire* opposition was once again encouraging the Spanish to be more resolute in the peace negotiations, at the time when the pope and Retz were also exhorting the clergy to protest against French foreign policy. The church in France proved generally reluctant to support this initiative, but a further attack on the apparently isolated Retz by Mazarin quickly rallied the *assemblée du clergé* to the cause of the archbishop. As Condé and the Spanish defeated the French at Valenciennes in July 1656, and hopes of peace rapidly retreated, the position of the central government seemed desperate indeed. The *parlement* now decided to exploit this confusion by launching a sustained attack on another aspect of royal policy, the increasing *évocation* of cases from its jurisdiction to the council, and this battle raged for the remaining months of 1656. In all these matters, Colbert was one of the advisers who counselled the minister to stand firm, in marked contrast with his attitude after 1661. However this future member of the government would have much to learn in the last turbulent five years of the ministry of Mazarin.

For all his skill in manipulating for money-markets, Foucquet now began to admit that, although he could still raise loans from the financiers, he simply could not hope to meet the expanding military expenditure of the crown. By the middle of 1658 he was prepared to concede that a declaration of general bankruptcy might be the only course of action, though he knew that this would perhaps permanently imperil the relations of the crown with its creditors. Already some financiers were falling into insolvency, as they had not received the proper return on the enormous commitment they had made. Foucquet also knew that he could not persuade the *parlement* to register any major financial innovations, and that it would be highly dangerous to take such action through other channels. The Paris judges had returned to the question of *évocations* with renewed vigour in the summer of 1658, because the king was seriously ill, the war was causing further problems, and there were aristocratic revolts in Normandy, Poitou and some other areas. In Aix, the *parlement* of Provence was at its most militant, speaking on behalf of many Provençaux who had a variety of different grievances as a result of recent arbitrary actions by the crown, the acting provincial governor, the army and the collectors of revenues.[23] The only problem which seemed to be diminishing was that of Retz and the disputed powers of the vicars-general in the diocese of Paris, but behind the new mood of compromise on this issue lay the seeds of further trouble. The more the hierarchy was prepared to be accommodating, the more did the *curés* take matters into their own hands.

The priests of Paris, with wide support from among their parishioners, had already given voice to some vigorous demands for moral stringency, reform of the episcopate, restraints on the power of the pope, the Jesuits and the regular orders, more power at parish level and stronger corporate organization for the lesser clergy. Indeed, of all the opposition groups which confronted the government in the 1640s and 1650s, this was the only one which wanted a readjustment of the social balance, and was therefore regarded by the crown, the church hierarchy, the judiciary and the municipal authorities as the most revolutionary. Some of these *curés* were Jansenist, but most were simply *richériste*, following the doctrine of Richer[24] that the parish clergy had been directly instituted by Christ and were not merely dependants of the higher-ranking bishops. Richer had claimed that it was for the priests to elect the episcopate and that the wider clergy formed the

[23]Kettering, *Judicial politics* pp. 298–328.

[24]Edmond Richer, the Parisian divine who in 1611 had written a tract on the distribution of authority in the church, reducing the primacy of the pope and raising the status of the *curés*, would not have gone to the extremes of those who were now developing his ideas. These ideas of Richer, and the term *richérisme* as understood in the 1650s and as used, sometimes carelessly, by historians, are succinctly summarized in Golden, *The godly rebellion*, pp. 72–5.

major constituent of any general council of the church, which was superior to the pope who was merely its president. The confusion in the organization of the Paris diocese in the mid 1650s had prompted the *curés* to take greater initiatives, and their assemblies had issued some uncompromising demands. In 1658, when the hierarchy was temporizing, the lower clergy of the capital decided on a new tactic, an appeal to the *parlement*. The judges were already annoyed by a further Bull from Rome in March 1657, not only censuring the Jansenists more vigorously but stating that the pope would appoint a commission of French bishops to try those who offended against its precepts. It was nine months before Mazarin dared to force the document through the *parlement* at a *lit de justice*, and then he persuaded the nuncio to add a statement that no new powers were being given by Rome to the episcopate.

If the sovereign courts were always on their guard against ecclesiastical attempts to usurp their jurisdiction, the right they most cherished was the *appel comme d'abus*, the procedure by which clerics could appeal to the *parlement* against decisions by the church tribunals.[25] Many clergy were equally passionate in their objections to this device, which was regarded by them as an unpardonable intrusion by the secular world into matters purely spiritual. Indeed, at an earlier stage of the Retz controversy, Colbert had even suggested that the *curés* loyal to the crown should invoke this procedure against the archbishop, knowing that this would force the judges to support the royalist side, but wise counsellors suggested that these devious tactics might be counterproductive.

In the first months of 1658, the *curés* of Paris approached the *parlementaires* on more than one occasion, seeking help in their attack on the Jesuits. Some provincial bishops supported their initiative as, after much hesitation, did the Sorbonne. The king forbade the judges to meddle in this affair because he feared the effect on French relations with the Holy See, although in other circumstances the crown sometimes positively welcomed the right of the secular courts to intervene in religious matters. This royal proscription particularly annoyed the judges because it meant that their hated rival, the

---

[25]The determination to safeguard this right caused the *parlement* to intervene in many religious disputes during the seventeenth and eighteenth centuries, sometimes supporting groups whose overtones of heterodoxy they would otherwise have found potentially dangerous. On the importance of these appeals in the later period, see B. Robert Kreiser, *Miracles, convulsions, and ecclesiastical politics in early eighteenth-century Paris* (Princeton, 1978). One eighteenth-century writer, d'Argenson, described *appels comme d'abus* as 'the finest jewel in the parlementary crown'.

council, would now assert its jurisdiction over cases arising out of the Bull. The *parlement* acted cautiously, despite the demands of its few Jansenist members for sterner decisions, but in July 1658 it ordered all bishops residing in Paris to return to their dioceses, on pain of forfeiting the revenues. This meant that the current assembly of court bishops would have to dissolve itself, and the judges insisted that it was an invalid gathering because it had not been authorized by the proper ecclesiastical provincial authorities. After two months of inactivity, the government gave way, and allowed the condemnation of the pro-Jesuit pamphlet, the *Apologie pour les casuistes contre les calomnies des jansénistes*, which lay at the heart of the whole debate. Although many of those who had campaigned against it were not Jansenists, it is not surprising that the term began to be applied to many of them. The Jansenists and Jesuits had been arch enemies for decades, and this appeared to be a further stage in their battle.

The following year, which also saw the belated conclusion of international peace, brought defeat to the Parisian *curés*. The episcopate shared the wish of Mazarin for an end to this seditious movement, and the crown took care to act with and through the bishops and the Retzian vicars-general. The parish clergy continued to hold assemblies for some years afterwards, but the combined forces of the government and the ecclesiastical hierarchy proved too much for them, especially as the inflammatory issue of the Jesuits had been extinguished for the time being. Their meetings would henceforth be a nuisance rather than a danger. Unfortunately for the royal ministers, the Peace of the Pyrenees did not end many of the other problems facing the crown. Indeed it exacerbated some of them.

The religious issue had not died down from the point of view of the *parlement*. It had been a reluctant ally of the *curés*, but it positively welcomed the *appel comme d'abus* which the bishop of Beauvais, Choart de Buzenval, brought against his own chapter, for insisting on wholesale submission to the Bull of 1657. Mazarin ordered the *évocation* of the case to the council, despite virulent protests from the judges, including the *premier président*, Lamoignon, who was a cousin of the Jansenist bishop. Yet this was not merely a matter of family solidarity. The president was most concerned at this unnecessary provocation of the sovereign court, and Foucquet, still a member of the court himself, shared this view. Ultimately therefore a compromise was reached, in which the crown confirmed the right of the judges to receive *appels comme d'abus* but with the proviso that the king himself would hear the Jansenist cases. The council would not be involved at all. Not that the general issue of *évocations* then died away, because there were other examples of this procedure in the last three years of the ministry of

Mazarin. Colbert had come round to the opinion of Lamoignon that caution was desirable in this contentious field of law, but the two men did not always succeed in persuading the other ministers. It was nevertheless clear that the crown could not win these disputes, and, by having to compromise, was in fact confirming the jurisdiction of the *parlement*. Thus one case, involving an appeal for justice from a monk, was evoked to the council, but after an outcry from the sovereign court was referred to the head of the religious order, so that neither body had to pass judgment. A further instance involved an *évocation*, not to the royal council, but to the *grand conseil*.[26] On this occasion the king stood firm, but he promised that this action would not become a precedent, and to show his goodwill towards the judges, he returned a case to them which had been evoked to the council in the preceding year.

The one issue on which the *parlement* was totally uncompromising was that of taxation, and the signing of the peace with Spain in 1659 prompted it to make demands for an immediate end to emergency measures. For the government, this was out of the question because it would take some years to repair the financial damage of the war. As a result, the judges soon began to receive and uphold appeals from municipalities and merchants against the wartime levies, and they took care to defend the traditional rights of financial officials. They also successfully thwarted government attempts to introduce other temporary fiscal measures. The chancellor admitted to Mazarin, early in 1660, that the Paris *parlement* had rendered the ministers powerless to execute these decisions, and added that the general public therefore regarded the judges as their protectors.

The sovereign court did not confine itself to restraining arbitrary government actions, in the last years of Mazarin. It also took the initiative, raising once again the need for general financial reform, as it had often done at moments of crisis in the past. It vigorously criticized the activities of tax-farmers and financiers, some of whom had bought high judicial office and were therefore debasing the standards of the bureaucracy. It insisted that such men should be excluded from these posts in future, and added that magistrates should even be forbidden to marry the daughters of tax-farmers. In voicing these feelings, the judges were not merely protesting against the illegality of new taxes and the corrupt practices of the financiers. They were sincerely

---

[26]The *grand conseil* was superior to the *parlements* and other sovereign courts, because it had the right to adjudicate when two or more of those bodies were in dispute; it was very rarely used in this way when Parisian courts were involved, although it had taken more cognizance of affairs in their provincial equivalents; the judges of the Paris *parlement* disliked its powers intensely, but they could not deny its traditional and long-established competence to act.

alarmed at the infiltration of their ranks by such base men, because they had a high sense of their duty as dispensers of justice. That professional integrity had been the principal factor which governed their actions during the Frondes. They were determined to preserve their judicial standards, and insisted that new purchasers of judgeships be fully conversant with the law. Although rules could be waived in deserving cases, they were not prepared to admit the young and the inexperienced, or to allow close consanguinity among members of a single court.

They were also deeply concerned about the present state of justice, and they therefore proposed many of the reforms which Colbert would implement in the first decade of the personal rule of Louis XIV. Frequently in 1658 and 1659 they called for speedier hearings, less complicated procedures, reductions in legal fees and the imposition of heavy fines on greedy lawyers, a ban on the soliciting of cases by judges, and in general for any change which would bring litigants cheaper, faster and more accessible justice. They also wanted a clearer delineation of the jurisdictions of the various levels and kinds of courts, so that there would be no doubt about the appropriate tribunal for every case. Too often hearings were prolonged by wrangles among rival groups of magistrates, each challenging the competence of the other. In addition, they called for greater uniformity in court procedures throughout the kingdom, although they assumed that Paris would provide the standard to which others would be made to conform, an attitude which would not find favour in the provinces themselves. Here was the constructive and reforming face of the *parlement*, and the government was prepared to look on these suggestions with favour, now that peace had returned and there would hopefully be less reason for the king and his judges to be at loggerheads.

A further distraction for the crown in 1659 was the continuing unrest in the provinces, notably in Provence where the *parlement* of Aix launched a strong attack on arbitrary government. Yet unlike the troubles of 1648–9, these disturbances revealed no strong unity of purpose among the Aixois citizenry, and internal disagreements helped to cause the collapse of the movement.[27] It was nevertheless clear to the royal ministers that the whole kingdom was in a very volatile state, and that the ending of the war might bring widespread demands for a return to peacetime taxation which the crown could not possibly meet at once. The government dared not show itself to be too conciliatory, lest it be accused of weakness. Past experience had taught

[27]Kettering, *Judicial Politics*, pp. 305–28.

ministers that, when taxes simply could not be collected and the crown
had accordingly waived the outstanding amounts as an act of apparent
royal clemency to hard pressed subjects, the taxpayers were
reinforced in their determination to resist on future occasions, hoping
for a similar volte-face by the government. The best course for the king
was to find some scapegoats, among the financiers and within his
circle of advisers, who could take the blame for past errors. Then a
new beginning could be made, in the long era of peace which it was
hoped would follow the Pyrenees treaty.

If financiers and tax-farmers were always vulnerable to this kind of
royal ingratitude, the crown knew that it must not repeat the mistake
of d'Emeri, and totally alienate the money-markets. Peace would be
less expensive than war, but the government would still need the
services of such men. Ministers were more expendable, however
talented they might have been, and their clienteles would be unlikely
to cause trouble. In contrast to the long-term dependence of lesser men
on aristocratic patrons, the relationship of minister and client was not
based on rank, geography or heredity. Power was the only concern,
and a fallen royal adviser aroused few feelings of loyalty or
compassion. Colbert and Hervart had their own candidate for
sacrifice. They seem to have disliked Foucquet from the moment they
began to work with him, and they intensified their intrigues in 1659,
although Mazarin did no more than encourage them. He had not
decided to act against the finance minister, because he was not yet sure
whether Colbert or Foucquet had the better answer to the problems
facing the government. Colbert advocated the creation of a *chambre de
justice* to investigate corruption among the financiers, and saw positive
advantages in declaring a royal bankruptcy. Such an attack on the
moneylenders would please the office-holders, and a prolonged spell of
peace should make the crown less dependent on borrowed money.
Foucquet thought such a plan to be disastrous. He had sustained the
government for some six years by means of his relations with the
financiers, when all other sources of money had proved insufficient,
and he feared that one more bankruptcy would damage relations
irrevocably. He had been prepared to consider such extreme measures
in the preceding year, but now that the war was ending, it was better
to try and wait for the recovery which would follow the signing of
peace. There were therefore real differences of strategy dividing
Colbert and Foucquet, but there was also the personal ambition of the
surintendant to remain in office and the determination of his rival to
oust him and take over his position.

Foucquet was already beginning to ameliorate the situation in the
treasury by the end of 1660. He had reallocated certain tax-farms, on

better terms for the crown, and he reduced payments to the *rentiers*, although his extensive use of secret grants of money may have been designed to compensate some of his victims behind the scenes. He was still borrowing very large amounts, and at high rates of interest, but at least the financiers were continuing to lend. Although Colbert would subsequently take more drastic action, it is far from clear that such steps could have been introduced in 1660, when France was only just beginning to recover from the war. Foucquet could therefore feel confident of his position in March 1661, when Mazarin died, especially as the cardinal had become extremely wealthy, had been highly unpopular and would thus make a good scapegoat on whom to blame recent ills. Here the *surintendant* was guilty of one major mis-judgement – he underestimated the cunning and the ambition of his rival, Jean-Baptiste Colbert.

The Frondes and the rest of the 1650s had taught Colbert and the royal ministers many lessons. They had learnt how easy it was to provoke very different, and often mutually hostile, groups into forming alliances against the government, and how very fragile such co-operation could be. They had also discovered the issues about which office-holders, clergy, merchants, townsmen and nobles felt passion-ately. The new regime, under the personal rule of Louis XIV, would exploit this knowledge very effectively, keeping local tensions sim-mering but preventing a united onslaught on the royal government. Such a policy would involve the abandonment, temporarily or perhaps permanently, of some reforms which the ministers would dearly have liked to introduce. They recognized that it was essential to have some support from within the kingdom for every royal action, even though the supporters would vary according to the particular purpose of each policy. To be able to impose arbitrary decisions on an unwilling population, the king would have needed to be absolute, and it did not occur to Colbert to use that adjective in 1661. The power of the crown had been violently shaken in recent years, and its ability to act of its own volition had sometimes been minimal. It depended on its creditors and on the office-holders, who fortunately also welcomed a return to stability but could still effectively prevent the government from acting in ways which they did not like. The only way forward was to proceed with caution, respecting traditional rights and privileges, seeking allies on every issue and maximizing the common ground which existed between the crown and its various corporate groups of subjects.

In particular the government needed to encourage competition among families and clienteles through the careful distribution of patronage, taking care not to show excessive favour to any one clan.

The king had to be seen to be impartial, both in his allocation of favours and, on occasions when family rivalries were put aside in order that one corporate body could make a united attack on the jurisdiction or privileges of another, as the mediator who resolved their dispute. Louis hoped that the more he gave an impression of evenhandedness, the more other notables would turn to him as the supreme arbiter.

4

The Personal Rule of Louis XIV:
The Kingly Areas of Government

INNOVATIONS IN GOVERNMENT AND THE RESTORATION
OF THE TRADITIONAL ORDER

The two Frondes and the turbulence of the years before and after them had one principal and general cause. Although the detailed pre-occupations of specific social groups were various, their common element was the defence of traditions, rights and liberties against arbitrary innovation and intervention by the government. The 'absolutist' historians have attempted to portray these conflicts in terms of selfish, vested interests versus a modernizing and reforming monarchy. Yet, apart from the problems of defining 'modern' and 'reform', and of deciding whether a government can be acting for the greater good of its subjects when the majority of the population is convinced that it is resisting an arbitrary regime, this old-fashioned and anachronistic interpretation accords Richelieu and Mazarin excessive status as conscious and far-sighted reformers. These writers have stressed new developments, like the wider use of  *intendants,* seeing them as deliberate preparations for the absolutism of the 1660s. Yet such novelties were in fact merely expedients, designed to ameliorate the terrible financial problems of the crown, and were not part of a carefully considered strategy for imposing a new structure on the French administration. A minister like d'Emeri had ultimately been compelled to use fiscal devices which he had initially tried to avoid, knowing how provocative they would be. Thus in all these recent confrontations, the crown was well aware that the only justification for its actions was the urgent need for funds to continue the war, whereas its opponents could convincingly and lucidly claim that their fundamental rights and privileges, originally granted by earlier kings and confirmed by many of their successors, were being violated. Some of these established liberties, like the hereditary nature of office and the very principle of venality, had themselves originated in the fiscal needs of former monarchs, but by the middle of the seventeenth century they too were now part of the whole corpus of privileges which had to be defended to the last.

With the exception of the princes and great magnates, who had sought a novel kind of authority at the very centre of government while pretending that there were only demanding a return to their traditional role, the other participants in the Frondes were sincerely and simply demanding the restoration of the status quo. Moreover, if the princes had not been able to snatch victory for themselves, the other social and administrative groups had forced the harassed government to accept many of their own demands because it had no choice but to give in to them. They had been granted major concessions in the settlements of 1649 and 1652, but there were many other occasions during the years of war when local elites had used the difficulties of the crown as a bargaining counter, promising to grant the treasury some financial relief in return for an unambiguous confirmation of their corporate rights. So these years of arbitrary royal action had both stiffened the resolve of privileged groups to resist further unwarranted intervention and given them an opportunity to negotiate a clearer definition of their own liberties. Colbert, with the realism which he increasingly exhibited in the later 1650s, was well aware that the emergency actions of the government had therefore been counterproductive in that they had produced little extra revenue, had aroused the animosity of many subjects, including those on whom the crown relied for the daily running of the administration, and had compelled ministers on many occasions to retreat and retract their threats. They had appeared to countenance overt disobedience towards royal authority, simply because they did not have the means to take effective measures against it. In 1661 Colbert knew that any major restructuring of the social and administrative systems was therefore out of the question. It would be provocative, and the crown, after the disastrous final years of the war, had neither the means nor the resources to embark on it. Moreover, despite the claims of some past historians that this minister was 'the great reformer' and that his period in office witnessed a 'revolution in government', he was not a visionary by nature. With a few exceptions, most of his so-called reforms were attempts to bring order and greater efficiency into the traditional system, not to change it. In no way did his policies anticipate the proposals for more sweeping reform which characterize the last twenty years of the reign. His mission was to improve the existing administrative structure in order to sustain the increased financial needs of the government in a volatile Europe, and it was his failure to meet this challenge which prompted his successors to realize that fundamental restructuring was the only solution. Only in reference to these later years could a historian justly claim that there was an attempted 'revolution in government'.[1]

The one theme which was not debated during the clamour of the Frondes was the very nature of monarchy itself. 'Vive le roi, point de Mazarin', and 'Long live the king, without taxation', were cries frequently heard on the streets. On the death of the cardinal in 1661, many Frenchmen, far from fearing the establishment of 'absolutism', assumed that Louis XIV would regard the restoration of the traditional order as a major part of his kingly mission. After the attempted usurpation of authority by evil ministers, he would surely wish to respect the privileges which his own ancestors had granted or confirmed. The *parlement* had reminded Mazarin on many occasions that it was the guardian of the *lois fondamentales*, but it did not expect that a personally ruling king would need to be apprised of this fact. Nor were the judges and the other elites disappointed in their initial optimism, because in many ways the new regime seemed to be taking great pains to be accommodating. Many subjects were prepared to give it a chance to substantiate its good intentions, especially as conditions within the kingdom seemed to be improving and a period of international peace appeared to be assured.

At the very centre, within the immediate entourage of the king, where he did have the right and also the ability to appoint and dismiss at will, there were some swift and dramatic changes, both in the organization of the government and in the personnel of the councils and the court. Yet even here, there was a greater amount of continuity than many earlier historians have perceived, because the purpose of the exercise was to create the impression of a new beginning, while retaining much of the expertise which had been available to the crown during the ministry of Mazarin. There was no need for Louis to

---

[1] The myth of Louis XIV's absolutism has been so deeply rooted in historiography that even writers like Harding and Bonney, who have done so much to demonstrate the weakness of the French crown and its need to coexist with powerful elite groups, have nevertheless given the impression that a much more powerful monarchy was established in the early personal rule of Louis XIV. Hamscher too, while demonstrating the continuing strength of the *parlement* and the need of the crown to co-operate with it, still couches his argument in absolutist terms by entitling his fifth chapter 'Parlement in submission, 1661–1673'. Only David Parker, while still using the word 'absolutism', gives an extended account of the very traditional approach to government of Louis XIV and Colbert, showing the considerable degree to which their freedom of action was limited – *The making of French absolutism* (London, 1983) pp. 118–151.

dissociate himself from any members of his inner circle of aristocratic advisers, because their closeness to the crown was a matter of courtly speculation rather than certain knowledge, and the wider public was unaware of their influence. Some of them also held office as provincial governors, but that was not necessarily an indication of complicity in governmental decisions as some of these aristocrats had been staunchly opposed to Mazarin during the Frondes. Even those who were close to the cardinal had taken care to distance themselves publicly from the worst excesses of the regency and the subsequent regime, because it was vital for them to retain the respect of their provincial subjects. Now that the ending of the war had removed much of the need for arbitrary action from the centre, they could return to their important role as patronage brokers and as champions both of royal policy and of local grievances. So, behind the few startling changes of ministers and secretaries of state, the same aristocratic names continued to be found among the intimate advisers of the king, whether they were primarily courtiers or also had responsibilities in the wider kingdom. The list included the d'Aumont as governors of the area around Boulogne, so vulnerable to enemy attack; the d'Estrées in diplomacy and in the highest levels of the church; the Gramont as governors of the Pyrenean frontier provinces of Béarn and Basse-Navarre; the Lesdiguières in Dauphiné; the d'Albert, with their dukedoms of Luynes, Chaulnes and Chevreuse, in the army, in diplomacy and in the provinces of Guyenne and later Brittany; Turenne in the upper échelons of the army; Montausier in Normandy; the Noailles in the army, the church and the provinces of Roussillon and Languedoc; the Saint-Aignan first in the army and then, in the person of Beauvillier, at the very centre of the ministry; the Béthune-Sully in the church, especially in the diocese of Bordeaux, in the navy and in diplomacy; and the Villeroy, where the archbishop ran the important *gouvernement* of the Lyonnais, so that his brother could carry out his duties at court as president of the new council of the finances. Lastly there was Condé, repatriated in 1659, and restored to his governorship of Burgundy. All these men offered and were asked for advice on many topics, sometimes well outside the scope of their official duties. There were other aristocrats, of course, whose names were equally familiar in court circles, who either never participated in royal decision making, or who had once done so but were now excluded because of past misdeeds or dubious loyalty during the Frondes. Some of those men were now honoured with purely ceremonial positions, although others were allowed to continue in ecclesiastical or military posts, because they still retained a limited amount of royal trust. Another group of nobles, who had never shown signs of disloyalty, could also be found in the hierarchies of the church and the army, but they too were not taken into the confidence of the king, were expected to confine themselves to the responsibilities associated with their posts, and were largely unknown at court.

The really striking changes in 1661 affected the ministers and the secretaries of state, men who did not have the protection afforded by a long aristocratic pedigree and who were therefore totally at the mercy of the sovereign. The most dramatic step was the first one, as Louis announced that he would not appoint a *premier ministre* to replace Mazarin and would personally shoulder the ultimate responsibility for government actions. In his *mémoires*, the king explained the reasons for this new departure.[2] His prime concern was that monarchy itself seemed to be diminished when the sovereign had only the aura of authority but a minister possessed all the effective power. Secondly, 'it was above all necessary to establish my own reputation and to make the public realize, by the very rank of those whom I selected, that it was not my intention to share my authority with them'. It was also essential for the ministers themselves to accept the fact that no single one of them had the entire confidence of the king. Lastly he was warning other ambitious members of society that this ruler was not prepared to allow any single subject or faction to dominate him.

If personal monarchy exposed the power of the crown and therefore necessitated greater caution by both king and subjects, lest they find themselves in a position where the monarch himself was being criticized, the existence of a group of ministers and secretaries of state gave the people, and on rare occasions the king himself, someone to blame. Many critics of the government would at times protest directly to the monarch that one of his secretaries had acted against the best interests of the people. Often his reply would be a declaration of support for his loyal servant, in which case the petitioners found themselves in the embarrassing position of having to withdraw or to criticize their sovereign. Sometimes, especially in the long years of war, the king would answer elliptically, blaming neither the complainants nor the minister. The opponents of specific royal policies therefore quickly devised new methods of proceeding, which avoided the possiblity of an awkward confrontation with the king. Instead of protesting against them, they simply failed to implement these royal directives, and became masters in the art of producing reasonable excuses while at the same time professing their undying loyalty to the crown. As the government very often could not compel obedience, and

[2]*Mémoires de Louis XIV*, ed. C. Dreyss (2 vols, Paris, 1860). The passage referred to here may conveniently be found in translation, in Roger Mettam (ed.), *Government and society in Louis XIV's France* (London, 1977), pp. 2–3.

as many of these extenuating circumstances sounded probable and might even be true, such covert obstructionism was soon practised by many different institutions. At least there was no overt defiance of the crown, as had occurred during the Frondes. In the early 1660s there was less need for such deception, because the ministers were trying, though not always successfully, to avoid taking provocative decisions, but by the 1670s one of the major tasks entrusted to the *intendants* was the investigation of the excuses made by provincial institutions in the hope of testing their veracity.

The chief casualty and scapegoat in the reorganization of the central conciliar structure in 1661 was the *surintendant des finances*, Nicolas Foucquet, and there were a number of reasons for his dismissal. First it was important for Louis to demonstrate that no subject, however powerful, could escape from the displeasure of the sovereign, especially when the offender stood accused, whether rightly or not, of misusing the revenues of the state for personal ends. The king was to make a number of similar gestures in these early years of his personal rule, in order to reinforce the point that he was supreme within his realm, although such bravura disguised the fact that there were many great aristocrats whom he could not have disciplined in this cavalier manner. Secondly, the arrest of Foucquet had the effect of distancing the new regime from the government of the late cardinal, and from the financiers on whom it had relied so heavily. It also gave the treasury an opportunity to default on the enormous debts which were owed to the minister, who was still advancing large sums to the crown during the months when the plans for his disgrace were being completed. It was only common sense for the king to borrow the maximum amount before announcing his intention to renounce the creditor and the debt. Moreover, the *surintendant* was generally regarded as the only possible candidate for the post of *premier ministre*, and his removal from the political scene underlined the determination of the monarch to share his power with no one, and to balance the ministerial factions in his new conciliar system. Lastly, there were the social reasons for the arrest, because many nobles, and the king himself, had been deeply offended by the extravagance of the life style and prodigality of Foucquet at Vaux-le-Vicomte. If some feared the political ambitions of this man, many more deeply resented the calculated insult to the hierarchy of rank and status which was implied in the ostentation of this parvenu.[3]

[3]The *affaire* Foucquet is discussed at length by Richard Bonney, *The king's debts: finance and politics in France, 1589–1661* (Oxford, 1981), pp. 258–71, and Daniel Dessert, *Argent, pouvoir et société au grand siècle* (Paris 1984), pp. 279–310; no doubt, further light

The principal dangers of arraigning the minister were that it might deal a fatal blow to the relations of the crown with the world of finance, and could also cause offence to the *parlement* of Paris which had held him in some esteem during the many years in which he had been its *procureur-général*. The financiers had trusted Foucquet, and although it was the intention of Colbert both to default on the royal debts and to put the blame on his predecessor, publicly castigating him for having overcommitted the treasury to its creditors, the experienced men of the money-markets would not be deceived. To them it would be yet another shameless declaration of bankruptcy and bad faith. The case against the *surintendant*, largely compiled by this ambitious rival, was made to seem as outrageous as possible, and included charges of massive corruption and treason. As so many of the inner machinations attending the preparation of the trial were in the form of verbal communications between the king and his advisers, it is difficult to identify all the prime movers in the *affaire* Foucquet. There are differing versions of the final instructions given by the dying Mazarin to the young king, in which he is supposed to have recommended some ministers and warned against others. The facts are that the *surintendant* was certainly persuaded to borrow further sums and then lend them to the crown after the death of the cardinal, and to sell his office in the *parlement* in order that he could advance the proceeds of the sale to the treasury as well – which did, of course, deprive him of his right to be tried by his fellow *parlementaires* when he was subsequently arrested. Moreover his actual confinement on 5 September 1661 was quickly followed by the creation of the new *conseil des finances* a mere ten days later. Within two months the crown had defaulted on its debts, as the financiers had feared, and had set up a *chambre de justice* to try them for corruption, two actions which were bound to please the *parlement* and many of the financial office-holders. Yet not all the moneylenders were so shabbily treated, because Colbert had already gathered together his own group, which would help the crown to survive during these years when order was still being restored to the royal finances.[4] Thus, whatever the political advantages to be derived from making an example of Foucquet, the whole procedure seemed to be tainted with villainy and personal ambition.

The Paris judges, happy to see a *chambre de justice*, were far from

will be shed by Daniel Dessert, *Fouquet*, soon to be published by Fayard; see also Albert N. Hamscher, *The parlement of Paris after the Fronde, 1653–1673* (Pittsburgh, 1976), pp. 123–6.

[1] D. Dessert and J.-L. Journet, 'Le lobby Colbert: un royaume ou une affaire de famille?', *Annales, ESC*, xxx, 6.

pleased by the trial of their former *procureur-général*. Some of the royal evidence against him was highly suspect, reviving memories of the *frondeur* trials which Mazarin had asked them to hold a decade before. Also the defendant justified his financial record very effectively, maintaining among other things that his allegedly treasonable purchase and fortification of the fortress of Belle-Ile was not a preliminary to a future conspiracy, but that he had bought it at the request of Mazarin because it was a vital stronghold, then belonging to the dangerous Retz family, which the crown could not afford to buy in 1658 as it lacked the funds. It was one more example of his willingness to use his private resources to relieve the poverty of the royal treasury. In its every aspect, this trial, which dragged on until 1664, cast a shadow over the early reconstruction of the central government.

When choosing his ministers, Louis remembered the advice he had received at the hands of Mazarin, and determined not to give too many positions of influence to any single family, a policy which he was to follow throughout his personal rule. Colbert, whose considerable skills were already recognized, did not become a secretary of state nor *contrôleur-général des finances*, and he was not appointed to the *surintendance* when Foucquet vacated it. He was simply made the *intendant des finances* on the new royal *conseil des finances*, which met under the presidency of the duc de Villeroy. Yet he did become a *ministre* after the arrest of the *surintendant*, replacing him on the *conseil d'en haut* where his colleagues were Le Tellier and Lionne. It was the fact of belonging to this innermost group of advisers which bestowed on the three men the status of *ministre*, because there was no such office, only a mere title. In the same way there had never been a post of *premier ministre*, although this appellation had been applied to both Richelieu and Mazarin. Of the new trio, only Le Tellier was also a secretary of state, while there were three more secretaries who were not designated as *ministres* – La Vrillière, Brienne and Du Plessis-Guénégaud. The last of these close counsellors, whose careers had been within the bureaucracy and whose influence depended primarily on the positions they held rather than on inherited prestige, was Pierre Séguier, the chancellor, and he was henceforward to play a smaller role in the non-judicial aspects of the administration. Thus only Le Tellier was both minister and secretary for one important area of government, the army. Lionne advised on foreign affairs, but Brienne held the official portfolio. Colbert was basically in charge of the finances, as both *ministre* and *intendant*, but he would dearly have liked to gain control of the navy, which was essential for his economic and colonial schemes. Yet it was not until 1669 that he was able to dislodge Du Plessis-Guénégaud from the secretaryship for the *marine*, and then only by accusing him of embezzling funds during the ministry of Foucquet.

Here, therefore, was a government organized in the way Louis described in his *mémoires*, with checks and balances, divided responsibilities, and no monopoly of power for any single individual. If the equilibrium were to be maintained, it would be necessary constantly to weigh the influence of the various ministerial factions, because these fluid associations could change rapidly as family alliances were abandoned and new liaisons formed. The rivalry most frequently identified by historians of Louis XIV has been that of the Le Tellier and the Colbert, but there was no sign of this tension in 1661. Eight years earlier, both of these families had been supporters of Foucquet, although they helped to dislodge him in the months following the death of Mazarin. Yet Colbert was still heavily reliant on Le Tellier, owing his new position as *ministre* as much to this trusted secretary of state as to his own talents. Similarly Brienne and Lionne were very close, as might be expected of uncle and nephew. La Vrillière belonged to a third and distinct network of patronage, that of the Phélypeaux family which always had some of its members near the centre of power. Every one of these ministers and secretaries was quick to seize any opportunity to advance the fortunes of his own relatives and clients, and by 1661 most of them had already been doing so for many years.

It has already been noted that the 'new men' in the royal councils of the personal rule were not middle-class, as the absolutist historians and the duc de Saint-Simon have claimed, the scholars portraying their appointment as a step into the modern world and the great memorialist regarding it as an insult to the nobility. Nor can these men meaningfully be called 'new'. La Vrillière had been a secretary of state since 1629, and would continue in office until 1678. During his tenure of this post, his family had intermarried with other houses which were close to the centre of power, and he himself was the son-in-law of Particelli d'Emeri. Louis XIV had no intention of removing this wise and faithful servant from office, and, though never a *ministre*, he continued to hold the portfolio for the RPR, that is to say the Huguenots, the *religion prétendue réformée*. As he had been responsible for this thorny problem since the Peace of Alais of 1629, his expertise was vital at a time when the king was hoping to eradicate heterodoxy in France, and he had also played an important role in dealing with some serious revolts in the provinces. It was only the nearness of his eightieth birthday which prompted him to relinquish his office in 1678, and then it was to his eldest surviving son, the marquis de Châteauneuf, who took over responsibility for Huguenot affairs as the climax of the persecution was drawing near.

Scarcely less senior was Pierre Séguier, chancellor since 1635 and keeper of the seals before that, who came from a family which had already arrived at the centre and continued to forge links with other important houses. His expertise included not only his detailed knowledge of the judicial hierarchy, especially during the turbulent years of the Frondes, but also the understanding of many provincial problems which he had acquired through his extensive correspondence with *intendants* and local officials.[5] Le Tellier too had been appointed by Louis XIII, just before his death in 1643, and had proved himself to be a highly able administrator. He had been staunchly loyal to the regent and the young king, although at the height of the Frondes this had meant his temporary estrangement from Mazarin because he had felt that the interests of the crown were not best served by his supporting the cardinal. After 1653 that conflict of interest disappeared, and he was one of the trusted servants whom Mazarin warmly bequeathed to Louis XIV. Here was another example of a family which, already powerful and well connected before 1661, remained so during the personal rule. Its status was further enhanced by the appointment of Le Tellier to the chancellorship on the death of Séguier, when his son, the marquis de Louvois, succeeded him as secretary of state for war. Also in 1643, Du Plessis-Guénégaud was appointed as holder of the marine portfolio, although Mazarin never shared the strong desire of Richelieu to expand the navy, and the secretary had therefore few major achievements to show for his first eighteen years of office. Indeed it is significant that, in his *mémoires* for 1661, the king praised the calibre of all these ministers and secretaries, but added that nothing of importance was happening in the naval and the Huguenot departments. Soon, of course, both of these portfolios would be bulging with new initiatives. The last of these families which had given long service to the crown before 1661 and continued to have members in high office under the personal rule was the Loménie de Brienne. It had now provided secretaries of state for three successive monarchs. Louis did not doubt the administrative abilities of the secretary for foreign affairs whom he inherited on the death of Mazarin, although there had been some suggestion in the past that Brienne had pro-Spanish sentiments. That was less worrying now that the 1659 peace had been signed with Spain and a royal marriage to a Spanish infanta had been solemnized, but the king still had some reservations about trusting the secretary wholeheartedly. Yet he did

---

[5]A clear idea of the range of Séguier's experience can be gained from: Roland Mousnier (ed.), *Lettres et mémoires adressés au chancelier Séguier, 1633–49* (2 vols, Paris, 1964); and A. D. Lublinskaya (ed.), *Lettres et mémoires adressés au chancelier P. Séguier, 1633–49* (2 separate vols, Moscow, 1966 and 1980).

not wish to insult the family by removing him from office and appearing ungrateful for its long service. Fortunately for Louis, a solution offered itself to him in the person of Hugues de Lionne, who had undertaken some crucial diplomatic missions for the late cardinal and had a profound understanding of international diplomacy. He not only seemed to be the ideal choice for the position of foreign minister, but he was also a member of the Brienne clan. A number of historians, some of them not realizing that the two men were so closely related, have made great play of the fact that Lionne guided policy while Brienne only wrote the letters, but there is no evidence to suggest that the uncle and nephew found this division of responsibilities particularly strange, and the younger man certainly consulted his older relative and drew upon his experience.

The only real newcomer was therefore Colbert, who was the first member of his family to be either a *ministre* or a secretary of state, even though some of his ancestors had held important offices and he himself had been able to use his earlier position as a household official of Mazarin to influence the making of policy. Having the strong support of Le Tellier at this time, he was able to insert some of his relatives into senior positions within months of his appointment as *intendant des finances*. He had already brought his brother Charles to the attention of Mazarin and Le Tellier, both of whom had entrusted to him a number of signifiant diplomatic and provincial missions. More responsibilities followed once Jean-Baptiste came to ministerial power, and in 1680 Charles was appointed secretary of state for foreign affairs. Other members of the Colbert clan who speedily benefited from the elevation of their kinsman to high office were Henri Pussort and Nicolas Colbert, uncle and brother respectively. Pussort was already a distinguished lawyer, but in 1661, when his nephew had been *intendant des finances* for only a matter of months, this man in his mid-forties was appointed to the new *chambre de justice*, and went on to undertake many sensitive tasks for the king, which included his playing a major role in the reform of justice and in preparing the great Civil Ordinance of 1667. Nicolas Colbert was quickly appointed to the bishopric of Luçon, and then to the see of Auxerre. Many more relatives and clients received patronage as the years passed, some acquiring key administrative positions, others with less talent contenting themselves with prestigious but largely ceremonial posts. It was soon clear that the Colbert family was no ephemeral presence in government, and its members were therefore able to arrange some very distinguished and influential marriages.

Despite both family rivalries and genuine ministerial disagreements about policy, the central government took care to appear unanimous when it proposed courses of action to the kingdom at large. Yet skilled observers of court politics were not deceived, and the Parisian and provincial elites knew that, on any individual issue, one minister or secretary might be more sympathetic than the others towards their own views or reservations. It would be tactless to approach someone who had no responsibility in the matter, but there was usually a choice of legitimate routes through which correspondence could be sent. There were, of course, the alternatives available in the locality itself – the governor, the bishop, the *intendant* and the prestigious noble – but there were others at the very centre. Each secretary of state was responsible not only for a departmental portfolio, but also for a geographical area equal to approximately one quarter of the kingdom. Theoretically, all communications from and to the ministers should pass through the hands of the secretary who was in charge of that part of France, regardless of whether the substance fell within his portfolio, but in practice both the government and the local notables used this channel only when it seemed convenient. Thus, when a province received a royal demand for increased levies to maintain the troops, for example, it might complain to the secretary for the region, to Colbert because it was a financial matter, to Le Tellier as it also involved the army, or even to the chancellor if it could claim that the law was being infringed. Usually a direct complaint to one or more of these ministers would be reinforced by a further appeal through the governor or some other great local spokesman.

In an attempt to prevent both the population in general and other members of the government from intervening in departmental matters, the secretaries of state sought to make themselves responsible for those parts of the kingdom which were also the areas of most concern to them in their governmental duties. Thus, when the marquis de Louvois succeeded his father as minister of war, he took over secretarial responsibility for a quarter of France which already included many crucial frontier areas, where military matters would always have a high priority in the daily administrative routine. Yet he was not responsible for the key provinces of Alsace and Lorraine, and he accordingly negotiated an exchange with Pomponne, who gave him these two vital areas in 1673 and received others in return. By the time such adjustments were completed, the war minister held secretarial responsibility for the complete chain of frontier provinces and newly conquered territories on the north-east and east of the kingdom from the Channel to the Mediterranean, with the exception of Champagne, Burgundy and Provence. Only the last of these shared a border of any significant length with a foreign state. He also held Roussillon, which was adjacent to the southern frontier with Spain. As a quid pro quo, he had relinquished the internal province of the Lyonnais and a swathe of territory which ran from the Limousin, north-west to the Atlantic seaboard of the Vendée, the pays d'Aunis and Saintonge. He tried, as did his colleagues, to appoint local administrators who shared his priorities, but many posts were in family hands and could not be touched. Moreover, if purely military officials might see it as in their own best interest to co-operate with the secretary of state for war, most civil administrators had to deal with many ministers on a variety of issues, and had no intention of committing their loyalty to a single member of the government.

The local elites quickly identified the main preoccupations of each *ministre* and secretary, making good use of this knowledge in their correspondence with the centre. For example, Le Tellier clearly wanted nothing to impede the improvement of both the army and the defences of the realm, whereas Colbert was concerned with the replenishment of the depleted funds in the treasury, the expansion of the navy, the creation of new industries, the development of international and colonial trade, the maintenance of road and river routes, the reduction of internal tolls and the exposure of administrative corruption. Thus provincial office-holders, town councillors and other notables used these ministerial preoccupations as bargaining counters in their dealings with the government. A municipality might lament to Colbert that it was sadly unable to inspire enthusiasm among its citizenry for some new economic scheme, but thought that the granting of a particular privilege, often one which would give the town greater status vis-à-vis other communities in its area, would make the wealthy bourgeois more willing to contribute towards this new enterprise.[6] If the proposed bargain seemed to be more beneficial than harmful to the crown, the minister would grant the wishes of the town, which would then fulfil its part of the agreement. Local communities and vested interest groups were prepared to pay heavily for these symbols of status and exclusiveness, and such rights did not necessarily affect the power of the government adversely. Other bodies in an area might protest at these actions, feeling themselves slighted by this display of favouritism towards a rival, in which case it might be possible for the ministers to placate them by striking yet another financially advantageous bargain. The same tactics were used by families and clienteles, who would pledge their support to a minister if

---

[6]See, for example, the attempt to persuade the bourgeois of Lyon to invest in the East India Company – Bibliothèque nationale, collection Mélanges Colbert (hereafter BN, Mél. Colb.), vol. 124, fol. 534; vol. 125, fol. 752; vol. 126, fols 230, 651.

one of their number had been appointed by him to an office which was also eagerly sought by rival houses and patronage networks. Here too the commitment would be honoured – for a time at least.

The central government, during the personal rule of Louis XIV, was therefore composed of a very few 'new men', some long-serving ministers, and a number of trusted nobles of the sword and the church. If some of their official titles were novel or different, and if some of the conciliar bodies on which they sat had been either reconstructed or recently invented, there was nevertheless considerable continuity with what had gone before. The only significant differences were that there was no *premier ministre* and that the war had ended. There was every sign that Lionne and Le Tellier would continue to advocate the foreign and military policies with which they were already associated. Only Colbert was a more unknown quantity. In the 1650s this household official of Mazarin was already in his thirties, so that youthful impetuosity could not have been the explanation for his fiery pronouncements about both abolishing the entire venal office system and treating the *parlement* of Paris with great firmness. Yet in 1661, whether just through experience or because the holder of the reins of government finds them less tractable than he had imagined, he was the cautious and moderate realist, as was quickly demonstrated.

Louis and his ministers shared a common view of kingship, namely that the prime concerns of the crown were foreign affairs, the making of war and peace and the defence of the realm. The task of Colbert, as *intendant des finances*, was to extract money from the kingdom in order to finance these purposes. Thus, contrary to the claims made by his biographers and admirers, he did not set out to extend the influence of central government into new fields, even though provincial Frenchmen frequently felt that he was indeed trying to do so. He knew that calm could be restored only by respecting privileges and returning to traditional and uncontroversial methods of administration. Prepared therefore to work within the existing bureaucratic system he was nevertheless determined to purge it of inefficiency and corruption, but he was willing to leave much responsibility for local affairs in the hands of long established corporate bodies and groups, whether they were municipal, judicial, ecclesiastical, provincial or seigneurial. He was concerned that they should carry out their responsibilities properly, because otherwise the raising of royal taxes might be affected, but he left their jurisdictions alone except where they were so ambiguously delineated that they gave rise to counterproductive squabbling. Some local tensions could be useful to a minister, but a few severely hampered the administrative process and Colbert hoped that in those instances he could lead the quarrelling parties along the path to compromise.

Only in commerce and industry did he really seem to be an innovator, but a closer examination of his policies reveals that in many ways he was merely continuing an established tradition. Many of the principles underlying his plans for economic expansion stemmed from theories which had been current in the reign of Henri IV, and in some cases earlier. Nor was he the first minister to attempt their implementation, although war and the financial problems of the crown had thwarted many of these earlier initiatives. Yet it is in describing the scope of his task as he himself conceived it that historians have been most prone to exaggerate. Many have talked of his 'New Deal', while Charles Woolsey Cole can claim that from the year of his death, '1683 to the inauguration of the five-year plan by the Soviet government in Russia, no conscious and directed effort to develop a nation's industrial life was so prolonged, so thorough, so permeating, so far-reaching as that of Colbert'.[7] Apart from the fact that many of his experiments were partially or totally unsuccessful, the principal objection to these claims is that the minister was concerned only with certain aspects of economic life. Just as he believed that the king was chiefly responsible for the international dimension of government, so too he saw his own commercial and industrial policies in terms of the French position in the wider world. He therefore regarded the colonies as vital, because possession of overseas territories could affect the balance of power in Europe, and France was already far behind in the colonial race. His industrial schemes were largely confined to meeting the requirements of the army and the navy, and to establishing within the kingdom those luxury industries which had hitherto been based abroad, with the consequence that precious gold and silver had been exported from the realm in order to obtain these costly commodities. The daily economic life of the French localities was of no interest to him, and his concern with agriculture was confined to the raising of better horses for the cavalry. His attempts at regulating commerce and industry within the kingdom were all geared to these internationally orientated aims, or, in the case of the grain trade, to ensuring that vital taxpayers did not starve because they could not obtain the means of survival.

It is only rarely that the historian can discover exactly what transpired in the *conseil d'en haut*, where Louis regularly met with Le Tellier, Lionne and Colbert, occasionally summoning some military or

[7]Charles Woolsey Cole, *Colbert and a century of French mercantilism* (2 vols, New York, 1939, reprinted 1964).

other expert to join their discussions. Similarly he can seldom listen in to the conversations of the king with individual ministers or other advisers, as few of them were summarized afterwards or reported in royal and ministerial letters to third parties. The decisions which resulted are known because there is plenty of documentation recording the attempts to implement them. Yet the way in which a consensus was reached on an issue, the variety of different views which were discussed, the extent to which one minister or adviser had a decisive effect on the outcome, the role taken by Louis himself – all these matters remain concealed behind the closed doors of the council chamber or the royal apartments, and the historian has not been permitted to enter. It certainly suited later critics of the king, like the duc de Saint-Simon, to claim that Louis did not seek advice outside the immediate ministerial and secretarial circle and that he was the virtual prisoner of these parvenu advisers. As he said in his anonymous letter to the king, 'France can no longer survive under this rule of five kings who are all equal in authority (if you will forgive me for speaking frankly)'.[8]

The part played by Louis XIV himself is further obscured because of the way his name was cited by the ministers and secretaries. Sometimes their assertions about the royal will can be checked from other sources, but often corroboration or refutation is impossible. These senior advisers were not, of course, being disloyal when they misrepresented the views of the king, but were using the authority of the sovereign in the manner which best suited their strategy. Thus Colbert might say that His Majesty had insisted on a course of action, when it was in fact his own initiative, concerned a minor matter, and had not even been discussed in the council or with the king. Alternatively he might threaten disobedient or reluctant officials by saying that he had not yet informed His Majesty of their behaviour, but that he would soon have to do so and that the reaction would be terrible indeed. On such occasions the king was often fully conversant with the continuing drama, but was choosing to feign ignorance in the hope of avoiding a direct confrontation. Sometimes Louis would personally intervene in a dispute, by writing directly to a high-ranking agent, usually the governor or the bishop, so that evidence of royal displeasure could actually be shown to the procrastinating local officials, but usually the will of the sovereign was conveyed by his ministers and secretaries of state. When the king did send a letter in his own hand, it had often been requested by the recipient, who

---

[8]The duc de Saint-Simon, 'Lettre anonyme au roi, avril 1712', *Ecrits inédits de Saint-Simon*, ed. M. P. Faugère (8 vols, Paris, 1880–93), vol. IV, p. 43.

wanted this dramatic reinforcement of his own negotiating position in his province or diocese.[9]

One enduring difficulty for Colbert was that Louis XIV, while undoubtedly eager to replenish his treasury, showed little interest in the workings of the financial machinery. His conception of his kingly mission led him to become an expert on foreign affairs, and the aristocratic values which he shared with his friends and courtiers gave him a passion for everything military. He readily praised the *intendant des finances* when economic and fiscal policies had been successful, and sometimes recorded his genuine surprise at the financial benefits they had yielded, but he did not wish to know the details of the methods which had been employed. Colbert tried to alert his master to the difficulties which confronted any reformer of the finances by asking his advice on many detailed points. Yet, while Louis might make lengthy comments on topics which attracted him, these financial proposals were often returned with comments such as 'it is for you to judge', or 'whichever you think is better', written one above the other in the margin.[10] Colbert was therefore rather like the household *intendant* in any aristocratic *ménage*, charged with keeping the family, and in this case the kingdom, solvent, and with maintaining the prodigious expenditure which the social position of the paterfamilias demanded – whether in the form of lavish building schemes, pensions, gifts, and, in the case of the monarch, subsidies to allies and to foreign writers who would extol the virtues of the 'Most Christian King'. Although Colbert frequently argued against policies which might rapidly lead to

[9] On Colbert's pretence that the king had not been informed of provincial obstructiveness, see, for example, Pierre Clément (ed.), *Lettres, instructions et mémoires de Colbert* (8 vols, Paris, 1861–82), vol. II (i), p. 79; vol. VI, p. 41. Instances of direct intervention by the king can be found in: Louis XIV, *Oeuvres*, eds P. A. Grouvelle and P. H. de Grimoard (6 vols, Paris, 1806), vol. V, pp. 74–5 (to encourage the export of Breton grain into more hard-pressed provinces), 78–80 (to rebuke Bordeaux for resisting the order to export grain) G. B. Depping (ed.), *Correspondance administrative sous le règne de Louis XIV*, 'Collection des documents inédits sur l'histoire de France', (4 vols, Paris, 1950–5) vol. III, pp. xxvii, note 1, and Clément, vol. II (ii), p. 426 (both to publicize, in Paris and Marseille respectively, the new council of commerce); Clément, vol. VI, p. 58 (against duelling); Depping, vol. I, p. 873 (to put added presure on a town to continue the term of office of a satisfactory mayor); C. J. Trouvé, *Essai historique sur les états-généraux de la province de Languedoc* (Paris, 1818), pp. 188–9 (to persuade the Languedoc Estates to give a pension to the widow of the royal *lieutenant-général*). The king might also intervene personally in the judicial process: to protect a man who had served him well – Depping, vol. II, pp. 208–9; or when he thought his judges were being too zealous – ibid, pp. 190–1. He might also issue a declaration on a matter where letters from his ministers and officials were being ignored, although even so that might not induce compliance in his subjects.

[10] For example Clément, vol. II (i), p. ccxxxii.

war and therefore reduce the treasury to chaos once again, he readily accepted that lavish spending on royal display and on building up a network of clients was an essential part of sustaining the reputation of the crown, in France and in Europe, and of keeping French society in equilibrium. Many examples could be quoted to show the way in which family and governmental business were intertwined. Colbert found that his tasks ranged from major matters of state to supervising the building of birdcages for Madame de Montespan during the construction of the new Versailles, while Madame Colbert was entrusted with the young children whom Louis had sired with his mistress, Louise de La Vallière. The government and the royal household were still one and the same thing.

The priorities of the king, as he contemplated the realm in 1661 at the time of his decision to rule personally, are clearly stated in his *mémoires*.[11] He began by acknowledging that 'disorder reigned everywhere'. His principal cause for concern will not surprise the historian who understands the values and attitudes of the age. It was the unsatisfactory condition of the royal court, and particularly the fact that, because of the weakness of the crown in recent years, the high-ranking members of society had been able to obtain favours by threatening the *premier ministre*, warning of dire consequences if their ambitions and demands were not satisfied. When the minister had capitulated to these pressures, rival families then became enraged, and concessions had to be made to them in turn. Louis accordingly decided that from this moment courtiers would have to request, not demand, royal favour, and that he would distribute his graces more evenly so as to create an orderly equilibrium. It was above all in the context of kingly splendour that he lamented the general shortage of funds in the treasury, because he found himself unable to spend adequate sums of money on personal adornment, on his household and on the distribution of largesse, all of which were essential to the very aura of kingship. He also deplored the fact that the monarch was being compelled to live on credit, and felt great distaste for the ostentatious affluence of the financiers who, he said, boasted of their wealth in the most vulgar way 'as if they were afraid that I might not notice it'.

Next among his concerns was the condition of the church where, 'in addition to its usual troubles', there was a serious threat of schism. He noted that even bishops were now infected with dangerous new

[11]See Mettam, *Government and society*, pp. 1–7 for some translated extracts, but see Dreyss (ed.), *Mémoires*, for the complete 1661 text. A further and more extended translation of many of the texts collated by Dreyss is that by Paul Sonnino – Louis XIV, *Mémoires for the instruction of the dauphin* (New York, 1970): the passages referred to here are on pp. 24–6.

doctrines, and could incite the populace to follow their lead, because, as the king rightly observed, many of these prelates were men who, if they had been more orthodox, would have been widely praised for their piety, charity and moral worth. Worse still, Retz favoured and was favoured by this rising sect. Louis does not actually use the term Jansenism in this passage, and he is obviously including both the adherents of that doctrine as well as the *richéristes*, but whether he thought that the latter group were also followers of Jansen or a separate undesirable sect he does not say.

Turning to the Second Estate, he castigated those nobles who had either usurped or purchased aristocratic rank, and among the true *noblesse* those who had tyrannized their underlings or neighbours, or who, despite years of prohibition, continued to fight duels, thus implying that they were denying the right of the king to be the sole fount of justice in the realm. Passing on to the office-holders, he did not make any general condemnation of the hereditary and venal aspects of the system. Instead he penned opinions which corresponded to the grievances of many senior *parlementaires*, namely that wealthy men were purchasing judicial posts when they lacked the necessary qualifications; that some judges were insufficiently learned and experienced; that royal edicts about the age of applicants and the preparatory training required for entry into the courts were being disregarded; that there were too many conflicting jurisdictions, which gave many lawyers opportunities for making money by prolonging litigation; and lastly, the most shameful of all, that his own council had further complicated this confusion by its unwarranted interference in the legitimate jurisdictions of other bodies. The effects of all this aristocratic, judicial and financial corruption fell most heavily on the poorest elements of society.

These statements might have seemed like the empty boasts of politicians, had they been a public manifesto for the new regime, but they were the private thoughts of the king for communication to his heir. Louis was as determined as Colbert to redress these wrongs, and a rapid beginning was made in the early years of the personal rule. It is true that the final text of the *mémoires* was compiled at a later date, and that Colbert had made many of the notes for the section on 1661, but at least the king was prepared to allow this version of his attitudes in that first year of his own government to stand as his own assessment of the immediate priorities. One final point which he made in these opening pages is most significant. While he stressed that it was necessary to keep an eye on the whole world, so that he could learn the opinions and weaknesses of all foreign princes and ministers, find out the secrets of their courts, acquire every possible piece of detailed information about other countries and know everything about the daily life of his own French provinces, he insisted that one task was more important than all of these. It was to discover the ideas, interests and ambitions of his own courtiers, and how they conflicted one with another. There was, he said, no pleasure so delightful that he would not abandon it if it meant his acquiring this kind of knowledge.

THE ESTABLISHMENT OF THE ROYAL REPUTATION AND THE RESTORATION OF EQUILIBRIUM IN FRENCH SOCIETY

A precondition for any successful period of personal rule was, as Louis XIV made plain in the early pages of his *mémoires*, the proclamation in Europe and throughout the kingdom of the grandeur, talents and virtues of the monarch. Mazarin and Lionne seemed to have achieved a desirable and lasting peace after so many years of terrible warfare, and the closing years of the 1650s had presented opportunities for a number of important diplomatic initiatives. It was hoped that a secure accord had been agreed with Spain and cemented by the marriage of Louis to the Infanta, who adopted the French orthography and became Queen Marie-Thérèse. Equally promising for the future was the accession of France to the League of the Rhine in 1658. Although the cardinal had not been able to bring the war to a speedy close, he had always believed that military solutions must be a last resort and that diplomacy offered the skilful statesman many routes by which to defer or even avoid international hostilities. His protégé, Lionne, was to continue his policy during the first decade of the personal rule, in marked contrast to the greater willingness shown by Richelieu before and Louvois after to engage the enemy in short and decisive campaigns. Mazarin knew that, once battle commenced, carefully laid plans for rapid victory could soon lie in ruins. The formation of the league of Rhenish princes was therefore an attempt at a diplomatic solution to a hitherto intractable problem – how to devise, in these border regions, a common frontier which suited both the French king and the Holy Roman Emperor. There was now to be a chain of 'neutral' princedoms, which would be protected by France in the case of any imperial inroads into their traditional liberties, but would otherwise ally with neither side. More princes joined the league between 1658 and 1665, adding substance to the claim that the problem of the Rhineland had been settled.

The only other potentially dangerous frontier was that with the Spanish Netherlands, from which France had been seriously threatened on more than one occasion in the past. The 1659 peace and the Spanish marriage reduced French fears of an invasion from this quarter, and further reassurance came when the old alliance with the Dutch Republic was renewed in 1662. These natural allies against Spain had parted in 1648, when the Dutch had made their separate peace with Philip IV without waiting for the Peace of Westphalia. Although there was a resumption of better relations in the 1650s, the Dutch 'treachery', as Mazarin saw it, had prevented the signing of a formal accord until he had left the international stage. French confidence was further boosted by the restoration of the monarchy in England, under the friendly Charles II, the purchase from that country in 1662 of the vital and strategic port of Dunkerque, and, in the same year, the submission by the duke of Lorraine to the suzerainty of the French king. Many of these apparent advantages were soon to appear hollow, but for the moment they added immensely to the feeling at the court of Louis XIV that the peace would endure.

The only cloud on the horizon was the question of the Spanish succession, which drew nearer in 1665 as Philip IV was succeeded by his only male heir, the sickly four-year-old Carlos II. That this moribund infant would live, in defiance of all probability, until 1700 could not have been foreseen, and therefore Louis immediately addressed himself to the problem of the Spanish Netherlands and its next ruler. He set in train the process of securing these provinces for his queen, whose renunciation of her claims to the Spanish inheritance in 1659 were not valid because the dowry conditional upon it had not been paid. Louis had no wish for her to claim peninsular Spain, although he hoped it would not pass into hostile hands, and indeed the Netherlander laws under which the queen claimed her patrimony could not have been applied to those southern territories. The French king always insisted that his foreign policy should have an underlying legality, even though his opponents frequently regarded his self-justification as highly dubious. The short War of Devolution of 1667–8, the opening skirmish in the Spanish succession struggle, displayed French military prowess and brought some useful territorial gains, after which the decade appeared to resume its peaceful course. Louis pressed ahead with his negotiations for an amicable division of the Spanish lands, and signed a partition treaty with the emperor in 1668. Lionne was proving to be a brilliant foreign minister in the moderate, Mazarinist mould. Yet already some powers were becoming uneasy, especially the Dutch Republic, which Louis believed to be totally preoccupied with its internal faction struggles. Many Englishmen were less than sanguine about the good intentions of the French king, and slowly therefore trouble was being stored up for the very near future.

Louis XIV used this spell of relative calm to assert his supremacy in European affairs, some of his tactics being as provocative as the War of Devolution itself. He demanded superiority over other princes, forcing the Spanish ambassadors to cede precedence to his own envoys. He insisted that other fleets should salute his ships first, as a mark of their respect, a requirement which caused English and French vessels to avoid any such encounters because they were allies and wished neither to give ground nor cause offence. In particular he proclaimed the liberties of his diplomats and their retainers in the city of Rome, as part of his wider policy of revenge on the papacy which had sheltered Retz and frequently tried to interfere in the internal and international concerns of the French monarchy. Scarcely less prestigious a target was the emperor, whose ceremonial position in the European hierarchy of secular princes was supreme. In his *mémoires*, Louis confided that he had no great opinion of the actual powers at the disposal of that elected potentate, a belief which was soon to be proved erroneous.[12] In the past, the Valois kings had often shown a desire to be elected to the Holy Roman throne, and even Mazarin entertained dreams of such an outcome to the election of 1658.[13] As a waking realist, the cardinal instead concentrated on advancing the claims of a pro-French candidate, a plan which came to a fruitless conclusion with the election of the Habsburg, Leopold I. So Louis had to content himself with harassing the emperor in the 1660s, and a number of French pamphlets appeared which claimed that the true descendants of Charlemagne had the sole right to rule the Empire. The king also talked of using his newly acquired dominion over Lorraine in order to take his seat on the imperial Diet, and in 1667 he caused concern in Vienna by proposing, unsuccessfully as it transpired, the election of Condé as king of Poland, which would have created a worrying French presence on the north-eastern flank of the imperial domains.

Much of this psychological warfare undoubtedly impressed Europe, but it did not make Louis XIV loved. Nevertheless it did not lead to a major war until 1672–3, and therefore the king and his ministers had a decade in which to solve the problems facing the monarchy within the kingdom, to restore the political and social equilibrium, to improve the army, to reform the finances, to resolve disputes within the church, to

[12]Louis XIV, trans. Sonnino, p. 27.
[13]See Gaston Zeller, 'Les rois de France candidats à l'empire', *Aspects de la politique française sous l'ancien régime* (Paris, 1964).

purge the nobility of corruption and to bring order to the judicial system. The restoration of the social balance at court, the most crucial of the tasks identified by Louis in his *mémoires* as remedies for the general state of disorder in the realm, is a subject which merits a complete book in its own right, and it is possible to give only a few examples here. As with his distribution of patronage to foreigners, the king relied heavily on the advice of his ministers and aristocratic intimates, but in the French context he also consulted a small group of churchmen because ecclesiastical posts were a major channel for his favour and an established part of the administrative mechanism. In 1661 the clerical advisers were his Jesuit confessor, père Annat; the archbishop of Toulouse, Marca, who had been a staunch royalist throughout the dispute with Retz; La Mothe-Houdancourt, the bishop of Rennes, 'because the queen my mother wished it'; and his former tutor, Hardouin de Beaumont de Péréfixe, bishop of Rodez. These men were therefore selected for their closeness to the crown and not because of the positions they held in the hierarchy.

Soon after his assumption of personal power, Louis made it known publicly that seekers after favour were welcome to approach him directly, and that they could rely on his fairness in considering their claims. Nevertheless, many supplicants continued to invoke the aid of an influential intermediary, although they knew that the more prestigious the advocate, the more likely he was to present an objective assessment of their candidature to the sovereign. Louis was not a totally free agent in the early 1660s, because he felt bound to honour most of the promises made by Mazarin, even though his own inclination would have been to offer less elevated titles to some of those on the list he inherited. He intended that his own creations should conform to the strict requirements of French aristocratic society. The highest titles should be awarded only to nobles who were already possessors of substantial rank, had families of ancient lineage and had a record of distinguished military valour, whatever other services they had performed for the crown and for the state. These criteria had to be balanced against his wish to reward some houses for their past loyalty, to give others greater status in order that they might have the additional backing of high social rank in their role as governors and senior administrators, and to flatter certain other families who were still potentially dangerous and might thus be won over to the royal cause. Yet no matter how pressing the political reasons, Louis very rarely waived the rule that satisfactory aristocratic antecedents were essential to the granting of a title.

An examination of the *duchés-pairies* created during the personal rule for native French families will demonstrate the attitude of Louis XIV to the social hierarchy.[14] Those destined for princes of the blood and for houses of foreign origin raise special problems, and will be excluded from this brief analysis. The title of *duc et pair* was the senior aristocratic hereditary rank which the king could confer, and, as it carried only social status, it could be used to add lustre to the powerful or to add further ceremonial precedence to the powerless. The letters which created a *pairie* were issued by the monarch, but had to be registered at the *parlement* of Paris. All *pairs* had the right to sit in that court, although they tended to exercise it only when matters affecting themselves, collectively or individually, were under discussion. Twelve such *pairies* were submitted for registration in December 1663, and a further four two years later. Then there was a long interval, until 1690,

[14] See Roger Mettam, *The role of the higher aristocracy in France under Louis XIV, with special reference to the 'faction of the duke of Burgundy' and the provincial governors* (Cambridge PhD thesis, 1967), pp. 129–203. Jean-Pierre Labatut, *Les ducs et pairs au XVIIe siècle* (Paris, 1972), does not address this particular question, nor does he consider each family and its influence individually; he is more concerned to describe the characteristics of the peerage as a whole. The reasons for the creations of the titles registered in 1663 and 1665 are to be found partly in Anselme de Sainte-Marie, *Histoire généalogique et chronologique de la maison royale de France, des pairs, grands officiers de la couronne & de la maison du roy* (the references here are to the third edition, 9 vols, Paris, 1726–33), and partly in Archives nationales (hereafter AN), séries K and KK. In the order the titles are listed here, they are: *La Rocheguyon*, Anselme, vol. IV, pp. 735–43, and vol. VI, pp. 209–19; AN, série K, no. 623, liasse 41 (the handwritten amendment 'males et femelles' being incorrect), série KK, vol. 611, fols 93–9, 269–73; *d'Estrées*, Anselme, vol. IV, pp. 592–5; AN, série K, no. 623, liasse 23, série KK, vol. 611, fols 203–10; *Gramont*, Anselme, vol. IV, pp. 605–10; AN, série K, no. 623, liasse 26, série KK, vol. 611, fols 211–18; *Tresmes*, Anselme, vol. IV, pp. 758–62; AN, série K, no. 616, liasse 33, série KK. vol. 611, fols 274–82; *Mortemart*, Anselme, vol. IV, pp. 645–9; AN, série K, no. 616, liasse 26, série KK, vol. 611, fols 247–52; *Villeroy*, Anselme, vol. IV, pp. 633–8; AN, série K, no. 616, liasse 37, série KK, vol. 611, fols 241–6; *Poix-Créquy*, Anselme, vol. IV, pp. 689–92; AN, série K, no. 616, liasse 16, série KK, vol. 611, fols 253–7; *Villars-Brancas*, Anselme, vol. V, pp. 270–6; *Randan*, Anselme, vol. VI, pp. 166–201; AN, série K, no. 616, liasse 29, série KK, vol. 611, fols 264–8; *Rethelois-Mazarin* and *La Meilleraye*, Anselme, vol. IV, pp. 619–24; AN, série K, no. 616, liasses 23–4, série KK, vol. 611, fols 219–40; *Coislin*, Anselme, vol. IV, pp. 797–800; AN, série K, no. 616, liasse 28; *Saint-Aignan*, Anselme, vol. IV, pp. 693–700; AN, série K, no. 616, liasse 31, série KK, vol. 611, fols 258–63; *Noailles*, Anselme, vol. IV, pp. 775–81; série K, no. 616, liasse 28, série KK, vol. 611, fols 283–8; *Montausier*, Anselme, vol. V, pp. 1–6; AN, série K, no. 616, liasse 25, série KK, vol. 611, fols 316–20; *Choiseul*, Anselme, vol. IV, pp. 811–16; AN, série K, no. 616, liasse 14, série KK, vol. 611, fols 299–305; *d'Aumont*, Anselme, vol. IV, pp. 865–9; AN, série K, no. 616, liasse 9, série KK, vol. 611, fols 305–10; *La Ferté-Senneterre*, Anselme, vol. IV, pp. 881–6; AN, série K, no. 616, liasse 18, série KK, vol. 611, fols 310–16; *Rouannais*, Anselme, vol. V, pp. 292–317; *Béthune-Charost*, Anselme, vol. V, pp. 30–5; AN, série K, no. 623, liasse 12; *Boufflers*, Anselme, vol. V, pp. 69–77; *Harcourt*, vol. V, pp. 114–25; *d'Antin*, Anselme, vol. V, pp. 167–73; *Fitz-James*, Anselme, vol. V, pp. 162–5; *Villars*, Anselme, vol. V, pp. 95–101; AN, série KK, vol. 611, fols 106–13; *Hostun*, Anselme, vol. V, pp. 248–58; *Joyeuse*, Anselme, vol. V, pp. 217–20.

when one title was registered, and then eight more were successfully put before the *parlement* between 1709 and 1715. Rapid social mobility was clearly not being encouraged by Louis XIV, who wanted neither to stimulate social ambitions nor to alienate the existing *pairs*. It is therefore instructive to examine the two periods in which there were so many registrations, 1663–5 and 1709–15.

Of the twelve names in 1663, seven had been proposed by Mazarin, but the cardinal had been either unable or unwilling to obtain their registration by the *parlement*. The first of these, La Rocheguyon, satisfied the criteria of antiquity and valour, because the family dated from 1300 and some of its members had given prolonged service in the royal armies, also playing leading roles at court. The royal letters creating their peerage had been issued in 1643, twenty years before they were finally registered. The d'Estrées, with letters granted in 1648, had given outstanding service in the army, the provinces, the church and in international diplomacy, although they could trace their line only to 1437, significantly short of the year 1400 which was the true test of legitimate antiquity. The Gramont, who also received their letters in 1648, did have fourteenth-century respectability, and they were singled out for their outstanding military and civil administration in the Pyrenean frontier provinces. The Tresmes, also from 1648, were not a family which Louis would have elevated by choice. They had served in a number of high administrative posts, but lacked both age and military valour. The eleventh-century Mortemart were clearly qualified on length of lineage, but they too had no history of distinguished service in the army. Nevertheless they had held many senior curial posts, and were therefore more suitable than the Tresmes. The peerage was registered some years before Mme de Montespan, sister of the second duc de Mortemart, became the mistress of Louis XIV and complicated the royal relationship with the family. The next family, the Villeroy, whose letters were issued in 1651, would almost certainly have been rejected for a peerage under the personal rule, because their genealogy began only in 1500. Yet their nomination by Mazarin doubtless pleased the king because they had provided an able secretary of state for Henri III and Henri IV, had been highly successful provincial governors of the Lyonnais, had shown valour in the field, and the first *duc et pair* had been governor of the person of the young Louis XIV and now became president of the new *conseil des finances*. The last of the seven registrations of 1663 which had been proposed by Mazarin was that of Poix-Créquy, the letters having been issued in 1652. This peerage was a further reward for continuing service, chiefly in diplomacy on this occasion, to a family which met every criterion, as it could trace its line back to the twelfth century, had received its first peerage of Lesdiguières in 1620, had produced outstanding governors of Dauphiné, and had a distinguished military record which included the last holder of the supreme post of *connétable*.

It is only with the remaining five registrations of 1663 that the personal views of Louis XIV can be discerned, because in each case the decision to create the title was his own, for Mazarin was no longer there to advise him. He also decided not to seek registration for the one remaining creation of the late cardinal, that of Villars-Brancas, because this title had been registered already at the *parlement* of Aix, on the initiative of the family, and Louis had no intention of becoming immediately embroiled in a jurisdictional dispute between the sovereign courts of Paris and Provence. It was not till after his death, in 1716, that the regent for Louis XV was persuaded to bring the Villars-Brancas peerage to the *parlement* in the capital and obtain its proper recognition. The first of the five, Randan, dating from the month when Mazarin died, was created for a woman, a rarity in this land of strict male inheritance. She had given devoted service as principal woman in the household of the queen, Anne of Austria, and had lavished much affection on the young Louis himself. Her family was entirely suitable for such an honour because it had the necessary age and valour as well as already possessing a *duché-pairie*, that of La Rochefoucauld. Indeed this was yet another of the purely ceremonial favours that Louis would shower upon this house which he so mistrusted. The other four were created in December 1663, immediately before their registration at the *parlement*. The first was simply the paying of a tribute to the late minister by honouring his heirs, although this particular family, the La Porte, had rendered good service to the crown in the posts which both their illustrious relative and his predecessor, Richelieu, had entrusted to them. The king accordingly created both a *duché-pairie* and a *duché*, so that the nephew by marriage of the cardinal, who was the designated heir to the great wealth which Mazarin had accumulated, was created duc de Rethelois-Mazarin, and would ultimately inherit the new peerage of La Meilleraye which was instituted at the same time for his own father. If the La Porte family tree went back only to the sixteenth century, the other ministerial tribute paid by the king in 1663, was socially more savoury. In 1663 Pierre Séguier had already been chancellor for nearly thirty years and was still in office. This highest judicial office of state was prestigious in its own right, but Mazarin had further honoured him with the creation of a *duché*, Villemor, and subsequently with a proposal to raise it to a *duché-pairie*. Séguier himself was unhappy about the elevation of a *robe* family to the peerage, and therefore suggested to Louis, who readily agreed, that a lasting monument to his own services should be created in the form of a peerage for his son-in-law, who was already a *marquis*, had a genealogy which stretched back to 1276, and came from a house which had given service in the army and the church, especially in senior positions at court. He accordingly became the first duc et pair de Coislin.

The creations of La Meilleraye and Coislin ended the tradition of raising ministerial families to the peerage. Henceforth they would have to marry into *pairies* if they wished their children to attain such high rank. The remaining two registrations of 1663 mark the determination of Louis XIV to restore the traditional criteria for high aristocratic titles. The Saint-Aignan, a twelfth-century house, had given extensive military service to the crown over many generations, as had the eleventh-century Noailles, who also had an established reputation as administrators of the dangerous south-western provinces. The same priorities were evident in the four registrations of 1665. The first was for the Montausier, a family dating from 1007, whose military tradition reached its highest point in the man designated as the first *duc et pair*. It was he who, having kept Saintonge and the Angoumois relatively calm during the Frondes, became effective governor of Normandy in place of Longueville. Prolonged and distinguished military service also characterized the other three creations of that year, for the Choiseul, dating from 1060, and for the two thirteenth-century families of d'Aumont and La Ferté-Senneterre, the former having used their martial and administrative talents brilliantly in the strategically vital area around Boulogne. Antiquity and military prowess, regardless of other services, continued to be essential components of most creations during the rest of the personal rule. In some instances the peerage served to bolster up the position of someone who was already a provincial governor, as in the cases of the d'Aumont, the Villeroy and others. Sometimes the appointment as governor came after the establishment of the title, but in both circumstances valour in the field was essential. Thus the ninth-century Aubusson de La Feuillade received the *pairie* of Rouannais in 1667, although it was not registered until 1716, and provided governors of Dauphiné, high churchmen, diplomats and other leading servants of the crown. The Béthune-Charost, who received their letters in 1672 and saw them registered in 1690, dated from 1213 and possessed more than adequate military distinction, although it was for their administrative roles in the upper strata of the church that they were most renowned under Louis XIV. In the closing years of the reign, the creation of peerages for the Boufflers, dating from 1133, the Harcourt, from 1001, and the d'Antin, from 1230, was also occasioned by the royal wish to reward valour in the field, especially in the current period of war. Even the *duché-pairie* of Fitz-James, erected in 1710 for a natural son of James II, was justified by the military prowess of the first *duc et pair*. The only peerage in these years which did not satisfy the criterion of a lengthy lineage was that of Villars, a sixteenth-century family, but not even a proud and self-conscious peer like Saint-Simon would have denied that the illustrious feats of this magnificent military commander outweighed his recent origins. Honour and glory had always been allowed to compensate for humble birth if they were present in sufficient quantity.

Only in the last twelve months of his reign did Louis have to depart from his strict qualifications for elevation to the highest stratum of the aristocracy. Although lobbying by courtiers had doubtless aided the fortunes of one candidate rather than another, until that time the king had made socially correct decisions, even if the families concerned had often rendered service, and would do so in the future, in other fields of government in addition to their having the required military qualifications. Now the politics of faction intruded upon the restored hierarchy which he had sustained so rigidly. The deaths of the dauphin and the duc de Bourgogne and the seeming inevitability of a prolonged regency inspired the great princely houses to play once again for the highest stakes. Such families had peerages of their own, among their many other titles, and it is not the intention of this present analysis, confining itself to native French houses, to consider whether any further titles were created for the houses of foreign origin. Yet in the closing months of the reign the great dynasties of Rohan and Lorraine combined to demand that some of their French clients be elevated to the peerage. Louis agreed as he was eager to secure their loyalty for the future king and his regent, and created the *duchés-pairies* of Hostun and Joyeuse and the *duché non pairie* of Rohan-Rohan. The families which received the two new peerages undoubtedly met the criterion of antiquity, but past service to the crown was not one of their distinctive features, and despite this royal bribe, might very well not be in the future.

It has already been noted that one of the few social errors committed by Louis XIV was his creation of a duchy for his mistress, Louise de La Vallière, but the greatest cause of offence to the entire peerage was not to occur until the last years of the reign, and would be a deliberate act on the part of the king. As a further way of mitigating the effects of the sudden deaths in the direct Bourbon line, he decided to raise his illegitimate sons to the status of princes of the blood, thereby giving them precedence over all the *ducs et pairs*. Thus the crown and the peerage were locked in a fierce dispute when the five-year-old king succeeded to the throne of his great-grandfather.

This brief examination of elevations to the peerage has revealed some of the social priorities and attitudes which can be identified at all levels of the social hierarchy during the personal rule of Louis XIV. Parvenus were prevented from fulfilling their ambitions, order and hierarchy were restored, excessive mobility was discouraged and appropriate rewards were distributed with ostentatious fairness. Therefore, some trusted royal advisers could not receive the social dignities which their service would have merited in more flexible days, because their lineage was deficient. Yet, in contrast to the picture painted by the 'absolutist' historians, with their 'new men', it is very striking how large a proportion of the senior military, ecclesiastical, diplomatic and administrative agents of Louis XIV were drawn from the peerage and from other high noble families, some being given additional honours by the king but many already well established in the aristocratic hierarchy. As he also showed his readiness to dispense purely ceremonial patronage to those nobles he did not trust, the *noblesse* soon accepted his boast that he would be traditional and fair. Some houses would have liked more administrative power, but none could say that they had been slighted, nor that their own titles were being devalued by the entry of parvenus into their ranks. Louis had solved the first of the problems which he listed in his *mémoires*, at least until 1712 when the weakening of the royal succession prompted some great courtiers to think that domination by one faction was again a possibility. There is no doubt that Louis himself was delighted to be sustaining the traditional hierarchical values, which he so admired, at the same time as he was pursuing the best policy for controlling potentially troublesome elements in French society, and it was a pity that his heir was too young to learn the wisdom of such tactics from his experienced predecessor. Apart from the added problems of a regency, Louis XV too often tended to show partiality for one faction, sometimes abandoning it impulsively, where his great-grandfather would have played off the rival forces one against the other.

Once the social priorities of Louis XIV became known in the early 1660s, the great debate about *noblesse*, which had dominated the salons for many decades, simply faded away. The abiding fear of the *épée* that the *robe* would encroach on its rightful preserves was now assuaged, as the king had no intention of appointing *robins* to posts traditionally reserved for the old nobility nor of countenancing marital *mésalliances* across this divide. The aristocracy of ancient birth was secure in its monopoly of high military posts, and its time-honoured pursuit of honour and glory was openly acknowledged by the king as the greatest of the services it could render to its sovereign. Yet Louis had determined, as his *mémoires* testify, to stamp out corruption within the nobility, and a beginning was rapidly made towards achieving this goal. In common with so many of the tasks confronting the government in 1661, this was an issue where it was possible to make a ringing declaration of royal intentions but much more difficult to implement them. The crown therefore made a determined start, then discreetly allowed its enthusiasm to lapse, and finally abandoned the whole attempt.

One aspect of the royal plan, no more successful than the rest, was the exposure and eradication of false nobles. Usurped *noblesse* was socially offensive, but it was also fiscally harmful because the undetected usurpers enjoyed the noble right of exemption from paying the direct taxes. The original declaration of February 1661, which began the attempt to identify and punish the false claimants, was so ineffective that a second one was issued in 1664, in order 'to interpret' its predecessor. This verb was frequently used by the government as a justification for reiterating an earlier command, when it did not wish to admit the fact that its orders had been overtly flouted. The second declaration was stronger than the first because it created a special commission to investigate these malpractices, the more traditional machinery having proved itself unable or unwilling to do so. In 1670 the whole process was abandoned, as it had done more harm than good. Many genuine nobles had been unable to prove the legality of their status, while some false ones had managed, through judicious bribery, to obtain confirmation of their rank. Of those who had been unmasked and declared to be commoners, many were still avoiding the payment of direct taxes after a number of years had elapsed. Worse than that, the inquest came to be associated with a cherished policy of Colbert. He wished to persuade nobles to enter colonial and wholesale trade, changing the law so that only retail commerce remained incompatible with noble status, instead of the whole range of commercial activity which past legislation proscribed. Most nobles had no intention of participating in such bourgeois practices, but their resolve was strengthened by rumours that the true policy of the crown was to trick them into trade, and then declare them to be false nobles because of their involvement in it, brand them as commoners and subject them to direct taxation. Nothing, of course, was further from the mind of the minister, who was keenly seeking more investors for his economic schemes. The witch-hunt against the usurpers of *noblesse* therefore remained little more than a royal declaration of intent.[15]

The next of the criticisms levelled against the nobles in the 1661 pages of the *mémoires* was that they persisted in duelling, which not

[15]See, for example, Clément, vol. II (i), pp. 77–8, 251–2, 304–5; vol. II (ii), p. 754.

only led to disorder but undermined the royal monopoly of justice. Richelieu had proved that he could make an example of a great noble like Montmorency-Bouteville, but had been able to do so only because the duel had taken place within easy reach of the palace guards regiments. Although Louis XIII had forbidden the practice throughout the realm, it continued, and many provincial instances went undetected. Mazarin made another unsuccessful attempt to end it, and after his death Colbert exhorted all officials to implement these past edicts as the matter was dear to the heart of Louis XIV. It was not until 1667 that the king decided to issue his own edict on the subject, which strongly reiterated the prohibition but also expressed the traditional views of the king on aristocratic values and the moderation for which much of his early legislation had become known. He accordingly stated plainly how highly he regarded the noble concept of *honneur*, and added that he fully understood the preoccupation of the *noblesse* with the preservation of its honour in an untarnished form. Nevertheless, duelling could not be condoned, and he charged provincial governors, *lieutenants-généraux*, bishops and indeed all his subjects to report violations of his proscription to the government. To encourage the forwarding of such information, he further ordered that henceforth the wealth seized from those found guilty of this crime should be given to the local poorhouse. As town councillors both disliked unbridled noble influence and aristocratic partiality for the duel, and feared the disorderly behaviour of the poor when they were not confined in secure institutions, there was a double incentive for these municipal officials to denounce the offenders to the authorities. Yet they did not always do so, especially if one of the combatants belonged to an influential local family, and more legislation was needed many years later in another attempt to solve this persistent problem.[16] Although the king insisted that the settling of disputes by means of the sword was a fundamental intrusion into the monopoly of royal justice, he never tried to undermine the legitimate seigneurial courts. Some 70,000 of these tribunals continued to co-exist in parallel with the lower levels of his own judicial system. They dealt with purely local matters, and the crown had no need to become involved in their proceedings unless an aggrieved litigant appealed to a royal court against the malpractices of a particular *seigneur* or his judge. The principle of separate seigneurial jurisdiction was therefore not a cause of offence to the king, and no attempt was made to change the system during the reforming 1660s.

[16]See, for example, Clément, vol. VI, p. 58; Depping, vol. II, pp. 171–2; F. A. Isambert (ed.), *Recueil général des anciennes lois françaises depuis l'an 920 jusqu'à la révolution de 1789* (29 vols, Paris, 1822–33), vol. XIX, pp. 209–13.

As with the case of Montmorency-Bouteville under Richelieu, the ministers of Louis XIV regularly used the tactic of seizing an important man and making an example of him, in areas of the realm where they had the power to do so. By this means they hoped to alarm others elsewhere who could not be arrested, often because the local forces of law and order sympathized with, or were in awe of, the culprit. Such a technique was employed by Louis and Colbert, in their continuing pursuit of corrupt nobles, through the medium of the *grands jours*. The decision to set up these grand assizes in various parts of the kingdom was taken by 1662, but ministerial correspondence reveals that the crown was not hoping for much success in the more distant provinces, which did indeed prove as unco-operative as it expected. Only within the jurisdiction of the Paris *parlement*, with its reforming judges, was it possible to create an effective tribunal. Also the Parisian court was responsible for a very large geographical area, in many parts of which the *parlementaires* did not have any vested interests. Therefore in 1665, the *grands jours* arrived in the Auvergne, a notoriously violent and corrupt province, and it did arraign and execute some very powerful nobles in that region. Many of the local judges would not have dared to take such action because, although they detested aristocratic tyranny, they feared the physical power of these men, many of whom still possessed the bands of armed retainers which had been condemned as far back as the *assemblée des notables* of 1626. Yet, as with the enquiry into false nobles, royal determination provoked an unforeseen and undesirable result. The fearlessness of the *grands jours* in attacking corruption, no matter how high up the social scale, prompted many lesser Auvergnats to appeal to the court for justice. Sometimes their grievances were justified, but on occasion the plaintiffs were using the tribunal in the hope of exacting new rights and status for themselves. The bishop of Nîmes remarked on how outspokenly the peasants gave evidence against their lords, and said that you had only to speak roughly to a humble tenant and he would threaten to take you before the grand assize. He cited the example of one noble lady, who complained that her peasants had bought themselves gloves, the sign of *noblesse*, and announced that they were no longer obliged to perform their labour services. On the basis of such reports, the crown deemed it wise to end the tribunal, lest it stir up new problems which were as dangerous as those it was trying to eradicate. Thus a mere two years after the first hearings of the assize, news was reaching the ministers that Auvergne had reverted to its traditional lawlessness.[17]

[17]See Depping, vol. II, pp. 9–10, 160–2, 165–7, 176–7; (Esprit Fléchier), *Mémoires de Fléchier sur les grands-jours d'Auvergne en 1665*, ed. Fernand Dauphin (Paris, 1930).

The *grands jours*, of course, dealt with criminal commoners as well as nobles. If it made no lasting impression on the Auvergne, it did play a significant role in the royal campaign to convince the nation that the king intended to attack noble corruption and to stamp out illegality and crime at all levels. It did not exactly frighten lawbreakers in other provinces, but it made them uneasy. The setting up of such investigative and executive tribunals immediately raised the question of how they should be staffed, and what role should be played in their proceedings by the traditional office-holders. The *parlement* of Paris had long been wary of special royal commissions and ad hoc bodies, because many of them in the past had been designed, or had seemed, to encroach on its own jurisdiction. The detailed plans for the creation of the *grands jours* immediately brought reassurance to the Paris judges on this point, for they were to staff the assize and they were given powers which were very sweeping indeed. This enterprise therefore gave them the opportunity to carry out, in one of the most lawless provinces within their jurisdiction, some of the reforms which they hoped to see introduced throughout the kingdom.

By 1665 the carefully orchestrated co-operation of the crown and the Paris *parlement* was firmly established, disproving the absurd claims by 'absolutist' historians that the crown had crushed its own principal law court. The judges approved the royal decision to set up a *chambre de justice* for the investigation of financial malpractice and, although this was another special tribunal, they were pleased that it was to have a substantial *parlementaire* membership. They were less happy that the king, under great pressure from the financiers to cease such persecution, began to reduce or commute some of the penalties imposed by the *chambre* for proven malversation. In 1669 the body was disbanded, so that once again a striking gesture by the monarch had produced a backlash, as the money-markets rounded on the crown for its ingratitude. Nevertheless the judges noticed that this *chambre* had achieved some victories over corruption, and had lasted much longer than many of its predecessors.[18]

If the creation of this tribunal in 1661 had been publicized as a generous royal concession to the *parlementaire* demand for an investigation into abuses in the royal finances, the judges were not wholly pleased that one of its first tasks was to be the trial of Foucquet. It was true that he had been associated with some of the recent arbitrary fiscal policies and was close to the world of the financiers, but he had always advocated the search for compromise, where possible, in the relations of crown and *parlement*. The judges knew that it was his

[18]See Clément, vol. II (ii), pp. 751–2, 758, 764–6.

influence on Mazarin which had facilitated the smooth renewal of the *paulette* in 1657, without any of the government threats associated with this procedure in the past. Colbert, on the other hand, they knew to have been aggressively hostile in his views on the *parlement*, and on venality in general, and the office-holders waited to see what tactics he would adopt now that Foucquet was removed from power. The judges were not yet to know that Louis himself, as his *mémoires* reveal, was opposed to the interference of the royal council in *parlementaire* matters, and they watched to see whether the hated policy of *évocations* would continue.

Whether or not, in some of the earlier pronouncements, Colbert was partly motivated by a wish to distance himself from Foucquet, it is clear that by late 1661 he believed compromise to be the only strategy for dealing with the *parlement* of Paris, especially as the ending of the war had removed the need for the emergency fiscal measures which had often been at the core of the disputes between the government and the judges. There were so many matters on which the *parlement* could help the king – given their mutual concern for the reform of justice, for religious harmony, for the maintenance of order in the city of Paris and for the efficient daily running of the judicial system. Nevertheless, the sovereign courts had to be given some form of public rebuke for their past behaviour, partly to establish the reputation of the monarch but also to reassure the financiers that the judges were not going to be dictators of financial policy. On 8 July 1661 Louis issued a decree which alarmed the *parlementaires*, because it confirmed the superior status of the royal council and therefore implied that it could supersede the jurisdictions of the sovereign courts, as it had tried to do so frequently in the recent past. Yet, at the same time, the king made it known to the judges, through a variety of personal channels, that he had no intention of allowing his council to use this supreme authority in ways which would undermine the legitimate functions of the courts. The Paris *parlementaires* waited to see what would actually happen when cases came up, and their apprehension was quickly stilled. There continued to be conciliar *évocations* from the provincial courts, but such cases were often handed over to the Paris *parlementaires* for judgment. On the few occasions when the judges of the capital did discover that the council was dealing with a matter which seemed to be their rightful responsibility, the ministers usually acceded rapidly and gracefully to their request for a transfer of the proceedings to their own jurisdiction.

The continuation of *évocations* from other parts of the kingdom raises an important historical point. In the 1660s the Parisian sovereign courts were prepared to be much more co-operative than their provincial colleagues, and yet even from these more distant tribunals there were fewer overt challenges to the government. There are three possible explanations for this apparent readiness to accede to the wishes of the crown. The wrong one is, of course, that the king was now 'absolute' and had crushed all opposition. A second possibility is that royal provocation had ceased and that co-operation was now feasible, as was undoubtedly the case with the Paris judges. Yet many provincial documents clearly reveal that this was not so. The third explanation is therefore the correct one, namely that the provincial courts, in common with the Estates, municipalities and other bodies, did not wish for a confrontation with a king who was ruling personally, and their experience of prolonged resistance to royal orders during the 1650s had taught them that it was not difficult to avoid carrying out instructions without openly refusing to do so. The contrast between the attitudes of the Parisian and the provincial sovereign courts was evident from the very beginning of the personal rule of Louis XIV. For example, whereas the Paris *parlementaires* were delighted with the intention to set up a *grands jours* in Auvergne, the *parlement* of Toulouse laid down impossible conditions for the creation of a similar tribunal within its own jurisdiction and the plan was accordingly abandoned. Many other instances of such contrasting behaviour could be quoted, and some will be discussed below.

Colbert never denied that, in an ideal world, he would have wished for an end to the venality of office, and he still voiced these feelings in private memoirs and letters to sympathetic recipients. He knew that, in practice, such a policy was not realistic, although the Paris judges agreed that too many offices had been created at the lower levels of the hierarchy, and hoped that one day the crown might have sufficient resources to buy back these lesser posts and then suppress them, compensating the holders for the loss of their investment. Little was achieved towards this goal, and, when the burdens of renewed war darkened the last half of his ministry, Colbert found that he once again had to create and sell such posts as a source of revenue. His successors would have to carry this policy to greater lengths, also introducing venality into areas of the administration where it had never existed hitherto.

The deceptions practised by local officials, as they failed to carry out the wishes of the government, made it essential to have a corps of reliable royal agents in the provinces, reporting to Paris on the doings of the venal and elected *officiers*. Colbert had inherited a team of experienced provincial governors and a number of able and loyal bishops, but there was a need for a stratum of bureaucrats which could perform the more detailed and humble tasks, and could spy on the local elites. The *intendants* were ideal for such a role, but there was the memory of the Frondes to allay, when the hatred felt for them had been amply demonstrated. Since 1653 there had been regular visits to the provinces by *maîtres des requêtes*, and they, taken together with the fact that these officials had been told to behave with circumspection, had seemed to cause less offence. The new minister therefore decided to prolong and rationalize this system. Although the word *intendant* soon began to be applied to these officials, in theory they were simply *maîtres des requêtes* on tour. Colbert was very careful not to fly in the face of the agreements reached in 1649 and 1652, at least not until these agents had become accepted as part of the provincial scene. He gave them strict instructions to avoid any provocative action, and especially to do nothing which might encroach upon the legitimate jurisdictions of local officials. They were to be basically observers, and it would be for the royal council to decide what action, if any, should be taken on the basis of the reports they sent back. Thus, although they were required to scrutinize the conduct of the judicial officials and to send their observations to the ministers, they were also enjoined to establish good relations with all levels of royal judges and with the elected municipal councillors.[19] Even in the years 1653–61 Mazarin had ensured that the touring *maîtres* would concentrate on the financial rather than the legal aspects of the administration, and the only grievance against them of the *parlements* in that period was therefore not that they interfered in the daily processes of law, but that cases arising from their fiscal activities were heard by the royal council, that odious rival jurisdiction. As the king reassured the judges in 1661 that arbitrary conciliar judgments would now cease, and as the travelling *maîtres* seemed to be respectful of local jurisdictions and continued to confine themselves largely to financial matters, the Paris *parlementaires* did not feel inclined to make a protest about the presence of these direct agents in the provinces. On this, as on so many other matters, they preferred to wait and to see whether the king did intend to respect traditional rights and privileges, as he was promising to do. The fact that the kingdom was at peace also encouraged their optimism, because most of the objectionable actions associated with the *intendants* in the decade before the Frondes had been occasioned by the poverty of the royal treasury in time of war. In 1648 these agents had also been accused of collaborating with the hated financiers, but that charge was not reiterated in 1661. No one suggested that any of them merited investigation by the *chambre de justice* because of any misappropriation of state funds.

[19]See, for example, Clément, vol. II (i), pp. 266–7; vol. IV, pp. 85–6.

There are a number of reasons why the *intendants* could not have been the cornerstones of 'absolutism' that some old-fashioned historians have maintained them to be. Given that the ideal *intendant* was to be a man from one area of the kingdom who was sent to another where he had no vested interests, and was not allowed to remain there for more than three years lest he became too involved with local affairs, it is clear that some parts of the realm did not even glimpse an official who conformed to this description during the first decade of the personal rule. That was particularly true in the *pays d'états*, those fiercely separatist provinces whose representative assemblies were often so difficult for the crown to manage. In many of them it would be the governor and some of the bishops who shouldered the burden of supervising their administration and of keeping these strategically vital frontier regions loyal to the crown. Brittany received its first permanent *intendant* only in 1689, and Béarn survived without one until 1682. In Provence the *premier président* of the *parlement* of Aix acted as *intendant* until 1671, and from 1690 these two offices were held by one man, the succession passing from father to son on more than one occasion. Except for transmitting royal orders to the appropriate provincial body, this official seems to have done little in his capacity as *intendant*, concentrating instead on his presidential duties in the *parlement*. Under Richelieu and Mazarin, the Aixois judges had sustained a turbulent relationship with both the *intendants* and the governors, and Louis was determined to establish a more cordial atmosphere between his government and this militarily and commercially vital province. He tried to find suitable members of local noble families to act as *lieutenant-général*, and rule the area on behalf of the nominal governor, but not all of those selected had the necessary talents. Increasingly, therefore, the king used the archbishops of Aix as his principal agents in Provence, choosing able men who were acceptable to the local elites. These churchmen were automatically presidents of the provincial Estates and of the *assemblée des communautés* which had effectively replaced them as the regular representative assembly of the province. In Provence, therefore, the *intendant* never exercised many of the powers which were associated with his commission in other parts of the kingdom.[20]

---

[20]See Bibliothèque nationale (hereafter BN), fonds français, no. 24166, 'Mémoire touchant le parlement de Provence', especially fols 317–19, 321, 336, 348, 367, 377; the detailed activities of the *intendant* can be found in BN, fonds français, nos 4289, 8820–964 (esp. 8820, 8879, 8952). Some of these documents have been summarized by J. Marchand, *Un intendant sous Louis XIV: étude sur l'administration de Lebret en Provence, 1687–1704* (Paris, 1889), but his purpose is to maximize the power of the *intendant* and he has to admit that many of these documents contradict his own thesis. A more balanced but

In the *pays d'états* of Burgundy and Languedoc, there were *intendants* but they cannot be said to have conformed to the ideal pattern of service for that official, with its insistence on short terms of office and on residence in provinces where he was not native. Bouchu was *intendant* in Burgundy from 1656 until 1683, and was the son of the *premier président* of the *parlement* in that province. Both of them were Burgundians, born in Dijon, and the family was already highly respected within the local administration. Bazin de Bezons was not a Languedocien, but he was *intendant* of Montpellier and of Toulouse, that large province being divided into two *généralités*, from 1656 until 1673. His successor d'Aguesseau, then held the same double commission for a further thirteen years. The effective royal power in Languedoc resided in the hands of the *lieutenant-général*, acting on behalf of the nominal governor, and he always worked closely and harmoniously with the current *intendant*, on whose appointment he had been asked to advise. It was not uncommon for a single man to be appointed as *intendant* in more than one *généralité*, though such pluralism was not often as lasting as that of Bazin and d'Aguesseau. Bordeaux and Montauban were united in 1658–62 and 1664–9, but had separate *intendants* in 1662–3 and after 1669. Similarly in 1663–4 and 1666–7, responsibility for Dunkerque and Soissons was handed to the *intendants* of Amiens, and then taken away from their successors.

The purpose of uniting two *généralités* under a single *intendant* might vary from one region of the kingdom to another. In Languedoc, for example, it made sense for the whole province to be brought together in this way, as there was one governor, one *lieutenant-général* and one Estates for the whole area. The union of the Lyonnais and Dauphiné from the late 1650s until 1679 was prompted by different considerations. Both these provinces had trusted governors, members of the Villeroy in Lyon and of first the Lesdiguières and then the La Feuillade in Dauphiné. The governors had themselves tried to draw their *gouvernements* closer together, as witnessed by a Lesdiguières-Villeroy marriage in 1617. During the ministry of Colbert, the governors and *lieutenants-généraux* were responsible for most internal administration, and the *intendant* concentrated on issues which traversed the provincial frontier. Lyon was an important trading centre, and many of its most vital routes passed through Dauphiné, which straddled the routes to Savoy and the river Rhône almost as far south as Avignon. Commerce, tolls on roads and rivers, smuggling and

shorter view is that of Raoul Busquet, *Histoire de Provence des origines à la Révolution française* (Monaco, 1954). On a number of occasions, the *intendant* had to inform the royal ministers that he was totally powerless to act in the face of sustained opposition from the local elites.

other such issues preoccupied the *intendant*.[21] As in Languedoc, the governors were always consulted on the appointment of this official, and here too the three-year rule was not enforced. The man chosen by Mazarin was still there in 1666, and his successor, Dugué, held Dauphiné until 1679 and Lyon until 1682. In contrast, many *intendants* did not stay in an area for as much as three years, often being moved to a different *généralité* for another brief tenure. Amiens, for example, saw the coming and going of six such *commissaires* within the first decade of the personal rule of Louis XIV, whereas Alençon received only one more, seven, in forty-five years. The ideal *intendant* seems to have remained on the ministerial drawing-board, alongside many other good ideas for improving the administration of the kingdom.

   If Colbert had decided that the *intendants* must be observers rather than executive officials, and should be cautious in their dealings with established local institutions and social groups, there were a number of other factors which also prevented them from becoming 'cornerstones of absolutism'. The first of these was the wish of the minister to receive very detailed information on many aspects of local administration. The more that new tasks were added to the already long list of his responsibilities, the less could the *intendant* devote sufficient time to any one of them. As the government began to publish additional regulations, especially on economic matters, the scope of his investigative duties became impossibly extended. His remit came to include every stage of the allocation and collection of the various taxes; the distribution of wealth among the population; the condition of roads, rivers and bridges; the levying of local tolls and duties; the regulations for the military and luxury industries; the provision of supplies and quarters for the troops; the efficacy of legislation against immorality and subsequently against the Huguenots; the integrity and behaviour of local officials; and the many provincial practices and traditions on which the government hoped to impose some national uniformity and rationalization. Numerous other burdens were added from time to time, some of them short-term enquiries to meet the needs of a specific

[21] See Mettam, *The role of the higher aristocracy*, pp. 209–49, esp. p. 222, for the amount of routine business done by the Villeroy acting-governor and his staff, and the minimal role of the *intendant* in Lyon; very occasionally the *intendant* was asked to provide factual information when no sensitive issue was involved and no judgment required – Clément, vol. II (i), p. 314. When the East India Company was being promoted, Villeroy took charge of the publicity in Lyon, but the *intendant* did it in Dauphiné – BN, Mél. Colb., vol. 124, fols 534 and 550 respectively. On customs dues and other matters which affected both the Lyonnais and Dauphiné, and sometimes other provinces as well, the *intendant* played a more major part – BN, Mél. Colb., vol. 109bis, fols 938–9; vol. 110, fols 220, 289, 495–6; vol 116bis, fol. 600; vol. 118, fol. 135; vol. 126, fol. 394; vol. 127, fols 40, 251.

situation. The ministerial instructions were sometimes conveyed in circular letters addressed to the *intendants* as a group, but many were sent as personal communications to individuals. It was only towards the end of his ministry that Colbert devised a lengthy summary of their duties which was issued almost every year thereafter, and amended only if the needs of the moment demanded.[22] Before then, the intendant tended to receive a host of small instructions, some general, others more specific, and a number which were clearly afterthoughts by the various ministers.

Confronted with so many daunting tasks, the *intendants* had to acquire some assistance. Under Richelieu and Mazarin, their predecessors had recruited helpers on an ad hoc basis, but after 1661 teams of *sub-délégués* began to be commonly found in most *généralités*. If Colbert realised that this was inevitable, he did not welcome it, because the most important characteristic of the ideal *intendant* was that he was an outsider, external to the social rivalries and vested interests of his administrative area. Most of his helpers, in contrast, were native to it, and therefore much less likely to be objective about local problems. Colbert was prepared officially to authorize the appointment of these men, sometimes in order to regularize the situation where the *intendant* had already selected them, and he recognized that, if the visiting royal official were seen to be relying on their advice, he might seem less of an alien presence in the *généralité*. Nevertheless the minister did insist that they should not be entrusted with duties which might offend the sensibilities of their fellow citizens. This requirement was often totally ignored by the *intendants*, perhaps wilfully but no doubt more often because there was no alternative. Either the *sub-délégués* would undertake the task, making sure that they did not prejudice the interests of their area, or no one would do it because the *intendant* himself had no time to spare.[23]

These decisions to disregard some instructions of Colbert raise the more general question of the motives and loyalty of the *intendants* as a group, and there is no single answer which can be given. Some of them were loyal, hard-working and enjoyed a degree of success. Others, equally diligent, were defeated by the opposition they faced, especially in the more distant and separatist provinces. Yet there were a number who were less than honest in their dealings with the ministers, and to such an extent that the government at one point considered creating some 'super-inspectors' who would scrutinize the *intendants* in the same way that they, in turn, observed other officials. In fact this plan was

[22]See Clément, vol. II (i), pp. 131–5, issued 1 June 1680.
[23]See, for example, Clément, vol. IV, pp. 108, 150, 155–6, 164.

never implemented, on the grounds that the process could be repeated ad infinitum. It was better to appoint only the most suitable candidates as *intendants*, to examine their reports with the utmost care, and to accept the inevitable fact that in an enormous kingdom there would always be some who successfully evaded their responsibilities. There is no doubt that the life of an *intendant* was frequently far from pleasant. He was away from his native province, his family connections and his estates, and was living in an area where most of the leading inhabitants regarded him with deep suspicion. Yet a period of service in such a post was often a stepping-stone towards higher office in his own province, and perhaps some welcome royal patronage for his family. So, while many approached their duties conscientiously, there were a few whose main aim was to give the appearance of efficiency without the reality, and thereby gain promotion to posts in their home area. The distance between some *généralités* and the capital made it impossible for the ministers to identify many of these deceptions. The best tactic for the unscrupulous *intendant* was to create a non-existent problem and then announce that he had solved it. For example, when the tax yield fell short of the sum required by the crown, it was possible for him to invent a bad harvest as a result of a late frost, in which case the sums collected could be presented as being remarkably high, given the alleged hardship suffered by so many of the taxpayers.

Colbert frequently rebuked *intendants* for repeating statements which seemed to him to be the special pleading of vested interest groups.[24] Yet he could never be quite sure whether his agent had been gullible, or had actually entered into an understanding with some of the local elites. Even when the *intendant* was totally honest and loyal, there were many insuperable obstacles in his path. If he toured his *généralité* too slowly, he was chastised for leaving some parts of it unsupervised. When he went too rapidly, he was rebuked for being superficial in his investigations. On fiscal matters the government recognized that he could not examine every aspect of the system in all areas each year. He was instructed to check the accounts of the tax officials every few months, but he was also to make more detailed enquiries in three or four towns as part of his annual tour of inspection. These were to include the questioning not only of the officials, but all the lesser collectors and the leading inhabitants of every parish, to ascertain whether they all agreed on the sums which had been demanded and had or had not been paid. As a single *généralité* contained many such centres, a town which had just received a visit could be confident that the next one was some years away. In the intervening period the

[21]See Clément, vol. II (i), pp. 200–1, 272, 274, 347–8.

intendant would have to rely solely on the figures provided by the financial officials, and there was ample opportunity for them to adjust these statistics in order to cover up any personal profit-making within the various groups of office-holders and tax-collectors.

Certain instances of disobedience by the *intendants* were not attributable to their own selfishness. Many of them were realists, and knew that some ministerial directives could not be implemented or would provoke an outcry and perhaps sabotage the working relationship they had reached with individual local officials. It was possible for them to raise many of these doubts in their letters to Colbert, but on issues where he, or worse still the king, felt passionately, it was better to say nothing. Thus in the southern provinces, some *intendants* and governors were not prepared to carry out the repressive policy of the crown towards the Huguenots, and later the Camisards. On other occasions the *intendant* did decide on strong action, and then found that the local commander of the royal troops refused to mobilize his forces as he did not think this to be a wise course to follow. Then Colbert would find himself bombarded by conflicting advice, not only from these civil and military agents, but from many other interested parties in the locality. Most *intendants* thought that the army should be called upon only when there was a real danger of revolt. The soldiery was too undisciplined, and, although there were some examples of its being used to coerce reluctant taxpayers, there were as many complaints from officials that troops, acting on their own initiative, were ambushing tax-collectors and making off with the money.[25]

The history of the *intendants* during the personal rule of Louis XIV is therefore a chequered one. They did provide the government with much valuable, and some false, information. They identified many aspects of local administration where reform was desirable, but the government was often powerless to take the required action. They uncovered much deception by local officials, and a few of them adopted similarly disingenuous tactics. Yet the principal weakness of even the most loyal and hard-working *intendant* was that he often lacked sympathy for the concerns of his *généralité*. He was a 'government man' in the sense that he could see why Colbert wished to effect certain reforms, but failed to grasp why the provinces found them so obnoxious. He might have agreed with the 'absolutist' historians who, failing to understand the provincial viewpoint, saw a progressive government being hampered by reactionary elites.

[25]See Depping, vol. III, p. 133 – a letter of 1664 from some financial officials in the provinces in which they complain of a number of recent instances where soldiers have ambushed tax-collectors.

Thus the personal rule of Louis XIV opened with a mixture of compromise and dramatic change, as the king sought to remedy the evils he identified in his *mémoires*. The assertion of his own power; some drastic changes in the ministry; the rebuke to the *parlement*; the fierce but short-lived attacks on false nobles, corrupt financiers and lawless Auvergnats; the restoration of the *intendants*, initially disguised as *mâitres des requêtes* on tour; and the boasting about French superiority in the courts of Europe – all of these actions savoured of absolute monarchy. Indeed, in his ability to dismiss his ministers at will, the king did have *pouvoir absolu*. Yet in fact most of the ministers and advisers were not new, the Paris judges were both rebuked and placated, duels continued, false nobles and financiers evaded justice, the *grands jours* had to be stopped, and behind the façade of change the king was labouring to restore the traditional social order and to rebuild good relations with the provincial and institutional elites.

Three of the problems listed in the *mémoires* for 1661 have not yet been discussed, because they were susceptible of no rapid and dramatic solution. These were the royal finances, the judicial system and the state of the church. Although the new ministry immediately took such matters in hand, they needed long-term solutions which could not be devised overnight. All of them continued to plague the crown for the rest of the reign, because as soon as one issue was resolved, another arose, or so it seemed to the increasingly frustrated ministers.

THE ARMY, THE POSTAL SYSTEM, FOREIGN AFFAIRS AND WAR

It has already been remarked that the ministers of the crown, under Louis XIV as under his predecessors, were chiefly concerned with the kingly areas of government – war, defence, foreign policy and religion – and that they interfered in local administration solely when the collection of royal revenues was at issue. They were interested, therefore, only in those aspects of financial, judicial and economic affairs, which were of 'national' rather than purely local concern. In contrast, the central government intended to have a monopoly of control over military and international affairs, and most Frenchmen had little reason to become involved in such matters. They might complain about increased taxes and take steps to evade them, but their objections were to the fiscal burden and not to the wars which had occasioned it. The king could attack whichever country he chose, as long as he did not expect them to foot the entire bill. Only very rarely did the actual foreign policy seem to be against their own interests, and then it was usually because the king had made war on a neighbouring state with which parts of the kingdom had close economic ties, or perhaps because enemy fleets made seaborne trading unsafe. Thus the Breton merchants condemned the Dutch War, the inhabitants of the north-eastern littoral disliked the attack on the Spanish Netherlands, the Bordeaux wine-traders wanted peaceful relations with England, the citizens of the southern and western ports wished for Mediterranean and *biscaïen* peace, all of these issues arising because royal and provincial perceptions of the outside world were at odds. On a few occasions disaffected subjects still looked to foreign powers for help against their repressive sovereign, as in the revolt of the Camisards during the later part of the reign, but fortunately for the crown, which dreaded internal rebellion in time of war, there were fewer insurrections and fewer treacherous overtures were made to the enemy than in the earlier years of the century. At the princely level of society, the dangerous defections to hostile countries of great generals and other magnates, as at the time of the Frondes, also seemed to be at an end. The only other issue which brought foreign policy into the internal affairs of the realm was the relationship between the French crown and the Holy See, and at times Rome was able to introduce a note of further confusion into the already complicated rivalries within the church in France while also threatening the international diplomatic objectives of Louis XIV.

All these problems came and went as the configuration of European politics changed, and as the extent of French involvement in that kaleidoscope of tensions fluctuated. Of more permanent concern to the crown was another aspect of foreign policy, and one in which some of its most powerful subjects had a vested interest. This was, of course, the army, which was both vital for the defence of the realm and important as the channel through which most nobles sought to advance themselves and their clients. To reform the military was, once again, to engage the forces of lineage, patronage and patrimonial politics. The creation of a mighty army is yet another of the achievements which the historians of 'absolutism' have attributed to their hero, Louis XIV, and, as with their other claims, the reality was not only less spectacular but his efforts formed part of a longer-term reform which had begun earlier in the century. That much had already been achieved is clear to the reader of the royal *mémoires*, because the condition of the troops does not feature on the list of disorders which were afflicting the kingdom in the first year of the personal rule. The king contented himself with talking about ways of further improving his forces.

As with his reform of his councils and his dealings with the *parlement* of Paris, so too in the military field it was essential for Louis to assert his authority, but without necessarily changing the personnel. Often it was the terms of service, rather than the men who served, which were changed. He began at the very top of the military hierarchy, and left vacant the post of *colonel-général de l'infanterie*, which became empty on the death in 1661 of the duc d'Epernon – in much the same way as Richelieu had allowed the position of *connétable* to remain unfilled after the death of Lesdiguières. Nevertheless, these supreme commands were key positions in the structure of the army, and remained in the published lists of senior officers. Thus in the 1658 *Etat de la France*, the title of *connétable* is still in its traditional place, and underneath is written 'the duc d'Estrées, fulfilling the functions of' that office. Moreover, whereas the death of d'Epernon had given Louis the opportunity to decide that he would appoint no successor, the corresponding post in the cavalry remained in active existence, because its holder, Turenne, was very much alive. The king had no intention of offending families by depriving them of an office in the army. Only death could take such decisive action, and then Louis would seize the chance to reward them with positions which were equally prestigious but did not entail personal aristocratic control and patronage over a section of the royal forces.

Although Louis treated noble officers with caution, he did continue the policy of slowly but steadily infiltrating civilian administrators into the preserves of the military. The *intendants* had been very unpopular under Richelieu and Mazarin, but the presence in the provinces of *intendants de l'armée* had come to be tolerated by 1661. The wider citizenry did not object to these agents of the crown, and indeed there was some sign that they helped to diminish the demands made by disorderly troops on the localities. It will be remembered that, at the 1626 *assemblée des notables*, there had been considerable support for the removal of private noble armies and for an end to the monopoly over senior military posts which belonged to certain great families. Yet, in 1626 as in 1661, the belief that the king should have the only army in the realm and the expectation that he would use it to defend his subjects were not accompanied by greater willingness to contribute more generously towards its maintenance. In wartime the ordinary people suffered much at the hands of the ill-disciplined soldiery and, despite the reforms of Le Tellier and Louvois, the prolonged wars which concluded the reign of Louis XIV proved that many deeply rooted abuses had not been eradicated. The ministers, the army *intendants* and the provincial governors laboured throughout the personal rule to stamp out corruption, but the shortage of funds in periods of war sabotaged their efforts.[26]

It has already been noted that the role of the *gendarmerie* had declined, ending a situation in which virtually hereditary officers had used their powers of patronage to sustain troops whose prime loyalty was to their immediate commander rather than to the crown. Yet military posts were mostly venal, and although they were not subject to the *paulette* and therefore could not be passed on automatically to kinsfolk, the crown found that it was as difficult to influence the buying and selling of these positions as it was with the sale of civil offices in the fields of justice and finance. Le Tellier had attempted to intervene in this process, but he had achieved little success by 1659 because the stresses of war made reform impossible. Other abuses abounded, and continued to plague the minister during the personal rule of Louis XIV. Captains exaggerated the number of troops that they had recruited, in order to claim extra funds for their maintenance from the treasury, and they were reluctant to report all deserters for the same reason. Both these practices meant that the strength of the forces was greater on paper than in reality. The army *intendants* attempted to verify these figures by inspecting the actual regiments, but there too deception was possible, the officers either enlisting men for the period of the inspection or moving troops from place to place, so that the inspector, travelling by a slower route, reviewed the same men twice and thought them to be two different companies. These abuses have often been attributed to greed on the part of the captains, but that was not always the case. The inclusion of imaginary soldiers on the rolls undoubtedly enabled those in command to extract more funds from the government than they should rightfully have received, but in wartime the crown was normally severely in arrears with its payments, and these additional sums could be used to give the real soldiers their back pay. Captains might also be reluctant to rebuke their troops for plundering the locality, because that too relieved their hardship and could encourage them to serve a little longer. Even when regiments were officially billeted on the population, they tended to exact more than their due, but in extenuation it could be said that the municipal officials charged with collecting funds for the army did not always hand over the full sums, preferring to spend the money on some civil enterprise. The real victim of this system was the citizen, who paid the military levy and found himself terrorized by the soldiers.[27]

There is no doubt that some effective reform of the army was

[26]On the attempt to reform the military administration and the care taken by ministers not to offend the existing hierarchy of command, see André Corvisier, *Louvois* (Paris, 1983), pp. 77–118.

[27]See, for example, Clément, vol. IV, pp. 79, 95–6, 171–2, 176–7.

undertaken in the first ten years of the personal rule, but it was largely a decade of peace, when the royal revenues were more stable. Also, as there was less urgency about the provisioning of the troops, the *intendants* were able to negotiate contracts for forage and supplies at much more reasonable terms. Nevertheless, the misuse of municipal funds which should have been destined for the military was a constant preoccupation of Colbert throughout his ministry, and his letters of 1683 suggest that little progress had been made, if any, in eradicating the corruption which he had identified in these procedures some twenty years before.[28] Although Colbert resented the extent to which prolonged wars undermined his plans for the economy, and wished that more money could be spent on the navy at the expense of the land forces, he devoted much time to those aspects of his governmental responsibilities which were designed to aid the reconstruction of the army, for he had no desire to see the kingdom undefended. He hoped that the strengthening of the military and the navy in peacetime would prevent war, because potential enemies would be dissuaded from engaging the might of the French king in battle. He tried to stimulate the military industries, seeking new weapons, better timber and stronger horses, and instructed his agents throughout Europe to persuade foreign experts that they would receive a warm welcome, and substantial privileges, if they would enter the service of the king of France.[29] Nevertheless he was in favour of short wars which furthered his colonial enterprises, and in that context was initially a supporter of the attack on the Dutch in 1672. Yet, when that limited engagement turned into six more years of general European war, wrecking his plans for internal reform and draining the financial resources which he had carefully accumulated, he did not disguise his feelings in the royal council that the war minister had blundered seriously.

Le Tellier, in common with the other ministers of the 1660s, was well aware that tact and caution must accompany any attempt to bring about long-term reform. Having served as an *intendant de l'armée*, he knew how difficult it was for a civil administrator to inspect the army with any real degree of objectivity. He also accepted that, although these officials had been tolerated by the military hierarchy, partly because they did help with the financing and provisioning of the troops, it would be unwise to let them interfere with the established chains of command. They would have to remain primarily as

[28]See Clément, vol. IV, pp. 172, 175.

[29]Depping, vol. III, pp. 727, 740–1, 751–3; and they were to continue to encourage those already in France – ibid, pp. 757–8, 851–2. Sometimes the initiative to ask for foreign help came from the provinces – as when the Estates of Languedoc asked for Swedish mining experts, ibid, pp. 803–5.

inspectors and as negotiators with the local civil authorities. There was a need to purge the army of its most disorderly elements, and the opportunity was provided by the signing of the peace. Le Tellier was determined to maintain a larger peacetime force than had been customary in past reigns, but he was still able to disband many of the least desirable regiments. This was not as inflammatory as suggesting that venal offices in the civil administration be suppressed, because the army had always grown in war and contracted in peace. He reassured the military that his intentions were honourable by issuing a declaration in 1660, which made it clear that the humbler civilian officials in the military administration, the *commissaires* and *contrôleurs des guerres*, would be responsible, not to the royal council or to some civil authority, but to the established military jurisdiction of the *connétablie* and the *maréchaux de France*. Here is further evidence that, although there was no *connétable* in post, the powers of that office were still intact.

One early concern of Le Tellier in reforming the army was shared by Colbert in his own plans for the civil administration. Neither wished dramatically to change the existing hierarchy and thereby risk offending those whose posts were to disappear, but both men wished to define the responsibilities of each level more precisely in order to end the constant disputes about precedence and duties. The war minister accordingly produced a number of ordinances on this subject, some adding to the content of earlier ones, others merely reiterating regulations which were obviously being disregarded, a pattern equally familiar in the reform of justice and finance. Le Tellier sought to resolve disputes between higher and lower ranks, between cavalry and artillery, between one French regiment and another, and between native and foreign troops. There were a number of exotic elements in the armies of the Bourbons, the Swiss guards being the most important. When it came to the purchase of military posts, the minister could do little, although in 1664 he did abolish venality in the royal guards, except for the rank of captain. Here was another example of the crown making a general point, but being able to implement it only in the immediate entourage of the monarch.

The recruitment of the smaller peacetime army proved very difficult. In time of war, especially if it was also a period of economic crisis, sheer personal poverty would prompt some men to enlist, and then the hardships of battle would lead many of them to desert. They might then repeat the process by joining and leaving a second regiment, being paid by both for offering their services. The 1660s were not a decade of bad harvests and the misery of war, and the recruiting sergeants found that few Frenchmen regarded army life as preferable to their current lot. Of those who were ready to sign up, many were fleeing from creditors, paternity suits or other legal processes. In these days before the wider establishment of poorhouses, many municipalities offered their vagabonds to the sergeants, although a high proportion of these most unwilling victims managed to escape before they reached their regiments. Those small numbers of men who did freely enlist, whether they were fugitives from justice or were genuinely attracted by the military life, were at least prepared to stay on and serve, so that the proportion of deserters declined drastically in these years. Few of these volunteers had to experience active service, save in the brief war of 1667–8.

Le Tellier was also determined to improve conditions in the armed forces, both to attract more recruits and to relieve the burden which the disorderly soldiery often imposed on the innocent population. He tried to ensure that they were properly clothed and fed, and that their wages were regularly and promptly paid. The rules for billeting were clarified, with financial alternatives for those citizens who preferred to pay a levy rather than to accommodate a soldier. None of these reforms worked satisfactorily in peacetime, and less so when prolonged war returned in 1672. Only some crack regiments received uniforms, corrupt officials misappropriated some of the designated funds, and both billeting and the alternative levy remained highly unpopular with the people. As citizens were reluctant to shoulder this burden in addition to that of providing victuals and forage – another part of the system where corruption flourished – the town councils sought to deflect ministerial anger and to relieve the citizenry by providing houses for the soldiery. Eager to spend as little as possible, they usually requisitioned abandoned dwellings for this purpose, and the conditions were often found by the *intendants* to be utterly appalling. Le Tellier was further concerned to improve the standard of medical care for the troops, as the imaginative proposals of Richelieu that every army and each frontier town should have proper facilities had progressed a very little way towards realization. Little more was done to advance these ideas in the 1660s, and neither did the plan for looking after old and critically wounded soldiers become actuality. A proportion of them were taken into religious houses as oblates, but most returned to burden their families and native villages or joined the already substantial ranks of the vagabonds.

The reform of the army in the early years of the personal rule therefore follows a course which can be discerned in other fields of government. At the very centre, a businesslike ministerial office, with efficient clerks keeping detailed records, sought to formulate a programme of improvement which contained some new ideas, and

224 The Personal Rule of Louis XIV

others which had been suggested but not implemented by previous ministers. In the provinces, there was the familiar resistance to change, among the people who resented the new demands which were being made upon them, and within the administration where far too many officials profited by the unreformed system. The *intendants de l'armée* and their subordinates, like the provincial governors and many leading generals, monitored this confusion and despaired of implementing any of the major reforms which were clearly essential – in a Europe where other armies were improving their capabilities, if the current foreign propaganda was to be believed. Only in the manufacture of better weaponry was France taking some forward strides, and here she was heavily dependent on the skills of foreigners. Yet once again Le Tellier had to be cautious, because many of these new armaments were designed to improve the performance of the infantry, and the nobility was on its guard against any innovation which suggested an attack on the pre-eminence enjoyed by the cavalry in the social hierarchy of the armed forces.

During the 1660s, Le Tellier slowly handed over the administration of the army to his son, the marquis de Louvois, whom he had carefully trained as his successor. They continued to work together until 1672, and it was only during the Dutch War that Louvois effectively became the war minister, although still consulting his father on very many matters. He was the first close adviser of Louis XIV to come from the younger generation, being only a few years younger than the king himself. Whereas his colleagues had vivid adult memories of the Frondes, and many of them could recall the days of Louis XIII and Richelieu, he had been a child during the turbulence of the civil wars. He was also unusual in never having served in a provincial office, and, although he made frequent tours of the frontier provinces and the troops, it was his Parisian viewpoint on every issue which most annoyed his many critics. He lacked sympathy for regional attitudes, and was abrasive in his dealings with senior commanders. Because he saw the overall needs of the military situation, whereas they were primarily concerned with their own part of the campaign, he was often obliged to allocate the limited resources at his disposal in ways which helped some regiments at the expense of others, causing the unlucky generals to complain bitterly. Instead of explaining the problem, he would then respond in a haughty manner, and it was often the king himself who had to soothe the ruffled feelings of his senior officers. As a result of these encounters, many serving commanders fiercely disliked this parvenu bureaucrat, and from their memoirs and letters has grown the legend, perpetuated by generations of historians, that Louvois was a loathsome monster. In fact he was an able, loyal and hard-working administrator, intelligent in planning strategy and in husbanding resources, but rather unimaginative when dealing with the elites of the army and the provinces. He was also eager to further the fortunes of his family and its clientele, but so was every other minister.

Two of his most abiding characteristics throughout his ministry were his passionate detestation of any disorder, whether religious, civil or military, and his almost obsessive desire to gather more and more information about the problems which faced him. Accordingly, he imposed a rigorous schedule on his immediate subordinates in the bureaucracy, and demanded regular and highly detailed reports from his network of agents throughout the kingdom and further afield. Yet he found it difficult to use the knowledge he gained as the basis for an effective series of reforms. He was therefore compelled to continue the policies of his father, slowly providing more uniforms and better conditions, but the abuses in recruitment and the misappropriation of funds persisted. He made sure that severe penalties were imposed on those miscreants who could be brought to justice and convicted, and he offered money to informers who would report corrupt practices. He also created a team of inspectors – military officers who were to complement the work of the *intendants* and other civilian officials. In the army therefore, as in other areas of the administration, the first decades of the personal rule saw a concerted attempt to banish corruption and to introduce greater efficiency, but no long-term plan for drastic structural reform.

In his search for information, Louvois made full use of the position which he purchased in 1668 and held until his death in 1691, the *surintendance général des postes*.[30] This office was not only vital to any minister who wished to know what was happening throughout the kingdom, but it was a source of considerable personal income for its holder. The existing system of *maîtres des couriers*, *maîtres des postes* and their subordinates was far from satisfactory, and the two groups of *maîtres* were often at odds. After an extended inquest into their activities, Louvois resolved to create a new network of couriers, and this was duly set up in an edict of 1672. Yet, in the first year of the Dutch War, the sheer size of the administration required by these new processes and the consequential cost to the treasury were too great for the government to bear, and so the right to run an internal postal service was farmed out to a company of financiers. The *surintendant*

---

[30]The definitive work on the postal system is that of Eugène Vaillé, *Histoire générale des postes françaises jusqu'à la Révolution* (6 vols, Paris, 1947–53). Its conclusions for the first half of the personal rule of Louis XIV are summarized, with the fruits of additional research, in Corvisier, *Louvois*, pp. 222–40.

remained in charge of the international post, and had overall control over the new company, but it was nevertheless not he but the farmers who appointed their own *sous-fermiers*, and they in turn who chose the lesser agents.

The first task for the *fermiers* was to reimburse the existing *maîtres* for the offices they had purchased, and those posts were then duly suppressed by the crown. As a further step towards achieving a monopoly of internal postal functions, they also sought to erode the position enjoyed by the many private networks of couriers which existed throughout the realm. Most of these systems had originally been instituted to serve a specific need, but they had attracted other customers once the service they offered was seen to be efficient. Notable among them were the university couriers, and the *fermiers* were prepared to offer generous compensation to these institutions in return for their agreement to abandon this wider and financially profitable role. Henceforth they would confine themselves to carrying letters relating to university business, together with the personal correspondence of staff and students. Local postal services, operating within a confined geographical area, were less easy to eradicate, especially as it might be costly to provide an alternative system, and they were therefore frequently allowed to survive, as long as they did not interfere with the monopoly of the farmers over the longer distance mails.

Thus Louvois had tried to set up a more efficient royal postal service, but had almost immediately sold it off to private interests, even if they were under his ultimate supervision. In fact the new arrangement seems to have worked more than adequately, because the *fermiers* and *sous-fermiers* received a substantial return for their initial investment and took care to appoint employees of a suitable standard. Moreover, Louvois issued a series of regulations which not only prescribed rules for the speedy, safe and regular conveyance of the mails, but afforded considerable protection and privileges to those involved in this enterprise. In return for these benefits, many officials obeyed the instruction of the *surintendant* that they should report to him any matters of interest which might have been gleaned from the letters they carried or from gossip heard on their travels. The *intendants* were instructed to observe the workings of the whole postal system, checking both that the employees were doing their duty and that their privileges were being respected by others, although Louvois was as insistent as Colbert that it was not for the *intendant* to interfere in the administration of such matters. If his reports contained matters of concern to the government, it was not for him, but for the council of the king, to take action.

The success of this royal, but privately organized, service was such that Louvois sent most of his communications by the post, using special couriers only for the most sensitive of matters. He was also satisfied in general with the information provided by the postal officials. Nevertheless, there were breaches of security and confidence, sometimes because an enemy had found hands willing to accept a bribe, but more often because newsmongers within France were prepared to pay for the knowledge which members of the clerical staff could provide. In 1706 twenty such clerks at the Paris postal bureau were brought to trial for this very offence, after an extensive interrogation of all personnel by the police authorities.

The international post was not entrusted to the *fermiers*, and the *surintendant* was able to place many of his own agents within its administration. These men not only reported on the contents of the mails, but were required to question travellers whom they encountered on their journeys. Bureaux were set up in certain foreign cities, where further intelligence was gathered by those charged with speeding the mails to and from France. For this task he tried to recruit men who had an intimate knowledge of these foreign lands, some of them natives and others Frenchmen residing abroad. He also relied heavily on the governors of the frontier provinces to seek out suitable and trustworthy men, especially those who had links with the neighbouring areas of adjacent states, for these delicate tasks. Much money was expended to foster loyalty in these officials, and to give them funds by which they in turn could reimburse their informants. Not surprisingly, there were rival claimants for their services, and Louvois was unsuccessful in exposing the many double-agents, among the officials and the purveyors of information, who made a good living from their duplicity.

Dissimulation was vital in these activities, and the minister was not averse to the employment of lawless methods if they would achieve his purpose. He engaged his own bands of highwaymen to ambush postal couriers, in order to create the impression that a letter, although lost, had not fallen into government hands. He also had considerable success in finding expert cryptographers, both to safeguard his own communications and to decipher those of his enemies, and this was one aspect of espionage where the French managed to outflank other powers. Although very secret matters of state were not entrusted to the post, the speed of the French couriers was so renowned that much government and private mail between Spain and the Empire was sent across France, because this route was so much faster than the longer journey by sea.

The almost obsessive desire of Louvois for information and his mania for deception were partly responsible for the changes in military strategy during his ministry. In his opinion, battles were unpredictable and victories might be Pyrrhic. The siege was tactically much more satisfactory and could be prepared with care, although the planning of such enterprises required the utmost secrecy. Louvois insisted that money was not to be raised in areas near to the stronghold which was to be besieged, lest suspicions be aroused. It was to be collected elsewhere and sent in small quantities by devious routes. Moreover, the choice of targets should be made to seem as random as possible, so that no town could foresee that it was soon to be invested. Nevertheless, these piecemeal attacks were part of a carefully prepared strategy which began to unfold in 1673, the year in which the short and swift campaign against the Dutch was transformed by the enemies of France into a major European conflict. The intention of Louvois was to build a strongly fortified frontier, whereas the preceding policy had been to defend the 'portes', the key gateways on the routes along which hostile armies might try to enter the kingdom or the French might sally forth to occupy neighbouring lands. The new plan involved the acquisition of territory to a limited degree, but for the most part it entailed the reinforcement of defences along the present frontiers. It was certainly preferable to the maintenance of advanced positions within enemy countries. Colbert was also in favour of this change in tactics, because it would enable him to police the regulations associated with his strict policy on imports, exports and tariffs. Yet in reality, although much of this defensive cordon was ultimately completed, it proved less effective than had been hoped, and it failed both to prevent smuggling and to halt the exodus of Huguenots after the persecution of the 1680s.[31]

Louvois and Louis XIV were both well aware that in the past Paris had lain open, on more than one occasion, to an invading enemy, and yet they refused to fortify the capital lest such defences become the bastions of future *frondeur* resistance to a royal army. This was an added reason for building a chain of strong frontier strongholds so that no foreign troops could enter French territory and give support to internal insurrection. Yet the creation and subsequent maintenance of a *pré carré*, a duelling field, in which battles could be concentrated, had some disadvantages. It meant that certain provinces bore an increasingly large proportion of the burdens imposed by war and defence, being regularly subjected to the presence of large garrisons and

[31]For a more extended discussion of the foreign and defence policies of the royal ministers, see Roger Mettam, 'Voltaire as historian of Louis XIV', in *Le siècle de Louis XIV*, eds S. S. B. Taylor et al, vols 11–13 of the complete *Oeuvres*, to be published shortly by the International Voltaire Foundation, Oxford.

frequently to the ravages of battles as well. The rest of the country experienced a corresponding reduction in these hardships, and the inner provinces therefore came to regard war as a distant happening which affected them but little. They consequently showed much greater reluctance than before towards contributing to its costs.[32]

The methods of Louvois pleased very few of those involved in the actual running of the army. His insistence on careful planning made him seem over cautious, although logistical considerations often impelled him to behave with restraint. Even Vauban, the architect of the *pré carré*, felt that the minister was half-hearted in his support for this new strategy, which was by no means true. Many generals, already aggrieved that he denied them adequate resources or recalled their forces just when further victories seemed assured, also disliked his regular requests for detailed information, knowing that it would be used to formulate the precise ministerial directives which they resented so bitterly. In the opening years of the Dutch War there were some direct confrontations between the minister and the military leaders, the proud generals putting aside their own rivalries in order to launch a combined attack upon him. The king had to intervene and calm their ruffled feelings, also making it clear to Louvois that greater tact was essential. Even so, the minister could seldom resist the temptation to complain about reversals in the field, but rarely praised those who had achieved success and victory. In contrast, Louis XIV took care both to laud the victorious and to treat the unsuccessful with courtesy. He knew that, in the turmoil of war, the loss of a battle was not necessarily to be blamed on those in command. Superior enemy forces, lack of resources, fatigue, illness, even geographical or meteorological chance might be partly or largely responsible. Those who lacked valour or wisdom could always be moved to a prestigious but less strategically vital post, and there was no reason to cause them, and therefore their whole family, to lose face by rebuking them publicly in front of the court.

If Louvois proved to be a poor psychologist in his dealings with the military commanders, he was sometimes no more perceptive in his treatment of foreign powers. His offer of the harshest peace terms to the Dutch after the initial invasion of the Republic in 1672, followed by atrocities such as the savage destruction of Zwammerdam and Bodengrave, only served to stiffen resistance when he expected it to crumble. His subsequent resolve to rase the Palatinate in 1688 showed that he had not learned this earlier lesson, although on this occasion

---

[32]See André Corvisier, *La France de Louis XIV, 1643–1715: ordre intérieur et place en Europe* (Paris, 1979), pp. 106–25.

the French generals refused to carry out the policy to the full extent which the minister required of them. It is not suggested that Louis XIV played no part in these decisions, nor that other ministers were opposed to them, but there is ample evidence that Louvois was often the architect of these severe measures. The king, as a truly aristocratic monarch, regarded diplomacy as a transaction between rulers, and took no account of the hostility which could be engendered among the subjects of enemy princes. Foreign policy was a royal monopoly, except in strange countries like England, Sweden and the Dutch Republic, where representative institutions sometimes interfered in these regal matters. Therefore Louis, negotiating with or fighting against rulers, not peoples, was as slow to realize the general hatred he had inspired among neighbouring populations as he was to comprehend the increasing dislike which his French subjects felt for his own expensive militarism. Thus he was lulled into a false sense of security during the mid-1680s, not realising that his enemies were awaiting their opportunity to humble him. As a result, he and his war minister miscalculated further, this time selecting the pope as their victim. Their seizure of papal Avignon, continuing the aggressively gallican religious policy that they had pursued for many years, had the effect both of provoking the pontiff into secretly excommunicating Louis – which would have been a disaster for the king if it had been made public – and of ensuring that the arbitration of Rome in the disputed election to the strategically vital archbishopric of Cologne would be exercised in favour of the imperial, not the French, candidate. When the Nine Years War broke out in 1688, taking the government at Versailles by surprise, it was soon evident to the king and his ministers that whole countries were out for revenge and that there were no major allies to be enlisted in support of the Bourbon cause.[33]

It is not the intention here to analyse in detail the diplomatic and military history of the reign, but a brief chronological survey is necessary for two reasons. First, it will provide a vital back-cloth for a discussion of the domestic administration of the kingdom, showing how far the incidence of war affected the ability of ministers to solve the problems of internal government. Secondly it will demonstrate the extent to which the reform of the armed forces was parallelled by similar changes in other areas of the bureaucracy. In 1672, the situation of France in Europe was very different from that of the early 1660s. The princes of the Rhenish league no longer trusted their French protector, the Dutch had ceased to be allies and were now

[33]See Geoffrey Symcox, 'Louis XIV and the outbreak of the Nine Years War', in Ragnhild Hatton (ed.), *Louis XIV and Europe* (London, 1976), pp. 179–212.

bitter enemies, and the Franco-imperial plans for an amicable division of the Spanish inheritance were in ruins. It was at this moment that the proposal, supported by Colbert as well as by Le Tellier and Louvois, for the rapid subjection of the Dutch Republic was implemented and came within sight of success, literally so because the advance troops could see the church towers of Amsterdam across the inundated lands which protected the Hollanders from their would-be conquerors. By the following year, this limited offensive against an apparently defenceless state had become a European war which would last for six years, and would have many disastrous consequences for Louvois, for Colbert and for France. During these prolonged hostilities, Charles II abandoned his French ally, the royal finances were thrown into such disarray that Colbert had to abandon all hope of realizing many of his cherished plans for reform, the great maréchal de Turenne was killed in battle and his death proved to be a severe blow to army morale, and a major revolt broke out in Brittany,[34] partly caused by merchant anger that the crown had forbidden further trade with the Dutch, whose ships were normally frequent and welcome visitors to the Breton ports. At the Peace of Nijmegen in 1678–9, Colbert had to agree that his aggressive national tariff policy should be abandoned, and it was only the moderate nature of French demands which enabled the ministers to claim a diplomatic victory in the negotiations. Nor had Louvois emerged from the conflict with too much distinction. Apart from the failure to crush the Dutch, he had quarrelled with the military commanders, compelling the king to intervene and mediate between the generals and the minister. Thus, although he and Colbert conspired to have Pomponne disgraced, the new foreign affairs minister was to be from the Colbertian clan and the Le Tellier candidate was rejected. Yet Louis did not want to humiliate Louvois and his family in public, and the king therefore cajoled the extremely reluctant duc de La Rochefoucauld into marrying his son, the duc de La Rocheguyon, to the daughter of the war minster. This social *coup* for the Le Tellier family undoubtedly compensated for its failure to secure the portfolio relinquished by Pomponne. Nevertheless the consequence was that diplomacy and defence were divided between the two leading ministerial factions. The Le Tellier retained control of the army, but the Colbert had both foreign affairs and the navy. In the 1690s Pomponne would return to his former office, and then be succeeded by his son-in-law, Colbert de Torcy, who was also the son of another foreign minister, Colbert de Croissy.

[31]See: Mettam, *The role of the higher aristocracy*, pp. 275–96; Mettam, *Government and society*, pp. 237–48.

With the signing of the Nijmegen peace, Louis XIV and Louvois hoped to resume the reform of the army, but further progress was painfully slow. A principal reason was that, with the cessation of hostilities, many officers wished for a relaxation of discipline after the rigours they and their troops had endured on the battlefield, and had no intention of tightening it in the way the minister required. It is true that better weapons were now being devised, but similar advances were also taking place in other countries. Moreover, the persecution of the Huguenots would cause many adherents of Protestantism, whether native Frenchmen or resident foreigners, to leave the country, and included among them would be many of the best designers and manufacturers of these novel French armaments. The strong frontier, devised by Vauban, proved unable to contain these emigrants, and they were soon putting their military skills at the disposal of enemy rulers. One great achievement during the Dutch War had been the completion of the spectacular hôtel des Invalides in Paris, a visible expression of royal concern for the returning wounded, but the expansion of this project in peacetime proved more difficult. Local authorities were reluctant to shoulder the costly burden, and the Paris hospital remained the unique showpiece of governmental good intentions, because the crown was always willing to alleviate the problems of the potentially aggrieved, and therefore possibly seditious, poor in its own locality of Paris, but had no intention of financing provincial schemes which should rightly fall upon the municipal treasuries. The number of those needing some assistance increased greatly in the later wars of the reign, as is seen by the fact that the workshops in the Invalides, designed both to raise money for the hospital and to employ those inmates whose injuries prevented them from working in the city, had to be converted into further dormitories in the 1690s as the demand for places rose. Some religious houses were persuaded to pay a levy, instead of receiving invalided soldiers as oblates as they had done in the past, but these funds permitted only a tentative assault on an expanding problem. Although Louvois was prepared to increase the amount spent on the relief of this suffering, Colbert was most reluctant to authorize the necessary funds. He was permanently aware that resources were inadequate, and he also had the needs of his cherished navy to consider. No matter how much effort the war minister devoted to improving the conditions of the currently and recently serving soldiery, these men remained in a state of penury which could only be improved by inflicting further suffering on the civil population in general. The other concern of Le Tellier and his son, the provision of medical facilities for the regiments, also showed no advance in the 1680s, and the splendid health care at the Invalides underlined the contrast between this Paris experiment in welfare and the lack of similar schemes in the army at large.

After 1679, Louvois determined to maintain a substantial peacetime military establishment, in order to minimize the difficulty of recruiting troops at the start of any future war, although some officers and many more of their men felt that they had served long enough, and wished to return to their homes. The minister was therefore eager to pursue the policy of *réunions*, the incorporation into France of bordering territories to which jurists had formulated a legitimate claim on the part of Louis XIV. This strategy justified the retention of a large army, and it was relatively successful in political terms, with most of the towns capitulating at the sight of the French regiments outside their walls and not waiting for the first shots to be fired. A further ruse for keeping extra soldiers in service was to employ them on the massive schemes, especially those for diverting rivers and transporting water, which attended the lavish embellishment of Versailles.

Yet Louvois was worried about the increasing hostility shown by the king towards the Huguenots, because approximately one-tenth of the serving manpower in the army belonged to the reformed religion. Attempts had been made to encourage such men to convert to 'the true faith', and indeed they were admitted to the Invalides only on the understanding that they would do so. Nevertheless the war minister was a realist, and knew that such abjuration was frequently insincere. Indeed, in the *réunion* lands he insisted on a token change to Catholicism but did not require the whole population to follow suit. In the existing frontier provinces of France, for which he had responsibility in his capacity as secretary of state, he tried to ensure that there were as few Huguenots as possible, because he feared that they might be tempted to side with enemy Protestant powers in future wars, especially if Louis proceeded with the policy of persecution. Within the army itself, the minister was prepared to be discreetly tolerant. Foreign regiments, like the Swiss, were not required to embrace the Roman faith, and he did not enquire closely into the sincerity of French Protestant officers who were prepared to join the ranks of the *nouveaux convertis*. Local commanders were instructed to persuade Huguenot soldiers to abjure, but only by gentle means, and all officers and men who underwent a change of heart were rewarded financially. The prospect of such rewards prompted many Catholics to profess the heretic faith, after which they speedily converted back again and pocketed the bribe. Although Louvois has always been associated with the policy of *dragonnades*, the billeting of troops on recalcitrant Huguenots, his own preference was for a peaceful solution to the Protestant problem, and he genuinely believed that conversions would be inevitable if the recompense were sufficiently substantial. He also gave strict orders about the enforcement of the rule that those who had abjured should henceforth be exempted from billeting. Yet many Protestant officers and men did leave the royal service, rather than abandon their beliefs, while some commanders simply ignored the demand for religious uniformity, preferring to retain their forces intact, whatever their personal beliefs. Only a year after the formal revocation, enshrined in the 1685 Edict of Fontainebleau, of the tolerance originally granted to French Calvinists by Henri IV, Louvois, who had now succeeded the deceased Colbert as secretary for manufactures, was trying to persuade foreign manufacturers to return to the France that they had recently left, and was issuing licences which guaranteed them freedom to practise their Protestant religion if they did so. This kind of bribery did not bring the desired results, so that the French economy and armed forces remained the poorer as a consequences of the Huguenot exodus.[35]

The insistence by Louvois on a strictly moral way of life for the inmates of the Invalides, and his demands that army *intendants* and commanders should ensure the observance of similarly high standards of behaviour by soldiers in camp, in special garrison houses and in billets – prescriptions which were very difficult to enforce – were part of his wider plan to improve the image of the soldier in society. To that end regular pay and uniforms were vital – and were equally beyond the administrative and financial resources of the crown. Although Louvois disliked the idea that governments should have to take account of public opinion, he nevertheless instructed a number of his spies to roam the streets and cafés of Paris, with a view to reporting everything they heard about the reputation of the soldiery, and about the military and diplomatic policies of the crown. He was also eager to use the image of an efficient and reformed army as a means of attracting more young nobles to the colours. An early plan for a cadet force in the royal guards, from which officers of new regiments would be selected, had been tried in 1664 but quickly abandoned. In 1682 the war minister created some new companies, strictly limited to the nobility, in which good officer training would be provided. The conditions of service in these corps were excellent, and many aristocratic scions were soon drawn to them, but they were so costly to run and their members quickly acquired such a reputation for disorderly behaviour that further recruitment was stopped in 1692 and they were abolished in 1694. Lesser nobles were lured into the army by

---

[35]See Roger Mettam, 'Louis XIV and the persecution of the Huguenots: the role of the ministers and royal officials', in Irene Scouloudi (ed.), *Huguenots in Britain and their French background, 1550–1800* (London, 1987).

being offered generous financial incentives, and by the promise of orders of chivalry for those who excelled.

Only good ordinary soldiers remained difficult to conscript, and the traditional abuses of recruitment procedures persisted. Too high a proportion of those enlisted still came from the prisons, the poorhouses and the vagabond population, and captains continued to invent fictitious troops in order to claim larger sums for maintenance, although this abuse was still motivated on many occasions by the desire to pay the real soldiers a higher wage than the regulations allowed, or more regular sums than the erratic provision of funds by the treasury permitted. Much against his will, because he knew it produced unwilling recruits who were quick to desert, Louvois was compelled to rely heavily on forced conscription. Indeed the rate of desertion was very high throughout the last two wars of the reign. Therefore, despite the sustained efforts of Le Tellier and his son, little had changed permanently for the better. Louvois continued to send out inspectors, who were to insist on tighter discipline, but officers knew that strict implementation of the rules would only increase the numbers of deserters. On the state of the army, as in so many other aspects of the administration, a massive amount of information was acquired by the ministers, but effective reform continued to elude them.

The last two wars of Louis XIV were fought on a much larger scale than that of 1672–9. More men were needed, but there was no possibility of providing the new weaponry in sufficient quantities to arm more than a small proportion of them. Moreover an increasing shortage of money, together with the problems of billeting and the lack of adequate garrison houses, began to affect the actual strategy of the campaigns. It became vital to move the troops as rapidly as possible into enemy territory, where they could tyrannize the local population, even though this was not always the best course of action on military grounds. The deficiency in manpower also compelled Louvois, in the three years before his death, to call up the provincial militias and add them to the royal forces. These local troops, which defended their towns in times of rebellion and helped to maintain order in their own area, had always been under the control of the elected urban authorities. They were therefore unpredictable because they, like their municipal masters, did not always agree with ministerial policies and decisions, and they had always been considered to be undesirable components of a royal army. In 1688 they were called to fight on the order of the king, instead of at the municipal behest, but this was a mere fiction. The scale of the problems confronting the war minister at the beginning of the Nine Years War is thus nowhere more clearly shown than in his recourse to these troops for which he had no liking, and which he would have rejected had there been any alternative. An attempt was made to guarantee their loyalty by offering fiscal exemptions to those who agreed to serve, but this was to increase manpower at a financial cost that the impoverished crown could ill afford to bear. The naval forces were supplemented by more bizarre methods, as lawless and piratical vessels were co-opted into the fleet. Their captains welcomed this legalization of their looting of enemy shipping, but they remained unreliable and were still likely to set upon French ships if the rewards were greater.

Many historians have claimed that Louvois was on the point of falling from royal favour in 1691, when death intervened to prevent his disgrace, but it is always difficult to prove that the king entertained such sentiments before he actually announced the dismissal of an adviser. It was never politic for him to reveal to his subjects that one of his ministers no longer enjoyed his confidence but was still in office. Very soon after the death of the war minister, but perhaps even before it, Louis XIV recognized that it was impossible to devise a strategy which offered any real chance of success. French policy-makers were being buffeted by forces beyond their control. Barbézieux, having succeeded his father as the holder of the military portfolio, was never highly esteemed by the king, who increasingly disregarded not only the views of this new adviser but also his position in the hierarchy of command. Instead, Louis wrote ever more frequently to those in the field who enjoyed his confidence, especially to governors and *lieutenants-généraux* such as the duc de Noailles in Languedoc, often following their counsel and ignoring the contradictory advice of Barbézieux.[36] The king seemed to have become his own war minister, and it was only his wish to honour the Le Tellier family for its past services which prevented him from dismissing the secretary of state from the government.

If the resumption of war in 1688 ended serious hopes of reforming the army, it had an equally devastating effect on plans for improving the internal administration of the kingdom. From 1690 a more moderate tone began to characterize French foreign policy, reminiscent of that during the early personal rule of Louis XIV, and therefore perhaps suggesting that the voice of Louvois was less prominent in the royal council during the last months of his life. Yet it could be that he

---

[36]See the letters of Louis XIV to Noailles, 1 August 1691 and 25 October 1694, and Pontchartrain to Noailles, 15 October 1694, quoted in abbé Millot, *Mémoires politiques et militaires . . . composés sur les pièces originales recueillies par Adrien-Maurice, duc de Noailles, maréchal de France & ministre d'état* (6 vols, Lausanne/Yverdon, 1778), vol. I, pp. 165, 276–8; see also pp. 248–82.

shared the general view of the present situation, which was that a French victory seemed impossible. Certainly the Colbert faction was predominant after 1691, with Croissy and then Pomponne, recalled from his fifteen years of disgrace, in charge of foreign affairs. Both men were convinced that negotiation, rather than military might, was the only way to obtain even minimal advantages for France in any forthcoming peace. Accordingly, in 1690 Croissy began his attempt to form a neutral group of states in the Rhineland, similar to the Rhenish league which had functioned so successfully in the 1650s and 1660s.[37] His efforts proved fruitless because French expansionism seemed a self-evident fact to the princes near her borders. A second resurrection of earlier policies was a plan for a diplomatic agreement on how to partition the Spanish inheritance, following on from the Partition Treaty of 1668, but this later initiative was also ultimately a failure, although some progress was made in the preparatory discussions. One restraining factor was that France dared not appear too eager to reach a settlement, lest she give the impression of weakness or of fearing defeat, and a further obstacle was the refusal of Louis XIV to recognize William III as monarch in England, even though the assent of the king-stadhouder would be essential to any enduring solution of the Spanish problem. Louis had to stand by his brother Catholic ruler, the exiled James II, in the same way that he felt obliged, during the subsequent War of the Spanish Succession, to support the royalty of James III, although on this second occasion all the French ministers advised him against doing so. At least the third strand in the more moderate foreign policy of the 1690s brought some diplomatic advantage, but this volte-face – the submission of the French crown to the claims of Rome and the abandonment of thirty years of royal gallicanism – aroused opposition within the kingdom which was soon to cause difficulties of a different kind. Louis found that, instead of the militant Innocent XI, his own judges were now the principal opponents of his religious policy, and that the Jansenists, whom he was determined to obliterate, were turning to the *parlement* of Paris, instead of to the pope, for protection against royal persecution.

The turbulent years of the Nine Years War were soon followed, after the failure to agree on a division of the Spanish inheritance, by the War of the Spanish Succession, with the extension of French military activity into the Iberian peninsula in order to establish Philip V on his new throne. With the royal finances in chaos and large areas of France suffering grievous economic hardship, there was an ever rising chorus of criticism directed against Louis himself, because his aggressive

[37]See Janine Fayard, 'Attempts to build a "third party" in North Germany, 1690–1694', in Hatton (ed.), *Louis XIV and Europe*, pp. 213–40.

militarism seemed to be the cause of all the present evils. Very few of his subjects would lament his death in 1715, although hardly any of them could remember the time when another king had ruled them. During this final war of the reign, Louis and his ministers felt themselves increasingly unable to devise any international strategy which offered a reasonable hope of success, and the aging monarch, who had always been courteous to defeated generals, was now doubly so because it appeared that no human efforts, however intelligently conceived, could bring France even a short respite from the enemies who beset her. When the direct Bourbon line was decimated by the premature royal deaths of 1711 and 1712, Louis became utterly convinced that divine justice was being wrought upon him for his past misdeeds, both military and moral. He had been troubled by this notion for many years, in fact since the reversals of the 1672–9 war, but now he felt that the evidence for celestial retribution was undeniable.

In the last years of his life, Louis XIV, although still regal and serene in public, was on occasion very testy in his dealings with ministers. Sometimes he seemed to reject their advice simply in order to remind them of his pre-eminence. As his counsellors did not always agree on the best solutions for the resilient problems which confronted them, Torcy began to consult them informally before the meetings of the council, in order to formulate a united, or an acceptable majority, opinion which would give the king less opportunity to propose a totally different course of action.[38] Although Louis had much more faith in Torcy than he had earlier shown towards Barbézieux, he still communicated directly with trusted royal agents, by-passing the foreign minister who thus had the additional task of finding out for himself what had been written by and to the king. At other times, Louis and Torcy discussed and decided matters without any reference to the other ministers and advisers. Thus a variety of personal relationships coexisted beside the formal deliberations of the king in his *conseil d'en haut*. No royal counsellor could be certain that he had been taken fully into the confidence of the sovereign, whose behaviour lacked the frankness which had characterized his relations with ministers in the 1660s and 1670s.

These last two wars cast a perpetual shadow over those members of the government who were charged with the internal administration of the kingdom. Plans for reforming the traditional administrative system had to be abandoned, and short-term financial expedients, which

[38]John C. Rule, 'Colbert de Torcy, an emergent bureaucracy, and the making of French foreign policy, 1698–1715', in Hatton (ed.), *Louis XIV and Europe*, pp. 260–88.

Colbert had tried to avoid in the peaceful 1660s, had to be revived and used with greater frequency than ever before. The situation was so disastrous that ministers and political commentators were forced to ask fundamental questions about the very nature of French society and administration, because it soon became clear that no reform of the existing structure would solve the problems of the crown. More drastic change was needed. Therefore, from the mid 1690s, there began to appear proposals which went far beyond anything that Colbert might have suggested. The first attempts to introduce them brought little success, because the pressures of war afforded the ministers no time for sustained planning, but a beginning was made which would be built upon by the ministers of Louis XV. This is not to say that these novelties were welcomed by the people of France, because some of them struck at the basic fiscal and jurisdictional liberties of social and institutional groups. The privileges which Colbert had accepted as legal facts were now being re-examined, and the new empirical philosophy offered additional evidence for regarding them as ana-chronistic and undesirable.

One final point must be made about the army, this time in the context of internal administration within the kingdom. Le Tellier and Louvois had made some piecemeal improvements in its discipline, efficiency and conditions of service, although it still more resembled the unsatisfactory body which they had taken over than the model force of which they dreamed. Yet it remained of dubious value as an agency of royal government in France. Apart from the unpopularity of its presence in the provinces and the disorder which its members caused, many of its aristocratic officers were persistently reluctant to act as a kind of police force, for it was not part of the honourable and glorious military career to which every true noble aspired. Moreover it would involve them in enforcing ministerial policies of which they personally disapproved, and which they would resist on their own estates. Thus the ordinary soldier was untrustworthy and the officer was unwilling, when the army was used in internal administration. The only issue where the consciences of Catholic captains would permit them to act against the population of an area, whether fellow nobles or commoners, was that of heresy. In the same way that the troops had enthusiastically attacked La Rochelle in the 1620s, so now in the 1680s the dragoons coerced recalcitrant Huguenots to abjure, and their brutality was a positive asset for the crown in making its policy effective. They were also used against pockets of Protestant resistance in subsequent years, although some leading commanders continued to question the wisdom of such forced conversions and implemented the repressive measures with less than wholehearted commitment.[39] A number of them actually stated that the Catholic church needed to be reformed before any dissenter could be expected to embrace its teachings. It was also safe to use the army against the peasant rebels in Lower Brittany in 1675 because they, unlike most insurgents in this period, had revolted against noble and clerical authority, as well as against the royal administration which was the usual target of such uprisings. Nevertheless, for the historian of the later seventeenth century the abiding impression is of how rarely the royal army was used in the internal government of the kingdom.

It has already been remarked that, although the war ministers created a larger and more efficient staff in their central bureaux at court, they were careful not to offend the noble army officers by allowing the new civil administrators to interfere too much in the daily running of the regiments. An *intendant* might be acceptable when he helped to improve the conditions of the troops, but any attempt by him to interfere with the legitimate powers of the captains and colonels would be doubly objectionable because he was their social inferior as well as a usurper of their authority. Gradations of status and rank caused less of a problem in the department of foreign affairs, where similar attempts were being made to create a larger and more expert team of bureaucrats. The royal ambassadors and envoys had to be treated with the respect due to their aristocratic rank, and therefore it was usually the secretary of state, or even the king, who personally replied to their correspondence and sent them further instructions. Despatches and titbits of information received from agents abroad and in the frontier provinces could be entrusted to humbler bureaucrats, because the informants were mostly merchants or other middling members of society, and there was no question of their being socially offended by having to deal with a career administrator of no great status. As in the office of the war minister, a particular need in the central bureaux for foreign affairs was for expert cryptographers, and there was also a mass of routine work to be done, such as the issuing of passports and the translating of documents. By the time of Torcy, the professionalism of this department was in marked contrast with the amateurism which persisted in many parts of the internal administrative machinery.

[39]See, for example, the letters from Châteauneuf to Noailles, 23 November 1682, and Noailles to Chateauneuf, 24 November 1682, in Millot, *Mémoires*, vol. I. pp. 14–18; Armand de Béthune to the secretary of Noailles, 20 January 1684, ibid, pp. 57–8; Noailles to Louvois, 27 October 1685, ibid, pp. 82–91; see also ibid, pp. 23, 26–7, 41–7, 61–2, 76–7.

If new experts appeared in the office of the foreign affairs minister, the lists of ambassadors and envoys, whether permanently resident at a foreign court or undertaking special missions and negotiations, contain few social surprises. Not only were these men always aristocrats, but most also held other significant official positions. Provincial governors and *lieutenants-généraux* were frequently entrusted with important diplomatic initiatives, as witnessed by the missions of the ducs d'Aumont, de Chaulnes, de Gramont and de Noailles. Distinguished and high ranking military men also undertook such tasks, their number including the duc d'Estrées and the maréchaux d'Harcourt, d'Huxelles, de Tallard and de Villars. Trusted senior churchmen from distinguished families formed a third group, as seen in the persons of the cardinaux d'Estrées, de Forbin-Janson and de La Trémoïlle. Ministers also frequently appointed one of their own relatives, provided that he had a noble or ecclesiastical title which gave him the necessary social status, although it is noticeable here that, while it was essential for the appointee to be a man of ability, the secretary for foreign affairs did not choose men only from his own faction. He selected some from every ministerial family and clientele, so that all these groups were associated with the workings of the diplomatic system. A final and untypical group of emissaries can be identified, who had been chosen because of the unusual characteristics of the countries to which they were to be sent. Most rulers were kings or princes, and the ambassador needed to be at least the social equal of the ministers and aristocratic advisers with whom he would have to negotiate. He had to have a personal social aura, in addition to that bestowed upon him as representative of his king. Such considerations did not obtain in those three extraordinary states – the Dutch Republic, the Swiss confederation and the Serene Republic of Venice. The rulers of these countries came from a different social background, and the envoys sent to them by Louis XIV were usually from a *noblesse de robe* family, although some of them had recently been elevated to the *épée*. Indeed the appropriate section of the *Etat de la France* for 1676 specifically makes this distinction: 'les ambassadeurs de Rome, de l'Empire, d'Espagne et d'Angleterre sont toujours pris d'entre les grands seigneurs de la cour; & ceux que l'on envoie à Venise, en Hollande et en Suisse sont d'ordinaire des gens de robe'. It continues by saying that either *robe* or *épée* nobles can be chosen for Savoy and for Constantinople, although in the latter case it is essential to raise the *robin* to the *épée*.

If some great nobles, and many more noble families, were involved in international diplomacy, the army and the internal administration of the kingdom, either concurrently or consecutively, and if some ministers held both domestic and foreign portfolios, such as finance and the navy, or war and the postal system, as well as having responsibility for a quarter of the French provinces, the central bureaux associated with each office remained discrete. There are two reasons why, during the reign of Louis XIV, the professionalism of the bureaucracy became so much more pronounced in the departments of war and foreign affairs than in the internal areas of administration. First, these kingly aspects of government were higher on the list of royal priorities, and secondly, the crown had a greater degree of control over them than over finance, justice, commerce and industry. In domestic matters, much of the routine work was carried out by local officials, many of them socially prestigious and self-conscious, who would not be prepared to accept instructions from inferior clerks in Paris or at Versailles. Also the office-holders, judges, tax-farmers, bishops and governors used their own agents for daily administrative tasks, so that there were fewer officials under the direct control of the ministerial departments of finance and justice than there were in the diplomatic and military hierarchies.

There were, of course, many areas of ministerial responsibility which overlapped and conflicted. It was therefore not just reasons of family prestige which prompted both Colbert and Louvois each to propose a foreign minister from his own clientele in 1679. Similarly, the war minister not only found it convenient to be in charge of the postal system, but was eager to take responsibility for manufactures, which included armaments, on the death of Colbert in 1683. There were numerous disputes between the secretaries for the army and the navy, each of whom might also be at odds with his colleague in foreign affairs. Louvois controlled the posts, but it was for Colbert to decide whether or not to improve the roads on which the couriers travelled. The war minister and postal superintendent wanted better access to and along the frontiers, but not always in the same areas as Colbert, who had two different and conflicting priorities. As finance minister he wished for improved routes between the capital and the provincial administrative centres, but as the secretary for commerce he knew that the greatest need was for roads and canals which would speed the transfer of goods from one area to another, and to the seaports, without necessarily passing near Paris. The one certainty was that the crown did not have sufficient funds to embark upon all these schemes at once. To finance ministers, who were always prudent housekeepers, wars seemed to consume enormous resources, although Louvois was personally very hostile to waste. Nevertheless, the expenses which seemed to him to be justified often found little favour with the *contrôleur-général des finances*, and he took his revenge by opposing expenditure on the navy, which was not only in Colbertian hands but was intimately linked with the colonial and international commercial policies of Colbert himself. (It is for this reason that the marine will be considered below, in conjunction with those policies.)

The one aspect of government which most frequently affected both the internal and the external branches of the royal administration was the church, because most religious problems had an international dimension, whether it was the support of rulers like William III for the Huguenots, or the interference of Rome in the debates about gallicanism, Jansenism, Jesuits and *richéristes*. These issues, which often caused dangerous divisions within the realm, were all the more alarming when they had consequences for French foreign policy.

THE CHURCH

If Louis XIV regarded the condition of the army and the defence of the realm as his highest priorities, the moral health of his kingdom and the state of the church were scarcely less important to him. In his *mémoires* for 1661, the king included three religious issues in his list of the disorders which were confronting the government on the death of Mazarin. These were the problem of the cardinal de Retz, the dissident *curés* who had challenged royal authority during the 1650s, and the Jansenists. All of these matters had given the papacy an opportunity for intervening in the internal affairs of France, and had provoked disputes between the crown and some of its secular officials. In contrast, the Huguenots were regarded as posing no immediate threat, and Louis contented himself with a long-term plan for their conversion, adding that meanwhile their liberties should be respected.[10] It was essential that heresy should ultimately be removed from the dominions of a ruler who was styled as 'Most Christian King', and he also noted the disruptive effects of this sect in the France of his predecessors and in other lands. Yet they had recently behaved as loyal subjects, and they did not alarm him to the degree that Retz, the *curés* and the Jansenists undoubtedly did.

The issue of Retz was speedily resolved. Alexander VII, like other European rulers and like many Frenchmen, waited to see what would be the effect of the death of Mazarin on the policies of France. In 1661 Louis XIV was exhibiting none of the aggression towards the Holy See which would erupt in the following year over the question of diplomatic privileges in Rome. The pope therefore showed himself

[10]See Mettam, 'Louis XIV and the persecution of the Huguenots'.

more willing than before to consider the French proposal that Retz be put on trial. The cardinal meanwhile made his final attempt to restore his reputation with his sovereign. He had always hoped to succeed Mazarin as *premier ministre*, but Louis both announced his intention to make no such appointment and rebuffed all the overtures made by intermediaries on behalf of the exiled prelate. To preserve his dignity, Retz duly resigned his see in February 1662, and the king was thus able to allow those who had supported him to return to Paris. The cardinal not only gave no further trouble, but his help was actually sought by the French crown in 1666 and he agreed to act as a mediator in a dispute between Rome and the Sorbonne.

The religious problems of the 1650s were in one respect similar to those created by the secular *frondeurs*, and therefore required the same tactics on the part of the government. This common factor was that, in the church as in the civil administration, a number of very different groups had come together and made a united onslaught on the policies of Mazarin. With the pressures of war now removed, it was vital for the crown to separate these often improbable allies, perhaps being able to sow tension among them as well. At times the supporters of Retz had included the pope, the Sorbonne, some canons and many lesser clergy in the city of Paris, a number of bishops and the judges of the *parlement*. A complicating consideration was that some of them, clerical and lay, also seemed to be Jansenists.

A necessary first step for the crown was to regain the support of the *parlementaires* for its religious policies. Their dislike of Rome, of Jansenism and any other form of heterodoxy, of the judicial powers of the church in general and the Sorbonne in particular, of the Jesuits and of the social pre-eminence accorded to nuncios and cardinals, suggested that they would be natural partners in many of the plans which Louis and his advisers were formulating. The *parlement*, as the principal law court in the realm and as the self-proclaimed champion of the *lois fondamentales* – a claim which it had often used against the government in the past – could give an air of both legality and national endorsement to royal decisions which violated the legitimate rights of the Holy See. Accordingly, Louis hurriedly reassured the judges on the one issue which had led them to involve themselves in the controversy about the cardinal de Retz – their right to hear *appels comme d'abus*. With this treasured power confirmed, the *parlement* began to act upon its interpretation of the term 'gallicanism', while the king set out to give greater reality to his rather different definition of that vague concept. At the same moment that Louis was asserting the rights of his diplomats in the city of Rome, the judges launched a vigorous and ultimately successful campaign against the Sorbonne for refusing to condemn some theses which contained unacceptably ultramontane views. The king let it be known to the court that he welcomed its actions, but he did not openly praise it because he still wanted papal support in his attempt to combat Jansenism. Most of the Paris judges had now reverted to their hatred of this sect, which they had put aside only while the dispute about *appels comme d'abus* had been raging. The *parlement* had further cause for rejoicing when Alexander VII agreed to act as Louis had requested, and the king therefore brought the Bull, together with his own subsequent declaration against those bishops who had refused to condemn the five propositions of Jansen, to the court for registration. The implication was unmistakable. Papal decrees required the endorsement of the *parlement*, and anyone who then disregarded their provisions, even if he were a bishop, was subject to the jurisdiction of that court.

The pope now took the initiative. He was not prepared to be humiliated by French diplomats in Rome, and then wooed by Louis XIV as if nothing had happened. He was prepared to condemn Jansenism, but he was no Bourbon puppet. Accordingly he intervened to deny the ability of the Sorbonne to approve or condemn articles of faith, because such decisions lay entirely within the papal prerogative. This action prompted the *assemblée du clergé* to display its own brand of gallicanism, first refuting the claim of the *parlement* to have cognizance of such matters and then complaining that Rome had also interfered to an unacceptable degree in the affairs of the French church. As the various interested parties were divided on many aspects of this dispute and united on very few, and as the king was preoccupied with the War of Devolution and the delicate partition negotiations with the emperor, the new pope, Clement IX, found that the French crown was prepared to compromise. The consequent Peace of the Church in 1668 wholly satisfied no one, but it established a religious truce and gave the Jansenists a reprieve for the moment at least. Louis XIV ignored their sect for most of the warlike 1670s, although he increased his policy of hostility to Rome, extending his claim to the *régale*[41] and ultimately issuing the fiercely gallican Four Articles of 1682. Such measures received the wholehearted support of the *parlement*, which eagerly registered the religious decrees that the king brought before them. Not

[41]The *régale*, the right of the French king to keep the revenues of vacant sees and to appoint secular clergy during an episcopal vacancy, had been conceded to François Ier by the pope in the Concordat of Bologna of 1516. It applied only to certain areas of France. Louis now not only tried to extend it to the whole kingdom, but claimed the right to appoint regulars as well as seculars. No matter how hard royal publicists ransacked the history of France in order to justify these steps – for Louis always liked to be seen to be acting legally – no justification could be found.

all the bishops were so supportive, but enough could be mustered to endow this legislation with the semblance of ecclesiastical approval. Yet the confidence of the king and his judges proved to be unfounded, and in the later 1680s the papacy began to take its very effective revenge on the arrogance of the French king.

The abandonment by Retz of his claims to the see of Paris did not solve the problem of the *curés* and their demands for the reform of the church, a rigorist cry which was supported by many Jansenists, by the more devout among the orthodox Catholics and by the popes as well. Nevertheless, their position seemed weaker in the first decade of the personal rule. The *parlement* had made peace with the king and saw no advantage in defending the *curés* or their Jansenist friends, while the abdication of Retz meant that their cause no longer had a political edge which the crown could not ignore. Nor, in the 1660s, was the kingdom disrupted by civil wars or local revolts on which they could capitalize. They therefore bided their time, until the mounting religious disorder of the 1680s gave them some further allies, although during these quiet years the number of *richériste* priests steadily grew and the movement spread through all the provinces of France.

If Louis resented the influence of Rome within his dominions, he was equally hostile to the regular orders of monks and friars, who seemed to be resident agents of the papacy inside his kingdom. Colbert disliked them with equal fervour, but for a different reason. To him they were an idle class, contributing nothing to the economy and hoarding wealth which could have been used to more constructive purpose. This was not wholly fair, as the monasteries did perform useful tasks in their locality, and it has already been noted that they cared for wounded and retired soldiers. They were certainly not interested in some of his new commercial and colonial enterprises, but neither were many other wealthy provincial Frenchmen. The only religious order for which the king did have some feelings of affection was the Society of Jesus, which was subtle enough to endorse his policies and therefore maintain its influence at the very centre of court life. Its moral and political flexibility was strongly disliked by both the rigorist Jansenists and the *richériste* lower clergy, who blamed the Jesuit confessors of the king for many of the religious misjudgements of the reign. The molinism of these priests seemed to have no limits, as was demonstrated when a Jansenist appeal to Rome evoked a sympathetic response from the pope, and the Jesuits accordingly stood firmly behind Louis XIV, despite the fact that the members of the Society took a special vow of direct obedience to the supreme pontiff.

The various approaches to religious issues – royalist, *parlementaire*, parochial, episcopal, Jesuit, Jansenist, ultramontane, gallican, rigorist, molinist and Huguenot – were not all mutually exclusive and therefore led to a changing pattern of alliances, as a particular ecclesiastical or theological issue prompted some groups to make common cause against others. The resulting tensions caused divisions, not only in Paris and the provinces, but at the royal court itself. Many leading courtiers held strong religious views, and the bishops too were drawn from the great aristocratic families which dominated the social world at the centre. The ministers were also much exercised about such matters of faith, even if their chief concern was often with the secular implications of these disputes. All these strains increased in the years after the Dutch War, when the king decided to pursue more aggressive policies towards Rome, the Protestants and the Jansenists. One prime consequence of this new royal fervour was that it raised grave doubts in the minds of hitherto loyal bishops, and prompted some of them to voice open criticism of their sovereign.[42]

The church played an important part in the civil administration of the kingdom, as well as guarding the moral and spiritual values of the population. Indeed some bishops were renowned more for their effective role in secular matters than for their advocacy of piety and reform. The ecclesiastical hierarchy stretched across France, from the court to the tiniest village, a direct chain of command which had no parallel in the secular institutional structure. Elected municipalities and venal office-holders had a considerable degree of independence and many privileges, but the parish clergy, in theory at least, were expected to obey their bishop who in turn should carry out the wishes of the king. It was he who had nominated these prelates to such high office, and he had further preferment in his gift. The role played by the bishop in the administrative affairs of his diocese made it highly desirable that he should be the social equal or superior of the leading laymen with whom he would come into contact, and the desire of Louis XIV for a strictly stratified society also meant that most

[12]See, for example: François de Pons de Salignac de La Motte Fenelon, 'Plans de gouvernement concertés avec le duc de Chevreuse pour être proposés au duc de Bourgogne', article IV, and 'Lettre à Louis XIV: remontrances à ce prince sur divers points de son administration', in *Ecrits et lettres politiques*, ed. Charles Urbain (Paris, 1920, reprinted Geneva, 1981) pp. 143–57, esp. pp. 153–7 – perhaps the sternest of all the criticism; but even the loyal Bossuet voiced his reservations – *Politique tirée des propres paroles de l'Ecriture sainte* (2 vols, Paris, 1709), seconde partie, livre VII, article III, propositions X and XI; Le Camus, the reforming bishop of Grenoble, began to defy the king on the harassment of the Protestants – see A. J. Krailsheimer (ed.), *The letters of Armand-Jean de Rancé, abbot and reformer of La Trappe* (2 vols, Kalamazoo, Michigan, 1984), vol. II, nos 870304, 900710, the latter recording the ultimate reconciliation of Le Camus with Louis XIV in 1690 after four years of strained relations over the Huguenot issue.

members of the episcopate were drawn from the upper social echelons. A bishopric was an important counter in the elaborate game of patronage which absorbed the attentions of the king and his greater subjects. In any one province there were often a few competing families within the high nobility who could each provide a socially and religiously suitable candidate for a vacant see, and the king seldom took the risk of choosing someone from outside such circles lest he offend these houses and prompt them to join forces against their unwelcome new diocesan. It was socially impossible for him to ask great noblemen of the cloth to carry out many mundane administrative tasks in their dioceses and parishes, but there were nevertheless some very important ways in which the bishops and lower clergy could help the crown to govern the kingdom. ⚊

At parish level, the power of the church could be exercised through the pulpit, the confessional and the less tangible influence of the priest over his flock.[43] Episcopal instructions and manuals listed the wrongdoings which the lesser clergy were to regard as most abhorrent, and in their compilation the hand of the royal government can be clearly identified. Indeed, many of their provisions bear a striking resemblance to those contained in the ministerial directives to the *intendants*. Thus, juxtaposed with prescriptions on purely moral questions of sexual behaviour were condemnations of usury, extortion, the use of false weights and measures, the clipping of coins, failure to pay taxes and other matters close to the heart of the finance ministers. These social crimes could be condemned by the church solely on the grounds that they offended against the laws of God, and therefore it was not obvious to the simple believer that his priest was acting as a government agent, although there are plenty of ministerial letters which reveal where the initiative for such measures originated. During the personal rule of Louis XIV, the bishops were entrusted with further tasks, such as identifying enfringements of the edicts against duelling and reporting them to the crown. Ecclesiastical power was a major weapon in the royal struggle to preserve law and order, and to impose docile acceptance of governmental directives on the population. Not surprisingly, this policy of social control was more impressive in

---

[13]See Robin Briggs. *Early modern France, 1560–1715* (Oxford, 1977), pp. 166–205, on the role of the church in society, although he does not give due weight to the secular tasks which were entrusted by the crown to bishops, and through them to priests – for example, on issues of law and order, Jean Lemoine, *La révolte dite du papier timbré ou des bonnets rouges en Bretagne en 1675, étude et documents* (Paris/Rennes, 1898), pp. 199–200; also Depping, vol. I, pp. 851, 859–61. They were also asked to help the crown in its economic policies – Clément, vol. II (ii), pp. 641, 660, 680; vol. VI, p. 58; Depping, vol. III, pp. 365–6, 369, 755, 757–9, 865; see also note 48 below.

theory than in practice, and the substantial bourgeois frequently took the clerical authorities to court when they thought that the moral imperatives of the bishops and *curés* were in conflict with the more worldly criteria of the market-place and the quest for wealth.

In the second half of the seventeenth century, the parish clergy became steadily less willing to implement these royally inspired instructions which were issued by their bishop, and before that they had regarded many episcopal commands with distaste. Their objections stemmed from a mixture of conviction and realism. The priest, often a local and relatively humble man, sympathized with his parishioners in their hostility to the fiscal demands of the distant Paris government, and felt compassion for them in their regular spells of poverty as harvests failed or disease overtook them. Even if he were rather more cynical about his mission, he would still have deemed it prudent to retain the support of his flock, as they paid a substantial proportion of the funds on which he lived. As the century progressed, the parish priests showed increasing concern about the hardships inflicted on the weaker members of their community. They denounced the excessive burdens imposed on the poor by the nobility, such as labour services and the despoiling of peasant land by hunting over it, and they refused to grant absolution to the wealthy sinner who had exploited the needy, until he had made full restitution for his misdeeds – another cause of conflict between the clergy and the wealthy bourgeoisie. Many aristocratic bishops were not pleased to learn of such socially impertinent actions by their subordinates. Yet a significant group was beginning to emerge from within the episcopate, which was calling for higher standards of morality in parish and presbytery, and it might be thought that this would have appealed to the growing *richérisme* of the lesser clergy. That it did not, emphasizes the differences between these two kinds of rigorism. The bishops were insisting on the purification of clerical life and the imposition of proper sexual and moral behaviour on the laity, neither of which was particularly attractive to the humble priest. Excessive puritanism on his part would be personally inconvenient, and would undoubtedly empty his church. His *richérisme* was a call for greater fairness at the upper echelons of the ecclesiastical hierarchy, with a more equitable distribution of wealth and a larger role for the local area in religious decisions which affected it. Bishops seemed too rich, too arbitrary and too remote. These demands, which had led the lesser clergy of Paris to seize the opportunity offered by the dispute of Retz with the crown, would prompt the *curés* of many parts of France to support the rigorism of the Jansenists in the 1680s and 1690s, and would lead them into an alliance with the *parlement* in the last years of the reign, when that illustrious law court became not only the defender of the Jansenists but the spearhead of the attack on episcopal power.[44]

Such an outcome could not have been foreseen in 1679, but it was from that year, when the end of the Dutch War gave Louis XIV some respite in which to attend to pressing internal problems, that the royal policies towards the Huguenots, the Jansenists and the Holy See became more aggressive, and at this time were eagerly supported by the *parlement* of Paris. The progress of this new religious fervour dramatically demonstrated the differing priorities and the tensions within French society, both ecclesiastical and secular. Among the bishops, the persecution of the Protestants called forth a variety of reactions. Harlay, the archbishop of Paris, was among the most fervent attackers of these heretics, but others were less strident. Even some of those who hoped to see a purely Catholic France were unhappy about conversion by force. Violent methods merely encouraged Huguenots to dissimulate, which meant that their souls were not truly saved. Another group went further, and openly said that it was essential to reform the Catholic church before expecting dissenters to embrace it.[45] Many bishops shared the concern of lay Frenchmen that the departure of both native and foreign Protestants would be a grievous blow to the economy of France, especially as their role in local society had often been highly constructive and seldom disruptive. Thus, once it became clear that, despite the exodus of many Huguenots, there were still far more remaining in France, whether masquerading as converts or overtly professing their old beliefs, a number of bishops and secular officials became reluctant to cause more disturbances by persecuting them further. In some dioceses they were required to make only the most superficial profession of orthodoxy, and no enquiries were made into their sincerity. Such bishops were therefore sympathetic to the letters from Louvois, in which he asked them to ensure that priests did not impose rigorous tests on Protestant soldiers who were prepared to go through the motions of conversion. The ordinary *curés* were often more fervent in their Catholicism than their more pragmatic ecclesiastical overlords. The military and secular authorities frequently shared episcopal reluctance to pursue both Huguenots and suspect *convertis* in provinces where they were not causing trouble, although in their letters to the ministers they continually reiterated their willingness to do so and

[11]See B. Robert Kreiser, *Miracles, convulsions, and ecclesiastical politics in early eighteenth-century Paris* (Princeton, 1978).
[15]See, for example, Fénelon to Noailles, 28 February 1697, in Millot, *Mémoires*, vol. I, pp. 351–5; and Fénelon, *Ecrits et lettres politiques*, pp. 105–16, 153–7.

found a series of logistical excuses to account for their lack of success.[46]

The whole history of this process of repression demonstrates the impossibility of generalizing about the internal administration of France during the personal rule of Louis XIV. Long before the sterner policy of 1679–85, there had been sustained attempts to persuade Huguenots to abjure, usually by fiscal incentives or direct bribery. If this was the approach advocated by the king in his *mémoires* for 1661, its effects were far from uniform. As with the plans to convert Protestant soldiers in the army, so in civil society there were many members of the RPR who were prepared to abjure, with varying degrees of sincerity, in order to obtain these financial rewards. Here too there were some Catholics who now pretended to be Huguenots and then professed their willingness to join the 'true faith' – and they also qualified for the same rewards, unless their trickery could be unambiguously proved. To the ordinary Catholic citizen, both of these groups were anathema. He had always been a loyal member of the official French church, and yet it was the heretics and dissimulators who were now receiving remission of taxes as a reward for perjuring themselves about their beliefs. In some towns, considerable tension and even outright disorder resulted, and there is no doubt that it was the reports of such unrest which greatly influenced the royal government in its decision to employ stronger methods against the remaining Huguenots. Yet there were towns where both faiths lived happily together, whether one was in a minority or both were evenly balanced. Further differences arose according to the vigour or gentleness of *intendants*, bishops and civil authorities in prosecuting the conversion policy, and that poses another difficult problem for the historian because some royal agents in the localities clearly exaggerated the number of converts in an attempt to win favour with the king.[47]

The increased hostility of Louis XIV in the 1680s towards Rome and towards the Jansenists also provoked a variety of reactions among lay and clerical Frenchmen. Innocent XI was a match for the French king, even without the support he received from discontented elements in France itself. Already enraged by the gallican policies of the crown and the *parlement* of Paris, he was not placated by the campaign against the Huguenots, regarding it as yet more evidence that Louis considered himself to be the master of the church. The arrogant assertion of French diplomatic franchises in Rome, the gallican articles of 1682, the unwarranted extension of the *régale* and the annexation of

[16]See, for example, Millot, *Mémoires*, vol. I, 14–18, 23, 26–7, 41–9, 59–62, 82–7.

[17]See Mettam, 'Louis XIV and the persecution of the Huguenots'; also Clément, vol. VI, pp. 131–2, 431–3, 438, 442–3; vol. VII, p. 274; Depping, vol. IV, pp. 319–21, 349–50, 385–8.

the papal domains at Avignon were all designed to intimidate the pope, but they only stiffened his resolve. Thus he seized the opportunity of the disputed election to the archbishopric of Cologne to ensure that the French candidate was unsuccessful in obtaining this strategically important Rhineland see, with its right to provide one of the Electors to the Holy Roman Empire, and, having publicly excommunicated the French ambassador in Rome, went on to anathematize the king himself, threatening to make public this decision which would have struck at the very foundation of the divine-right monarchy in France. Moreover, Innocent championed the cause of the Jansenists, whom Louis was trying to eradicate, because the pope sincerely shared their concern for a rigorist reform of the church.

The appeal of the Jansenists to Rome revived the demands of the *curés* for a moral purge of the ecclesiastical hierarchy, so that once again there was an alliance of *richériste* parish priests and Jansenists, as in the days of Retz. A very few bishops openly supported Jansenism, but a growing number in the 1680s were calling for the moral renewal of the church and sympathized with the appeal for papal intervention. Moreover many other bishops, whether out of conviction or pragmatism, were concerned at the encroachment of the monarchy, with enthusiastic *parlementaire* support, on the authority of Rome and indeed on that of the church within the kingdom. The episcopate knew it was under attack from the lower clergy and that the secular judiciary would never cease to challenge its jurisdictional powers, but there was the further problem for the bishops that they owed allegiance to both pope and king, and there were considerable advantages to be obtained from being on good terms with both. Louis knew that it could be very dangerous to alienate such powerful prelates, because not only would he forfeit the help they gave him towards maintaining law and order, but they might decide to use their extensive influence in their diocese, their powers of patronage and their important family connections to thwart his policies. In the *pays d'états*, the bishops could greatly aid or obstruct royal business in the provincial Estates, and in some provinces a particular archbishop was *ex officio* president of either the clerical estate or of all three.[48] Nor could the *assemblée générale du clergé*

---

[18]For examples of the many tasks undertaken by archbishops and bishops as both presidents and leading members of provincial Estates, see Depping, vol. I, pp. 58–61, 63–7, 95–8, 182–7, 289–93, 295–6, 308–9, 539–40, 542–3, 546–50; and by Villeroy as acting-governor of Lyon and by the archbishop of Aix in Provence, both of whom regularly took the initiative in secular administration without waiting for instructions from the crown, see Mettam, *The role of the higher aristocracy*, pp. 209–49, 363–81; they also sometimes asked the king and his ministers to help their diocese, for example Depping, vol. I, pp. 857–9, or to support them against other local power groups, for example ibid, p. 844; they also reported the problems of their province to the crown, for example ibid, pp. 353, 387–8.

be ignored, because it was not only an influential voice when it favoured royal policy, but its financial contributions had saved the monarchy from insolvency on many occasions in the past.

Contrary to the claims of many historians, the gallican articles of 1682 were not submitted to, and approved by, a regular meeting of this clerical assembly. The king and his ministers knew that such a body was likely to voice as much criticism as support. Accordingly, he summoned a special assembly of those clergy who were at court, some because they had posts in the royal household and others because they were there in search of favours. Both groups would therefore be likely to approve the proposals which Louis intended to place before them. Yet he deemed it wise not to invite the attendance of the archbishop of Lyon, knowing that this great prelate, who was a wise and effective governor in the Lyonnais and a close collaborator of Colbert, would nevertheless find himself unable to endorse a course of action which was so insulting to the Holy See. The special meeting opened in November 1681, and within four months it had confirmed the extension of the royal right to collect the *régale* and passed the four articles. Those pronouncements, although ambiguous in their detailed provisions, clearly asserted that kings were subject to no ecclesiastical power in temporal matters and that, even in matters of faith, the church had to approve the decisions of the supreme pontiff. Rome reacted swiftly, denying further preferment to anyone who had taken part in the proceedings. Louis in return decided that future promotions must be concentrated upon those very participants.

In the years of deadlock which followed, Louis could not win the contest because of the resilience shown by Innocent XI. The pope refused to accept gallican candidates for bishoprics, and many sees therefore remained vacant. The fact that their revenues went to the king, under his claim to the *régale*, did not weaken the resolve of the papacy, and soon there was the very real problem that the functions of the episcopate could not be carried out in many areas of France. Priests could not be ordained, and some chapters were divided on how to proceed in the absence of a superior. In certain dioceses, conflicting appointments of ecclesiastical officials were made by the crown and by the local clergy, a situation reminiscent of the days when there were rival vicars-general in Paris during the Retzian controversy of the 1650s. No sooner had the pope made it known that he refused to be intimidated by the seizure of Avignon, and instead took an offensive stance over the Cologne election and the secret excommunication of the king, than the Nine Years War suddenly plunged Europe into chaos, and Louis knew that he would have to give in to Rome. Yet this would surely alienate the *parlement*, which had been so co-operative for

254 *The Personal Rule of Louis XIV*

nearly three decades, as well as the other interested groups in the realm who favoured various kinds of gallicanism. Yet at least it could make the Jansenist problem easier to solve, because a friendlier pope might be less eager to protect them. By the end of 1693, after the two-year pontificate of Alexander VIII, from 1689 to 1691, and a series of negotiations with his successor, Innocent XII, Louis had made his peace with the Holy See. The terms of his capitulation were sometimes vague, but he did not renegue on most of them during the remaining years of his reign. Avignon was restored, diplomatic franchises in Rome were waived, the gallican articles of 1682 were suspended, the innovations in the *régale* were countermanded, and every prelate who had participated in the 1682 assembly had to sign a most apologetic retraction of any offensive views which had been promulgated by its members.

The last twenty years of the personal rule were therefore decades of *rapprochement* for the French king and the popes, and that was to cause increasing resentment within the kingdom. The two rulers worked together in repressing Quietism, a new mystical movement of the kind which always alarmed the institutional church and the secular state. More importantly, they combined in a fierce assault on Jansenism which, they hoped, would bring its activities to a permanent end. In the 1670s and 1680s, the appeals by Jansenists to Innocent XI, demanding a moral revival in the church and condemning the royal extension of the *régale*, had lost them the support of many anti-Roman elements in France, although some *curés* had approved their campaign for spiritual rigorism and were therefore thought by the crown to be Jansenists themselves. Louis continued to suspect the sect of seditious designs which it did not in fact harbour, and the Jesuits in his entourage seized every opportunity to encourage his suspicions of these men who were their most hated enemies. As increasingly damning evidence against the Jansenists was unearthed, Rome and Versailles worked together on their plans, although at the same time Louis was still trying to give no offence to the *parlement* and to the more gallican of the French clergy. It was that attempt at compromise which undermined the effectiveness of the Bull *Vineam domini* of 1705, or such at least was the opinion of the pope. He had issued this revocation of the 1668 Peace of Clement IX, and was furious that Louis asked both the *parlement* and the *assemblée du clergé* to agree to its adoption in France. Those bodies, pleased to find that the king thought their consent to be necessary before a papal pronouncement could be implemented in the kingdom, were not in fact to blame for the difficulty of enforcing its provisions. The Jansenists had more friends than Louis or the pope had realized.

The king therefore resolved to take more drastic action against the sect, but found that Rome was initially reluctant to support him, fearing that its decisions would again be disregarded. Then, seeing the determination of the French monarch, the pope decided to take a more aggressive stance, imposing stern conditions for his further co-operation. He would issue another Bull, but only if it were not to be subject to ratification by secular and ecclesiastical bodies within France. Louis, increasingly obsessed by the Jansenist threat, agreed to the papal terms and assumed that he would be fully consulted on the drafting of the Bull. Some consultations did take place, but the final text of *Unigenitus* took Versailles by surprise when it was published, without any advance notification of its contents, in the autumn of 1713. In the years between the two Bulls, the king had continued to harass the Jansenists, and in 1709 he had finally expelled the aging nuns from Port-Royal-des-Champs, to which they had been forced to retreat after the closure of the Parisian Port-Royal earlier in the personal rule. The closing of the Paris house had revealed that the sect, far from being absorbed with inward spirituality, had won popularity in the capital for its charitable works. The expulsion of 1709, and the destruction of the buildings and cemetery two years later, aroused considerable anger among the public and prompted senior churchmen, many with no love for the Jansenists, to denounce this unwarranted brutality. It was in this atmosphere that the Bull condemning them was thrust upon the French kingdom.

Although Louis could clearly not reject the Bull, he wished that some of its clauses had been worded more tactfully. Accordingly, he employed the same method that he had used in 1682, and summoned a special assembly of prelates who were currently at court. Even at that earlier gathering, when they had been asked to consider gallican measures which enhanced their power, they had used the opportunity to exact some other concessions from the king. Now they were being required to endorse a document which, because it contained papal pronouncements on the interpretation of doctrine, implied the anti-gallican idea that the pope was the sole authority on matters of faith. This specially chosen assembly therefore withheld its consent and began to examine the propositions in detail. After they had added a number of qualifications, forty bishops accepted the Bull in January 1714. Yet nine of them, led by the cardinal de Noailles, refused to do so, attacking it on gallican and doctrinal grounds. Although Louis sent the bishops back to their dioceses and forbade them to communicate directly with Rome, it was clear that the division of opinion within the assembly seriously undermined the Bull, and made it difficult for the king to recommend its acceptance by every bishop and priest throughout the kingdom. The Sorbonne also debated *Unigenitus*, uttering some strong sentiments in the process, but it finally succumbed to royal pressure and agreed to it in March 1714.

The *parlement* of Paris, normally no friend of the episcopate, was delighted by the gallican stance of the bishops, and by the fact that the assembly was divided. The judges vigorously debated the Bull, protesting strongly against some of the papal claims which were stated or implied within it, and finally registered it with the rider that it should be accepted in so far as it did not violate the gallican liberties of France and its church. Another group which saw an opportunity for self-assertion by attacking the Bull was the *richériste* lower clergy. They had been increasingly irritated by the way in which Louis had championed episcopal authority in recent years, and had allowed the wealthy bishops to purchase personal exemption from the *capitation* tax of 1695. The *curés* therefore now declared that, if the bishops were claiming a right to adjudicate on matters of faith, as equals of the pope, then every priest should have that same equality extended to him. Louis did not live long enough to see the consequences of *Unigenitus*, but a strange alliance of *richéristes*, gallicans, Jansenists and *parlementaires* would make common cause against it on many occasions during the reign of his successor, Louis XV.

At the end of his life, Louis XIV could see few gains and many losses as a result of his religious policies. The Huguenots were still present in his realm, and had recently played a dangerous part in the revolt of the Camisards, which had shaken parts of southern France in the years 1702–5. Other members of that faith continued to conspire against him from the safety of foreign lands. His episcopate was divided, and there was a widening rift between the lower and higher clergy. The Jansenists had resisted him, and were apparently gaining supporters daily. The *parlement*, whose enthusiasm for his earlier gallican policies had proved to be a basis for even wider co-operation, was disaffected once again. Even some of the carefully selected bishops, on whom he had placed so much reliance, had now deserted him, and no one was more important in that regard than the archbishop of Paris, the cardinal de Noailles. Coming from a trusted family of able provincial governors, generals and advisers, he had seemed an ideal successor to Harlay in the Parisian see which had often been so troublesome in the past. Yet the *rapprochement* of Louis and the pope and its climax in *Unigenitus* not only forced him to take a stand, but it left the ministers of Louis XV with the same situation which had confronted Mazarin in the 1650s – a powerful archbishop, popular in the capital, who was a hero to the parish clergy and to many Jansenists.

5

Domestic Administration, 1661–1715

If the royal ministers of the 1660s did not wish to extend the direct authority of the crown into areas of local administration which were traditionally the responsibility of provincial and municipal institutions, they were nevertheless eager to ensure that those bodies carried out their tasks efficiently and honestly. It was not that the central government cared about the welfare of the ordinary Frenchman, for such matters were the responsibility of the communities themselves. Its concern stemmed from the fact that, if local officials were profligate, corrupt or even merely inept, much money would be squandered and the royal taxes would be more difficult to collect. Only in the implementation of some new economic policies did Colbert require the active co-operation of provincial and urban institutions. For the most part he simply demanded that they carry out their traditional administrative functions with the minimum of expenditure. Apart from the misappropriation of funds by unscrupulous individuals, which it was the duty of the criminal courts to punish, the principal causes of extravagance were the lengthy litigation initiated by local bodies whose jurisdictions overlapped and the lavish spending by rival elites on architecture and ceremony as

Note: throughout this chapter, an attempt has been made to avoid overlap with Roger Mettam, *Government and society in Louis XIV's France* (London, 1977). As that book was concerned with the extent to which royal policies were executed in the provinces, and as the present text concentrates on the mechanisms of power, it has been possible to maintain a considerable difference of approach and content in the two works. It should also be noted that, when in this chapter an aspect of the mechanism has been discussed and where it did not subsequently change significantly, it has not been thought necessary to give examples of it throughout the reign. Therefore some topics are considered only in the context of the early personal rule, while others are taken as far as 1715.

expressions of their status.[1] Thus, although the ministers did not want to assume responsibility for the details of everyday administration, they did wish to ensure that the criminal judges would enforce the law, no matter how influential in local society the offender might be, that jurisdictions be more clearly delineated, and that needless waste be prevented. In all these matters they were bound to trespass upon the rights, prejudices and social pride of some prestigious local groups. All that they could hope for was, in each individual dispute, to win the temporary support of those whose claims they had upheld. Moreover it was important that the crown should not consistently favour one institution in a whole series of disputes, lest local society polarize into supporters and opponents of the royal government. The king had to seem impartial, so that everyone might expect true justice at his hands. In fact the local elites were often reluctant to submit their claims to his arbitration, for fear that the decision would go against them, but a wide variety of small groups and individuals did appeal to him directly when they could not obtain redress from a powerful individual or institution in their own area. Such demands could easily embarrass the royal ministers, as they did not always have the effective power to right these wrongs.

JUSTICE

The problem of overlapping jurisdictions was doubly distasteful to Colbert. Not only did they cause costly lawsuits and delay the daily routine of administration, but they offended against his love of order and system. Seigneurial, ecclesiastical, municipal and royal tribunals disputed among themselves about their right to hear cases; litigants chose the court which was most likely to agree with them, so that one lawsuit might be taken by the respective parties involved in it to two different jurisdictions; higher courts might evoke cases from lower ones; appeals might be made by the litigants or by the judges to even higher courts or to the royal council; and every aspect of these procedures delayed the dispensing of justice and increased the costs of the cases. One consequence of this confusion was that many humbler men did not dare turn to the law for the resolution of their disputes with neighbours, and therefore an informal system of justice grew up. This involved an agreement by the two parties to submit their quarrel to a prestigious figure in their locality, on whose objectivity they were

[1] These aspects of rivalry among the social elites form the twin themes of Roger Mettam, *Images of power: social and political propaganda in Louis XIV's France*, (London, to be published in 1987/88).

agreed. He would hear the evidence, and then deliver his informal verdict. The petitioners would abide by this decision, each having the right to go to a formal law court if the other subsequently broke his promise. As that would involve both of them in considerable expense, it seems that these informal adjudications were frequently respected by both sides.[2]

Louis XIV had cited the condition of the judicial system as one of the worst disorders in his kingdom at his assumption of personal power. Such chaos and malpractice was particularly alarming to him, because it was only through the courts that he could hope to reform other abuses in the administration. Yet they themselves were in even greater need of purification and, as he acknowledged in his *mémoires*, there was no section of the bureaucracy which it would be more difficult to purge of chicanery and greed. Most offensive of all, he added, was that all the conflicting decisions made by the rival courts were issued in his name, because they were his courts and he was the fount of justice, and this confusion clearly diminished the dignity of the crown.[3] Fortunately for the king, the Paris *parlement* was equally eager to see a wholesale reform of justice, and so the royal ministers had its co-operation in this field as well as in their gallican religious policies. Yet the judges were not invited to join the council which would draw up the proposals for judicial reform. They had been allowed to staff the *chambre de justice* and the *grands jours*, sitting as individuals on specially created royal tribunals but nevertheless de facto representing the range of *parlementaire* opinion. The new royal *conseil de justice* was to contain none of them, and the 'absolutist' historians have therefore maintained that its reforms were a further attack on the views and powers of the sovereign courts. A more subtle scrutiny of events between the beginning of the personal rule in 1661 and the publication of the Civil Ordinance in 1667 will show that this is a gross and incorrect over-simplification.

The new council was not created until the autumn of 1665, by which time the *parlement* of Paris was able to judge the general attitude of the

[2]On conflicting rights and jurisdictions, see, for example: Pierre Clément (ed.), *Lettres, instructions et mémoires de Colbert* (8 vols, Paris, 1861–82), vol. II (i), pp. 118–19, 231; vol. II (ii), pp. 511–12; vol. VII, p. 298; G. B. Depping (ed.), *Correspondance administrative sous le règne de Louis XIV*, 'Collection des documents inédits sur l'histoire de France' (4 vols, Paris, 1850–5), vol. I, pp. 705–6, 717–19, 763–4, 788–9, 859–61, 878–80, 924–5; vol. II, pp. 145–6, 210–11, 217; vol. III, pp. 216–19, 241–2, 345–6, 839–40; sometimes informal tribunals were set up by local groups, like the *compagnies des oeuvres fortes* (courts of mighty works) in Paris and elsewhere, whose very existence Louis XIV felt obliged to condemn – see Clément, vol. VI, pp. 32–3.

[3]Louis XIV, *Mémoires*, in Mettam, *Government and society*, p. 2.

young monarch and his ministers towards its own role in the kingdom.[4] It was far from despondent about the way in which it had been treated. Not only had it been invited to aid the sovereign in his religious policies, and to take part in the attack on corrupt financiers and on the lawlessness of the Auvergne, but it had received a number of more tangible benefits from the crown as well. First, the king was respecting its jurisdiction by ending the practice of the *évocation* of cases to the royal council. Moreover, the resumption of more traditional fiscal policies, made possible by the signing of international peace, took away one of the major causes of past conflicts between the judges and the ministers. The king had issued stricter rules for the admission of candidates to the judiciary, but the *parlementaires* themselves were eager to keep up the standards of their court and it was useful to have royal support for the exclusion of an undesirable applicant. The ministers also showed that they were willing to waive these prescriptions, for a fee, when an otherwise well qualified man was being considered as a potential judge. It was also soon evident that the government had no intention of bargaining with the office-holders about the renewal of the *paulette*, but was prepared to accept the hereditary transmission of posts as a fact of life. Even the edict of 1665, which reduced the official value of offices and limited the maximum price, always many times greater, which could be paid for them in the market-place, was not the savage blow which some historians have claimed. The reduction in the first of these ipso facto lowered the amount which had to be paid for the *annuel*, the yearly payment under the terms of the *paulette*, because this was calculated on the basis of one-sixtieth of the offical value. The restraint on market prices did not affect the profits of individual office-holders because, even though the new limits were some 30% below current levels, the recent rapid rise in values ensured that the seller would still obtain much more money than he had originally paid. Also it was still possible to obtain a *pot de vin*, an undercover payment, from the purchaser as a means of by-passing the regulations. Yet it often suited the judges to accept the new level of prices, as the inflated official values of recent years had put many offices beyond the reach of many *noblesse de robe* families. As a result the hated tax-farmers, financiers and bourgeois had begun to infiltrate the court. The new rules of 1665 ensured that *robins* could re-

[1]On the views of the *parlement*, see Albert N. Hamscher, *The parlement of Paris after the Fronde, 1653–1673* (Pittsburgh, 1976), pp. 155–95; on the *conseil de justice*, see Clément, vol. VI, pp. viii–ix, 3–11, 369–79, 396–401; on new regulations about offices and the personnel of the courts, see F. A. Isambert (ed.), *Recueil général des anciennes lois françaises depuis l'an 420 jusqu'à la révolution de 1789* (29 vols, Paris, 1822–33), vol. XVIII, pp. 66–7, 325–7; vol. XIX, pp. 1–2.

enter the market for *parlementaire* posts, and many sellers of office were prepared to forgo the extra profits of the *pot de vin* in the knowledge that the social integrity of the judiciary was being preserved. After all, many of their relatives still sat in these elite tribunals, where social pre-eminence was a vital factor.

The stricter rules for entry into the sovereign courts were frequently useful to the judges in their internal power struggles within the judiciary itself. They could take a firm stand in support of them, when one family and clientage group appeared to be gaining too much influence, or they could apply for them to be waived when that would help to balance the patrimonial factions more satisfactorily. These factional rivalries also gave the crown an opportunity for intervention in the business of the courts, although it was acknowledged by both king and judges that the royal ministers were unable to exert direct influence over the sale of offices. That remained a matter for buyer and seller, subject always to the willingness of the judges to accept the new candidate. Yet royal patronage, in both social and financial forms, was still a useful weapon for the crown, especially as the prestige and wealth of the judges varied considerably. One such stratagem concerned the payment of salaries. Within weeks of assuming personal power, Louis XIV announced that promised salary increases, against which the judges had been prepared to advance loans to the crown, would now be reduced by one third. If this caused alarm at first, it was soon evident that the government was also adhering to a commitment that these sums would be paid promptly. As payments had often been many years in arrears, the office-holders quickly accepted that it was better to receive a lower sum regularly than to wait a long time for the full amount. Moreover, Colbert negotiated privately with some of the key magistrates and agreed to pay them the total salary they had expected, thereby hoping to win their support in resolving cases to the liking of the crown. Secondly the king was prepared to sell parts of the royal demesne lands to selected judges, often at very low prices. As the *robe* nobles were always trying to make themselves more like the old landed nobility, they welcomed this development, especially as Louis was frequently prepared to raise the status of these estates so that the owners acquired an aristocratic title. He also granted them seigneurial rights which both increased their revenues and enhanced their prestige. With his insistence on strict hierarchy, he was never prepared to allow excessive social mobility, but the *parlementaires* were already high in the hierarchy and so these extra rewards were not inappropriate. Further, he was willing to grant lesser posts in the royal household to members of their families, although he excluded them from any positions which might have offended the great courtiers.

Some sons of the magistrates had entered the church, and they too received royal largesse in the form of benefices. By 1665 many judges could rightly feel that they had been well treated by the new regime, both socially and as a court of law. At the same time, the king was pleased that the Paris judges, in common with many other levels of the social hierarchy, were tending more and more to marry within their own narrow social circle, and so his patronage was enhancing their status as an elite but was not falling upon parvenus who had recently married above themselves into these illustrious ranks. Nor was he prepared to show similarly great favour to any member of the *robe* below this uppermost stratum of the judiciary.

There is much evidence to show that, during the years 1661–5, public pronouncements by the crown which might have offended the *parlement* were accompanied by private reassurances, either to individual judges or, on occasion, to the court as a whole. Also the ministers were prepared to allow it to negotiate modifications to offensive aspects of royal decisions. Unfortunately for the historian, neither the secretaries of state nor the judges were willing to record the details of these informal initiatives, and all that remains is clear evidence that a change of heart occurred at some stage of the negotiations. Older scholars, if they had troubled to examine these happenings in depth, would have attributed the outcome to the absolutism of the king, but that explanation is no longer convincing. One example concerned the attack on the *rentes* in 1662 and 1663, as part of the wider attempts by Colbert to reduce the indebtedness of the royal treasury to a variety of creditors. Initially, the judges were very hostile to these proposals, which promised to compensate the *rentiers* at a much lower rate than they had the right to expect from the value of the bonds they held. Yet a compromise was reached which more than satisfied the *parlementaires*. Most of their investments were in older issues of *rentes*, and these were now excluded from the present proposals. Also, the crown promised that it would never liquidate bonds which were in the hands of royal officials and that its level of compensation would henceforth be higher. In addition, the right of the court to supervise the administration of the whole system was confirmed. The judges were aware that the crown was having difficulty in restoring its finances to a state of order, and this compromise therefore seemed very reasonable in the circumstances. The only group to be severely affected were the *rentiers* who were not royal officials, but that band of financiers and speculators commanded no affection in the *parlement*.[5]

[5]For a commentary on all these events from a judicial point of view, see Olivier Lefèvre d'Ormesson, *Journal*, 'Collection des documents inédits sur l'histoire de France' (2 vols, Paris, 1860–1).

By the time that the council to reform justice was created in 1665, the Paris judges had received not only some public rebukes from the king about their conduct during the Frondes, but also many specific signs of royal favour, goodwill and willingness to compromise, together with requests for their support in religious and judicial matters. Moreover, the composition of the new *conseil de justice* did not alarm them, although they were not invited to sit on it, and its proceedings soon reassured them even further. It sent out *maîtres des requêtes* to consult with the provincial *parlements*, and it contained six senior advocates from the Paris court who were closely in touch with the judges of the capital. Its plans for improving the judicial system were also much in tune with proposals which the Parisian *parlementaires* had been voicing for many years, and therefore they largely welcomed the provisions of the 1667 Civil Ordinance in which the council published its conclusions. They had called for cheaper and faster justice, an end to conflicting jurisdictions and a uniformity of court procedures throughout the realm. Indeed in 1665 they issued very detailed and lengthy decrees on these subjects which in many ways anticipated the 1667 Ordinance. The main difference was that the Paris judges could prescribe only for the lesser courts within their own jurisdiction, whereas the Ordinance referred to the whole kingdom, and it was in those more distant provinces that the abuses of justice were most flagrant and the judiciary less eager to remedy them.

Behind closed doors, the royal council of justice considered many matters which would have caused great offence if they had been enshrined in the final ordinance. Complaints were made against the whole venal system, the excessive number of officials, the laziness and corruption of individuals, the inflated levels of fees and the dominance in certain courts of powerful family interests.[6] On none of these matters was it safe for the crown to legislate, because it had to accept venality, it could not afford to repurchase and suppress surplus posts, and it was faced with patrimonial power in every aspect of the administration. Fortunately for the king, the Paris judges were themselves quick to maintain the balance of power in their courts and to stamp out corruption. On the subject of fees, Louis did say that in the future he hoped to eliminate such payments altogether, but that this would obviously necessitate the raising of judicial salaries in compensation. In fact this plan was never implemented, and fees remained, although both the crown and the Paris judges tried hard to ensure that they were kept within reasonable limits.

[6]See Depping, vol. II, pp. 33–98, for the surveys of judicial personnel, their strengths, weaknesses, patrons and clients made by the *intendants* in 1663; for the instructions of Colbert on the compilation of these reports, see Clément, vol. IV, pp. 27–32.

The draft of the 1667 Ordinance avoided these emotive matters, and concentrated on standardizing procedures within the courts of the realm. Therefore, when the *parlement* of Paris was consulted on the text, it found that almost every article was satisfactory, although it carefully discussed each one in order to demonstrate that it had the right to do so. Only the suggestion that judges could be prosecuted by litigants for violating the terms of the Ordinance was hotly debated, not because such behaviour ought to be condoned, but because the *parlement* maintained that it should have the responsibility for disciplining the magistrature. To allow ordinary citizens to proceed against them was to lower the prestige of the judiciary as a whole. On this issue the judges lost, as the crown was clearly not going to give way and they did not want a confrontation. On balance, therefore, they were satisfied with the 1667 Ordinance on civil cases, and with its criminal counterpart of 1670. The two documents gave royal authority to many of their own reform proposals, and avoided offending their pride. It was known, for example, that some members of the *conseil de justice* had wished to substitute the term 'superior courts' for 'sovereign courts', and had used the novel term during the negotiations with the judges on the draft ordinance. When the final text was published, neither adjective was used, and the unexceptionable phrase, 'our courts of *parlement* and our other courts', was substituted.

If the 1667 and 1670 ordinances did not strain relations between the crown and the Paris *parlement*, neither were they such a legal landmark as their own preambles, and some later historians, have claimed.[7] They have been likened in their scope to the Code Napoléon, but they were in fact confined to detailed matters of procedure. The wide variety of French laws and customs remained, and, although *intendants* were asked to investigate the ways in which greater uniformity might be introduced, very little could be done. Nor were these two ordinances implemented with enthusiasm throughout the whole kingdom. Both the ministers and the Paris judges complained that provincial *parlements* and lesser courts continually evaded their prescriptions, and that jurisdictional disputes and costly delays in justice persisted.

The pattern of justice in the provinces continued to be variegated. Sometimes courts tried to act but failed because the criminals whom they were pursuing were simply too powerful in their locality. On

[7]For the text of the ordinances, see: Isambert, vol. XVIII, pp. 103–80, for the Civil Ordinance of 1667, and pp. 341–61 for the supplementary ordinance of 1669; pp. 219–311 for the general regulations for the rivers and forests; pp. 371–423 for the Criminal Ordinance of 1670; and vol. XIX, pp. 70–2, for the 1673 regulations for the registration of letters patent.

other occasions, the courts delayed the preparation of a case for years, because pressure had been put upon them to avoid reaching a decision about a defendant who would certainly be found guilty if the trial actually took place. When litigation involved a senior judicial official, it was sometimes impossible to obtain justice, as witnessed by the abbot and community of Saint-Antoine-de-Viennois who in 1671 complained that, after twenty-three years, their suit against a president of the local *parlement* was still unresolved in the court of first instance.[8] If members of the provincial elites could thwart the law, more general forms of lawlessness persisted too. Travellers were at the mercy of highwaymen; vagabonds made urban streets unsafe, because the authorities had not followed the Parisian example of shutting them up in poorhouses, which were expensive to build and maintain; servants carried swords and attacked passers-by; and if the authorities sometimes pursued these miscreants with vigour, they were often able to seek effective sanctuary in the privileged lands of the church. Even in the city of Paris, where the crown, the *parlement* and the municipality co-operated closely in maintaining order and in confining seditious elements within poorhouses, there were still large areas of private jurisdiction into which the police authorities had no right of access. Most of the Left Bank was under the control of the university, the palace of the Luxembourg and the abbey of Saint-Germain-des-Prés, and although those jurisdictions did not wish to encourage crime and disorder, they were determined to yield none of their privileges to the crown, the city or the courts.[9] In order to improve the policing of the capital, the crown divided the responsibilities of the *lieutenant-civil* between two officials in 1667, one of them continuing to hold that title and the other being designated as the first *lieutenant-général de police*. The royal justification for this action was that justice and policing should be separated and that too much work was involved for a single official effectively to supervise both functions. There is no doubt that the duties of the new officer overlapped with certain aspects of *parlementaire* responsibilities in the city, and absolutist historians have added this fact to their evidence that the king was allegedly attempting to humble the sovereign courts. Yet the judges did not regard the

[8]See, for example, Clément, vol. VI, pp. 31, 36–7, including p. 37 note 2; Depping, vol. II, pp. 145–6; for one of many instances of overt disobedience against the 1667 ordinance, see Depping, vol. II p. 224.

[9]See, for example, Depping, vol. I, pp. 837–8, 924–5, the latter showing that the abbey of Saint-Germain-des-Prés was still providing a haven for undesirables as late as 1703, despite persistent attempts by the crown and the city authorities, since 1674, to reduce its rights.

lieutenant-général in this light. They co-operated closely with him in their common purpose of maintaining law and order, and the judges did not complain that their jurisdiction was being usurped, not surprisingly, because the *lieutenant* took very great care to ensure that they were consulted and allowed to exercise their authority on all appropriate matters.

The final aspect of the judicial reforms which has been persistently misunderstood by historians is the royal decision of 1673 that henceforth the *parlement* had to register edicts at once, and only afterwards could it remonstrate against provisions which it did not like. It could still hope that the king would act upon its reservations and reissue the edict in an amended form, but it could no longer delay the first registration, as it had frequently done in the past. These facts have not been in dispute, but the interpretation put upon them has frequently been wide of the mark. For the absolutist historians, the events of 1673 were the final stage in the total humiliation of the *parlement*. Yet the behaviour of the Paris judges does not suggest that they considered it to be so. An earlier attempt to expedite the registration of royal decrees had been made in the 1667 Civil Ordinance, whose first article announced that, when a court was accompanying the monarch, it had six days to remonstrate against an edict, after which it would be deemed that the document had been registered. If the court and the king were in different locations, then the period was to be six weeks. When the sovereign was physically present among the judges, then registration was automatic as at all such *lits de justice*. During the discussions between the judges and the members of the *conseil de justice*, in the months before the publication of the Civil Ordinance, the Paris *parlement* did not show any alarm at the prescriptions contained in this article. They were much more excited about the suggestion that litigants could sue magistrates for incorrectly interpreting the law, and they were pleased that their jurisdiction had not been reformed in any important way. A week was not an unreasonable length of time, especially as the king could always prevent all debate by attending the court in person. The most significant factor for them was that, in recent years, there had not been any unacceptable royal edicts, either at *lits de justice* or at ordinary sessions.

The 1673 letters patent were undoubtedly more fiercely worded, because they insisted that registration had to be effected before any remonstrances could be formulated. They were issued on 24 February, a few days after the king and his advisers had decided that the Dutch War was not going to be concluded with the speed that they had originally intended. A possible prolonged international conflict was accordingly cited as the explicit reason why immediate registration of royal edicts was vital, as the royal ministers well remembered the threat posed to the foreign policy of Mazarin by the delaying tactics of the *frondeur parlement*. Once again the Paris judges did not object. In the years 1667–73, they had not found the need to initiate a single remonstrance, and they did not envisage a sudden return to the illegalities of Mazarin after the recent decade in which they had co-operated so well with the personally ruling king. Also, through informal channels, they received plenty of reassurance on this point, and it seems to have been sincerely given. In 1682 the chancellor, Le Tellier, reiterated it in a letter to the first president of the Paris *parlement*, saying that the right to remonstrate was fundamental and that all such remonstrances would be treated with the same seriousness as in the days when they preceded registration. Yet there is one further piece of careful phraseology in the 1673 letters which every historian seems to have missed, but it was no royal drafting error. Those letters referred back to the 1667 Ordinance, and noted that a delay of six days, or six weeks when the court was away from the king, was allowed for discussion of all ordinances, edicts, declarations and letters patent. Under the new rules, it was only letters patent which were to be registered without time for remonstrating. There was no mention of ordinances, edicts and declarations. Therefore, unless the king began to use letters patent for matters which would normally appear in one of those other forms, the judges would have even less cause for apprehension.

To any historian who has studied the relations of the crown with the Parisian and the provincial sovereign courts, the message of both 1667 and 1673 is clear. It was an assault on the delaying tactics of the provincial courts, who had the right to register royal commands in those distant *pays d'états* which were troublesome for other reasons, not least because they were highly separatist and near to the frontiers of the kingdom. It was geographically impossible for the king to visit these proud tribunals in person in order to hold a *lit de justice*, and it would have been dangerous to engineer such an encounter in which the sovereign exposed his authority before judges who might have been less reluctant than their Parisian confrères to defy him. The wisdom of this royal caution is substantiated by the history of the subsequent twenty years. Not only the crown, but the Paris judges as well, regularly complained about the persistently obstructive behaviour of these provincial *parlements*, *cours des aides* and *chambres des comptes*, which ignored the prescriptions of 1667 and 1673 as cavalierly as they disregarded many other instructions from the royal government. At the centre, in contrast, the king and the principal law court of both his capital and his realm preserved their harmonious relations on many matters, especially on Huguenots, gallican issues, Jansenists, law and order. Not until the royal *rapprochement* with Rome would this co-operation be severely shaken.

In the reform of the law, as in other aspects of the internal administration, the crown tried to achieve its purposes by public pronouncements made in ringing tones, by private reassurances given behind the scenes and by the liberal use of patronage and favour. Yet in all fields, the provinces proved themselves much less amenable than the capital. Also, the dynamic proposals of the years 1667–72, which would always have been difficult to implement, became totally inappropriate when renewed war undermined the royal finances once again. Colbert was quickly forced to reintroduce emergency measures, and to depend on those very groups which he had hoped to reform.

FINANCE

In attempting to overhaul the fiscal system, Colbert was faced with a whole series of problems, some very similar to, others different from, those he encountered in his role as a legal reformer. Although he once again wished to restore and work within the traditional mechanisms, here too he was confronted by inefficiency, corruption, and by conflicting jurisdictions which gave rise to continual litigation. He had to take account of the powers of the sovereign courts – not the *parlements*, but the *cours des aides* and the *chambres des comptes*. Once again he found that those in Paris were more co-operative than their provincial counterparts. Yet there was an added dimension here, because he planned to use the *intendants* more widely in the financial administration than in judicial affairs. Where the *parlement* of Paris had barely mentioned these officials in the 1660s, because the judges did not feel threatened by them, the financial sovereign courts saw them as potential challengers, even though the minister endlessly exhorted them to respect the rights of office-holders. Another major difference was that the crown had less direct control over the fiscal administration. At least the magistrature, even that in the obstreporous provincial *parlements*, was composed of royal judges. In contrast only a proportion of the funds in the treasury came through the agency of direct crown officials in the venal bureaucracy. Much money came in the form of loans from the financiers, other sums depended on investors in government bonds, the most profitable taxes were advanced by tax-farmers and subsequently collected by their own appointees, while in the *pays d'états* it was the Estates themselves which took responsibility for the *taille* and had the right to negotiate with the crown about the exact amount which was to be levied.

The *pays d'états* raised a number of administrative issues which were uniquely their own. These provinces were proudly independent, many of them having been relatively recent acquisitions of the French crown, and they were mostly frontier areas. They often had stronger economic links with neighbouring countries than with the rest of France, and this might pose problems in wartime when those neighbours became enemies. The need to defend the kingdom in war and peace also necessitated the permanent presence of troops in these areas, with all the attendant costs and distress for the population. As the Estates were responsible for many aspects of the local administration which in the *pays d'élections* would have been under the direct supervision of the central government, there was a long-established tradition of reluctance to pay high taxes to the crown. Local levies were at least spent on matters which affected life in the area, and were under the supervision of the Estates, which was an elected body and enjoyed a certain amount of respect and trust. The taxes paid to Paris were not regarded as beneficial to the province. They were frequently used to finance wars on distant and therefore irrelevant frontiers, or sometimes against peoples whom the province regarded as friendly neighbours and economic partners. It was accepted that a certain amount would be paid to the king in peacetime, but a higher demand then, and an even more exorbitant one in war, would arouse the ire of the people and of the Estates which they had elected. Ironically, as Colbert would have admitted, the *pays d'états* were in many ways more efficiently administered than the *pays d'élections*. In the latter areas, the office-holders might obstruct the crown, but the various *officiers* were often at odds, and the general citizenry had no love for any of them – even though they might at times make common cause against an even greater evil. The Estates, in contrast, were able to achieve more because they were elected, they appointed officials from the localities and supervised them carefully, and were in no sense agents from distant Paris. The problem for the crown was to persuade the deputies in the Estates to endorse royal policies. Once that had been done, there would be a reasonable chance of their implementation. Whereas in the *pays d'élections* the crown could issue any instruction it chose, but would then have to threaten and cajole in order to stand a chance of its being obeyed, in the *pays d'états* the task was to reach agreement with the Estates, always involving protracted negotiations and ultimate compromise, after which the deputies would see that the decision was implemented. That at least was the theory, and for much of the 1660s it was an accurate description of the practice.[10]

Even in that first peaceful decade of the personal rule, it is nevertheless clear that the crown needed all its patronage and personal links with provincial worthies if it was to reach agreement on taxation with the Estates. A first requirement was to have some trusted advisers who could take rapid decisions without reference to Paris, because debates in elected assemblies have a way of changing direction unexpectedly. There would be no time to write for further instructions from the capital, if a new issue was suddenly raised at a critical moment of the discussion about the level of taxation. There is accordingly a striking difference between the very restrained behaviour required of the *intendant* in the *pays d'élections* and the considerable freedom of action granted to the governor and certain bishops in the *pays d'états*. The commissions of the *intendants* accorded them very few executive powers, and most of those were temporary and subject to reversal – on appeal to the sovereign courts – by the local office-holders. Their principal role was as observers, reporting their findings to the royal council which alone would decide on the action to be taken, and would usually seek to implement that decision through the traditional channels of the venal bureaucracy. The governors and trusted bishops were given a general mandate to react in whatever way they deemed appropriate to local circumstances, using every means to further the best interests of the crown. It has already been noted that, in the *pays d'états*, the *intendants* were often drawn from local families, and were therefore not open to the charge of being intruders from outside the area which made them so suspect in the *pays d'élections*. Also they were normally chosen in consultation with the governor, and their principal role was to supervise the routine of daily administration, a task which would have been socially demeaning for this high aristocratic officer of the crown. The *intendant* was present at the Estates, but it was the governor who negotiated with the local elites because he alone had both the social pre-eminence to command their

[10]In addition to subsequent references, see: on the Estates of Artois, Depping, vol. I, pp. 591–2; on the Breton Estates, Bibliothèque nationale, collection Mélanges Colbert (hereafter BN, Mél. Colb.), vol. 171bis, fols 662–3; vol. 174bis, fols 339–40, 381; Clément, vol. II (i), pp. 309–10, 315–17; Jean Lemoine, *La révolte dite du papier timbré ou des bonnets rouges en Bretagne en 1675: étude et documents* (Paris/Rennes, 1898), docs CI, CIX, CXII, CXIII, CXXVIbis, CLXIII, CLXIV; on the Estates of Languedoc, Clément, vol. IV, pp. 81–2; Depping, vol. I, pp. 3–8, 95–8, 133–4, 182–7, 289–93, 308–10; vol. III, pp. 803–5; vol. IV, pp. 27–8, 63–4; abbé Millot, *Mémoires politiques et militaires . . . composés sur les pièces originales recueillies par Adrien-Maurice, duc de Noailles, maréchal de France & ministre d'état* (6 vols, Lausanne/Yverdon, 1778), vol. I, pp. 59–60, 69; C. J. Trouvé, *Essai historique sur les états-généraux de la province de Languedoc* (Paris 1818), pp. 188–9.

respect, and the powers of patronage to enlist the support of key individuals in the provincial hierarchy.

The constitution and practices of the individual Estates varied from one province to another. In some areas the three estates sat and voted together, and in Languedoc the Third Estate was twice the size of the other two so that its voting strength was equal to the combined forces of the clergy and nobility. In other provinces the three estates deliberated and voted in separate chambers, and it was for the governor to win the support of two of them in order to outvote the third. In Brittany the nobles were the most difficult to control; in Languedoc it was the Third Estate deputies who proved most intractable. Some Estates met annually, others every two or three years, but in each case they approved the levy of the direct taxes until the date scheduled for their next meeting.

Considerable effort went into the selection of presidents for these meetings. In Languedoc, where all three estates debated in a single forum, the chair was taken by the archbishop of either Toulouse or Narbonne, and great care was exercised therefore in appointing the holders of those sees. In Brittany it was necessary to find three suitable men, one for each chamber. The clergy were chaired by the bishop in whose diocese the assembly was held, and much correspondence passed between the governor and the ministers before the venue was finally chosen.[11] Over the selection of the noble president, there was some room for manoeuvre, but only if the duc de Rohan and the duc de La Trémoïlle waived their right to preside at alternate meetings. Even then, the candidate had to be a Breton noble of very high rank or extremely ancient lineage, if he were to command the necessary respect from the Second Estate.

Once each assembly and its officers were duly constituted, the crown and the governor used all their influence and patronage behind the scenes to facilitate a successful outcome.[12] This was never an easy task, and there were always powerful nobles and bishops, from the great landed families of the province, who were equally skilful in using their personal connections and prestige to thwart the royal will. Some of the most loyal prelates were also prepared to force the government to compromise, if they sincerely thought that the fiscal demands of the crown were excessive and failed to make allowance for economic difficulties which were causing hardship in the area. The problem for the ministers was to decide which of the pleas for moderation were

[11]See BN, Mél. Colb., vol. 165bis, fols 404–5; vol. 171bis, fols 772–5; Depping, vol. I, pp. 546–50.

[12]See Depping, vol. I, pp. 49–51, 56–61, 63–7, 97–8, 540, 542–3.

sincere, and which were special pleading by the leaders of provincial society.

After each meeting of an Estates, much money was given, and many favours granted, to those who had played a constructive role, in the hope that they would be encouraged to behave in a similar way at the next session. Thus, in 1673, the governor of Brittany asked Colbert to reward the marquis de Lavardin, the *lieutenant-général*; Boucherat, one of the two royal commissioners to the assembly; the prince de Tarente and his mother for their good offices in making the nobility more tractable; the marquis de La Coste for the same reason; the bishop of Rennes for his excellent service as clerical president; and the bishops of Dol, Saint-Malo and Nantes for seconding his efforts in that role. The assemblies might also initiate the payment of gratifications, in order to ingratiate themselves in high places. Thus, in 1679, the Estates of the Mâconnais authorized the payment of 4,000 *livres* to the provincial governor, 1,000 to Colbert, 500 to one of the *intendants* on the royal *conseil des finances*, 500 to the local *intendant*, 500 to a member of the Paris *parlement*, 200 to the private secretary of Colbert and the same sum to the private secretary of the *secrétaire d'état* for Protestant affairs.[13]

Despite this careful use of bribery and patronage, there were often prolonged negotiations between the governors and the Estates about the precise level of the taxes, and the king knew that his agents would have to haggle in this manner. The provincial deputies were always insistent on their great loyalty to the crown, but that did not extend to their blind acceptance of royal demands. In 1662, when the ministers were requesting modest sums, the Estates of Burgundy concluded their deliberations in only six days. The governor was the duc de Bourbon, the former prince de Condé, and he had been instructed to ask for 1,500,000 *livres*, although he had full authority to accept whatever sum he could obtain. The deputies offered exactly one third of that amount, raising it under persuasion from Bourbon, to 600, 800, and finally 900,000. At that point the governor revealed that he would be willing to lower his demand to 1,200,000. After some reflection, the delegation from the assembly came once more to his house and announced that they could just manage 1,000,000. He made one last appeal to their generosity, and the final sum of 1,050,000 was agreed, a moral victory for the crown because it had conceded 450,000 and the assembly had raised its offer by 550,000. As the governor wrily noted in his report, the Third Estate had been much more difficult than the nobles and the clergy in these negotiations, 'but that is excusable,

[13]See Clément, vol. IV, pp. 539, 596–8.

seeing that it is they who carry the burden of almost all the taxes'.[14]

As fiscal needs rose during the Dutch War of 1672–9, the crown found it increasingly difficult to obtain higher sums from the *pays d'états*. Yet here, once again, the absolutist historians have fallen into a trap of their own making. They have noticed that, when Estates were negotiating the customary fiscal compromise with the governor, the agreements which were finally reached included surprisingly high levels of taxation, and their conclusion is that the absolutism of Louis XIV must have humbled these proud provincial bodies. That argument does not stand up to close scrutiny. These elected bodies, in common with many other institutions, were undoubtedly eager to avoid an overt confrontation with a monarch who was ruling personally, but there were other ways of avoiding his orders without the need for a resort to open defiance. Accordingly many Estates adopted two tactical strategems. The first was to exploit the financial difficulties of the treasury and ask the government for new privileges or for the confirmation of existing liberties. If these requests should be granted, the province would increase its tax contribution, or so it assured the governor. Often the impoverished ministers had no choice but to accept these terms, and a relatively high fiscal levy was then duly agreed. It was at this point that the second strategem was needed, as it would not be long before Colbert began to enquire why the province was falling into arrears with its payments of this tax which had been jointly accepted by both governor and Estates. It was essential for the deputies to prepare convincing explanations for the delay. The excuses offered were of many kinds, often plausible and always difficult for the Paris ministers to verify – the olive crop had failed; late hailstorms had destroyed the flowers on the fruit trees; the province had been required to contribute extra sums towards the provisioning of troops, which they knew to be a major concern of His Majesty; the Estates had spend extra funds on dredging the ports, which they felt compelled to do because their principal wish was to aid Monsieur Colbert in his plans for the revival of overseas trade; or even the incredulous reply that the local treasurers had indeed sent off the money and were amazed to hear that it had not arrived. Sometimes it was true that highwaymen had ambushed one of these lucrative convoys, and it was certainly extremely likely. If that had indeed happened, it was impossible for Colbert to ask the province to levy a further tax in order to replace the missing sums. Such were the deceptions practised by the apparently acquiescent officials of the *pays d'états*, and both governor and *intendant* spent much time trying to test

[11]See Depping, vol. I, pp. 426–31.

the veracity of these extenuating circumstances. Despite their best endeavours, fiscal arrears mounted steadily in wartime, and in 1673, the archbishop of Narbonne could write ruefully to Colbert that, on the day that the Estates of Languedoc had agreed to pay 2,000,000 *livres* in tax for the present year, they had collected only 700,000 of the 1,700,000 which they had pledged to raise in the preceding twelve months.[15]

The proceedings of the provincial Estates were also disrupted by the squabbles among the local elites themselves. An immense amount of time was wasted on disputes about precedence, whether in processions, in the allocation of seats, in the order of speaking and voting, indeed on any matter where there was a social or institutional point to be scored. Sometimes whole estates were at odds with others, but frequently the conflicts arose within a single order. Nobles disputed the lineage of their fellows, bishops questioned the claims to seniority of others on their benches, and in the meetings of the Third Estate some urban deputies used this forum to assert the pre-eminence of their town over its rivals. As the archbishop of Toulouse remarked in 1662, it was strange how the delegates from his city behaved in the Estates 'as if they were tribunes of the people, in opposition to the service of the King', and spoke loudly against taxes which their own citizens did not have to pay because the Toulousains had long ago purchased exemption from them. Nevertheless, these disputes sometimes provided opportunities for the governor and the bishops to win some short-term allies, by offering to champion the claims of one party.[16]

There were, of course, occasions when the provinces really were afflicted by unforeseen economic hardship, and in such cases the governor and some of the bishops would write to the ministers and plead for a reduction in the tax burden. As these were trusted advisers, the central government would pay great attention to their requests and would frequently make whatever concessions were possible, given the other demands on royal revenues. In contrast the governors would also advise Colbert on the means by which he might extract further sums from the provincial Estates in order to compensate for their reluctance to shoulder the fiscal responsibilities which the crown imposed upon them. The best method was to propose overtly, or to start a rumour, that certain local privileges would be reduced or abolished, and then wait to see whether the Estates were prepared to pay for their preservation. Such tactics could rebound upon the ministers, if care were not taken, as Colbert discovered in 1675 when

[15]See Depping, vol. I, pp. 295–6.
[16]See Depping, vol. I, pp. 63–6, 95–8.

Brittany revolted against the central government.[17] In 1672 he had begun his provocation by including in a royal declaration the statement that henceforth the Estates would be denied the opportunity of criticizing edicts, even when they were aimed against the privileges of that assembly itself. He had also set up a chamber to investigate seigneurial jurisdictions, which were more extensive there than in other provinces of the realm. A third piece of ministerial aggression was the opening of hostilities against the Dutch, seriously disrupting Breton trade to the Republic, with which close economic links had long been maintained. When the Estates began their 1673 session, Colbert wanted them to grant 2,600,000 *livres* for the direct taxes, and therefore initially asked for 3,000,000, in order to be able to concede the sum of 400,000 in the course of the negotiations. The deputies immediately showed themselves willing to buy off the chamber looking into seigneurial jurisidictions and the declaration of 1672. Thus, when the governor announced, in the third week of the meeting, that the king would make this concession of 400,000 on his original request, the Estates promptly offered the full 3,000,000 on condition that the chamber and the declaration were withdrawn. When the governor pretended that he did not have the authority to accept such a bargain, the deputies offered to pay 2,600,000 for the taxes and prepared further memoirs about the offensive attacks on the privileges of the province. Within the next thirteen days, as a result of skilful diplomacy by the governor, the prince de Tarente and the bishops of Rennes and Saint-Malo, the three estates offered a supplementary sum and then increased it first to 2,200,000 and finally to 2,600,000, the same amount that they had already agreed to pay in direct taxes. The governor now graciously accepted this combined grant of 5,200,000 and consented to end both the chamber and the restriction on the right of the Estates to debate matters of privilege. As he confided to Colbert, it would never have been possible to implement either of these royal decisions, because the likelihood of insurrection would have been too great, and therefore the extra 2,600,000 *livres* was a very substantial bonus in the circumstances. Yet this victory seems to have given the

---

[17]See BN, Mél. Colb., vol. 156bis, fol. 579; vol. 157, fols 186–7, 202–7, 230–1, 256, 260–5, 296–9, 331–5, 374–6, 400–1, 408; vol. 157bis, fols 436–9, 458; vol. 159, fols 185–7; vol. 165bis, fols 528, 675–8; vol. 166, fols 226, 268–9; vol. 166bis, fols 510–13, 559–60, 679–82; vol. 167, fols 110–11, 140–3; vol. 175, fols 120–1, 179, 204, 238; vol. 176bis, fols 831–2; Depping, vol. I, pp. 521, 523–4, 526–32, 537, 541–4; Madame de Sévigné, *Lettres*, ed. Gérard-Gailly (3 vols, Paris, 1953–7), vol. I, pp. 665–7. See also Roger Mettam, *The role of the higher aristocracy in France under Louis XIV, with special reference to the 'faction of the duke of Burgundy' and the provincial governors* (Cambridge, PhD thesis, 1967), pp. 266–74, 285–9; Bibliothèque nationale (hereafter BN), fonds français, no. 22346, fols 323–520.

minister too much confidence, and within two years he imposed three controversial new taxes on this proud province. The result was a full-scale revolt, in which the crown had ultimately to compromise and admit almost total defeat.[18]

Scarcely less difficult than the provincial Estates, when it came to raising royal revenue, were the elected municipal councils in the *pays d'élections*. They too were responsible for much routine local administration, and they and their citizenry preferred to finance those matters which brought immediate benefit to the town rather than contribute to the treasury in distant Paris. Moreover, whereas the Estates at least took their provincial responsibilities seriously, the town elites were often extravagant and spent a high proportion of their revenues on litigation against rival groups of citizens and royal officials. Although the crown did not imagine that it could dispense with these elected bodies, and it certainly had no wish to take over their daily administrative tasks, it did try to influence elections and to enlist the aid of nobles and bishops in order to make the councils less intractable. Its prime aim, which took over thirty years to achieve, was to establish the right of the king to designate the mayor in every town, so that at least the chairman of the council would be sympathetic to the interests of the crown.[19]

Some historians have greatly overestimated the extent to which the king already enjoyed the right to appoint mayors and, in certain towns, the whole of the council. As the mayor became ex officio a royal magistrate, the monarch had to approve the appointment, but the important historical question concerns the extent to which the crown could choose the nominee. Often the final choice was a compromise. The citizens gave the king a list of their preferred candidates, and he chose one of them. There was considerable advantage to be gained for the government and for the town in the selection of a mayor who was acceptable to both of them. There were always conflicts about detailed matters of administration, especially when royal taxes rose in wartime, but there was nothing to be gained for either side by suggesting a mayor who was totally unacceptable to the other. In the *pays d'états* the search for suitable urban leaders was entrusted to the provincial governor, and Colbert was reluctant to interfere. He said so specifically to his brother who, as bishop of Auxerre, wrote to him about the forthcoming mayoral appointment in that town. Colbert reminded him that 'the choice must be left to Monseigneur le duc de Bourbon', and added, some weeks later and after further communications from the bishop, that 'I will see if I can find some appropriate

[18]See pp. 313–16 below.
[19]See Depping, vol. I, pp. 715–7, 811, 873, 877.

moment to speak to Monseigneur le Duc; but, to tell you the truth, I shall not make a great effort to do so, because I am reluctant to meddle in this kind of matter'.[20]

Once the towns had been reassured by the care which the crown took, over many years, to appoint acceptable mayors, they were prepared to accept a royal offer of extra privileges in return for allowing the king to nominate his own candidate in future. Thus, it was eventually possible for the government in 1692 to publish an edict which said that henceforth the crown would select the mayor in every town of the kingdom. The council members were still to be elected, of course, and with varying amounts of pressure from royal agents and from powerful local interests, but at least the chairman would be a royal appointee, even if one likely to be accepted by the municipality. Only two months later, as the Nine Years War emptied the treasury, the city of Dijon was allowed to purchase the right to elect its mayor for 100,000 *livres*, and other similar agreements quickly followed. Very soon all the posts on the town councils were offered for sale, and thus a new stratum of urban venal office-holders was created. If the first holders of these posts were grateful to the crown for this new security of tenure, it prevented the government from exercising further influence over these appointments. The offices would henceforth be passed on within families, or would be sold to the highest bidder.

Throughout his ministry, Colbert tried to persuade the towns to appoint some councillors who came from the world of commerce, but the tenacious grasp of office-holding families on these positions was normally too strong. In consequence, there were many disputes between the civic authorities and the merchants or gildsmen. There were also lengthy battles in the courts between councillors and office-holders, even though many of them came from the same families. Sometimes totally unsuitable men were elected to municipal office, as in 1664, when two men who had been condemned to death, and who had been hanged in effigy because they could not be apprehended, were made councillors at Nérac and Condom. Although not all urban officials were of such dubious pedigree, Colbert received numerous reports of their maladministration, about which he could often do very little.[21]

A characteristic incident occurred at Bourges in 1667. The keeper of the town hall was arrested for non-payment of taxes and imprisoned. The mayor and councillors promptly seized the gaoler for five hours and, when they pretended to return him to his prison, took the keys in order to free their keeper. In retaliation the *intendant* succeeded in

[20]See Depping, vol. I, pp. 851–3.
[21]See Depping, vol. I, pp. 683–4, 692, 705–6, 717–19, 844, 859–61, 866.

capturing the son of the keeper, and expressed his alarm to Colbert that the mayor, who was supposed to prosecute on behalf of the crown in the local *présidial* court, was now harbouring one of the criminals whom he should have been prosecuting. On another occasion, the mayor of Bayonne showed remarkable disinclination to investigate the assassination of an agent working for the navy in 1670.[22]

To the great distress of the minister, many towns were so heavily in debt that they could neither run the administration of their locality nor pay their dues to the treasury. In Beaune, the debts amounted to 600,000 *livres* in 1663, not including the unpaid contribution to the direct taxes. As the *intendant* noted, this had been largely brought about by the lavish spending of the councillors on banquets, gifts and travelling expenses. The minister issued numerous directives to the effect that all municipal levies and borrowings had to be approved by the government, but these prescriptions were disregarded. The *intendant* could not be everywhere at once, and usually discovered these abuses after they had occurred. The crown could then issue demands for strict observation of the regulations in the future, but these had a hollow ring in view of such persistent municipal disobedience. In the last year of his life, Colbert was still writing to *intendants* on this matter, and noting that, after a twenty-two year campaign, municipal debts were as high as ever. Moreover, he added, the towns had been allowed to levy extra taxes in order to repay these sums and restore their solvency, but all they had done was to seize this opportunity for raising extra revenue, and then spend it on other matters without repaying any of the capital they had borrowed.[23]

Another regular complaint by Colbert was that either towns failed to collect the sums destined for garrisoning and provisioning the army when it was quartered in the locality, or that, when the money had been raised, the municipal officials failed to pass it on to the military authorities, using it instead for civic or personal expenditure. It was very difficult to bring the perpetrators of such corrupt practices to justice, seeing that the local judges were often sympathetic to them and might be from the same municipal families. The one major consolation for Colbert was that the town councils did share his concern for maintaining order among the lesser citizenry, because it was in their own interest to do so. They would therefore provide a civic militia to contain the danger of local sedition, and they would seek to improve hygiene, prevent epidemics, and perhaps build poorhouses in which to contain the potentially rebellious poor.

[22]See Depping, vol. I, pp. 763–4, 813.
[23]See Clément, vol. IV, pp. 59–60, 132, 138, 144, 146–7, 164–5, 172, 175; Depping, vol. I, pp. 666–9, 679–80, 816–8.

As the *pays d'états* authorized lower taxes than the crown required or else failed to deliver the whole amount, and as the towns in the *pays d'élections* were so obstructive, the finance ministers had to depend for the direct tax revenues on the peasantry, the poorest element in society, in the areas of *taille personelle*. Here too there was much corruption, both among the collectors and among those who had sufficient influence to affect the just apportionment of the tax burden. This latter group included not only the more prosperous peasants, who were known as the 'cocks of the parish' and used their resources to bribe the assessors, but also the nobles, who were concerned that, if the ordinary peasant paid excessive royal taxation, he would be unable to pay his various seigneurial dues. He also was required to pay indirect taxes to the crown and the tithe to the church, as well as municipal levies on goods going to and coming from market. With so many demands upon his pocket, the peasant gave priority to those which brought him some benefit, and the direct royal impositions therefore came lowest on his list.

Although Colbert abandoned his attempt to identify false nobles, who were wrongfully claiming exemption from direct taxation, he continued to pursue those genuine aristocrats who were trying to influence the allocation of the *taille*. The principal obstacle here was that the local assessors and collectors were in awe of these great landowners and dared not defy them. In 1681, after twenty years in office, Colbert was still complaining that the apportionment of the *taille* was regularly taking place in the houses of local nobles on their instructions, and that the richer taxpayers were avoiding their obligations as well, the poor acquiescing in this inequality because they obtained employment from these more prosperous members of society. The *intendants* tried to identify the worst examples of these practices, but frequently a local conspiracy of silence prevented them from discovering the true malefactors. Sometimes the senior fiscal office-holders, the *receveurs-généraux*, enlisted the aid of the minister. Thus, in 1662 Colbert wrote to the duc d'Arpajon, asking him if he would kindly tell his peasants to pay the outstanding *taille*, as they were refusing to do so in the absence of specific instructions from their lord. On that occasion Colbert even threatened to send in troops in support of the collectors, but this was mere pretence because his correspondence contains many references to the undesirability of using military force in such matters. The soldiers could not be trusted, and they inflicted grievous harm upon the populace.[24]

---

[21]See Clément, vol.II (i), pp. 62–3, 67, 75, 118–19, 154–5, 170–1, 175, 224, 226–7, 258, 294–5, 373, 381–2; vol. II (ii), p. 762; Depping, vol. III, pp. 24, 133, 168–73.

The minister also received regular reports of illegal extensions of the seigneurial and ecclesiastical levies, further sapping the ability of the peasant to pay his *taille*, but once again it was difficult to punish these abuses because the nobles and high clergy were too dominant in their area. Wealthier peasants had rather different means of defrauding the royal collectors. An effective ruse was to place a son in the church, and make over to him all the family wealth. Then it qualified for the clerical exemption from the *taille*, although the father still had access to his money and the use of the property. No matter where Colbert looked, there seemed to be successful deception. The more the *intendants* appointed *sub-délégués* to help them with their increasing burden of work, the more the minister suspected that these local men were taking care not to discover corrupt practices. Moreover, he was increasingly convinced that a significant number of *intendants* were either failing to discover fiscal abuses or even condoning them. Although he often voiced these suspicions to them in the plainest language, it was impossible for him to be certain about such trickery and he very seldom carried out his threat to dismiss these officials from their posts.[25]

At the same time as he was criticizing men from all levels of the social and administrative hierarchy for the abuses they introduced into the assessment and collection of the direct taxes, Colbert also had to deliver regular rebukes to officials who were over zealous. Despite his insistence that collectors should not seize the livestock of peasants as payment for outstanding tax, because that would condemn these humble farmers to imminent starvation, the practice continued. Yet he readily acknowledged that, given the deceptions practised by tax-payers and nobles alike, the collector was not always to blame if he failed to amass the revenues for which he was responsible. He should be punished only if he had deliberately misused his position. To imprison a collector who had tried to do his job was to ensure that he would not be in a position to collect any more taxes, and it was better for him to remain at work than to be behind bars. Although Colbert repeated this point many times, the higher office-holders frequently ignored it and committed many of their subordinates to prison. Thus, in 1680, the minister discovered that there were 102 collectors of the *taille* in the gaols of Angers and some three hundred more imprisoned in other parts of that one *généralité*.[26]

One final aspect of the system of direct taxation caused particular annoyance to the finance minister. In the hope of reducing inequalities

[25]See Clément, vol. II (i), pp. 200–1, vol. IV, pp.108, 143–4, 150, 155–6, 164; Depping, vol. III, pp. 165–6, 185–6.
[26]See Clément, vol. II (i), pp. 70–3, 88–9, 137, 168, 172; vol. IV, p. 578.

in the allocation of the *taille*, he had given the *intendants* the power to impose temporary *taxes d'office*. These took the form of upward adjustments to the original assessment and had to be paid at once, although the taxpayer then had the right of appeal to the *cour des aides*, which would consider the increase and, if it were found to be unwarranted, order the extra sum to be repaid. In a letter to all *intendants* in 1670, Colbert acknowledged that his plan had not worked. He had hoped, he said, that as the *taxe d'office* had to be paid immediately it would discourage taxpayers from launching appeals, risking further expense if their claim was turned down by the court. He had since discovered that the *cours des aides* always upheld these pleas, often with scant regard for the circumstances of the case, and all taxpayers knew that it was therefore worth their while to take the *intendant* to court. He instructed them, in consequence of this, to send him full details of every such decision made by the *cours des aides*, in the hope that the royal council could evolve some plan for arresting this practice. Unfortunately for the minister the courts were acting perfectly legally in annulling these temporary levies, and the council soon decided that it could do nothing except make known to them the displeasure of the king.[27] As the kingdom was very soon plunged into the Dutch War, further provocation of these sovereign courts was not a wise course.

Thus, in finance as in justice, a newly reformed council at the centre encountered endless obstruction from officials and from subjects in the localities. After initially lowering the *taille* at the beginning of the personal rule of Louis XIV, in order to impress Frenchmen with the benevolence of the young monarch and to convince foreigners that this was a stable country in which to invest, Colbert had to demand ever larger sums in the war years of the 1670s, and found that the people would not pay what was required. Like every minister before him, he therefore had to rely more and more heavily on the financiers, on the issuing of government bonds, on the tax-farmers and even on the sale of new offices, on all of which he had initially hoped to reduce royal dependence. Yet the money-markets were only just recovering from the shock of the concessions given to the taxpayers in the early 1660s. Not only had the assessment of the direct taxes been at a lower rate, but the sums outstanding from the last years of the war, when it had been impossible to collect much revenue, had been cancelled so that a fresh start could be made. This measure doubly alarmed the financiers. They considered it unwise to give people the impression that resistance to high taxation would ultimately lead to a retreat by the ministers, and more importantly, they were painfully aware that

[27]See Clément, vol. II (i), pp. 294–5; Depping, vol. III, pp. 33–6.

the money which they had advanced to the crown in the 1650s had been secured against the yield from the taxes in subsequent years. Many lenders were therefore expecting to recoup their investments from the revenues of those taxes which the government now cancelled. Their promissory notes from the crown became valueless, and their royal debtor had defaulted on his obligations to them. Although some of these men slowly began to lend again in the peaceful years of the 1660s, the commencement of another war caused them to worry that the crown might once more be compelled to take similarly drastic measures, if the conflict were to be prolonged. Nevertheless, Colbert had to seek their aid so that he could anticipate the yield of the indirect taxes, *rentes* and newly created offices.

The indirect taxes had certain advantages over the *taille*, from the ministerial point of view. They fell upon all consumers, whether nobles, ecclesiastics or commoners, and they were collected by tax-farmers whose agents were prepared to employ considerable brutality as they recouped the sums which they had advanced to the crown at the beginning of the fiscal year. In consequence these collectors were hated by the population, especially as their methods were often remarkably effective. Colbert hoped to raise the additional revenue he needed by increasing only those indirect levies which fell on luxuries, making no change in the tax on salt which he regarded as a necessary commodity for everyone. Yet in wartime that too had to be increased. There were restraints on the tax-farmers and their agents, but their accounts were not subject to detailed scrutiny by the *intendants*, as was the case with records of the *tailles*. The levels of indirect taxation were fixed and the farmers were exhorted to refrain from seizing livestock in lieu of payment, but both of these limitations were disregarded on many occasions. In the peaceful years of the 1660s, these abuses were less widespread, as the yield of the taxes was more certain, and for that same reason Colbert was able to persuade the farmers to pay more generously for the right to collect these levies. Under Mazarin groups of financiers had worked together, agreeing on which of their number would bid for each tax and then offering the crown a low price because no rivals were bidding against them. With the new confidence which came from European peace and the assumption of power by Louis XIV himself, Colbert made it plain that such deception would not be tolerated. Financiers could pay a just price, or the contract would simply not be awarded to anyone. As this was the time when the *chambre de justice* was investigating financial corruption, a number of these men of the money-markets decided that it was better to make a higher bid. They still stood to gain very substantial profits.[28]

[28]Louis XIV, *Mémoires* – see Mettam, *Government and society*, p. 7.

The Dutch War brought this period of relative harmony to an end. Not only did the crown increase the indirect taxes, and therefore demand higher advances from the farmers, but there were soon many complaints that these entrepreneurs were trying to guarantee their profits in the uncertainty of wartime by illegally raising the rates still further. The Normans informed Colbert that the wine duty had been doubled during the war, and from many provinces it was reported that the farmers of the salt tax were permitting men to take this vital commodity on credit, but only if they took far more than they needed. Then, when payment was due, the agents of the farmer seized the livestock and chattels of those who could not find the money which was owing. The *intendants* were instructed to investigate these abuses, but it was difficult to eradicate them. Moreover the crown relied on these sources of revenue, and Colbert intervened on many occasions in support of a tax-farmer who had been the victim of popular agitation or had even been denounced by royal officials. In wartime the government needed to create more such taxes, as well as raising existing ones, and it must be remembered that it was the imposition of three new levies which helped to provoke the Breton revolt of 1675.[29]

The attempt to improve the existing fiscal system absorbed most of the energy which Colbert could expend on his financial portfolio, for he had many further responsibilities in other fields of government. Very little time was left for any long-term reform of the finances, and his few initiatives in this direction were largely unsuccessful. Although the irregularities and inconsistencies which necessitated these changes had been brought to his attention by *intendants* and other officials throughout the 1660s, it was not until the end of the Dutch War in 1679 that the minister began to prepare the way for greater rationalization of the fiscal structure. It was not simply the death of Colbert in 1683 which brought these plans to an inconclusive halt, because he had already realized that there were immense obstacles to be surmounted before they could be implemented. His successors therefore lacked not the will but the means to continue this policy.

A major problem was that the boundaries of the various tax districts did not coincide. As the *intendant* of Tours reported in 1667, there were sixty-four parishes in the *élection* of Laval, all of whom paid their *taille* to the bureau in that town. Yet only twenty-nine of them also paid the salt tax at Laval. The others had to make a separate journey – twenty-six to La Gravelle, seven to Château-Gontier, one to Craon and one to

---

[29]See Clément, vol. II (i), pp. 163–4, 183–4, 381; vol. II (ii), pp. 753–4, 768–9; Isambert, vol. XIX, pp. 88–90, 145–6. Colbert subsequently regretted imposing these levies and determined to abolish them – Clément, vol. II (i), pp. 125–7.

Mayenne. As the rate of the salt tax might vary from one bureau to another, it meant that some villagers were more heavily burdened than others, and also had to journey to two different collection centres instead of only to Laval. In many areas the fiscal offices were not located in the middle of their jurisdiction, so that some taxpayers had to travel a considerable distance although they lived much nearer to the bureau of the adjacent tax region. Such confusion caused added expenditure for taxpayers and collectors, as revenues and salt had to be transported over longer distances. Also, if it proved necessary to arrest a reluctant contributor, it cost only twenty-five *sous* if the parish were nearby but as much as six *livres* if it were much more distant. Yet it was not until July 1679 that Colbert wrote to every *intendant*, telling him to embark upon the first stage in the rationalization of these boundaries. This involved his compiling of a map, showing every parish in his *généralité* and the distances between it and the various tax bureaux at which its taxes were paid. With this information, the king could redistribute the parishes among the *élections* and establish common boundaries for the direct and indirect levies.[30]

It was quickly realized that this project was too grandiose, and that vested interests would oppose any change. Colbert therefore resigned himself to accepting the inconsistencies in the various boundaries, but at the same time tried to bring uniformity to the actual rates of the taxes. He wanted to discourage taxpayers from migrating to nearby parishes where the assessment was lower. Even this plan proved to be too ambitious, and nothing of substance was achieved. At least he gathered together all the decisions about the salt tax, which had been formulated piecemeal over the years, and combined them into a single ordinance in May 1680, but this was a convenient way of cataloguing the variations in current practice rather than an attempt at rationalization.[31]

Another method of fiscal reform which attracted Colbert was to increase the number of taxpayers. In furtherance of that long-term goal, he granted exemption from the direct taxes to men who married when young and fathered more than ten children, all of whom had to be still alive, thereby substantially enlarging the future taxpaying population. This decision was taken in 1666, but Colbert soon realized that it led to a variety of abuses. Dead children were recorded as living, and attempts by officials to prove that a father was not, or was no longer, eligible for fiscal relief were regularly negated by the local courts. It also imposed a heavier burden on the rest of the population,

[30]See Clément, vol. II (i), p. 110; Depping, vol. III, pp. 157–60.
[31]See Clément, vol. II (i), pp.164, 169–70, 211; vol. II (ii), p. 770.

who had to pay higher taxes to compensate for the revenue lost through this concession. That situation was made worse when further fiscal exemptions were granted to Huguenots who converted to 'the true faith'.[32]

The minister also revived the tentative attempts of his predecessors to extend the fairer assessment of the *taille réelle* to the *pays d'élection*, beginning with the two provinces of Guyenne and Provence where both the *réelle* and *personnelle* forms of the tax coexisted in some confusion. He instructed the *intendant* of Guyenne to consult his confrères in neighbouring Languedoc, a rare example of concerted action by officials across the boundaries of *généralités*. In 1681, two years after this initial decision, he noted with exasperation that the local officials were managing to make these discussions as difficult as possible, and in 1682 he acknowledged that it was going to be 'almost impossible to effect a compromise between the good order and principles worthy of a legislator and the customs of Languedoc'. These reforms were therefore abandoned, like so many others.[33]

The attempt to stamp out corruption and inefficiency in the collection of revenues, if marginally successful in the peaceful 1660s, was sabotaged by the expense of the Dutch War. When peace resumed in the 1680s, the costly building of Versailles, the *réunions* policy and the persecution of the Huguenots did not permit any real respite. The outbreak of the Nine Years War in 1688 and the bad harvests of the early 1690s quickly reduced both the treasury and the population at large to the depths of poverty. Old financial expedients were revived and new ones, like the sale of municipal offices, were introduced. Yet there were plenty of wealthy men, exempt from most taxation, among the aristocratic, bureaucratic and ecclesiastical elites. It was therefore a combination of royal penury on the one hand, and a new trend in political theory which questioned the very justification of hereditary privilege on the other, which prompted ministers to formulate a novel kind of tax which would affect all but the poorest members of society, and would be assessed on the basis of wealth without regard to social status. It was an idea which had never occurred to Colbert. Thus the *capitation* of 1695 was devised, although it was presented, like most other administrative novelties, as an emergency measure which was justified only by the military needs of

[32]See Isambert, vol. XVIII, pp. 90–1; vol. XIX, p. 413; also Roger Mettam, 'Louis XIV and the persecution of the Huguenots: the role of the ministers and royal officials', in Irene Scouloudi (ed.), *Huguenots in Britain and their French background, 1550–1800* (London, 1987).

[33]See Clément, vol. II (i), pp. 106–7, 149–50, 196 note 2.

wartime. The ministers promised, and kept their word, that it would be removed once peace was signed.[34]

Many old-fashioned political historians have ignored this measure, but some administrative scholars have regarded it as a fundamental advance in French social history, the start of the debate about universal taxation which would recur throughout the eighteenth century and the first blow in a self-conscious governmental campaign to destroy privilege.[35] In fact the *capitation* merits neither the disregard of one group nor the ridiculously inflated claims of the other. The first tariff for the tax was issued in January 1695 and contained 301 titles, offices and occupations. After two supplementary lists were published in February and another one in the following January, the number had increased to 596. They were divided into 22 classes, according to the amount of the levy imposed upon them. The first class paid 2,000 *livres*, the twenty-second only one *livre*. Those in the most heavily assessed category included the dauphin, the duc d'Orléans and his son, the prince de Condé and some other princes of the blood, the two illegitimate sons of the king, the chancellor, the ministers and secretaries of state, the treasurers of the navy and the farmers general of the taxes. At 1,500 livres, in the second class, came the princes, the dukes, the marshals of France, the officers of the crown, the first president of the Paris *parlement*, the provincial governors and some senior financial officials. Almost all of those in classes three to six were officials and administrators of various sorts, and it was only with the seventh grade, at 250 *livres*, that marquesses, counts, viscounts and barons made their appearance, keeping company with many middle-ranking fiscal agents. Lesser civil and military bureaucrats and their junior staffs dominated the remaining classes, but ordinary citizens began to make an appearance. For example wholesale merchants were ranked in the eleventh class, at 100 *livres*, two grades and 40 *livres* above the mayors of lesser towns. Only in the final division, with its obligation of a single *livre*, did the simple soldier appear, together with apprentices, ordinary workers, shepherds and the humblest levels of the administration.

The institutional historians have sometimes claimed that this was a revolutionary way of classifying French society, evaluating individuals

[31]François Bluche and Jean-François Solnon (eds), *La véritable hiérarchie sociale de l'ancienne France: le tarif de la première capitation, 1695* (Geneva,1983); S. Le P. de Vauban, *Projet d'une dixme royale qui supprimant la taille . . .*, *produiroit au roy un revenu certain et suffisant . . .*; P. Le P. de Boisguillebert, 'Le factum de la France', ch. 13, in *Economistes-financiers du XVIIIe siècle*, ed. E. Daire (Paris, 1843).

[35]See Roland Mousnier, *The institutions of France under the absolute monarchy, 1589–1789*, tr. Brian Pearce (2 vols, Paris, 1974–9), vol. I, *Society and the state*, pp.148, 167–8.

according to wealth or usefulness and therefore striking a savage blow against the hierarchy of rank, but the Frenchmen of the time, always so sensitive to any social pretensions or to signs of rapid mobility, did not seem to regard it as such. There were murmurs of annoyance, particularly in 1713 during the arguments about *Unigenitus*, that the wealthy bishops had managed to obtain exemption, but the *nobles d'épée* seem to have been pleased at the heavy burden placed on senior *noblesse de robe*, rather than affronted at their own inclusion in only the seventh class. It was possible to argue that such a low position on the table of obligation was a tribute to their birth and lineage, because some of them were wealthy enough to have afforded a much higher level of contribution. A number of social groups seem to have welcomed the *capitation*, because it was being rumoured that this new duty would soon replace the confused mass of direct and indirect levies which were always erratic and frequently crippling. That is not to say, of course, that everyone paid the full sum required of him in these wartime years of hardship, but an interesting fiscal experiment had been undertaken. During the subsequent war a further tax, the *dixième*, would be tried, although that too was never paid at the required rate. Many Frenchmen were simply too impoverished to find such sums, and it was a time of mounting hostility to the king and resentment of the prolonged misery which his international belligerence had inflicted on his subjects. The ministers toyed with other financial initiatives, including the introduction of some kind of paper currency, which would reduce dependence on frequently scarce supplies of precious metals, but these years of dearth and of unstable royal finances were not the time to inspire confidence in pieces of paper of whose worth the government was the guarantor. It would be left to the ministers of Louis XV, in a lengthy period of international peace, to build on these ideas for major financial reform.[36]

Recent historians of France are generally agreed that the ministers of the later reign of Louis XIV were much abler than has been allowed hitherto. Unlike the more traditional Colbert, they formulated some daring ideas for lasting reform, and it was the disastrous economic situation during the Nine Years War and the War of the Spanish Succession which sabotaged their efforts. Nothing testifies more dramatically to royal impoverishment than the decision of Louis XIV to sell off, or melt down, some of the treasures at Versailles, those trappings of monarchy which were essential in this ostentatious age where social display was a tangible sign of rank. The king was

---

[36]On the financial crisis of the later reign of Louis XIV and the first measures subsequently taken by the regent, see Daniel Dessert, *Argent, pouvoir et société au grand siècle* (Paris, 1984).

Bad was had destroyed France

profoundly distressed at the endless litany of woes and poverty which poured in from the *intendants*, office-holders, nobles and even the poor themselves, who petitioned their sovereign for bread. It was said that starving children were resorting to cannibalism, even in the forests around Versailles, and a host of seditious libels, pamphlets and popular songs placed the blame on one man, the king who had ruled for as long as anyone could remember. In his last years the majority of his subjects devoutly wished for his death, and those in high places paid increasing attention to the men who were likely to dominate the next reign.

COMMERCE, INDUSTRY AND THE NAVY

Nowhere has the hyperbole of absolutist historians reached greater heights than in their assessment of both the aims and the successes of Colbert in the field of economic policy. Moreover, this was the aspect of government in which it was most difficult for the minister to arouse the enthusiasm of even some groups in society. Far from being able to play off one faction against another, he found that many of his initiatives in trade and industry were greeted with stony hostility throughout the kingdom. Louis XIV himself showed no interest in these lowly pursuits, and neither did most of his courtiers. The fact that nobles had always been forbidden by law to indulge in such activities was an indication of the gulf between the social elites and the bourgeois world of economics, and there was no general aristocratic pressure for the removal of this prohibition. Office-holders took great care to 'live nobly', stressing the length of time since their ancestors had left the middle levels of society, while many members of the bourgeoisie eagerly awaited their own opportunity to ascend into the higher stratum of the bureaucracy. Even those merchants and craftsmen who were still engaged in commerce or trade regarded Colbertian interference with undisguised hostility. Not only was the government imposing arbitrary regulations upon them, but its policies assumed the desirability of considering France to be an economic unit. This *dirigiste*, centralizing and 'nationalist' approach to economic matters seemed to threaten many provincial liberties and profitable local tariffs, while at the same time jeopardizing the close trading relations which some provinces had long enjoyed with other countries.

Colbert was never as doctrinaire in his theories as both his admirers and detractors have often claimed. Although he subscribed to some of the principles which would later be included among the tenets of 'mercantilism', he would not have seen his own theories as an economic system in the sense implied by that term. He had preferences and he was undoubtedly attracted by the new rationalist philosophy, which reinforced his conviction that internal tolls and customs were harmful to the prosperity of the kingdom. Yet he knew that provincialism was deeply rooted, and that much persuasion would be needed before merchants would change their trading habits and craftsmen would establish new industries. He often reiterated to his closest agents that, while it was sometimes possible physically to interrupt patterns of commerce, by naval blockades or other means, it was impossible to force men to invest money in alternative enterprises if they were not convinced of their profitability.[37] Unfortunately for Colbert, very few were attracted to his new schemes, no matter how much propaganda was produced in favour of them.

It has already been noted that Colbert was chiefly concerned with the economic aspects of the kingly areas of government – that is to say with the military industries and with any matter which had international implications. One of his fundamental assumptions was that every state should play a role in world trade proportionate to its geographical area and its own native resources. It was therefore vital for France to acquire a large share of the new overseas territories and the wealth which could be obtained from them, and yet she was far behind in the race for the colonies. She should also possess a strong navy and a substantial merchant marine, for it was intolerable that so much French trade was dependent on Dutch ships. It had long been believed by economic theorists that France was potentially self-sufficient, and another priority was therefore to develop indigenous natural resources in order to minimize the need to import them. The export of manufactured goods should be encouraged, because they could be exchanged for much needed gold and silver, but anything which caused those precious metals to leave the country should be firmly discouraged. The purchasers of foreign luxury goods were the chief offenders against this dictum, and it was essential to stimulate the production of these manufactures within the realm, because it was evident that the aristocracy would never abandon its passion for obtaining them. If foreigners had to be enticed into France, because only they had the skills needed to produce these commodities, then that was a small price to pay. At least it would prevent the exodus of the gold and silver. Few of these ideas were original. They had been voiced by theorists at the beginning of the century, and all the ministers of the Bourbon kings had made some attempt to implement them. They had been defeated by a combination of French inertia and international conflict.

[37]See Clément, vol. II (ii), pp. 632, 645–6, 787–9; Depping, vol. III, pp. 489, 532–3.

As in other areas of the administration, Colbert again tried to put these policies into practice within the traditional social system. He did not initiate any fundamental reforms of the kind which would be envisaged by the ministers of the 1690s and early 1700s. Once again the historian is struck by the conservatism of Colbert and the adventurousness of his successors, both in the last twenty years of Louis XIV and under the regency for Louis XV. During those periods the novelty of the *capitation* and the *dixième* would be paralleled by new plans for more sophisticated methods of international credit which would reduce the slavish dependence on precious metals. There would also be a reaction against the *dirigisme* of Colbert, which was thought to have been a major cause of the Dutch War, and a powerful lobby in favour of free trade would emerge. Even so, it did not find favour with the wealthiest section of the nation, the nobility, which continued to dismiss the commercial and industrial world as bourgeois and base.

Many of the economic policies which Colbert considered to be essential preliminaries for any revival of French prosperity were thwarted from the outset by influential vested interests. He changed the law so that overseas and wholesale commerce were no longer incompatible with *noblesse*, but that did not encourage many nobles to enter trade. There had always been a few aristocrats who had invested some of their wealth in such enterprises, often using middlemen as a shield, but most of these were very rich and belonged to the circle of provincial governors and favoured courtiers close to the king.[38] Some of them may have supported these ministerial schemes merely in the hope of further patronage, but many were genuinely sympathetic to the economic aims of Colbert. They were therefore very untypical of the wider nobility, which felt that no amount of royal legislation could free commerce from its social stigma. Moreover, most nobles could barely sustain the lavish style of life which their rank demanded of them, and had no funds to spare. Landed estates and hereditary offices were investments which also brought added social status, and no member of the *épée* or the *robe* was eager to sell these family assets in order to obtain capital for reinvestment in the often precarious world of trade.

The minister had no greater success in implementing his plans for a single scale of weights and measures which would be effective

[38]See: BN, Mél. Colb., vol. 133, fols 86–7; Clément, vol. II (ii), p. 660; Depping, vol. III, pp. 365–70; François Véron de Forbonnais, *Recherches et considérations sur les finances de France depuis l'année 1595 jusqu'à l'année 1721* (2 vols, Basel, 1758), vol. I, pp. 436–7; Jacques Savary, *La parfait négociant* (1675), chapter 42; R. B. Grassby, 'Social status and commercial enterprise under Louis XIV', *Economic History Review*, xiii, 1960–1, pp. 19–38.

throughout the realm. Provincial merchants did not want to change over to this new system, because it would confuse their existing trading partners. One hundred *livres* on the Parisian scale of weights was equivalent to 123½ *livres* in Marseille and 120½ in Avignon, Toulouse and Montpellier, but Provence, Languedoc and the papal state of Avignon had few commercial contacts with the capital, not least because a series of tolls were levied on the road and river routes passing up the Rhône. The Mediterranean merchants who traded with these southern towns were not involved with Parisian commerce either, and so there was no incentive to accept the Colbertian plan for rationalization. Other peripheral provinces in the east, north and west of the kingdom similarly ignored these governmental directives, and no reform was achieved.[39]

Even less enthusiasm greeted the attempt by the minister to abolish internal customs dues and impose a single tariff area which coincided with the frontiers of the kingdom. In 1661, when Louis XIV assumed personal power, France was still divided into a number of customs areas. Most of the northern provinces were within the *cinq grosses fermes*, within which internal dues had been abolished, but there were heavy duties on goods passing into and out of these territories. Some of the trading cities in the seaward provinces therefore encountered no such barriers when they traded with the outside world but were heavily penalized if they sent commodities to their own capital city of Paris. The initial tariff reform of 1664 recognized this situation, and tried only to simplify the levies imposed on merchandise entering or leaving the *cinq grosses fermes*. The measure was reasonably effective because it had the support of the merchants involved in this trade. Under the new regulations, they now paid a single duty on each item, instead of the numerous small sums which had been levied in the past and varied according to the point of entry into the *fermes*. In contrast vigorous hostility greeted the tariff of 1667, which was designed to establish customs dues at all points of entry into and exit from the entire realm. Unfortunately, Colbert had not been able to abolish the internal customs barriers between provinces and between the *cinq grosses fermes* and the rest of France. The merchants of the seaward provinces therefore found that a novel imposition was placed upon their international commerce but that no reduction in tolls and duties on landward routes had been effected. As always, the crown found it difficult to persuade local officials to enforce these new regulations, which did not seem to be in the best interests of their area, and even in wartime, when Colbert tried to blockade defiant ports, the fleet was

[39]See Savary, *Le parfait négociant*, chapters 9 and 11; also Mettam, *Government and society*, p. 201.

too small both to keep effective guard at harbour mouths and to play its full naval role in the maritime wars which necessitated a presence in many southern, western and northern seas. The prohibition on trade with the Dutch during the war of 1672–9 was a major cause of bourgeois disaffection during the Breton revolt in 1675, and even the loyal governor of the region around Boulogne, the duc d'Aumont, pleaded with Colbert in the second year of the war to allow the traders of that coast to continue their commerce with the hostile Spanish Netherlands. He was already in a position to state that the authorities in Brussels would be favourable to such a scheme, if the French king would agree. Louis and Colbert were not prepared to condone such a seemingly treacherous plan. Eventually, the 1667 tariff was removed as a condition of the 1679 Peace of Nijmegen, but the very next year Colbert was still saying privately that its re-establishment was vital to French prosperity. Nevertheless, the international traders proved as effective in resisting the revival of this initiative as a variety of provincial elites had been in preventing him from abolishing the local customs dues from which they derived considerable revenue.[40]

If wars necessitated the suspension of trade between the French and their present enemies, they also caused major problems on the commercial routes which it was still desirable to keep open – those to friendly powers and to the French colonies. Again Colbert encountered the hostility of merchants to his proposals. He tried to persuade them that it was advisable for their ships to travel in convoy, protected by naval vessels, but most ship owners preferred to take their chance. The best profits from the hazardous voyages to other continents were obtained by individual enterprise rather than by state organization. Higher prices could be charged when a merchantman arrived unexpectedly in a French port, bearing a cargo which was much in demand. To return home in a convoy, with rival vessels carrying identical commodities, was to lose the rarity value of these exotic luxuries, and merchants had to reduce their prices in order to undersell their competitors.[41]

[10]See Clément, vol. II (i), p. 139; vol. II (ii), pp. 486, 787–93; Depping, vol. III, pp. 549–50; Isambert, vol. XIX, pp. 242, 251. For provincial fears about the effect of the Dutch War on commerce, see BN, Mél. Colb., vol. 157, fol. 256; vol. 160, fols 1004–9; vol. 161, fols 64–5; vol. 166, fols 163–4; vol. 168bis, fols 446–7, 519, 560, 564–7, 569, 575; vol. 169, fol. 301; A. Hamy, *Essai sur les ducs d'Aumont, gouverneurs du Boulonnais 1622–1789; Guerre dite de Lustucru, 1662; documents inédits* (Boulogne-sur-mer 1906–7), pp. 48, 101, 104–5.

[11]See BN, Mél. Colb., vol. 159, fols 231–3; vol. 161, fols 329–30, 343–4, 365–6, 460; vol.163, fol. 330; Clément, vol. II (ii), pp. 482–3, 646–7, 652–3, 726; Depping, vol. III pp. 599–600; but Louis XIV and Colbert did not like private protectors of shipping – Clément, vol. II (ii), pp. 683–4.

Most other aspects of government intervention in the colonial trade received equally cool responses, both from the mercantile community and from the ranks of potential investors. Once again these policies were not new, but Colbert had no more success in implementing them than Richelieu and Sully before him. The crown put every kind of pressure upon the wealthy elements in society, as it attempted to create effective colonial companies with a monopoly on each group of trade routes. If the merchants themselves disliked such regulation and were often sceptical about developing some of these routes on any basis, the office-holders were even more reluctant to become involved because commerce was a socially demeaning business for men of their elite status. They therefore did everything in their power to resist the pleas of the king that they should invest heavily in these organizations. Louis always presented his case carefully, as with his attempt to raise money for the East India Company in 1664. He stated then that this new exercise was not primarily a commercial one, but that it was an opportunity for every Frenchman to gain merit in the eyes of God because its chief aim was to bring the Gospel to the pagans of distant lands. Moreover, he was able to list an impressive array of princes, persons of quality and senior office-holders who had already given both willingly and generously to this divine mission. Some courtiers, mindful of the need to remain in favour if they were to obtain further royal patronage, had deemed it wise to contribute, and many of the provincial governors were strongly supportive of the whole scheme, as they were of other commercial and industrial suggestions by Colbert. The Paris office-holders had been less enthusiastic, but some had been put in an impossible position. For example, the chancellor had personally confronted the *conseil de la grande direction*, one of the financial commissions of the council, announcing first the devotion of the king to the East India Company and then his own contribution of 40,000 *livres*. The duc de Villeroy quickly did the same, and the royal appointees on the *conseil* hastened to follow suit. Then the subscription list was offered to the other members, who were totally taken aback. One refused at first, but when the chancellor whispered something in his ear he changed his mind, although he was still muttering to himself as he signed. All the others then committed themselves to a variety of small sums, although a man who offered 1,000 *livres* was so ridiculed by Colbert that he trebled his initial contribution.[42]

As always, the personal influence of the king and his ministers was much more impressive at the royal court than in the provinces, and the provincial office-holders had time to plan an obstructive strategy when

[12]See Clément, vol. II (ii), pp. 428–9; Isambert, vol. XVIII, pp. 38–9; d'Ormesson, *Journal*, August 1664.

they received this account of the enthusiasm shown by the central government and the court for the company. Some *officiers* made a financial commitment and then defaulted on paying the greater part of it. Others saw a splendid opportunity for obtaining new privileges from the crown, in return for their co-operation. Some law courts sent in a list of their members who had invested as soon as they received the royal request, adding an apology that very few names appeared on it because some posts were vacant, and the occupants of others were either away on business or were simply too poor to make a contribution. They promised to continue their efforts to raise more money, but they did not try very hard. Although Colbert exhorted them to do more, he had no way of compelling them to give more generously. Behind the scenes, governors and other ministerial confidants used all their powers of patronage and influence to rally the local elites to the royal cause, frequently offering privileges as an incentive. Camille de Villeroy, the archbishop of Lyon, persuaded the merchants of his diocese to give 1,000,000 *livres*, but they agreed only on condition that one of the regional chambers of the East India Company should be established in their city, as a tribute to its economic status in the realm. Once this proviso had been accepted by Colbert, the investors and the government honoured their respective commitments, so that the money was paid and the chamber was created. Encouraged by this success, the merchants tried the same tactics when Colbert asked them to invest in the Levant Company some years later. This time they demanded a total monopoly of the trade for their city. The minister refused to entertain such a sweeping demand and the Lyonnais accordingly declined to invest.[43]

The companies were not mourned when they faded away. They had been inefficiently administered, had failed to pay adequate dividends to their investors, had been unable to prevent merchants from trading independently of their monopoly and had found that some of their routes simply could not be made profitable. The crown did not openly acknowledge defeat. Indeed the edict which disbanded the West India Company in 1674, ten years after its foundation, claimed that the company was no longer necessary because it had been so successful in opening up both those colonies and the trade between them and the motherland. Nothing could have been further from the truth.

[13]See BN, Mél. Colb., vol. 119, fol. 73; vol. 124, fols 534, 550; vol. 125, fol. 752; vol. 126, fols 230, 651; vol. 127, fols 511, 584; vol. 127bis, fols 586–7, 767–8, 1091–3; vol. 128, fols 194, 358, 487; vol. 128bis, fols 779–82; vol. 131bis, fol. 1160; vol. 132bis, fols 466, 755, 772; vol. 149, fol. 308; Clément, vol. II (ii), pp. 439, 507–8; Depping, vol. III, pp. 354–5, 358–66, 370–3, 382–6, 520–1, 636–7.

Provision was made for the reimbursement of investors but, given the shortage of funds in the treasury during the Dutch War, it is to be wondered whether this pledge was honoured in full or even in part. At all levels the colonial trade had been unpopular, and often riddled with corruption. Perhaps the most unsavoury aspect for Colbert was that his cherished navy, far from confining itself to its task of patrolling the colonial seas, began to carry cargoes of merchandise back to France, thus violating the monopoly of the companies.[44]

By the outbreak of the Dutch War in 1672, Colbert had realized that, in commerce as in justice, major innovations were impossible, and he must concentrate on stamping out abuses within the existing and traditional system. That therefore was the prime concern of the Commercial Ordinance which he published a year later. It sought to prescribe better training for apprentices; stricter tests, covering all aspects of trade and finance, for merchants who were applying to be admitted as masters; rigid rules for scrutinizing the accounts of merchants and bankers; more thorough procedures for investigating insolvency and thereby exposing fraudulent bankrupts; and a detailed delineation of the jurisdictional powers enjoyed by the commercial courts. Honest merchants welcomed many of these rules, and in particular those concerning the special courts, which gave them rapid justice and allowed them to go on their way. In contrast, many local officials strongly disliked these tribunals, and there were many less honourable members of the commercial world who did not welcome the tightening of mercantile practices either. This ordinance, like the Civil Ordinance of 1667, was prefaced by a wide-ranging preamble, but in both documents the contents were less ambitious and confined largely to procedural matters. Moreover they shared the same fate of being extensively disregarded by the provincial bureaucrats.[45]

Seeing that he was unlikely to effect any major changes in bourgeois, noble and bureaucratic attitudes to commerce, Colbert resigned himself to concentrating on small-scale incentives rather than on major schemes. In the early years of the personal rule, he had assured merchants that they would be received at court with the greatest goodwill and would be given a fitting lodging in the royal apartments, although very few of them subsequently accepted his offer. The minister realized that a better plan was to help them to rise in their own local hierarchies. He sought to persuade towns that there should be a mercantile presence on the municipal council, and in some

[11]See Clément, vol. II (ii), pp. 482–3, 601–2; Depping, vol. III, p. 374; Isambert, vol. XIX, pp. 152–4; S. L. Mims, *Colbert's West India policy* (New Haven, 1912).
[15]See Isambert, vol. XIX, pp. 92–107.

instances this did come about, although in most places the office-holding urban elite had a monopoly of such posts. In Amiens the opposite extreme obtained, and a merchant oligarchy controlled the entire council, exercising an economic tyranny over the craftsmen who were forced to sell their wares to them alone and at ridiculously low prices. The traders of Marseille were even more unwilling to co-operate with Colbert in increasing the prosperity of the kingdom. They not only used every device to discourage foreign merchants but also, as the *intendant* of the galleys reported, spent their time seeking orders of chivalry and swaggering along the quays with swords and pistols at their side. Worse still, they flouted the bullionist principles of the minister by paying for their Levantine imports in precious metals instead of identifying French goods which could be exported in exchange. In some cities the king had granted the privileges of full citizenship to anyone who owned a ship of a certain tonnage, as part of a plan to increase French shipping and reduce dependence on the Dutch. This concession was also difficult to police, and it became common practice to obtain a vessel for the time required to ascend into the citizenry and then sell it, perhaps to someone else who had the same intention.[46]

One final aspect of commercial policy at which Colbert laboured for many years was the improvement of routes, in order to speed trade. Better roads with fewer highwaymen, more navigable rivers and safer harbours were essential preliminaries for greater prosperity. Most audacious of all was the plan to link the Mediterranean and the Bay of Biscay by a new waterway, the 'canal des deux mers'. The principal problem was how to finance such enterprises, because the crown had many demands on its purse in peacetime and even more during periods of war. Also Colbert was always insistent that the king should not be expected to pay for major public works in the *pays d'états*. As he said in a letter of 1670, 'there is nothing more universally accepted in this kingdom than that public works are carried out at the King's expense throughout those provinces where His Majesty has the right to impose whatever levy seems fitting to him; but with regard to those provinces which have Estates, public works are at their expense, and the King never interferes save to see that they are well and thoroughly carried out'. The proposed canal passed through *pays d'états* and *pays d'élections*, and so Colbert was prepared to contribute to the part of the project which was within Guyenne and largely involved the improvement of existing waterways. The really difficult and novel part of the

[16]See Clément, vol. II (ii), pp. 645–6, 673, 679–80, 695, 697–8, 711–12, 778–9; Depping, vol. I, pp. 788–9, 866; vol. III, pp. 615–16, 839–40.

canal lay entirely in the jurisdiction of the Languedoc Estates, and it was therefore their responsibility to provide funds.[47]

In fact neither Paris nor the Estates financed the entire enterprise because with this, as with other road and water routes, the normal practice was to find an entrepreneur who would be willing to mastermind the construction process, supplement provincial and government funds by borrowing on the money-markets and use some of his own wealth as well. Then, when the scheme was completed, he would be given the right to impose a toll on the new route as a means of recouping his investment. It was beyond the administrative resources of either crown or province to organize such large-scale public works through their own officials, but this use of enterprising individuals clearly ran counter to another Colbertian policy. Whereas the minister was generally concerned to reduce tolls because they restricted trade, he now had to authorize new ones as the only way of paying for expensive engineering projects. Pierre-Paul Riquet presented his detailed plan for the canal in 1662, and its construction was authorized in 1666. The completion was due in eight years, but it was not until 1681 that the whole waterway, with its sixty-five locks, was finally opened. It had cost about 17,000,000 *livres*, of which 7,500,000 had come from the crown and a little less than 6,000,000 from the Estates of Languedoc. Eventually that province would admit that its trade had benefited, but at the time when the canal was under construction the Estates were less convinced and used every ruse to delay payment of their contribution. In fact the government had subsidized them in this enterprise, because it decided to waive part of the tax burden which had been agreed by both crown and Estates, if the deputies would authorize larger sums for Monsieur Riquet. When the canal was finally completed, both Colbert and Louis XIV acknowledged it as perhaps the greatest achievement of the reign, and yet it was not they who had formulated the original idea. The proposer of the project had been the archbishop of Toulouse, who had forceseen the benefits at a time when his diocese could not conceive of them. It was he who found Riquet and introduced him to the minister, and throughout the construction he was a principal propagandist in the financial debates of the Estates. When the most difficult section was completed, he made a triumphant progress through the locks by boat, in order to stimulate the enthusiasm of the people for the last expensive stages.

Other canals were begun or completed, but none was so spectacular.

[17]Clément, vol. IV, pp. 81–2, 451; Depping, vol. I, pp. 289–93; vol. IV, pp. 27–8, 63–4.

Perhaps inspired by the success of Riquet, the entrepreneur who offered his services in order to construct a waterway from the Loire to a tributary of the Seine was none other than the brother of the king, the duc d'Orléans, and the canal was duly named after him. In considering overland routes, Colbert had to balance the need of the government for speedy contact between the centre and the provinces, against the benefits which would result for commerce. The administrative and commercial road networks were very different, and the minister was always more eager to develop the latter. He also received numerous requests from Louvois for the building and repair of highways which would improve the postal services and facilitate the deployment of troops. Once again Colbert insisted that the *pays d'états* should finance their own roadworks, although they often disagreed with him about which routes should have priority. Even in the *pays d'élections*, he told the *intendants* to make clear to the municipalities that the crown would undertake only major bridge and road schemes, and that routine repairs were to devolve upon them – a burden which they were frequently very tardy in shouldering. In the countryside there was an obligation on the peasantry to spend a number of days per year working without wages on the maintenance of roads, but this labour service was often difficult to enforce. When it was replaced by a financial levy, that proved to be no easier to collect. The king also authorized additional taxes for the specific purpose of road and river works, but although these were often collected, the local officials diverted the funds to other projects. In 1664 Colbert was irritated to learn that the *robinage* tax in Narbonne, which was designed to maintain the *robine*, or channel, connecting that city to the sea, was being spent by the municipal council 'according to their pleasure', and his informant, the *lieutenant-général* of the admiralty, frankly admitted that he had no power to prevent it.[48]

If the commercial initiatives devised in the councils of the king were rarely regarded with favour by the provincial elites, the plans prepared by the governors were often more successful. Unlike the *intendants*, who tended to look at local matters from a Parisian viewpoint, the governors combined an understanding of governmental priorities with a pragmatic assessment of feelings within their province. Although they were great aristocrats, who might have been prepared to disdain commerce and industry, they in fact studied these economic matters in great detail. Chaulnes in Brittany, Noailles in Languedoc, Bourbon in Burgundy, d'Aumont in the Boulonnais and Villeroy in Lyon all examined their *gouvernements* with painstaking care and sent letters and

[18]Clément, vol. IV, pp. 471–2, 478–9, 518–9, 539; Depping, vol. III, pp. 345–6; vol. IV, pp. 65–6.

[handwritten margin notes: Size of France needed more Provincial Intervention]

extended memoirs, often in their own hand, to Colbert, suggesting ways in which trade could be extended, new manufactures introduced and commercial barriers reduced. Many of these proposals were different from those of Colbert, because the province and the government did not share the same conception of economic expansion, but they did go some way towards the goals of the minister. Thus, whereas he found that his own attempts to reduce tolls were often thwarted by vested interest groups which both profited from them and resented government interference, the duc de Noailles and the archbishop of Lyon were able to abolish many such levies on the Rhône because the merchants of Languedoc and the Lyonnais favoured this course of action, and because a wave of popular unrest against these tolls frightened their collectors into acquiescence. Similarly many Estates, officials and town councils did maintain the roads, bridges and river routes which seemed important to them, even though these were often not the ones which Colbert regarded as vital.[49] Once more therefore the power of the crown to coerce its subjects against their will was minimal, but there was some opportunity for co-operation. Nevertheless, this meant that the most grandiose economic schemes of Colbert were doomed to failure from the beginning. After his death in 1683, French commerce and industry entered upon a stagnant period, affected by the Huguenot persecution and soon crippled by the Nine Years War. When international commerce did revive after the 1697 Peace of Rijswijk, it was through the spontaneous enterprise of the merchants. By then, reformers were condemning *dirigisme* and advocating free trade, and, whether because of their theories or of unsuccessful attempts at intervention in the past, the government did not seek to co-ordinate this expansion from the centre. Colbertism was a thing of the past.

The one aspect of international commerce for which the crown claimed total responsibility was the protection of merchant shipping by the navy. Although merchants did not like organized convoys, there

[49]BN, Mél. Colb., vol. 109, fols 938–9; vol. 109bis, fols 1014–15; vol. 110, fols 220, 286, 379, 495–6; vol. 111, fols 46, 264; vol. 112, fol. 538; vol. 116bis, fols 827–8, 1037; vol. 117, fol.188; vol. 118, fol. 135; vol. 119, fol. 571; vol. 125, fols 675–6; vol. 126, fol. 230; vol. 127, fols 74–7, 172, 174–5, 511, 576; vol. 127bis, fols 841, 1084; vol. 128, fol. 348; vol. 132bis, fol. 772; vol. 133, fols 92–3, 232–3, 449–51, 638–9; vol. 146, fols 29, 359–60, 406–7; vol. 147, fols 196, 198–9; vol. 148bis, fols 641–2; vol. 149, fol. 252; vol. 150bis, fols 789–93; vol.155, fols 454, 486, 492, 508; vol. 156, fol. 180; vol. 157, fols 1–3, 296–9, 331–5, 374–6; vol. 161, fols 135–8, 318–22; vol. 162, fol. 89; vol. 171, fols 323–5; Clément, vol. II (ii), pp. 623, 660; Depping, vol. III, pp. 365–70; abbé Millot, *Mémoires politiques et militaires . . . composés sur les pièces originales recueillies par Adrien-Maurice, duc de Noailles, maréchal de France & ministre d'état* (6 vols, Lausanne/Yverdon, 1778), vol. I, pp. 26–30, 55, 67–8.

were plenty of other commercial duties for the fleet to perform. In wartime there were the rival maritime nations to combat, and even in peacetime the problem of piracy was ever present. It is well known that Colbert encouraged the designing of better ships and the invention of more dangerous weapons. He also advocated the incarceration of convicted criminals in the galleys, where they were more useful than when languishing in prison. Yet much mercantile tonnage fell prey to pirates and maritime enemies, and the aggressive naval tactics of the French fleet provoked countermeasures. The Mediterranean pirates even began to hunt in large groups, more effectively to resist the sea power of Louis XIV. In the wars of the later reign, some of these corsairs were actually encouraged to fight for France, although they remained most unreliable allies who would seize any opportunity for profit.[50]

Although concessions were offered to shipbuilders who constructed commercial vessels, and warships were taking shape in the various royal dockyards, it was far from easy to find native Frenchmen willing to serve below decks. Nevertheless, the royal navy was a respectable career for an aristocrat, and so it was less difficult to recruit officers than seaman. Moreover, the officer class remained a virtually noble monopoly, despite the sneers of Saint-Simon that men were promoted from the ranks. Unheard of in the army, there were some examples of such mobility in the fleet, but they remained very few indeed. Training schools were set up, and many officers became well versed in the nautical skills and sciences. In contrast, the ordinary sailors were often men of undesirable character and were unwilling conscripts. An elaborate system of conscription was instituted, but evasion was widespread, despite the attempts of Colbert to ensure that recruits were well treated and adequately paid. As in the army, vagabonds and prisoners were therefore drafted into service, and many foreign slaves were purchased for the galleys. Although Colbert and Louvois were equally passionate about their respective armed services, there is no doubt that the marine was low on the royal list of priorities. It took Colbert nineteen years to persuade the king to visit a naval port, but when he finally did so he was enthralled by what he saw. In the later reign, when the French fleet had some successes in wars which had an increasingly large maritime element, it seems that Louis did acquire a greater interest in this aspect of his power.[51]

[50]See: Paul W. Bamford, *Fighting ships and prisons: the Mediterranean galleys of France in the age of Louis XIV* (Minneapolis, 1973); Geoffrey W. Symcox, *The crisis of French sea power, 1688–1697: from the guerre d'escadre to the guerre de course* (The Hague, 1974).

[51]Eugène L. Asher, *The resistance to the maritime classes: the survival of feudalism in the France of Colbert* (Berkeley/Los Angeles, 1960).

The most serious obstacle to the economic policies of Colbert was the inability of France to defeat the economic power of the Dutch, either by tariffs or by war. As long as that nation survived, the French would use its ships in preference to building their own, and his plans for a self-sufficient kingdom would be retarded. He was rather more successful in the field of manufactures where, although he could not persuade many Frenchmen to start new industries, he was at least able to lure foreign craftsmen into the kingdom so that their products no longer had to be imported. French envoys resident abroad, special emissaries and trusted merchants were all instructed to seek out mining engineers, designers of armaments and makers of luxury goods in Sweden, Bohemia, Italy, the Dutch Republic, the Spanish Netherlands and other likely locations, offering privileges and promising royal favour to any who would enter the service of Louis XIV. Those who undertook this task of recruitment were also generously rewarded when their efforts produced results. A sizable number of immigrants was gathered together, but many of them did not remain in their new country for any length of time. Some were lured elsewhere by rival rulers who offered greater incentives, others left when fellow members of their Protestant religion began to be persecuted. The armaments manufacturers, as many governors frequently reminded Colbert, were at the mercy of their only customer, the central government, and at times when the royal need of weapons declined they were threatened with bankruptcy.[52]

The fortunes of those who did decide to remain in France were also very variable. Some new crafts became well established, but the illness or death of a foreign craftsman could lead to the closure of his workshop because no one had been trained to succeed him, although on occasion it was possible to find another foreigner who would take over a flourishing business. Colbert exhorted these visitors to teach and pass on their skills to Frenchmen, but they often refused to obey him. In many towns the senior citizenry paid no attention to these immigrants, and the ordinary workers entered their service with no qualms, but in some urban centres gildsmen saw the attraction of these new enterprises and petitioned the minister to revoke the privileged status of the visitor, so that they too could take up the craft. In such cases, as Colbert saw that the manufacture would continue

[52]BN, Mél. Colb., vol. 127, fol. 333; vol. 127bis, fols 586–7; vol. 128, fol. 358; vol. 128bis, fol. 612; vol. 134, fol. 271; vol. 134bis, fol. 820; vol. 136, fols 82, 507; Clément, vol. II (ii), pp. 850–1; Depping, vol. III, pp. 369, 740–1, 751–3, 755, 757–9, 803–5; père Guichenon, *La vie d'illustrissime et reverendissime Camille de Neufville archevêque et comte de Lyon* . . . (Lyon, 1695), livre 3, pp. 248–56. Also French émigrés were to be encouraged to return – Clément, vol. II (ii), pp. 492–3.

whatever decision he made, he preferred to encourage the French petitioners, revoke the monopoly and permit local competition. The disillusioned foreigner, robbed of his royal protection, often left speedily for home. Some of these visiting craftsmen were further dismayed at the restrictions imposed by the minister on the use of luxury goods, which diminished the profits they had been led to expect by the royal agents who had lured them to France.[53]

This sumptuary legislation was not new, and it had always been partly justified in the past by citing the Christian abhorrence of waste. Colbert did not give that as a reason, but preferred the twofold argument of restricting imports and bolstering up the hierarchy of rank. Many aristocrats welcomed the second reason because, as long as the rules were enforced upon everyone, it reduced their lavish expenditure on living in high society. Only the uppermost levels of the nobility were now entitled to indulge in such prodigious display. As in all matters affecting the court and the ordering of society, the royal rules were very precise, and could be made into a vehicle for expressing signs of extra kingly favour. An ordinance of January 1665 prohibited everyone from decorating his jerkin with any braid, lace or embroidery which contained either gold or silver, but three weeks later Louis XIV issued letters patent concerning the prince de Condé, saying that 'in order to give to him some particular sign of the goodwill he feels for him and one which would distinguish His Highness from the other men around his royal person and at his court, he has permitted and permits him to wear a jerkin, blue in colour, adorned with galloons, braid, lace or embroidery of gold or silver, in the manner and fashion which will be prescribed to him by His Majesty'. Breaches of these new rules were easily discovered because, once it had been made plain that the king was determined to enforce them, nobles were quick to report and complain about infringements of them by other ambitious families. Thus both the duc de Bouillon and the duchesse de Rohan fell foul of wider aristocratic opinion for the over-elaborate gilding on their carriages.[54]

If foreign craftsmen often grew disillusioned about the treatment they received in France, many native manufacturers felt that Colbert was inconsistent in his encouragement of their own activities. They too included many Protestants, and the minister was unable to prevent the growing restraints placed upon them by the king. Nor did he always champion them in their disputes with the local elites. He would have

[53]Clément, vol. II (ii), p. 705; Depping, vol. III, pp. 696–7, 727, 790.
[51]Louis XIV, *Oeuvres*, eds P. A. Grouvelle and P. H. de Grimoard (6 vols, Paris, 1806), vol. VI, p. 375; Clément, vol. VI, pp. 54, 71–2.

wished to do so, but it was not always politic to alienate town councils and other influential groups which might be useful to the crown in various ways. As Colbert was prepared to grant those who established new crafts both manufacturing monopolies and exemptions from taxes and from the billeting of soldiers, their fellow citizens often became very jealous and petitioned the government for redress. As a result, privileges were abolished and concessions revoked on many occasions, often prompting the craftsman to close his business and perhaps to go elsewhere. Sometimes others would seize this opportunity to set up a similar workshop, but more commonly the craft was allowed to die because it was the fiscal concessions, not the economic monopoly, which had been the real cause for concern.

Apart from seeking to make France self-sufficient in armaments and in luxury goods, Colbert confined his industrial interests to the making of high quality exports which, when sold abroad, might attract payment in gold and silver. Agriculture was of little concern to him. He laboured long to encourage the raising of better horses, importing high quality bloodstock from abroad, but this enterprise was geared to the military needs of the cavalry. He also legislated, like ministers before and after him, about the trade in grain, but that was to prevent both the export of this vital commodity from the kingdom and the hoarding and price-fixing by some provinces while other areas of the kingdom experienced dearth. His prime purpose was therefore to ensure the survival of his taxpayers, and he showed no interest in better methods of producing crops and increasing yields. He also paid attention to the fishing industry, but only because it was a vital training school for sailors. His abiding concern was with the quality crafts, and here he immediately came face to face with the monopolistic gilds. Elaborate attempts were made to institute a system of royal inspectors, but it was soon clear that they could be effective only if these closed corporations were prepared to be co-operative.[55] In one respect they shared the priorities of the minister, because they were determined to maintain quality and to impose strict tests on candidates who wished to enter their closed circle. Yet they were not at one with Colbert on the desirability of expanding production. Their chief purpose was to ensure that everyone inscribed on their rolls made a good living. Expansion might lead to over-production and fluctuations in prices. In an ideal world the minister would have wished to destroy these restrictive bodies, but that was impossible. By working

[55]Louis XIV, *Oeuvres*, vol. V, pp. 74–5, 79–80; Clément, vol. II (ii), pp. 511–2, 543, 607–8, 641, 650–1, 680, 705, 728–30, 740, 832–41; vol. IV, 223–4, 273 note 1, 294 note 3; vol. VII, p. 448; Depping, vol. I, pp. 879–80; vol. III, pp. 663, 687–9, 839–41, 851–2; Isambert, vol. XVIII, pp. 63–4.

with them, he at least obtained the quality he desired, although not the quantity. His ministry therefore had the effect of strengthening the gilds, and they continued to enjoy their privileged status long after Louis XIV was dead.

As in the fields of justice and commerce, the extensive regulations promulgated by the crown were designed to banish corruption and regularize procedures, rather than to effect any drastic reform or innovation in the world of industry. The gilds, in conjunction with the royal inspectors, tried to implement many of them, but the town councils were often obstructive when an opportunity presented itself to them. The lack of commercial and industrial participation on these municipal bodies meant that the urban elites and the privileged gilds were often sworn enemies. So too the merchants resented the monopolies of the corporations of craftsmen. It became increasingly rare for major families to be in all three spheres of influence. The mercantile, industrial and administrative dynasties were all distinct, and that intensified their rivalries. Despite the commitment of many gildsmen to the high quality of their products, there were still many complaints about craftsmen who evaded the rules and gave a particular manufacture a bad reputation among its customers. The gilds themselves tried to prevent such abuses, but deception was all too easy and Colbert received many letters from aggrieved merchants who had discovered the wares they had purchased to be below standard. Not that they could be trusted any more than the craftsmen, because in both circles there were individuals who would distort the truth for their own personal advantage. Indeed a recurrent theme in the correspondence of Colbert, whether on commerce, industry, justice, finance or the navy, is that it was dangerous to trust anyone, even the *intendants*. As his economic initiatives continued to be thwarted over the years, he came to one further conclusion, which he voiced with increasing frequency – that the people of France were simply lazy and did not want to prosper.[56] For what other reason, he wondered, could Frenchmen so stubbornly resist schemes which, to him, were self-evidently beneficial. He failed to realize how irrelevant, or even positively undesirable, his *dirigisme* seemed to be in distant provincial centres, far away from the court. There the conception of an economically united France had no appeal.

The governors, who shared the priorities of the minister but understood the reluctance of their *gouvernement* to endorse them, laboured to bridge the gap. Yet they found it particularly difficult to explain away those points where different royal policies themselves

[56]For example, Clément, vol. II (ii), p. 490.

conflicted. For example Colbert, as secretary of state for manufactures, wanted to increase the production of quality wines for export, but as *contrôleur-général des finances* he had raised the indirect tax on those same products because he wished to lower direct taxation. To the provincial Frenchman there was only one explanation – the crown was prepared to use every kind of trickery in order to extract more money from him. Nevertheless, the governors never ceased both inspecting local economic activity and suggesting possible innovations, sometimes pleasantly surprised the king and Colbert. The monarch specifically mentioned his unexpected delight when he congratulated the duc de Bourbon on the skill he had shown in his detailed analysis of the industries at Auxerre. These great aristocrats told the minister many things which he did not know, as when the duc de Chaulnes informed him of the hardship afflicting the sugar refineries of Nantes, because of the heavy duties imposed on goods travelling along the Loire. Colbert, who had not known of these establishments, had assumed that the sugar had been refined abroad. Once he discovered that it had been processed with native labour, he adjusted the levies and the Nantes industry prospered. In the Boulonnais the second duc d'Aumont personally devised a plan to prospect for coal, organizing the search, guiding the process of exploiting the finds, arranging for the compensation of the landowners whose property was mined, and helping to find markets. Most remarkable of all was the work of the archbishop of Lyon, who governed the province on behalf of his brother. He has already been identified as a promoter of the colonial companies and a simplifier of tolls on the Rhône. He personally encouraged and protected foreign craftsmen, inspecting their products with care, and sent detailed reports to Paris about the performance of new weapons which he had seen with his own eyes. Yet his really distinctive contribution was to establish, with his own money and upon his own estates, a series of pilot industrial schemes which had not commended themselves to the city of Lyon. These included a new kind of steel furnace and a factory producing Bolognese organzine. They were so successful that he was soon able to persuade the Lyonnais bourgeois that these were indeed profitable ventures, and they followed his example.[57]

[57]BN, Mél. Colb., vol. 118bis, fol. 810; vol. 126, fols 230, 236–8; vol. 127, fols 74–7, 174–5, 333, 576; vol. 127bis, fols 586–7, 841, 1084; vol. 128, fols 358, 552; vol. 128bis, fol. 612; vol. 132bis, fol. 772; vol. 133, fols 92–3, 232–3, 449–51, 638–9; vol.134, fol. 271; vol. 134bis, fol. 820; vol. 136, fols 82, 507; vol. 146, fols 29, 359–60; vol. 147, fol. 196; vol. 148bis, fol. 641–2; vol. 155, fols 454, 486, 492, 508; vol. 156, fol. 180; vol. 157, fols 1–3, 296–9, 374–6; vol. 161, fols 135–8, 318–22; vol. 171, fols 323–5; Clément, vol. II (ii), p. 660; vol. IV, pp. 57–8; Depping, vol. III, pp. 365–70, 608–11; Guichenon, *La vie,*

One further aspect of the work undertaken by Colbert, in his capacity as *surintendant* of arts, buildings and manufactures, was to support the existing royal academies and to increase their number. Despite his efforts, these illustrious bodies remained adornments of the court rather than becoming, as their founders had hoped, a means of imposing throughout the entire kingdom royally approved criteria of language, literature, arts and science. They impressed foreign diplomats, but their prescriptions were disregarded in intellectual circles far from Paris.[58] The provincial learned societies and salons had their own dynamism and were disinclined to accept such alien commands.

When Louvois succeeded to the *surintendance* on the death of Colbert, he was determined to take his new responsibilities as seriously as his predecessor had done. Yet he was unable to reverse the defeats Colbert had suffered in his attempts to rationalize and expand the economic life of the kingdom, and the times were now even less propitious for the expansion of wealth. The exodus of both native and foreign Protestants after the persecution of 1680–7 had dealt a savage blow at both trade and industry, and the attempts of Louvois to lure them back to France bore little fruit. His approach to the economy was in many ways Colbertian, emphasizing the need for direction from the centre and for the granting of incentives in the form of privileges and monopolies. The local commercial and industrial elites therefore felt that nothing had changed, and that the intervention of the government in their daily life was as unwelcome as before. Nor did Louvois have greater success than Colbert in promoting the royal academies, and their intended role as national arbiters in the arts and sciences became even less appealing when the 'quarrel of the ancients and the moderns' divided the Parisian intellectual world into warring factions. It was therefore impossible to reach a consensus, even in the academies, on the principles of art, architecture, philosophy and science, let alone to impose it on distant provinces with very different cultural traditions. The only aspect of his duties as *surintendant* where Louvois could point to some positive achievements was in furthering the royal building programme at Versailles and in the capital, although before the end of

---

livre 3, pp. 248–56; Hamy, *Essai sur les ducs d'Aumont*, pp. 68–9; Daniel Haigneré, *Recueil historique de Boulonnais. . .*, (2 vols, Boulogne-sur-mer, 1897–8), p. 269; J. H. de Rosny, *Histoire du Boulonnais* (4 vols, Amiens, 1868–73), vol. IV, p. 135.

[58] Much has been written on the royal academies but it has not seemed wise to list some of the books and articles here. The best of them have regretfully been written by art historians who have displayed a scholarly knowledge of the visual arts but have set it in a context of 'absolutism' which has rendered their conclusions largely useless for the social historian.

the 1680s the demands of war would severely curtail these ambitious and expensive plans.[59]

Soon after his death in 1691, the whole notion of government interference in the economy began to be loudly challenged, and the ministers seemed to accept the fact that the provinces would not change their economic practices in order to support a nationwide ministerial plan. The crown therefore deemed it wiser to support the initiatives which the local elites were prepared to take, especially in these years of war, bad harvests, poverty and general economic depression. Political and economic theorists were also advocating the abandonment of *dirigisme* in favour of free trade, both to increase prosperity within kingdoms and to remove a major cause of international war. Some royal advisers accepted the wisdom of these proposals, just as they had welcomed the plans of those same writers for the abolition of fiscal privileges and the establishment of a universal tax. Yet they also knew that one aspect of this *laisser-faire* policy would not command general support among the elites of provincial France. They would approve the abolition of tariffs on trade between countries, but many of them would not wish to see the removal of all local tolls and duties, because they either made a substantial profit from collecting them or benefited from their restraining effect on the activities of rival economic groups.

The ministers therefore deemed it needlessly provocative to campaign for free trade within the realm, during these years of war and hardship, but they were prepared to reduce, or even remove, the restrictions on foreign commerce. Their new approach to the participation of the government in economic matters is well demonstrated by their creation of a *conseil de commerce* in 1700. This body was very different in composition and in tone from the regulatory councils and companies set up by Colbert. Many of its members were practising merchants, and it was a forum in which the crown could discuss commercial matters with the mercantile community and ask how it could best give government support to economic enterprises. The council had not been created in response to demands from the world of trade, because the merchants had not felt the need for such an institution and indeed had found that, since the 1697 Peace of Rijswijk, international trade was reviving without any stimulus from the government. Yet they soon realized that the ministers had their best interests at heart, and were no longer seeking to impose arbitrary regulations and directives upon the economic life of the realm. They therefore used the council as a means of soliciting royal help, although

---

[59]Corvisier, *Louvois* (Paris, 1983), pp. 375–404.

some groups of merchants continued to make use of other channels to the court. Whichever method they used, they found that the ministerial response was more sympathetic than it had been at any earlier stage of the personal rule of Louis XIV. When the War of the Spanish Succession brought inevitable insecurity to international sea and land routes, some mercantile groups seriously questioned the wisdom of French foreign policy, but once again they had to admit that the government was being more reasonable in its attitude to economic matters. During the Dutch War of 1672–9 it had imposed a total ban on trade with the enemy, but now, although it was not prepared to issue merchants with any general permission to maintain all their commercial activities, it did not forbid all economic links with hostile powers. Passports were issued to individuals, and a number of commodities were exempted from the wartime ban on trade. In particular, much trade with England and Scotland was allowed to continue largely uninterrupted.

Despite these important shifts in emphasis, the commercial life of the French provinces preserved many of the characteristics which have already been discussed in the context of the ministry of Colbert. There was no national tariff barrier, and peripheral regions of the kingdom were still outside the customs area of northern France. They could trade freely with the outside world, but came up against a variety of tolls and other levies if they sent goods to many other parts of the kingdom. The economic privileges of papal Avignon remained intact, so that it continued to prosper as a commercial and industrial centre, as well as being a haven where disaffected Frenchmen could escape the power of the French legal system. The gilds still preserved their authority in the towns of France, and their disputes with the corporations of merchants or with the municipal authorities went on as before. The only indication that there had once been a minister, Jean-Baptiste Colbert, who had tried to rationalize and expand the economy of the kingdom, was to be found in the wariness shown by these local elites towards every government pronouncement on economic matters. The crown seemed to have abandoned its *dirigiste* policies, but it was still not wholly to be trusted.[60]

[60]Charles Woolsey Cole, *French mercantilism, 1683–1700* (New York, 1971); Thomas J. Schaeper, *The French council of commerce, 1700–1715: a study of mercantilism after Colbert* (Columbus, Ohio, 1983).

Conclusion: Disobedience, Disorder and Dissent

After the turbulence of the Frondes, the 1660s seemed remarkably peaceful. That is generally accepted both by the old school of historians, who have explained the calm in terms of a ruthless absolute monarchy which crushed all opposition, and by more recent scholars, who have identified a sincere wish on the part of the crown and the local elites to revive more traditional and cautious methods of government. The chroniclers of absolutism, as the logic of their interpretation dictates, have also minimized the incidence of revolt and dissent during the later decades of the reign, arguing that there was no rebellious manifestation comparable with the civil wars of 1648–53. Yet a study of ministerial correspondence, local archives and the writings of social commentators quickly reveals that many people thought France to be in turmoil during the years 1690–1713, and numerous examples of disorder can be found from the very beginning of the personal rule in 1661.

The preceding chapters have considered some aspects of opposition to the royal government and to other forms of authority during the years in which Louis was his own first minister, although they have stressed that the two Frondes had resulted from a coincidence of circumstances which was not likely to be repeated. A personally ruling monarch and the lack of popular support prevented the princes from fomenting provincial rebellions after 1661, but their ability to cabal at court and to use their extensive family influence meant that the crown could not ignore their claims. The office-holders had abandoned their *frondeur* alliance and had resumed their internecine disputes, but groups of them could still obstruct royal policy and the ministers could not always play one off against another. It has also been noted at some length that new methods of opposition were devised by the administrative and social elites, so that the government could be ignored and obstructed without the need for open defiance. There were further dangerous movements within the church, where the crown felt that a popular religious radicalism was threatening the whole hier-archical structure. On all sides the ministers were experiencing resistance to their reforms, even in the early years of the personal rule when they sought only to restore efficiency and remove corruption from the traditional social and administrative structures.

Many of these jurisdictional battles either culminated in protracted law suits or were allowed to simmer for many years because neither side could successfully arraign the other. Very different, but in many ways far more dangerous, both to the king and to the local administrations, was the ever present streak of lawlessness in French society which occasionally took the form of open revolt. Even in the 1660s, when higher society seemed to be living more harmoniously, this subversive current was never far below the surface. Indeed that very spirit of co-operation between local and central bodies was sometimes a cause of the unrest, as the populace, used to being at loggerheads with the Paris ministers, suspected the officials in their area of betraying their interests by making treacherous alliances with the crown. Such an incident occurred in 1665, when more than three hundred townsmen of Bordeaux marooned the *cour des aides* in its own courthouse, bombarding the windows with stones and snowballs. The judges decided to send for the city council, being certain that their very presence would restore order, but those municipal worthies declined to come as they wanted no part in the affair.[1]

If the local judicial and police authorities could sometimes identify the leaders of such troubles, which was frequently impossible, they still found it difficult to apprehend them. Many had bands of men to protect them, and some holders of legal offices lamented to Colbert that the sergeants-at-arms simply dared not try to make an arrest. These complaints were far from uncommon in the 1660s, and when the Dutch War began, the shortage of royal and local funds gave rise to an additional problem. The law-enforcement officers, whose pay was in arrears, flatly refused to perform their duties until they received what was due to them. Thus in 1679, to take one of many examples, the executioner at Laval insisted that he would carry out a death sentence only when he had been given the fee in advance.[2]

In the countryside, there continued to be many dangers for the

[1]G. B. Depping (ed.), *Correspondance administrative sous le règne de Louis XIV*, 'Collection des documents inédits sur l'histoire de France' (4 vols, Paris, 1850–5), vol. II, pp. 144–5.
[2]Pierre Clément (ed.), *Lettres, instructions et mémoires de Colbert* (8 vols, Paris, 1861–82), vol. VI, p. 59.

resident population and the traveller. Highwaymen, groups of army deserters, bands of retainers whose activities were condoned or even encouraged by rogue landowners who were too powerful to be brought to justice – all these miscreants were familiar features of rural life. In the towns there were some officials and judges who imposed their will by hiring gangs of ruffians, but usually the disturbances were popular movements and were directed against government agents, municipal office-holders or wealthy individuals. In Bourges a mob carried off the collectors of the wine tax in 1664, but on this occasion the magistrates did risk their lives to save them, as the governor reported to Colbert. In 1670 an agent of the marine was assassinated on his way to work by the people of Bayonne, one of many such incidents.[3] Robbery was a common occurrence, and the urban militias could not stamp it out. As La Bruyère commented:

> what do I or any of his subjects care if the prince is happy and showered with glory through his own actions and those of his followers, or if my country is powerful and feared, when I, anxious and miserable, lead a life of oppression and poverty; if, protected from enemy attacks, I find myself perpetually threatened by an assassin's dagger in the streets and squares of the city, so that I am afraid of being robbed not so much in dense forests as at the corner of my own street; if town life lacks the security, order and cleanliness which would make it pleasant, and which would bring calm and prosperity to the community.[4]

In addition to this general undercurrent of violence and lawlessness, there were a number of occasions when the personal rule of Louis XIV was disturbed by full-scale revolts, some of which were very serious indeed. The initial manifestation of provincial sedition, the 'guerre de Lustucru' in the area around Boulogne, occurred during the first full calendar year after the death of Mazarin. It was caused by the determination of the crown to turn an emergency wartime tax into a small peacetime levy, despite the exemption from all direct taxation of the Boulonnais which, in return for this privilege, provided an effective militia to guard the coast. This uprising nevertheless took the government completely by surprise. It showed the king how tenaciously his subjects were prepared to defend their liberties, even when the fiscal consequences of their abrogation were minimal. The governor, the duc d'Aumont, managed to persuade the nobility to remain neutral but he could not inspire them to help in repressing the troubles. Thus the revolt was basically a peasant movement, with aristocratic connivance, although a few nobles were subsequently

---

[3]Depping, vol. I, pp. 725, 813.
[4]Jean de La Bruyère, *Oeuvres*, nouvelle édition, ed. G. Servois (3 vols, Paris, 1865–1912), *Caractères*, 'On the sovereign and the state', no. 24 (1689).

attacked by the insurgents for refusing actively to support their cause. Fortunately for the government, the neighbouring Picards and Artésiens, at all social levels, refused to aid the rebels, because they had long been jealous of the privileged fiscal status which the Boulonnais enjoyed. As it was peacetime and royal troops could easily be spared, the crown had little difficulty in suppressing these disturbances, although it decided that only a few rebel leaders should be savagely punished, to serve as an example. A royal order to send many of the lesser rebels to the galleys was only partially implemented by the authorities in the area, and the ministers, contented themselves with two reprimands, one symbolic and the other economic. The bells were taken down for a year in two villages where they had been used to sound the alarm, and in those same settlements there were to be no fairs and markets during that same period. In his *mémoires*, Louis XIV claimed that the outcome of this confrontation was a triumph for the crown, but there is no doubt that the ministers had been alarmed at the time by these unexpected events. In future they would be much more careful in their attempts to undermine cherished local rights and liberties.[5]

Two years later there was an even more worrying revolt in Guyenne. Although generations of historians have perpetuated the mistake that this was a reaction to the salt tax, it was in fact occasioned by hostility to a special Bordelais levy on wines, which was not part of the regular duties on liquor. A group of villages in the province had made earlier attacks on the collectors of this imposition but, as the *intendant* reported to Colbert, they had always been pardoned out of respect for their lord, who was that worthy soldier and provincial governor, the duc de Gramont. In 1664, after further violent incidents, the *intendant* recommended that an example should be made of them, and, as with the Boulogne revolt, it was peacetime when there were troops to spare for such an enterprise. The minister agreed, but he underestimated the support which the insurgents enjoyed in their locality. Soon the *intendant* was inundated with complaints about the brutality and lawlessness of the soldiers, but no one spoke against the rebels who continued their effective resistance to the tax-collectors.

[5]Louis XIV, *Oeuvres*, eds P. A. Grouvelle and P. H. de Grimoard (6 vols, Paris, 1806), vol. I, p. 213; A. Hamy, *Essai sur les ducs d'Aumont, gouverneurs du Boulonnais, 1622–1789; Guerre dite de Lustucru, 1662; documents inédits* (Boulogne-sur-mer, 1906–7), esp. pp. 269, 280–2, 287–90, 298–300, 318–20; J. H. de Rosny, *Histoire du Boulonnais* (4 vols, Amiens, 1868–73), pp. 65, 74. See also the role of the d'Aumont governor in the Boulonnais troubles of 1694 and 1702, Hamy, p. 135; *Mémoires du marquis de Sourches sur le règne de Louis XIV* (13 vols, Paris, 1882–93), vol. VII, pp. 282, 380; the duc de Saint-Simon, *Mémoires*, ed. A. de Boislisle (45 vols, Paris, 1879–1930), vol. II, p.140.

Although the leaders of the movement could not be caught, the royal judges passed severe sentences upon them and their principal accomplices, who included some members of the nobility, so that there would be no need to delay their punishment if ever they were apprehended in the future. Two were hanged in effigy, as a warning to all. Six weeks later some more collectors of the wine tax were killed and others wounded in an ambush, forcing the *intendant* to acknowledge that the terrain was very difficult for the troops and offered numerous vantage points and refuges to those who wished to harass them. The following summer more soldiers, armed with a warrant from the Béarn *parlement*, set out after their quarry, but all the church bells sounded, from village to village, and the whole population came out to obstruct their progress. In the same month a mass meeting of the inhabitants sent a deputation to the king, asking for the confirmation of their privileges and exemption from the wine tax. This was not granted but instead the *intendant* recommended that the whole area be pardoned, save for some ten ringleaders of the rebellion. After that, the crown seems to have resigned itself to defeat. The troops ceased their activities, and a year later the *intendant* reported that the wanted men were still looting and pillaging, although they were now ignoring the tax-collectors and venting their wrath on those few citizens who were thought to have betrayed them. At this inconclusive point, the Guyenne rebellion disappears from the historical archives.[6]

Other local insurrections of this kind occurred in a number of areas during the 1660s, all of them irritating to the crown and difficult to repress. Yet they were as nothing when compared to the major revolt which erupted in Brittany in 1675, the 'révolte du papier timbré'. It will be remembered from an earlier chapter that the 1673 Breton Estates had paid an enormous sum in order to obtain the suspension of the enquiry into seigneurial jurisdictions and the withdrawal of the edict forbidding them to discuss any royal decision which affected their own privileges.[7] Now the government introduced three more offensive measures – a ruling that all legal procedures should henceforth be transmitted upon specially designed documents, prescribing standardized forms of words for the entire kingdom and liable to a stamp duty; a levy on tobacco; and a tax payable on the compulsory hallmarking of all pewter vesels. In addition, the merchants were incensed at the wartime ban on their regular trading contacts with the Dutch Republic. When the news reached Brittany that there had been a revolt against the new edicts in Bordeaux, the

---

[6]See Depping, vol. III, pp. 68–73, 79, 84, 87–90, 114–15, 121–2.
[7]See pp. 275–6 above.

Bretons quickly followed suit. The first demonstrations took place in the city and suburbs of Rennes, and the mob included many women and children. To the fury of the governor, the *parlement* refused to condemn these happenings and, like its sister court in Bordeaux, actually stimulated them by allowing its officials 'to spread a thousand slanders against the authority of the King'. The bourgeois militia was prepared to guard the municipal buildings, lest they too become objects of hatred for the rioters, but, when the governor tried to raise further civic forces to protect the offices of the collectors who were responsible for the new taxes, the men handed back their pay as soon as they discovered what their task was to be. The disturbances continued for some weeks, and the tax-farmers angrily demanded action because they had paid for these farms and yet could not collect the money from the people. Some of them realized that it would never be possible to establish these novel levies, and therefore that their best plan was to force the crown to refund their initial investment. Accordingly, they positively encouraged the rebels, bribing them to continue their sedition. One official was finally forced to admit that he himself had fired shots during the evening in order to stimulate a riot, and had looted his own room so that he could prove how dangerous his position was.

As this sedition spread to other towns in Upper Brittany, a very different revolt was gaining ground in the west of the province. There the church bells were rallying hordes of peasants whose targets were not only the royal officials, but the noble and ecclesiastical landlords as well. They killed aristocrats or forced them to march with their ragged forces, they looted inns and they ransacked the houses of the bourgeoisie. They protested against the introduction of the salt tax into the province, which was a reaction to deliberate rumourmongering because the government had no such intention, and they subscribed to an extraordinary document, the Peasant Code, which contained some revolutionary social demands: an end to labour services; the right of male peasants to marry the daughters of nobles and by that means acquire nobility for themselves and their descendants, as well as the entitlement to the equal division among all the children of the wealth brought into the partnership by the noble mother – a demand which both flouted property laws and challenged the principle that rank was transferred only through the male line; a limit on the wine tax; the employment of the hearth tax to purchase tobacco which should be given out gratis with the consecrated bread at mass, for the pleasure of the parishioners; an end to the stamp duty; the right for the ordinary people to elect their judges from among themselves; a ban on hunting during the growing and harvest seasons; and free access to mills, with a prescription that the millers should be forced to give back in flour the same weight that they had received in corn. Anyone who violated these rules was to be declared an enemy of Armorican freedom, and serious offenders were to have their skulls broken. The document was signed by 'The Skullbreaker and the People'.

Faced with these two very different revolts, which occurred at a time when few troops could be spared from the European phase of the Dutch War, the government tried a policy which involved both compromise and an assertion of authority. It hoped that many of the peasant rebels would return to their fields when it was time to gather in the harvest, and this supposition proved to be correct. At the same time a Breton-speaking priest was sent to tour the area, explaining as he went that the king had only the best interests of the people at heart, did not intend to levy a tax on salt or corn, and would pardon them if they laid down their arms. Many villages accepted this offer, although disturbances continued. In the turbulent urban centres of Upper Brittany, the governor decided that repression was impossible. Indeed false rumours that royal troops were approaching inflamed the rioters still further. He therefore announced the summoning of the provincial Estates, at which everyone would have an opportunity to voice his grievances, and the news that this cherished assembly was to meet had the desired effect. Almost all the townsmen laid down their arms. Only after these gestures of conciliation had calmed many passionate spirits did the governor think it safe to bring in a limited number of royal troops, not to punish the province but to remind it of the sovereign power to which it owed allegiance. He also insisted that the commanders should take great care to avoid inconvenience to any Bretons who had not actively participated in the uprising. The one punishment which the duc de Chaulnes did inflict on the city of Rennes, where the sedition had commenced, was to transfer the *parlement* under guard to the town of Vannes. He could not manage without these judges and he dared not risk further disorder by suspending them, but at least he made their lives uncomfortable and at the same time delivered a blow at the pride and the economy of Rennes.

The Estates duly met and deemed it prudent to offer the king the full sum of 3,000,000 *livres* for the direct taxes. In return the offensive new levies were abandoned. A deputation went to Paris and begged forgiveness, which gave the king an opportunity to grant a gracious amnesty. Some twenty-five rebels, who had been seized at random, were put to death as an example, but that was the extent of royal 'repression' of the revolt. The crown and the governor were very relieved that calm had returned to the province, because the newspapers in enemy capitals had been publishing numerous details of this revolt which had threatened to deflect Louis XIV from his international purposes. Now he could again concentrate on them, which did not please the foreign news writers. The Bretons had resisted the hated new taxes, and in a few years, at the Peace of Nijmegen, the merchants would see the lifting of the embargo on trade with the Dutch and the abrogation of the 1667 tariff which they so detested.[8]

Popular unrest continued spasmodically for the rest of the reign, but there were few occasions when the forces of law and order encouraged it, as had happened in Rennes. In the 1680s the repression of the Huguenots became an additional cause of grievance in some areas, as did revived *richériste* calls for an assault on episcopal wealth. Obstruction by officials persisted, the recruitment of soldiers was often thwarted and desertion frequent, and two new kinds of fierce criticism began to circulate in the realm. First came the violently hostile pamphlets from the Huguenots and their friends, some resident abroad and others in hiding within France. Then followed the wider and more thoughtful attacks from aristocrats like Fénelon and Saint-Simon, who proposed detailed plans for the greater prosperity and better government of this impoverished and besieged monarchy. One source of comfort for the crown was that the municipal officials of the 1690s, especially once they had been allowed venal and hereditary tenure of office, did not ally with the disorderly elements in the towns. These elites appreciated that they had little to gain from such involvement, because the king had no further concessions to offer them. It was better to give priority to their other enduring concern – the maintenance of order within the walls of the town.

The aristocratic reformers, who have been dismissed by absolutist historians as a group of feudal reactionaries, made an intelligent assessment of the difficulties besetting France before offering detailed methods of avoiding them in future. Their ranks included not only theorists but provincial governors and trusted royal advisers, like the ducs de Chevreuse and de Beauvillier. They certainly favoured a

[8]Clément, vol. II (ii), pp. 768–9; vol. IV, p. 133; Depping, vol. II, pp. 175–6, 201–2; vol. III, pp. 254–6, 260–1; F. A. Isambert (ed.), *Recueil général des anciennes lois françaises depuis l'an 420 jusqu'à la révolution de 1789* (29 vols, Paris, 1822–33), vol. XIX, pp. 89–90, 145–6; Jean Lemoine, *La révolte dite du papier timbré ou des bonnets rouges en Bretagne en 1675: étude et documents* (Paris/Rennes, 1898), pp. 114–16, 125–30, 149–50, 170–1, 182–3, 189–90, 194–7, 199–200, 211, 214–15, 230–1, 258–9; Madame de Sevigné, *Lettres*, ed. Gérard-Gailly (3 vols, Paris, 1953–7), vol. I, 767–71, 859–60, 884–5, 891–2. See also A. de La Borderie, *La révolte du papier timbré advenue en Bretagne en 1675: histoire et documents* (Saint-Brieuc, 1884), which contains the text of the 'Code paysan' (1–2 July 1675).

largely aristocratic government, although it should be chosen by merit rather than by hereditary right, but this was not just class pride. They sincerely believed that the secretaries of state and the venal office-holders had been responsible for many past ills, and the role they proposed for their own social order was far removed from that dictated by the traditional aristocratic ethic. These high noble administrators would have to concern themselves with the minutiae of economics, commerce, industry and finance, as many of the governors in their midst already did to great effect. They also advocated universal taxation, rejecting the exemption of their own estate from the *taille* as a privilege which could not be justified. Many of them castigated the *dirigiste* economic policies of Colbert, which provoked wars and upset native merchants. Free trade was the only route to French and international prosperity.

A fundamental problem, which to these reformers was the root cause of almost every tension within the kingdom, was the failure of crown and provinces to appreciate each other's attitudes, priorities and interests. Some of these strains would disappear with a cessation of governmental *dirigisme*, but more had to be done if harmony were to be restored. The provincial Estates worked well in their own local context, even if they were often at odds with the crown. Consultation and representation clearly had their merits, and therefore the system should be extended. A hierarchy of consultative bodies should be established, with an Estates-general at the centre, provincial Estates in every province, and more local assemblies below them. Also those respected men who linked the royal court and the periphery, the aristocratic governors, should be the effective administrative head in every province, instead of in certain areas as at present. Here was a plan of reform which took the desirable parts of the present system and added some major innovations. It is needless to say that some of these ideas, especially the establishment of a universal and permanent tax, did not find favour with the majority of their fellow nobles and other privileged elite groups, although some royal ministers approved and tried to implement a number of their suggestions.[9]

[9]See: P. Le P. de Boisguillebert, 'Le factum de la France', in *Economistes-financiers du XVIIIᵉ siècle*, ed. E. Daire (Paris, 1843); Henri de Boulainvilliers, *Essais sur la noblesse de France* (Amsterdam, 1732), *Etat de la France* (3 vols, London, 1727–8), *Mémoires présentés à Monseigneur le duc d'Orléans* (The Hague/Amsterdam, 1727); François de Pons de Salignac de La Motte Fénelon, 'Lettre à Louis XIV: remontrances à ce prince sur divers points de son administration' and 'Plans de gouvernement concertés avec le duc de Chevreuse pour être proposés au duc du Bourgogne', in *Ecrits et lettres politiques*, ed. Charles Urbain (Paris, 1920, reprinted Geneva, 1981), *Dialogues des grands hommes aux champs élisées appliquez aux moeurs de ce siècle* (Paris, 1713), *Nouveaux dialogues des morts* (2

A number of wise governors had been alarmed at the added note of provocation, in these difficult times, that the decision to persecute the Huguenots had introduced into royal policy, and they steadfastly avoided implementing it in so far as this was possible without overtly defying their sovereign. The duc de Noailles in Languedoc, a close friend of the reforming aristocratic writers, was much exercised by this dilemma. When he had been seriously ill in 1684, many Protestants had been among the well-wishers who prayed for his recovery and assured him that they had nothing but the highest regard for him. Their faith in him was soon justified because he strongly attacked the revocation of the Nantes edict, condemned the uselessness of forced conversions and demanded the reform of corruption in the Roman church. He deplored the *dragonnades* and pointed out that in his province industrial prosperity and Protestantism were intimately associated. He voiced these severe strictures in private letters to the ministers, because he wished to be outwardly loyal and he was aware that the Estates of Languedoc contained many vehement opponents of the Huguenot cause. He therefore acquiesced in some public gestures against these heretics, like the destruction of their temple at Montpellier, but he contrived to fail in his task of rooting them out of their strongholds in the Cévennes. He found good reaons for his failure, because the Nine Years War soon distracted his attention and that of the king, funds were short and above all he could claim that the inhospitable mountain terrain exposed his troops to ambushes as the heretics commanded the heights above the narrow defiles which he was forced to use. In fact, as his friend Fénelon knew, Noailles had not tried very hard to pursue this campaign.[10]

Despite this moderation by a wise governor of Languedoc, it was Protestantism which added extra dangers to the last major revolt of the reign, that of the Camisards. At a time when poverty and disorder

---

vols, Amsterdam, 1719), *Avantures de Télémaque, fils d'Ulysse* (The Hague, 1708), *Examen de conscience pour un roi* (London, 1747); the duc de Saint-Simon, 'Lettre anonyme au roi' and 'Parallèle des trois premiers rois bourbons', in *Ecrits inédits de Saint-Simon*, ed. M. P. Faugère (8 vols, Paris, 1880–93), vol. I, *Projets de gouvernement du duc de Bourgogne*; S. Le P. de Vauban, *Projet d'une dixme royale qui supprimant la taille . . ., produiroit au roy un revenu certain et suffisant . . . .* (The editions given here are the most complete and accurate, although the works were all drafted or completed between 1690 and the very early years of the d'Orléans regency.) See Roger Mettam, *The role of the higher aristocracy in France under Louis XIV, with special reference to the 'faction of the duke of Burgundy' and the provincial governors* (Cambridge PhD thesis, 1967), pp. 67–106, for other works by these reformers.

[10]See abbé Millot, *Mémoires politiques et militaires . . . composés sur les pièces originales recueillies par Adrien-Maurice, duc de Noailles, maréchal de France & ministre d'état* (6 vols, Lausanne/Yverdon, 1778), vol. I, pp. 14–18, 23, 26–7, 41–9, 59–62, 76–7, 82–7, 351–5.

were still rife throughout the kingdom, and when Louis XIV was confronting a mighty coalition of enemies in the War of the Spanish Succession, the people of the Cévennes rose in revolt. Inspired by fervent religious prophets, this movement was particularly dangerous because enemy powers offered to support its aims. As at La Rochelle many years before, here was a group of Frenchmen which was prepared to enlist foreign aid against a tyrannical ruler who was persecuting its faith. The insurrection was at its fiercest in the years 1702–5, and eventually Louis had to compromise with the rebels he could not defeat. After agreement had been reached, the Camisards rejected further advances from their allies outside France. They were not prepared to behave treacherously now that their demand for religious toleration had been conceded. It was the last time that the king would initiate an attempt to extirpate Protestants, and they would henceforth be permitted by the crown to pursue their beliefs. Some royal ministers of the future, and many provincial elites too, would continue to bar their way to offices, but the policy of 1685, denying them any place in France, was at an end. Voltaire was not the only Frenchmen to derive wry amusement from the ending of the Camisards affair, when the mighty Bourbon monarch had been forced to negotiate with the son of a baker.[11]

When Louis XIV died in 1715, France was impoverished, vanquished, riddled with internal dissent and buzzing with criticism of the government. The strong royal line had been decimated by premature deaths. The passionate quarrel about *Unigenitus* was at its height, and the aristocratic factions were jockeying for position around their respective candidates for the supremely difficult task of governing France on behalf of the five-year-old Louis XV. Yet some verdict must be passed on the king who had ruled France for seventy-two years. The absolutist historians have been quick to do so, rivalling each other in their wild and anachronistic eulogies of this amazing monarch. Those who disagree with their interpretation have wisely resisted the desire to offer a contradictory, but equally glib, judgement on a man who lived for so long and during such a complicated period of history. The most appealing course of action is to leave the last word to someone who had seen these events at first hand, was renowned for his wisdom and eloquence, was favoured by Louis XIV and was entrusted with the great honour of delivering a funeral oration on his late royal patron in the Sainte Chapelle of Paris. He was Jean-Baptiste Massillon, a cleric so respected for his moral integrity that his listeners

[11]See: P. Joutard, *Les Camisards* (Paris, 1976); F. Puaux (ed.), *Jean Cavalier: mémoires sur la guerre des Camisards* (Paris, 1918, reprinted 1973); A. Ducasse, *La guerre des Camisards: la résistance huguenote sous Louis XIV* (Paris, 1978).

would have regarded his assessment of their deceased sovereign as a wholly fair one. Here is part of his text.[12]

God alone is great, my brothers, and never more so than of late, when he presides over the death of earthly kings. . . .

This King, the terror of his neighbours, the marvel of the universe, the father of kings; greater than all his ancestors, more magnificent than Solomon in all his glory, has acknowledged with him that all was vanity. The world was dazzled by the glitter which surrounded him; his enemies envied his power; strangers came from the furthest isles to lower their eyes before the splendour of his Majesty; his subjects have set up virtual altars to him; and the prestige which grew up around him captivated even his own mind. . . .

After the troubles of a long minority had been calmed by a virtuous regent and an able minister . . . , France put on once more the air of well-being which a new reign always seems to inspire in empires. . . . Success soon crowned our efforts. First Flanders was claimed as part of the patrimony of the Queen. . . . Then Holland, that bulwark which we ourselves had constructed against the Spanish, fell to our assault. . . .

Already the fires of war were burning throughout Europe; the number of our victories increased the number of our enemies; and the more our enemies grew, so too the more our victories multiplied. . . .

The earth alone did not offer sufficient scope for our triumphs. The sea as well groaned beneath the number and massive grandeur of our fleets. . . .

Such was the greatness of Louis in war. Never before had France raised such formidable armies; never had the art of war, that is to say the deadly art which teaches men to exterminate each other, been taken to such lengths; never so many famous generals. . . .

But alas! it is a sad reminder of our victories which you recall to us. What of these fine monuments, which have been erected in the middle of our public squares to immortalize your memory, when, as the Israelites did before them, 'your children ask their fathers in time to come, saying, what mean ye by these stones?', *Quando interrogaverint vos filii vestri, dicentes; quid sibi volunt isti lapides?* (Jos. IV, 6); you will bring to their minds a whole century of terror and carnage; the cream of the French nobility flung into the tomb; many ancient families falling into extinction; so many inconsolable mothers who still weep for their children; our countryside deserted and, instead of the riches which are locked up in its bosom, yielding up nothing but brambles to the small groups of ploughmen who are unable to keep them down; our towns laid waste; our people exhausted; crafts *in extremis* through lack of competition; trade languishing; you will remind them more of our losses than

---

[12]Jean-Baptiste Massillon, 'Oraison funèbre de Louis le Grand', *Oraisons funébres choisies de Mascaron* . . . . (Paris, 1802).

our conquests: *Quando interrogaverint vos filii vestri, dicentes: quid sibi volunt isti lapides?* You will bring back the memory of so many holy places which have been desecrated; so much licentiousness that even the most lawful enterprises can incur the wrath of Heaven; burning, bloodshed, blasphemy, atrocities and all the horrors of which war is the father; you will recall for them our crimes rather than our victories. . . .

Such a long series of unparalleled successes, for which we knew that one day we would have to pay, soon lifted the kingdom to a peak of glory and magnificence which previous centuries had never seen. France became the most renowned spectacle in all Europe. Royal palaces were built, the superb residences of Louis, where all the wonders of Asia and Italy were gathered together, as if in homage to his greatness! Paris, like triumphant Rome, adorned herself with the spoils taken from other nations. The court, following the example of the sovereign, was more brilliant and splendid than ever, and prided itself on having eclipsed all foreign courts. The city, eternal imitator of the court, copied its ostentation. The provinces, seeking to emulate, followed behind in the footsteps of the city. The simplicity of ancient ways changed; no trace remained of the modesty of our ancestors save their old and sober portraits, which decorated the walls of our palaces and whispered reproachfully against our extravagance. Luxury, which is always the herald of poverty, by corrupting our morals has dried up the source of our well-being; even misery, of which it is the father, cannot restrain it; the ever changing fashions in adornments became a national characteristic; eccentricity was made into a cult; our neighbours also, who found our lavishness so odious, nevertheless tried to model themselves upon us; so that, having exhausted them by our victories, we then went on to corrupt them by our example.

Yet every passing day added glory to the reign of Louis. The merchant fleet, more flourishing than in any previous reign, spread our commerce throughout all parts of the known world. . . . Our ships brought us every year, like those of Solomon, the treasures of the new world. Alas! these simple and insular peoples have sent us their gold and their silver, and we perhaps have taken them in exchange, not our faith, but our profligacy and our vices.

Our commerce, extending so far beyond our shores, has been improved within our country by works worthy of the greatness of Rome. Rivers have been joined, despite the land and the hills which separated them, and now bring to the walls of the capital the tribute and varied riches of each province. The two seas which surround and afford prosperity to this vast realm have, so to say, linked hands; and a miraculous canal, the product of daring and of unbelievable feats of enterprise, has brought together what nature had divided by such immense distance.

To Louis was reserved the opportunity to achieve what preceding centuries of the monarchy would not even have dared to wish for; it was the reign of marvels; our fathers had not imagined them, and our children will never see their like again; but happier than us, they will perhaps see the rule of peace, frugality and innocence. . . .

Great God! send your mercy upon this ravaged monarchy. . . . Spread the wings of your protection over this precious child whom you have placed at the head of your people; this august scion of so many kings; this innocent victim who alone has escaped the shafts of your anger and the extinction of the entire royal line. Give him a heart which will be willing to learn from good example; and ensure that piety, mercy, humanity and all the other virtues, which are to watch over his education, shall be spread throughout the whole length of his reign. Be his God and his father, in order to teach him to be the father of his subjects; and lead us all to a happy life hereafter.

Amen.

Bibliography

This list does not seek to include every document, article and book which either the author has read, or the reader could read, on the period; nor does it repeat every title which appears in the footnotes; section 1 records the principal archival collections which have proved useful, listing only the volume numbers (although many individual folios have been identified in the footnotes); section 2 presents some of the more important printed collections of documents, many of them with expert commentary; section 3 lists major works by selected seventeenth-century and early eighteenth-century writers; and section 4 confines itself to works by historians who have made a significant advance in the study of early modern France, mostly in recent years.

1 ARCHIVAL COLLECTIONS

Archives nationales: série K, nos 556, 619–24; série KK, vols. 610–13, 624 (documents about the creation of peerages, the privileges of the peers and disputes between peers and the Paris *parlement*), 1103–4 (on the administration of the Breton governor and the report of the *intendant* in 1698).

Bibliothèque nationale: fonds français, ancien fonds, vol. 1925 (the duties of a provincial governor); fonds français, vols 14190 (disputes between governors and *maréchaux de France*), 16511–13 (on *lits de justice*), 17399 (letters to chancellor Séguier), 21750 (on the Breton governorship), 22346 (on the Breton Estates); Mélanges Colbert, vols 107, 107bis, 108, 109, 109bis, 110, 111, 112, 116bis, 117, 117bis, 118, 118bis, 119, 124, 125, 126, 127, 127bis, 128, 128bis, 131bis, 132bis, 133, 134, 134bis, 136, 142bis 144, 146, 147, 148, 149, 150bis, 155, 156, 156bis, 157, 157bis, 158, 159, 160, 161, 162, 163, 164, 165, 165bis, 166, 166bis, 167, 168, 168bis, 169, 171, 171bis, 172, 172bis, 174, 174bis, 175, 176bis (letters from governors, *intendants*, other provincial officials and citizens to Colbert).

Ministère des affaires étrangères (now Ministère des relations extérieures): vols 215 (on the peerage), 1508–9, 1511–13, 1515–16 (papers from the central government about the administration of Brittany), 1687 (and about the Boulonnais), 8149 (the 1698 report of the Languedocien *intendant*), 8829 (the intendancy of Lebret in Provence), 24166 (papers about the dispute between the governor and the *parlement* of Aix).

2 COLLECTIONS OF PRINTED DOCUMENTS, LISTED UNDER EDITOR

Anselme de Sainte-Marie, *Histoire généalogique et chronologique de la maison royale de France, des pairs, grands officiers de la couronne & de la maison du roy . . .*, 3rd edn (9 vols, Paris, 1726–33). (Prints many documents on the aristocracy as well as providing full genealogies.)

Boislisle, A. de, *Correspondance des contrôleurs généraux des finances avec les intendants des provinces* (3 vols, Paris, 1874–97).

Champollion Figeac, M., *Documents historiques inédits* (4 vols, Paris, 1841–8).

Clément, Pierre, *Lettres, instructions et mémoires de Colbert* (8 vols, Paris, 1861–82).

Depping, G. B., *Correspondance administrative sous le règne de Louis XIV*, 'Collection des documents inédits sur l'histoire de France' (4 vols, Paris, 1850–5).

Hamy, A., *Essai sur les ducs d'Aumont, gouverneurs de Boulonnais, 1622–1789; Guerre dite de Lustucru, 1662; documents inédits* (Boulogne-sur-mer, 1906–7).

Isambert, F. A., *Recueil général des anciennes lois françaises depuis l'an 420 jusqu'a la révolution de 1789* (29 vols, Paris, 1822–33).

Lemoine, Jean, *La révolte dite du papier timbré ou des bonnets rouges en Bretagne en 1675: étude et documents* (Paris/Rennes, 1898).

Mettam, Roger, *Government and society in Louis XIV's France* (London, 1977).

Millot, abbé, *Mémoires politiques et militaires . . . composés sur les pièces originales recueillies par Adrien-Maurice, duc de Noailles, maréchal de France & ministre d'état* (6 vols, Lausanne/Yverdon, 1778).

Véron de Forbonnais, François, *Recherches et considérations sur les finances de France depuis l'année 1595 jusqu'à l'année 1721* (2 vols, Basel, 1758).

3 SEVENTEENTH- AND EARLY EIGHTEENTH-CENTURY WRITINGS

(Complex aristocratic names have been rendered in the form in which they appear in most major library catalogues.)

Boisguillebert, P. Le P. de, 'Le factum de la France', in *Economistes-financiers du XVIIIᵉ siècle*, ed. E. Daire (Paris, 1843).

Boulainvilliers, Henri de, *Essais sur la noblesse de France* (Amsterdam, 1732).

Boulainvilliers, Henri de, *Etat de la France* (London, 1727–8).

Boulainvilliers, Henri de, *Mémoires présentés à Monseigneur le duc d'Orléans* (The Hague/Amsterdam, 1727).

Coeffeteau, N., *Tableau des passions humaines: de leurs causes et de leurs effects* (Paris, 1635).

Fénelon, F. de, *Avantures de Télémaque, fils d'Ulysse* (The Hague, 1708).

Fénelon, F. de, *Dialogues des grands hommes aux champs élisées appliquez aux moeurs de ce siècle* (Paris, 1713).

Fénelon, F. de, *Ecrits et lettres politiques*, ed. Charles Urbain (Paris, 1920, reprinted Geneva, 1981).

Fénelon, F. de, *Examen de conscience pour un roi* (London, 1747).

Fénelon, F. de, *Nouveaux dialogues des morts* (2 vols, Amsterdam, 1719).

(Guez de Balzac), *Les oeuvres de Monsieur de Balzac* (2 vols, Paris, 1665).

La Mothe Le Vayer, F. de, *Oeuvres* (2 vols, Paris, 1656).

(La Rochefoucauld, the duc de), *Reflexions ou sentences et maximes morales* (Paris, 1671).

Les soupirs de la France esclave qui aspire après la liberté (1689–90: variously attributed to M. Levassor, P. Jurieu et al).

Louis XIV, *Mémoires pour l'instruction du dauphin . . .*, ed. Charles Dreyss (2 vols, Paris, 1860). Partially translated by Paul Sonnino, as *Louis XIV: Mémoires for the instruction of the dauphin* (New York, 1970).

Louis XIV, *Oeuvres*, eds P. A. Grouvelle and P. H. de Grimoard (6 vols, Paris, 1806).

Loyseau, Charles, *Cinq livres du droict des offices avec le livre des seigneuries et celuy des ordres* (Paris, 1614).

Montchrétien, A. de, *Traicté de l'oeconomie politique*, ed. Th. Funck-Brentano (Paris, 1889).

(Nicole, Pierre), *De l'éducation d'un prince* (Paris, 1670).

Ormesson, O. L. d', *Journal*, 'Collection des documents inédits sur l'histoire de France' (2 vols, Paris, 1860–1).

Pascal, B., *Opuscules et lettres* (Paris, 1955).

Saint-Simon, the duc de, *Ecrits inédits de Saint-Simon*, ed. M. P. Faugère (8 vols, Paris, 1880–93).

Saint-Simon, the duc de, *Mémoires*, ed. A. de Boislisle (45 vols, Paris, 1879–1930).

Saint-Simon, the duc de, *Projets de gouvernement du duc de Bourgogne* (Paris, 1860).

Vauban, S. Le P. de, 'Idée d'une excellente noblesse et des moyens de la distinguer par les générations', *Vauban: sa famille et ses écrits; ses oisivetés et sa correspondance*, ed. Lieutenant-colonel de Rochas d'Aiglun (2 vols, Paris/Grenoble, 1910).

Vauban, S. Le P. de, *Projet d'une dixme royale qui supprimant la taille . . ., produiroit au roy un revenu certain et suffisant. . . .*

4 MODERN WORKS

Asher, Eugène L., *The resistance to the maritime classes: the survival of feudalism in the France of Colbert* (Berkeley/Los Angeles, 1960).

Beik, William, *Absolutism and society in seventeenth-century France: state power and provincial aristocracy in Languedoc* (Cambridge, 1985).

Bergin, Joseph, *Cardinal Richelieu: power and the pursuit of wealth* (London, 1985).

Bonney, Richard, *Political change in France under Richelieu and Mazarin, 1624–1661* (Oxford, 1978).

Bonney, Richard, *The king's debts: finance and politics in France, 1589–1661* (Oxford, 1981).

Briggs, Robin, *Early modern France, 1560–1715* (Oxford, 1977).

Church, William Farr, *Constitutional thought in sixteenth-century France: a study in the evolution of ideas* (Cambridge, Mass, 1941).

Cole, Charles Woolsey, *French mercantilist doctrines before Colbert* (New York, 1931).

Cole, Charles Woolsey, *Colbert and a century of French mercantilism* (2 vols, New York, 1939, reprinted 1964).

Cole, Charles Woolsey, *French mercantilism, 1683–1700* (New York, 1971).

Corvisier, André, *La France de Louis XIV, 1643–1715: ordre intérieur et place en Europe* (Paris, 1979).

Corvisier, André, *Louvois* (Paris, 1983).

Coveney, P. J., (ed.), *France in crisis, 1620–75* (London, 1977).

Dent, J., *Crisis in finance: crown, financiers and society in seventeenth-century France* (New York, 1973).

Dessert, Daniel, *Argent, pouvoir et société au grand siècle* (Paris, 1984).

Dessert, D. and J.-L. Journet, 'Le lobby Colbert: un royaume ou une affaire de famille?', *Annales, ESC*, xxx, 6.

Diefendorf, Barbara B., *Paris city councillors in the sixteenth century: the politics of patrimony* (Princeton, 1983).

Elias, Norbert, *The court society*, tr. Edmund Jephcott (Oxford, 1983).

Golden, Richard M., *The godly rebellion: Parisian curés and the religious Fronde, 1652–62* (Chapel Hill, NC, 1981).

Hamscher, Albert N., *The parlement of Paris after the Fronde, 1653–1673* (Pittsburgh, 1976).

Harding, Robert R., *Anatomy of a power elite: the provincial governors of early modern France* (New Haven/London, 1978).

Hatton, Ragnhild (ed.), *Louis XIV and absolutism* (London, 1976).

Hatton, Ragnhild (ed.), *Louis XIV and Europe* (London, 1976).

Hayden, J. Michael, *France and the estates general of 1614* (Cambridge, 1974).

Kettering, Sharon, *Judicial politics and urban revolt in seventeenth-century France: the parlement of Aix, 1629–1659* (Princeton, 1978).

Kettering, Sharon, *Patrons, brokers and clients in seventeenth-century France* (New York, 1986).

Kossmann, E. H., *La Fronde* (Leiden, 1954).

Kreiser, B. Robert, *Miracles, convulsions, and ecclesiastical politics in early eighteenth-century Paris* (Princeton, 1978).

Lublinskaya, A. D., *French absolutism: the crucial phase, 1620–1629*, tr. Brian Pearce (Cambridge, 1968).

Marchand, J., *Un intendant sous Louis XIV: étude sur l'administration de Lebret en Provence, 1687–1704* (Paris, 1889).

Moote, A. Lloyd, *The revolt of the judges: the Parlement of Paris and the Fronde, 1643–1652* (Princeton, 1971).

Parker, David, *La Rochelle and the French monarchy: conflict and order in seventeenth-century France* (London, 1980).

Parker, David, *The making of French absolutism* (London, 1983).

Salmon, J. H. M., *Society in crisis: France in the sixteenth century* (London, 1975).

Schaeper, Thomas J., *The French council of commerce, 1700–1715: a study of mercantilism after Colbert* (Columbus, Ohio, 1983).

Sutcliffe, F. E., *Guez de Balzac et son temps: littérature et politique* (Paris, 1959).

Wolfe, Michael, *The fiscal system of Renaissance France* (New Haven/London, 1972).

Index

280, 319; subsidies to the crown, 122, 149, 165, 245, 252–4, 256
Coislin, peerage 1663: 198, 201
Colbert, Jean-Baptiste, marquis de Seignelay (*see also* economy; finance; justice; ministers; navy): 17, 23, 29, 55, 72, 81; family of, 88–9, 94–5, 96, 97; Charles, marquis de Croissy, brother of, 93, 97, 98, 185, 231, 237; Nicolas, brother of, 96, 185, 276–7; Henri Pussort, uncle of, 185; Jean-Baptiste, marquis de Seignelay, son of, 97; Jean-Baptiste, marquis de Torcy, son of Croissy, 99, 231, 238, 240; rivalry with Le Tellier family, 183, 185, 187, 221, 231, 232, 237, 242–3, 298, 300; apprenticeship under Mazarin, 147, 159, 166, 168, 170, 172–3, 185, 188; takes charge of finances, 182; attitude to royal largesse and cost of court, 61, 63, 191–2, 285; attitude to war and the army, 190, 221, 223, 242; overall economic and administrative aims, 24, 91, 176–7, 182, 187, 188–9, 221, 246, 281, 288–90; rationalization of the kingdom, 29–31, 37–41, 75, 176–7, 210, 213, 221, 258, 264, 283, 288–9, 290–2, 295, 298–300, 303–4, 306, 307, 308, 313; conflicting priorities of, 204, 242, 297, 298, 304–5; respect for privileges and traditional administrative bodies, 78, 170, 176, 188, 207–13, 239, 257, 268, 276–7, 281, 290, 310; caution in use of *intendants*, 23–4, 132–3, 209–14, 217, 263, 268, 270, 280–1, 283; relations with governors, 88–91, 209, 253, 270, 271–2, 274–6, 298–9, 305, 317
Condé, princes of: 99; Henri, prince de, 118, 120; Louis II, prince de, subsequently duc de Bourbon, governor of Burgundy and Guyenne, during regency for Louis XIV and ministry of Mazarin, 52, 135, 137, 141, 144–52, 154, 158–9, 162; and during personal rule of Louis XIV, 52, 158, 178, 196, 272–3, 276–7, 286, 298–9, 302, 305
Conti, Armand, prince de: 147, 149, 159

Corneille, Pierre: 76–7, 79
court (*see also* princes: conspiracies at): government as part of the royal household, 10, 47–8, 81, 89, 191–2, 199, 200; as royal propaganda, 15, 59; less itinerant, 82; its embellishment and establishment at Versailles, 20, 26, 82, 233, 285, 306–7, 321; elaboration of life at, 61–2, 86, 321; as centre of patronage, 8, 28, 44, 48, 56–7, 84, 253; foreign envoys at, 25–8; royal authority greater at, than in rest of kingdom, 30, 205–6, 222, 293–4; curial offices as reward for service, 92, 177–8, 261; high offices for untrustworthy nobles, 21, 61, 92–3, 158, 178, 197, 202–3; rotation of court offices, 92; intrigue at, 28, 52, 87, 193–4; length of nobles' residence at, 18, 20–1, 25–6, 48, 54, 92–3
Courtin, Honoré: 93, 97, 98, 231

Desmarets de Saint-Sorlin, Jean: 77, 79
Du Plessis-Guénégaud, Henri: 182–3, 184

economy: limited aims of Colbert's policies for, 189, 303; lack of interest by Louis XIV in, 49–50, 288; economic theorists, 79–80, 288–9, 299, 307, 317; mercantilism, 34, 122, 288; bullionism, 15, 111, 189, 287, 290, 296, 303; *dirigisme* and reactions to it, 15, 24, 79–80, 122, 124, 189, 213, 218, 228, 231, 288–9, 290–5, 299, 302, 304, 305, 306, 307, 308, 317; plans for uniform weights and measures, 39, 248, 290–1; effects of royal attacks on Protestants, 109–10, 122, 232, 234, 250, 299, 301, 302, 306, 318; role of foreign experts, craftsmen and merchants, 221, 224, 232, 234, 250, 289, 291, 292, 296, 301–2, 305, 306, 308; condition and improvement of merchant marine, 289, 296, 299–301, 303, 321; commerce, 15, 122, 187, 189, 204, 212–13, 218, 236, 242–3, 274, 295, 299, 320–1; *conseil de commerce*, 191, 307–8; Colbert's attempts to raise the social image of trade, 75, 204, 290,